BLOODSTAIN PATTERNS

For Donald M. Harding (1917–2005), who in 1977 gave me a chance to work in the real world of forensic investigation.

BLOODSTAIN PATTERNS

IDENTIFICATION, INTERPRETATION, AND APPLICATION

ANITA Y. WONDER

with

G. MICHELE YEZZO

AMSTERDAM • BOSTON • HEIDELBERG • LONDON
NEW YORK • OXFORD • PARIS • SAN DIEGO
SAN FRANCISCO • SINGAPORE • SYDNEY • TOKYO
Academic Press is an imprint of Elsevier

Academic Press is an imprint of Elsevier
The Boulevard, Langford Lane, Kidlington, Oxford, OX5 1GB
525 B Street, Suite 1800, San Diego, CA 92101-4495, USA

Notices
Knowledge and best practice in this field are constantly changing. As new research and experience broaden our understanding, changes in research methods, professional practices, or medical treatment may become necessary.

Practitioners and researchers must always rely on their own experience and knowledge in evaluating and using any information, methods, compounds, or experiments described herein. In using such information or methods they should be mindful of their own safety and the safety of others, including parties for whom they have a professional responsibility.

To the fullest extent of the law, neither the Publisher nor the authors, contributors, or editors, assume any liability for any injury and/or damage to persons or property as a matter of products liability, negligence or otherwise, or from any use or operation of any methods, products, instructions, or ideas contained in the material herein.

British Library Cataloguing in Publication Data
A catalogue record for this book is available from the British Library

Library of Congress Cataloging-in-Publication Data
A catalog record for this book is available from the Library of Congress

ISBN: 978-0-12-415930-3

For information on all Academic Press publications visit
our website at store.elsevier.com

Printed and bound in China

15 16 17 18   10 9 8 7 6 5 4 3 2 1

Working together
to grow libraries in
developing countries

www.elsevier.com • www.bookaid.org

Contents

I

INTRODUCTION

1. Introduction

2. The Science of Bloodstain Pattern Evidence

3. Discussion on Terminology

II

IDENTIFICATION

4. Review of Historical Approaches to Bloodstain Pattern Identification

5. Differentiations Between Similar Patterns

6. How Many Pieces of Evidence?

III

INTERPRETATION

7. Information for Interpretation

8. Investigative Leads: Suggested Questions and Answers

9. Staging

IV

APPLICATION

10. Expanding Applications in Bloodstain Pattern Evidence

11. Applications of Bloodstain Pattern Evidence to Crime Scene Investigation

12. Bloodstain Pattern Application in Court

Acknowledgments

As with the previous books, this one would not have been possible without the input from several conscientious and knowledgeable contributors. Because of the scope and complexity of this work, there were many more individuals involved before the end product was completed. The groups of individuals can be divided into types of contributions.

Those proofreading the chapters and contributing suggestions to modify, improve accuracy, and verify facts were as follows: first and foremost was Lorie Teichert, defense attorney and Spanish interpreter. Lorie was essential in explaining the legal viewpoint and applications to criminal defense. Richard Saferstein provided time and concerned comments with regard to criminalistics viewpoints and a much-needed revision of the first four chapters. All comments were appreciated. Professor Edward Imwinkelried not only commented on Chapter 12 but also provided suggestions to greatly improve the application to law.

Those who contributed opinions regarding the concepts associated with bloodstain pattern evidence include the following: Karl Hutchinson was generous with his information regarding administration and budget considerations from a retired chief of police. Angela Gallop, as in the past, provided comments regarding the international appreciation of bloodstain pattern evidence. Dennis Dolezal continues to keep the author updated on in-house training and investigative applications for the evidence. Christie Davis, Ph.D., is a main source of information regarding DNA for anyone who needs her. Cynthia Windsor, San Diego prosecutor, whom I met at a workshop on "How to be a Better Expert Witness" during an AAFS meeting, continues to answer my questions regarding prosecution and application of physical evidence in California.

Those who contributed material and articles, and helped construct experiments: Nancy Shelton gave of herself as well as needed items for research. Harry Holmes has always been helpful in putting on workshops, proving opinions from an identification technician viewpoint, and sharing literature he has received in regard to the evidence. Peter Pizzola shared photographs as well as his viewpoint from considerable experience. No list of acknowledgments would be complete without including my cousins who helped with computer applications, construction of dynamics, and photography of patterns found around the world. Linda Smith, Daniel Long, and David Long are my family. Wayne Jeffery has continued to share professional information with me since our initial gig together in England while training individuals from the Forensic Science Society. Thanks also to my friend and confidante who helped with experiments, finding files, and sharing experiences, Angela Santos.

All the above is credited to my major source for proofing every chapter and sharing experiences for the past 30 years, G. Michele Yezzo.

I also owe a great deal of appreciation to my patient and encouraging editor, Joslyn Paguio.

Anita Y. Wonder
May 2014

About the Author

ANITA Y. WONDER

Ms. Wonder received her B.S. in Microbiology from the University of California—Davis in 1966. After applying her education to industrial microbiology at the California Almond Growers Exchange, she studied clinical lab science at California State University in Sacramento. Working in three different hospitals and engaging in medical research simultaneously failed to satisfy her desire for discovering new pathways to knowledge. In 1982, she embarked on a totally new career by obtaining a Master of Arts degree from CSUS in Criminal Justice, with emphasis on Forensic Science. Her thesis was on bloodstain pattern evidence, a discipline she has consistently viewed as a scientific field, but one she feels is underappreciated in the applications to casework and court trials. Ms. Wonder has been involved in casework for both prosecution and defense. This is the third book she has written with the objective of passing on to the next generation all her information and concepts in science. She is presently semi-retired, accepting only those cases of particular interest to further the scientific recognition of bloodstain pattern evidence.

G. MICHELE YEZZO

Ms. Yezzo received a B.S. in Comprehensive Sciences with a concentration in Biology and Chemistry, and a minor in Criminal Justice from Youngstown State University, Youngstown, Ohio, in 1976. She is a retired forensic scientist from the State of Ohio Attorney General's Office, Bureau of Criminal Identification and Investigation with more than 32 years of experience in the analysis of trace evidence, blood, physiological fluids, and bloodstain pattern evidence. Her work involved the analysis, reporting, and testimony on criminal cases primarily in Ohio. However, she has also consulted on cases in various jurisdictions including Ontario and Quebec, Canada, and Sydney, Australia. She has provided training to other scientists, law enforcement, medical and nursing personnel, and attorneys on these topics and presented papers for numerous regional, national, and international forensic organizations. While in retirement from the lab, she is presently consulting and training within her areas of expertise.

List of Figures

INTRODUCTION

1

Introduction

TO SOLVE A PROBLEM, YOU IDENTIFY IT

In 1977, following a Frye Hearing, a trial judge denied bloodstain pattern testimony in an assault case because he had never heard of it as a forensic discipline. At a 2009 meeting of the American Academy of Forensic Sciences in Washington, D.C., a renowned judge sitting on a panel discussing the National Academy of Sciences Report (NAS Report) stated that it, applied to pattern match types of evidence including fingerprints, tool marks, and *blood spatters* [sic]. In 2011, a trial judge denied the inclusion, within bloodstain pattern testimony, of information regarding the way blood was distributed from inside the body to outside pattern arrangements from an expert with 40 years of experience as a clinical laboratory scientist and 35 years as a forensic scientist.

If true detective programs on television are any indication, bloodstain pattern evidence is now widely recognized for its use in solving complex and confusing violent crimes. However, unlike pattern match types of evidence, bloodstain patterns more closely resemble 3D dynamic events, like bomb blasts. In addition, arterial damage patterns require that bloodstain pattern experts provide explanations of anatomy, or qualified medical experts explain how arteries end up distributing blood drops in unique and identifiable patterns. Then, there are the misconceptions from popular pulp fiction, films, television, and media reports repeating confusion regarding how this evidence is applied. From all of this, there is adequate need for clarification and explanations of bloodstain pattern evidence as an acceptable forensic science discipline.

Before suggesting explanations and clarifications, we must understand why misconceptions occur, why they presently exist, and how we should update and clarify the scientific foundations. The importance of this evidence as a forensic discipline must be accepted because it is, or definitely can be, one of the most cost-efficacious methodologies in the investigation of violent crime.

The textbook *Bloodstain Dynamics* was published in 2001 by Academic Press with the primary objective of presenting a broader, and updated, scientific foundation for the forensic discipline of bloodstain pattern analysis. A few other available publications followed traditional approaches recovered in print from 1939 (Balthazard et al., 1939) and continued in 1971 (MacDonell and Bialousz, 1971) after the death of Dr. Paul Leland Kirk. They were based primarily on scientific principles recognized in the early 1900s (MacDonell, 1991, p. 820). Although *Blood Dynamics* received favorable reviews, some readers claimed that the science used to describe principles was too complicated for practical applications and would not be accessible to those looking

3

to obtain investigative leads in actual casework. The objective of the book, however, was for science-based criminalists in crime laboratories to update their scientific foundation in regard to bloodstain patterns and add support to identification testimony. Many otherwise highly qualified experts ignore the science behind the evidence and conclude that the task is simply "police work." It is police work, but it is also scientific evidence requiring support and understanding from qualified forensic scientists. Bloodstain pattern evidence works extremely well in team approaches.

Bloodstain Pattern Evidence, Objective Approaches and Case Applications, published in 2007 under Elsevier's acquired AP Forensics label, was received well for practical work and also found favorable scientific reviews (Hulse-Smith, 2008, p. 1015). Although references and scientific sources were provided, some practitioners still felt that the scientific principles mentioned were not necessary for bloodstain pattern analysis. Earlier simplified concepts were retained that would not satisfy the National Institute of Standards and Technology's (NIST's) push to improve material for science data committees.

Feedback regarding criticisms and misperceptions from other authors regarding the first two publications from the present author did not arrive intime for clarification in the latter work, *Bloodstain Pattern Evidence, Criteria Approach and Case Applications*.

It follows that a third work is necessary to, hopefully, accomplish the following objectives:

1. clarify misperceptions and misunderstandings from previous publications, presented papers, and lectures;
2. re-emphasize recent scientific discoveries and update and further explain a need for correction in logic for bloodstain pattern interpretation and research;
3. repeat and confirm the importance of blood substance composition, mainly as non-Newtonian fluid influenced by red blood cell content, in applications for bloodstain pattern analysis in casework and research experimental design;
4. provide an interpretation scheme for the purpose of obtaining initial, economically beneficial investigative leads before persons of interest are identified; and
5. encourage and extend legal applications of bloodstain pattern analysis as an economical methodology before as well as during and after trial.

Most books and articles regarding bloodstain patterns present some history, beginning in Europe and later reaching the United States predominantly through the applications and lectures in the 1950 and 1960s by Paul L. Kirk, a professor at the University of California, Berkeley, campus. Dr. Kirk was primarily a chemist who viewed bloodstain pattern evidence as a science akin to that field. Recently, a popular magazine article claimed that forensic science started with law enforcement investigators applying what was deemed science, whether or not it was actually based on such principles (Regan, 2008. p. 51). This description may not have been a fair historical reference, but it sounded good to the usual readership. Early pioneers of forensic evidence, up to and including Dr. Kirk, had backgrounds in science, albeit as acquired science available from the late 1800s through the 1930s (Walcher, 1939). Because the idea of using a crime lab to handle physical evidence was supported by some in civilian science, scientific principles developed during the 1960s to 1990s were modified applications from clinical disciplines such as serology, chemistry, and genetics. As crime labs became staffed with individuals who had scientific backgrounds, some new scientific principles, techniques, methodologies, and instrumentation were developed directly for forensics applications, such as investigative information, especially regarding DNA.

A realignment process, which began in 2012, may have had an effect on the establishment of scientific principles for the various forensic disciplines. This shift in viewpoint might result from the control and direction for crime lab design reverting from scientific-based formats to administration by law enforcement officers, lawyers, and the private sector with the objective of economy (LinkedIn website, 2012–2013). There are assumed benefits and detriments to this change of management. Controversy exists between forensic experts, those employed in the labs that are shifting directorships, and those making demands from the legal profession. Financial emphasis is not necessarily science-based by its very nature but often is politically influenced. Acceptance and rejection of techniques, methodology, terminology, and scientific principles are evaluated relative to continued business success. It is difficult to defend innocence of bias when one's livelihood is involved in the interpretation.

In 2014, the National Institute of Standards and Technology (NIST) used the 66th annual meeting of the American Academy of Forensic Sciences (AAFS) in Seattle, Washington, to lobby for a shift in forensics toward the same scientific data base as chemistry and other pure sciences. Ironically, this would revert bloodstain pattern evidence back to the level Dr. Kirk introduced, i.e., a science aligned with chemistry. One objective for forensic divisions of NIST is to set up committees, Organization of Scientific Area Committees (OSACs), possibly derived from Scientific Working Group on Bloodstain Pattern Analysis (SWGSTAIN) designations, but also to include review and revision systems for reporting. The task of reviewing and updating revisions, although possibly tedious, is very much necessary in a changing field such as bloodstain pattern evidence because of the volume of research and progress in the subject of blood substance alone. Toward this future goal of scientific data, this book is offered to provide preliminary suggestions and discussions of science gleaned from the advances in understanding blood.

Fingerprints, tool marks, and bloodstain patterns appear to have no obvious scientific foundation in civilian science disciplines, although applications for fingerprints are involved in civilian employment and identity records. All three applied to crime investigation, however, are regarded as derived and applied solely from law enforcement requirements. In the 1980s, some students of bloodstain pattern workshops felt they were dealing with a new subject. Actually, indication exists that recognition by prehistoric humanoids, many millennia ago, equated bloodstains with violence, as interpreted from records in European cave paintings.

Figure 1.1 is a reproduction of a cave painting in South Africa (Smith, 2011). The patterns show handprints. A detail is shown in Figure 1.2, where handprints were transferred to the cave walls as multiples in red ochre. Red ochre is suggested as a pigment associated with blood in works found in Australia with links associated with Neolithic culture. This prehistoric evidence was also illustrated in *Blood Dynamics* and *Bloodstain Pattern Evidence, Objective Approaches and Case Applications,* with cave paintings in Spain (Wonder, 2001, p. 36) and France and stone carvings in the Middle East (Wonder, 2007, pp. 2-4).

Hands and finger patterns transferred in blood periodically occur in physical evidence of violence. Examples from a crime scene work-up are shown in Figure 1.3, which shows a victim's or assailant's attempt to grasp a sheet. In this case, the assailant was considered more likely to have made these marks based on the position and association with tool mark/weapon transfers. In Figure 1.4, the example is, perhaps, representative of a victim's attempt to write in blood.

The historical association between bloodstain pattern evidence, tool marks, and fingerprints, however, creates one of the most common misunderstandings in forensic investigation. It is often believed that bloodstain patterns are *pattern match evidence* equivalent to fingerprints and tool marks. If this were true, it would imply that one could memorize simplified exercises from workshops and lectures and then encounter the same thing at actual crime scenes. Students in workshops often do

FIGURE 1.1   South African cave painting. *(Photograph by Linda Sue Smith)*

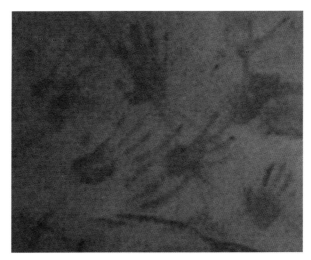

FIGURE 1.2   Detail from South African cave paintings.

attempt to memorize case examples as labeled by the lecturers and then assume they will find the same patterns during their own crime scene work. First, they must accept the identity given to the case examples and then recognize the dynamics of the events that distributed blood during violence, often under or over other patterns. If the connection isn't there, the students don't see similarities, or if they don't remember how the patterns looked during the workshop exercises, their workshop training may not be applied. The truth is that bloodstain patterns cannot be easily memorized and remembered. Crime scenes also are far more complex than workshop exercises. This point is illustrated in Section II of this book.

FIGURE 1.3   Handprint in blood on a bed sheet from a crime scene. *(Photo from G. Michele Yezzo of Ohio)*

FIGURE 1.4   Victim of violence attempts to write in blood on a wall. *(Photograph from Peter Pizzola of New York)*

Encountering scenes that do not resemble workshop exercises may impede learning to recognize blood spatter patterns without bias. More recent books on the subject emphasize that the predominance of stain size be used (Bevel and Gardner, 2002, p. 104). Even providing a given predominance of stain size and shape may lead to misinterpretation. Mist-sized stains, associated with gunshot (Bevel and Gardner, 2002, p. 74), may actually result from respiration-released blood drops, high pressure with pin-hole-sized arterial breach, or high-speed cutting action from power tools. Without elimination of reasonable alternatives, size alone can be misleading.

Distribution of spatters occurs in a three-dimensional context with too many permutations to re-create all possible arrangements in a 40-hour workshop. Analysts may claim that reconstruction experiments can be used to re-create crime scene patterns. Again, the number of parameters involved makes exact reproduction unlikely and may lead to improper interpretation of both the crime scene and the experiment. The reconstruction, if designed to be pattern match, will reproduce less than reliable proof of identity. Blood spatter patterns follow the dynamics of a bomb blast more reliably than a simple pattern match. Transfers can be considered pattern match, but moving transfers are again 3D dynamics and provide valuable information when analyzed as such. Although indication exists that experts believe they are using criteria formats to classify patterns, one may encounter casework in which conclusions were based solely on size and shape of spatters without justification of the classification for dynamic events distributing the blood drops that formed the spatters. This is often insufficient information for identification.

Some analysts disagree that bloodstain pattern expertise requires more than a single 40-hour workshop to apply to casework. Others argue experience is all that is needed for expertise. Experience and training together are required for the complete analysis, perhaps because experienced experts learn, consciously or subconsciously, to use multiple criteria in their identification scheme. After training, not before, one begins to accumulate experience and knowledge applicable to crime scene investigation.

CHANGED HISTORY

Dr. Paul Kirk brought bloodstain pattern evidence to the U.S. from his conferences and associations in Europe. An indication of his scientific applications in regard to "blood dynamics," his title for the evidence, can be gleaned from his lectures to lawyers. He introduced some of his terminology in such a lecture before the Annual Meeting of the California Trial Lawyers Association. Most noteworthy was his concept of "velocity impact spatters" (Kirk, 1968). Dr. Kirk recognized that the speed a drop of blood is traveling at the moment it makes contact with a recording surface (called a "target" by bloodstain pattern analysts) influences the shape of the resultant stain. This point should be obvious but may be ignored in books and lectures on blood spatter evidence which cite spatter shape as dependent on angle and surface textures alone (James, 1998, p. 162). A blood drop hitting a recording surface at low velocity will lose forward momentum sooner than a blood drop traveling at high velocity. The length of a blood spatter is determined by the time the blood drop continues to travel after the footprint records on the target until forward momentum is lost, and thus can be longer or shorter depending on the velocity of the blood drop at contact with the target.

Figure 1.5 compares a theoretical blood drop impacting a target compared with another drop going twice as fast. At zero time, the slower drop makes a greater and wider contact with the target before continuing travel. The faster drop touches but continues traveling to deposit blood over a longer and narrower path.

The width of a stain results from a drop making initial contact and the microsecond of time to collapse and be recorded against the surface during forward travel. The initial contact is the footprint of the sphere with the elongation of an oval, tear shape, or exclamation symbol marking continued travel between initial contact and the end of forward momentum. A bloodstain narrows in the direction of travel because some blood is lost in the initial footprint, while the traveling drop will continue to leave blood along the surface depending on the speed the drop is traveling while staining the target. Less blood is available when completing forward travel. Thus, drops traveling at high velocity will be narrower than drops traveling at low velocity because they travel farther, as well

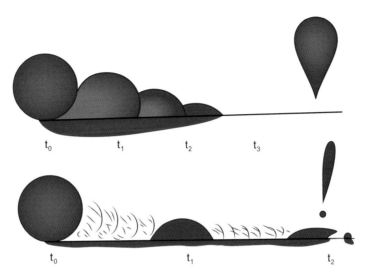

FIGURE 1.5   Two blood drops making contact at different velocities. The bottom one is theoretically going twice as fast as the drop illustrated at the top.

as faster, while leaving the content from the blood drop. High velocity impact spatters may be seen as streaks or exclamation marks that result from gunshot, sneeze, or high blood pressure arterial breach–distributed blood drops. A final exclamation mark shape is characteristic, but not exclusive, of firearms-distributed drops. The last part of an exclamation mark blood stain may be seen as a dot. High-speed photography (Bevel and Gardner, p. 130) has shown that a blood drop traveling while in touch with a recording surface may form a wave much like the ocean cresting. When the wave breaks at the end of travel, the remaining fluid may be deposited or cast ahead as a dot. To avoid confusing these with primary spatters, we call this ending drop a secondary spatter forming from a "parent" stain (James and Eckert, 1999, p. 305).

TERMINOLOGY SHIFT

A booklet submitted for publication around 1970 (MacDonell and Bialousz, 1971, p. 1), after the death of Dr. Kirk, changed the definitions Dr. Kirk developed for the terms of "velocity impact spatters" (VIS). Instead of applying to the speed of the blood drops at contact with recording surfaces, the terms were said to relate to the velocity of an impact that then distributed blood drops. In subsequent workshops, the VIS terms were defined as relative velocity of an object impacting with a blood source. Some differences between Dr. Kirk's format and the changes in 1970 were included in *Bloodstain Pattern Evidence, Objective Approaches and Case Applications* (Wonder, 2007, p. 51). In addition to those listed, changing the definition of velocity impact spatters created an ambiguous situation in which classification became subjective. The definition is in terms of the velocity for something hitting a blood source but does not define how the spatters themselves can be classified when found at a crime scene. A study in 1986 (Laber, 1986, pp. 12-16) illustrated the considerable overlap of blood spatter sizes, which makes classification on the basis of size of individual stains alone subjective.

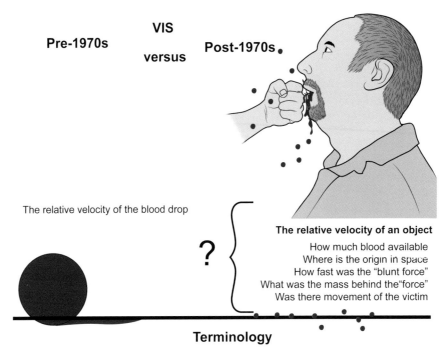

FIGURE 1.6   Comparison of terminology application pre-1970s versus post-1970s.

Instead of an identification scheme based on characteristics of a group of spatters from a dynamic event, classification for the new definitions of velocity impact spatters was based on size and shape of the individual spatters. These are equated to an *estimate of the velocity* of an impact to a blood source. More recently, a caution has been listed in regard to jumping to visual conclusions regarding predominant size ranges (Bevel and Gardner, p. 200). A *predominant size* is a better fit for investigation but still may lead to bias if the cause of assault/death is provided initially. The shift in velocity terms can lead to shoe-horning the spatter label into whatever weapon is suspected; i.e., in a recognized beating, any spatters are identified as medium velocity impact spatters (MVIS), and a group of spatters where gunshot occurred may be identified as high velocity impact spatters (HVIS). Instead of a scientific application, use of velocity impact spatter terms can be applied as an opinion qualified by experience and stated as "consistent with" whatever conclusion may be desired. More should be required for conclusions.

Figure 1.6 provides a schematic comparison of the change in terminology. The pre-1970s' application was simple and relative to the final shape of spatters as interpreted from dynamics. Post-1970s' terms could be considered ambiguous because they assume too much that is not known at crime scenes. The list of unknowns associated with the velocity impact spatter terminology applied to an object impacting a blood source must include the velocity and mass of the object, the composition of the blood source, and its amount of breakup into drops, with the initial velocity of the drops distributed, and the position in space that will contribute air friction to slow drops. The issue here is that the interpretation is not made at the impact with the blood source but rather with the various spatters that might have resulted from such an impact or some other dynamic that is not necessarily impact. In short, too many variables exist for this to satisfy the need for scientific-based technique.

Terminology of any discipline is based on knowledge of the applicable principles and lexicon recognized at the time and by the practitioners when defined. After 1970, the shift in definition of what is impacting for low velocity impact spatter (LVIS) led to the phrase becoming ambiguous. The original definitions of the velocity of the blood drops recorded made sense because blood drops dripping off something onto a recording surface were drops traveling by the pull of gravity alone; thus, drops were traveling at a relatively low velocity at impact with the target. When the force applied to a blood source became the definition, such was lacking for the LVIS designation; i.e., no separate low velocity force was applied. Gravity is technically applied to all the classifications—high, medium, and low impacts.

An indication that the original meaning was understanding is shown in the workshop exercise in which blood is dropped from increasing heights. Such drops will accelerate by the force of gravity until the upward force of the air column beneath the drop equals the downward pull of gravity. At this point, travel will be at a steady velocity, labeled *terminal velocity*. In other words, a velocity for a blood drop at impact would be equal to the value of the terminal velocity if the height of fall was sufficient to reach terminal velocity. This was assumed associated with forward momentum, i.e., the speed of the drop projected by impact. The application to forward momentum is a misunderstanding of the term because terminal velocity applies only to the pull by gravity, not slowing of forward motion. A consideration for forward movement should include wind shear, and air friction.

Another workshop experiment was devised suggesting attention to the velocity of drops rather than the velocity of an object impacting a blood source. A motor with paddles spinning inside a box was used in this experiment. A hole over the paddles allowed blood to be dropped onto the paddles and then thrown (cast off) out of the front opening of the box. The velocity of the paddles could be measured with a tachometer and was assumed to apply to the speed of blood drops distributed. Again, too many parameters exist to make this approach logical. The main facts missing from interpretation based on this experiment are the composition of the blood dropped into the fan and the surface characteristics of the paddles themselves. This latter characteristic results from surface texture adhesion affecting the retention or release of blood drops from the paddles. Observations depend on the composition of blood used in the experiments. This experiment is discussed further later in this book.

A suggested replacement for LVIS is "passive drops," assuming the applied force of gravity could be considered a passive force, not an applied force such as gunshot or blunt force. Switching to the term "passive" may confuse two different concepts in physics: kinetics and kinematics. Kinetics describes motion and the force which creates that motion, such as the original label applied by Dr. Kirk: "blood dynamics." Kinematics defines location and motion without specifying force. "Passive" and "active" are terms of kinematics, not usually applied to kinetics. Passive does describe a pool of blood because it has the potential of becoming active. Drops falling by gravity are active. Further confusion may exist in the difference between the classical mechanics of Sir Isaac Newton's day and modern mechanics of the present century. This topic is discussed in more detail in Chapter 2.

CORRECTING MISPERCEPTIONS

Clarification is necessary for Figure 2.5 in *Blood Dynamics* (shown here as Figure 1.7) (Wonder, 2001, p. 25).

Background: In December 2010, the author was cross-examined in court regarding statements made by well-regarded authors in their book (Bevel and Gardner, 2008, p. 13). The questions asked on

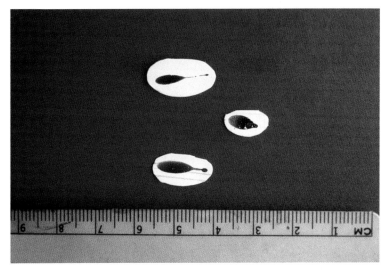

FIGURE 1.7   Figure 2.5 Individual stains from Patterns Illustrating Known Dynamics, reprinted from *Blood Dynamics*.
(Used by permission of Elsevier, Inc.)

cross-examination related to claims that this author advocated identification of dynamic events from one or two individual spatters. Although such a claim could apply to others, it was a misperception in regard to this author. Throughout training and publications, this author has emphasized that no two or even a few stains can adequately identify the violent events which distributed blood drops. Such contradictory claims led the author to inquire for the background from which the misstatements were derived. The cause was identified as misinterpretation of the figure shown here as presented in *Blood Dynamics*.

The three spatter stains shown were to illustrate manufactured patterns from known dynamics including *impact* (with a spring-trap device), *castoff* (from an overhand swing with a crowbar), and *arterial spurt* (from a punctured latex tubing attached to a recirculating pump). The reader was asked to identify which dynamic applied to which stain, with the answers given at the end of the chapter. What was not stated and led to the misunderstanding was that the size and shape of all three stains were deliberately selected to be similar. The objective of the exhibit, however, was not specifically stated.

Based on size and shape of the individual stains, *the dynamic events could **not** be identified*. Unfortunately, such identity may be claimed as the basis for opinions of classification with blood spatters. The association of identity solely based on size and shape of spatters has been suggested for dynamics classification to fit the VIS terms shifted in definition. The illustration was presented in *Blood Dynamics* to show the unreliability of size and shape of *individual* spatters in identifying and classifying the dynamic events that distributed blood drops. Size and shape of groups of spatters do help determine degree of force, although they are not sufficient as individual stains alone. The classification requires whole spatter pattern groups, with the predominance of specific sizes included and consideration to alignments and distribution among the included spatters.

What may have created the misperceptions of the figure in *Blood Dynamics* is that some readers attempted to identify the individual stains as requested and were not correct when they checked the answers. Instead of accepting that size and shape of individual stains did not help in identifying the dynamic acts, readers criticized the author for presenting such a question initially, with implication that there was an answer. A requirement of any expert witness, although a difficult position in forensics, is that it is acceptable to say, "I can't answer that question given the material I have to work with," which was the unstated objective of the author. The desired answer was "I can't identify the actions from those individual stains."

The stains were chosen to illustrate the inaccuracy of using individual size and shape to identify events from known actions and were deliberately chosen to confuse readers. Each stain, individually, could lead to misidentification. The top stain was from swing castoffs. The extended tail, more tear drop shape, and smaller overall size suggested impact spatter but was castoff shaped in position and alignment shown because of the speed of the swing at that point when the drop left the crowbar that distributed it. The crowbar surface did not retain sufficient blood for larger drops. The mass of the crowbar also acted to influence the size and shape of the spatters recorded. Less blood adhering to the weapon surface resulted in less blood, smaller drops, and castoff in the swing with greater centripetal force (note spelling is not *centrifugal*). In other words, the speed of blood drops is not uniform for impact and castoff spatters but could be uniform for a segment of arterial-distributed drops projected at the same amount of force from blood pressure. Thus, size and shape uniformity of a group of spatters, or lack of uniformity, could be helpful to differentiate between impact and castoff or arterial damage *whole* patterns (arrangement of several spatters from one dynamic event). Alone, as individual spatters, concluding action identification is not reliable.

The middle stain was from gunshot-distributed blood drops; no other event occurred. The shape, however, was fat and short, which would suggest castoff or arterial dynamics. The purpose of this example was to illustrate that spatter shape was influenced by location in space and distance from the impact in relation to a blood source. The size was larger than the traditional association of gunshot with mist-sized recorded spatter because of the distance the drop traveled beyond the range that mist low-mass drops can carry. The farther medium-sized drops traveled, the less reliable size alone would be in suggesting gunshot dynamics. One must see a group of blood spatters from a single event to classify them according to dynamic act of distribution.

The bottom stain was from a puncture in latex tubing of similar size to main arterial blood vessels. The single stain more closely resembled blunt force trauma distribution but lacked the group of stains that would show parallel arrangement of uniform-sized individual spatters. Thus, all three stains were selected to emphasize that one *cannot identify what event distributed the blood drops forming the three stains on the basis of individual spatter appearance alone.* Other criteria must be included to identify the dynamic events involved, with size and shape considered after identification to determine the degree of force. Size and shape of spatters help to fine-tune interpretation of the series of events in the total crime sequence. Dr. Kirk originally used criteria other than just size of spatters to differentiate dynamics.

The last choice of the three unknown stains, which represents an arterial damage blood spatter, also introduces a common misunderstanding that contributes to errors in investigations. Books on bloodstain patterns claim the sizes of blood spatters resulting from arterial spurts identify arterial damage patterns (James and Eckert, 1999, p. 42). Because the source of blood, an artery, creates the identifying features of the classification, the resultant pattern totally depends on the nature of the arterial breach for patterns, i.e., size, shape, alignment, and distribution of blood drops. Because arteries are not uniform in size and/or flow rate, nor is it possible to standardize the injury that causes a breach, arterial-distributed blood drops are not of a standard, typical, or uniform size for the range of patterns possible. Spatter size from arterial distribution may range from mist to multiple large drops. The former size may occur for initial breach and a pinhole puncture, whereas the latter size may occur from overlapping of several individual drops hitting together in a chain. This not only influences identification but also provides widely differing interpretations when found at crime scenes. Refer to Section II of this book for identification and Section III for interpretation of arterial damage bloodstain patterns.

In May 1998, during a spring meeting of the California Association of Criminalists, the author made a statement within a presentation equating force and energy. A common mistake occurs when a colloquial use is mixed with a scientific term. The challenge from someone more versed in physics was justified and appreciated. Force and energy are not the same thing, although studies show that there is some link between the two quantities. Force has direction, whereas energy does not. Energy is studied as potentials, whereas force has stated direction from specific events. Between classical physics and modern physics, with regard to force and energy, meaning of the terms shifted in interpretation (Parker, 1998, pp. 1068-1069). Kinematic energy is related to mass and velocity as $E = \frac{1}{2} mv$, while in classical kinetics, force was equated to mass and acceleration as $F = ma$. Kinematics is modern physics as contrasted with classical physics.

The reason for error in comparing energy with force for the lecture during the California Association of Criminalists meeting was that energy was used in a colloquial sense, equated with force, whereas force was taken from the study of classical mechanics from textbooks published prior to 1962—still relatively early, but later revisions showed updating (White, 1962, pp. 18, 118). The author tenders apologies for any misspoken principles regarding these terms. The point that needs to be made is that although one can debate physics applications and accuracy, such discussions do not necessarily provide technical and practical procedures to apply bloodstain pattern evidence to actual case processing. This is not to say doing so isn't important, but rather other principles may need to be considered first.

PREVIOUS CONFUSION CORRECTED

Does bloodstain pattern evidence follow Newton's laws? A misunderstanding occurred with an advertising blurb for *Blood Dynamics*. The blurb stated that the book included material suggesting that blood does not follow Newton's laws of motion. Because the majority of practitioners of bloodstain pattern analysis rely on physics to explain blood behavior, and Newton's laws form an integral basis for modern physics, an objection was spread in personal discussions. In fact, a common introduction to testimony is that "blood is a fluid like any other fluid that behaves according to the laws of physics" (MacDonell, 1982, p. 2). The cross-examination question should be, "which laws of physics?" The assumption for the misleading advertisement was that "non-Newtonian fluid behavior" meant that blood didn't follow Newton's laws. The statement should have been that blood does not follow the fluid mechanics suggested by Newton. Such deviation from fluid mechanics that apply to water and aqueous substances must be considered in any scientific definitions for bloodstain pattern evidence.

Bloodstain Pattern Evidence, Objective Approaches and Case Applications clarified the error that Newtonian flow was derived from suggestions, not laws, proposed by Sir Isaac Newton (Wonder, 2007, p. 23), and that non-Newtonian behavior was discovered and labeled hundreds of years after Newton's death. Thus, the existence of non-Newtonian fluid behavior does not deal directly with

Newton's laws of motion. Further explanation of the sequence and knowledge regarding non-Newtonian behavior is available in Chapter 2.

THE ECONOMICS OF BLOODSTAIN PATTERN TRAINING

Although a new approach to bloodstain pattern evidence as a scientific discipline can be beneficial to any investigation of violent crime, a background is necessary from an introductory bloodstain pattern workshop. Several such programs are available from private and in-house formats. Unfortunately, administration may limit attendance to specific individual duty stations due to decreasing budgets. Justification of the training requires economic consideration, and many requests have been encountered that this need should be addressed in books regarding applications of the evidence. The difficulty of supplying specific cost savings became clear in interviews with administrators, detectives, and commanding officers. The discussions established that a case may take as little as a day with one detective to months, years, or even decades with many officers, plus crime lab and prosecuting attorney time. Cases featured on reality TV detective series have taken years and scores of investigator time and travel to reach adjudication or other resolution. All those interviewed claimed there was no way to predict budgets for homicide investigations. One retired chief of police claimed no law enforcement administrator wanted to know in advance how much a high-profile investigation might cost.

The first point in considering economics is deciding whether the scene of death is a homicide, suicide, or accident. Suicides and accidents may not be viewed as justifying the same extensive devotion of time and expense with multiple DNA testing, complete CSI work-up, and/or volume of interviews. This is not to say that accidents and suicides are ignored but rather that the classification can then lead to a more speedy resolution than those immediately classified as homicide. Therefore, the first determinant of how much cost outlay will result from an investigation is how the case is classified. There are many examples available of homicides classed as suicides or accidents, as well as accidental deaths classed as homicides, plus suicides classed as homicides for insurance or religious purposes. The tighter the budget, the more likely a case could be quickly resolved by calling it an accident or suicide. Such a call may result in empowering a murderer to kill again, in addition to the injustice to family and friends of the victim. Law enforcement officers are very aware of the danger of miscalling a crime scene but may be forced into a quick decision by demands on time and expense. Bloodstain pattern evidence is the cheapest and most rapid path to a correct call for cases in which blood has been shed. However, to make the most effective use of such training, one must apply some recognition to first-line patrol officers as well as later identification technicians and homicide detectives. Sending homicide detectives to a bloodstain workshop but not the identification personnel usually results in the evidence not being fully applied, especially if considerable contamination occurs before the detectives arrive at a crime scene. Assumptions may be, erroneously, made that no probative evidence exists, and/or essential patterns may be ignored because they were considered contaminated by first-line responders. Short 1- to 2-hour presentations within the usual basic law enforcement academy and/or peripheral service training repays in the long run.

In at least one jurisdiction, the erroneous classifying of a suicide, which was in fact a homicide, by coroner's deputies resulted in all death investigations being processed by homicide personnel thereafter. Identification, or CSI, preprocessing would be a more economical approach. Even so, the assigned prosecution may be making the final decisions and thus need to be aware of how the evidence can be applied to quickly resolve questions and decide the proper charges. In recent case-work, this author has encountered substantial staging of crime scenes. Jurors are blamed for expecting CSI-style evidence, but assailants also watch CSI-type programs. Charging the wrong person based on misreading staged evidence can destroy lives and allow a murderer to kill again.

Patrol officers benefit from some preliminary training in bloodstain pattern evidence so that they do not get sick at the sight of a bloody crime scene. Understanding what various bloodstain patterns mean provides a duty to perform, a need to seal the scene, and a desire to protect the evidence. When the patterns are understood, thoughts of where the blood came from become less intimidating. Understanding the probative value of bloodstains increases the chance that first responders won't contaminate the scene.

The FBI Uniform Crime Reporting lists reported murders for the first half of 2013 (Federal Bureau of Investigation website). Those include only the known and reported murders. The statistics do not include suicides and accidents and may not include all homicides if such is suspected but not confirmed; i.e., cold cases are not necessarily included. Of these reported murders, percentages were provided for cities around the continental United States. Examples include New York City (155 murders), Miami (29), Dallas (62), Chicago (179), and Los Angeles (133). Salaries for detectives who would be involved with the cases vary per state and city. California, for example, may pay a homicide detective more than $50,000 per year base salary for 2,080 hours, vacations included. This breaks down to roughly $24–$25 per hour. An 8-hour day would be close to $200 with possible overtime 1½ times hourly. For Los Angeles, the cost for murder investigations would be a minimum of $26,600 if each of its 133 murders was cleared in one day with one detective. If detectives always work with partners, the price doubles to $53,200. But seldom does a case take only one day. Consequently, the cost escalates exponentially.

Budget constraints are strongest in cities with higher crime rates, while one high-profile case could bankrupt a small town's law enforcement budget. The answer isn't more money for the budget but rather use of CSI techniques that provide increased benefits to clearing cases without the need for more funds. Quick resolution of a violent scene with preliminary investigative leads information can provide budget boosts of immeasurable benefit. This information may be applied in requests for all personnel to attend some form of bloodstain pattern training and bring the information back to the department for justification to set up an in-house program to fit each duty station. No one workshop is viewed as the best. All provide something, and most provide emphasis on one or more categories of patterns. Sending officers to different programs is of benefit to the department. Setting up in-house programs may be limited to the information gleaned from only one workshop, but adding to the in-house program from different outside programs would benefit the sum of knowledge for the entire department.

The economic meltdown of the twenty-first century requires considerable cost savings for all investigative work and violent crime investigation. Specifically, aggravated assault and homicide are the most costly procedures handled by law enforcement. Bloodstain pattern evidence provides instant investigative leads, while not requiring expensive equipment, extended personnel time, and/or storage of volatile/corrosive/carcinogenic chemicals. To not use this information completely, correctly, and competently in cases of violent crime is a waste of time and funds that no agency can presently afford. This becomes an even greater loss if violent serial criminals are not identified early in their career. Competent applications do require accurate and quality training, yet any training to appreciate bloodstain pattern evidence benefits the course of criminal justice. The purpose of this book is to add to training and experience, not to replace it.

The following information is directed toward those who have never attended a workshop as well as those who feel they are presently qualified as experts in bloodstain pattern evidence.

REFERENCES

Balthazard, V., Piedelievre, R., Desoille, H., DeRobert, L., 1939. Etude des gouttes de sang projecte. Presented at the 22nd Congress of Forensic Medicine, Paris.

Bevel, T., Gardner, R.M., 2002. Bloodstain Pattern Analysis With an Introduction to Crime Scene Reconstruction, 2nd ed. CRC Press, Boca Raton, FL. pp. 74, 104.

Bevel, T., Gardner, R.M., 2008. Bloodstain Pattern Analysis With an Introduction to Crime Scene Reconstruction, 3rd ed. CRC Press, Boca Raton, FL. p. 13.

Federal Bureau of Investigation website. Crime in the United States Preliminary Statistics for 2013 January-June. http://www.fbi.gov/about-us/cjis/ucr/crime-in-the-u.s/2011/crime-in-the-u.s.-2011 (accessed August, 2014).

Hulse-Smith, L., 2008. Book review. Journal of the Forensic Sciences 53 (4): 1015. July.

James, S.H. (Ed.), 1998. Scientific and Legal Applications of Bloodstain Pattern Interpretation. CRC Press, Boca Raton, FL, p. 162.

James, S.H., Eckert, W.G., 1999. Interpretation of Bloodstain Evidence at Crime Scenes, 2nd ed. CRC Press, Boca Raton, FL. pp. 42, 305.

Kirk, P.L., 1968. Presentation Notes for a Lecture at the 4th Annual Criminal Law Seminar, San Francisco, CA. Paul Kirk Papers. Blood Spot Analysis. UC Berkeley Library, Berkeley, CA.

Laber, T., 1986. Diameter of Bloodstain as a Function of Origin, Distance Fallen, and Volume of the Drop. IABPA News 1 (2), 12–16.

LinkedIn website, 2012-2013. Discussions between several forensic scientists regarding closure of FSS government crime laboratories in the UK.

MacDonell, H.L., Bialousz, L.F., 1971. Flight Characteristics and Stain Patterns of Human Blood. National Institute of Law Enforcement and Criminal Justice, Washington, D.C. p. 1.

MacDonell, H.L., 1982. Bloodstain Pattern Interpretation, Revision. Painted Post Press, Corning, NY. p. 2.

MacDonell, H.L., 1991. Transcript of testimony in the Alexander Lindsay Inquiry, May 27. p. 820.

Parker, S.P. (Ed.), 1998. Concise Encyclopedia of Science and Technology. , 4th ed.McGraw-Hill, New York, NY, pp. 1068–1069.

Regan, B., 2008. The Truth about Forensics. Popular Mechanics, August, 51.

Smith, L.S., 2011. Photograph of a prehistoric cave painting. Photography exhibit at the South African Museum in Cape Town, South Africa.

Walcher, K., 1939. Ein Leitfaden fur Studiereende Arzte und Kriminalisten. In: Bluntuntersuchung, Gerrichtlich-medizinische und Kriminalistische.

White, H.E., 1962. Modern College Physics. D. Van Nostrand Company, Inc, Princeton, NJ. pp. 18, 118.

Wonder, A.Y., 2001. Blood Dynamics. Academic Press, London. pp. 25, 36.

Wonder, A.Y., 2007. Bloodstain Pattern Evidence, Objective Approaches and Case Applications. Elsevier, San Diego, CA. pp. 2–4, 23, 51.

The Science of Bloodstain Pattern Evidence

Although there is proof that bloodstain patterns have been recognized for thousands of years (Wonder, 2007, pp. 2–4), and concepts from 100 years ago are still appreciated as the basis for principles (Scientific Working Group on Bloodstain Pattern Analysis, 2009) to justify some subjectivity, changes within the past 50 years should be considered when doing reviews and revising guidelines regarding bloodstain pattern evidence. References that follow, although not from the most recent publications, are offered to orient the reader to search engines that provide a history of changes in the scientific bases of bloodstain pattern evidence.

The question of whether or not blood is a non-Newtonian fluid is important to bloodstain pattern evidence and must be answered. It is essential that time and money aren't wasted considering technical material that will not benefit the discipline. It is equally important not to ignore applicable technical advances before designing research experiments. An abstract for the 2012 American Academy of Forensic Sciences (AAFS) meeting in Atlanta (Park and Cho, 2012) suggested alternative logic for estimating the size of drops and distance fallen by counting the spines around blood spatters. The study acknowledged blood as being non-Newtonian in behavior but did not consider what factors contribute to that classification and how the classification affects blood drop behavior. The size of drops formed and the edge characteristics, or spines, which result from drop contact with a surface are very much influenced by the ratio of red blood cells to plasma in the blood drops. The fact that red blood cell content contributes to blood being non-Newtonian was recognized before the 1980s (Lowe, 1988, p. 5).

The simple statement that it doesn't matter whether or not blood is a non-Newtonian fluid from anyone who is not offering proof to support his or her claim unjustly prevents acquisition of knowledge to resolve the issue. Some of the scientific principles commonly mentioned in publications defining bloodstain pattern evidence are based on pre–World War II concepts. The explanations in those terms may be accepted in court because law is based on precedents from the foundation of the applicable legal system itself, whether that be adversarial, Napoleonic Code, or other. Each change in a law requires adequate discussion and approval by an authoritative body, so stating principles in words established hundreds of years ago keeps law orderly; however, such order may provide nothing toward expanding applications or clarification of a science. In keeping things simple, one can consider that law is words, whereas science is things.

The scientific emphasis placed on bloodstain pattern evidence predominantly comes from the disciplines of mathematics and physics. Does physics accurately and completely describe blood fluid behavior? The answer to that question is "no," especially in modern times after hundreds of years of discoveries in related biological fields. Living systems have many surprises, and blood is a living, respiring system. Advances in science show that fluid mechanics of some substances, especially blood, are not like all other fluids and do not behave according to the classical mechanics formula derived from Newton's suggestions, i.e., Newtonian fluid mechanics. Water is the classical example of a Newtonian fluid, as described and studied in hydraulics (King et al., 1949, pp. 7–13). Blood is not the same as water; thus, it is classified with many other complex materials as non-Newtonian and studied in rheology (Connes et al., 2013, pp. 283–293).

In general, physics is considered a steady scientific discipline with two cautions. First, new discoveries do, in fact, occur, although they may not be as frequent as in fields such as DNA and computer technology. Second, new applications require changes in viewpoint of historically accepted principles. To expand the applications of bloodstain pattern evidence, we must acknowledge both of these cautions with regard to what we accept as the forensic science discipline of bloodstain pattern analysis (BPA). Most of the introductory workshops on bloodstain patterns rely on scientific principles that may date to the late 1930s (Testimony, 1991, pp. 820–821; Piotrowski, 1895) or even earlier. Educators who teach this subject may have learned their basic science years previously to providing instruction or accepted a background from instructors who, in turn, learned their approach to the field decades ago. To say nothing has changed since then may mean that lectures lack important updates to information that would be beneficial to future applications.

In addition to advances in the whole discipline of physics, classical mechanics experienced some changes to become modern mechanics (Parker, 1998, p. 412). Other sciences—notably hematology, clinical chemistry, and physiology—have provided volumes of research information regarding blood behavior because of the involvement of blood in medicine. These additional scientific basics also provide engineering validity, i.e., the importance in flow and behavior of fluids, including blood, both inside and outside the body.

One discovery occurred in the mid-1940s following World War II, when industrialization of flow mechanics gave rise to a whole new field of discovery: rheology. Hydraulics is the flow of water, or watery substances (King et al., 1949, p. 1) and thus classified as Newtonian fluid, based on suggestions by Newton discovered years after his death. "Rheology" was a new term to designate non-Newtonian fluids that behave differently from water and watery fluids. This followed the discovery that some substances—most noteworthy at the time were processed food stuffs and synthetic rubber and plastics—did not flow according to formulas derived from suggestions made by Newton. This was not in violation of any of Newton's motion laws. It was, however, considerable deviation from a formula developed from his suggestions sufficient to cause manufacturing design problems for industrial processing. Blood behavior gave rise to the biorheology discipline of bioengineering and applications to vascular medicine. Blood flow and behavior are influenced by rheological classification both within and outside the body, while hydraulics is used to understand the distribution of water, such as the behavior of rain drops and other aqueous fluids.

When traditionalists are challenged regarding blood not being a fluid comparable to water, the answer is usually that it's just a matter of viscosity. Yes, viscosity is involved, but blood behavior is not a simple matter of viscosity. Watery fluids have a direct, linear relationship with viscosity, whereas blood has a changing, logarithmic relationship between flow and viscosity; this is studied as "viscoelasticity." The difference in concepts between viscoelasticity and viscosity should not be confusing, except for a misunderstanding that blood is a uniform substance. If that were true, the increasing number of tests available for analysis of blood in a clinical laboratory and the considerable research to find proper vessel replacements for implants wouldn't be necessary. Blood does not have uniform consistency, measured with standard ratios of components, nor simple uniform viscosity. In fact, a test in a 1970s clinical lab included a tube method of estimating viscosity for a single patient's blood (Tietz, 1983, p. 502). If blood was viewed as uniform, a test for variance would be irrelevant.

To know how non-Newtonian behavior affects bloodstain pattern formation, we must first understand in what way behaviors differ between blood and water because water has been used as a comparable study medium for comparison to blood (Raymond et al., 1996). and blood is confirmed as a non-Newtonian fluid (Lowe, 1988, p. 5). Viscoelasticity influences flow via a characteristic that is called "stress" in rheology but may be better known as "friction" between layers of fluids and surfaces. This is also regarded as resistance to flow. The faster water flows, the more stress, or friction, it exerts against the surface or other fluid that it flows against. Blood, on the other hand, is "thixotrophic." This is a term exclusive to rheology and non-Newtonian fluids. It means that the faster blood flows, the influence from stress changes. At first, the faster blood flows, the greater the stress, but as it continues to flow faster still, the stress reverses and becomes less. This happens because of blood's composition.

In *Blood Dynamics,* this author pointed out that blood does not normally flow homogeneously, or evenly, mixed (Wonder, 2001, p. 10). As described in the 1980s, blood behavior in vessels flows with red cells forming a central core in the middle with plasma and circulating platelets around the center core in the vessel. This composition can facilitate smooth flow and resist friction, or stress. However, with blood, at a point in the higher velocity of flow, the column of red blood cells destabilizes. Instead of the smooth, less viscous, outer fluid flowing through the vessel, a random mixture of particulate blood cells bumps against the vessel walls. When blood is destabilized due to fast flow and/or high blood pressure, the friction against the blood vessel increases. In the human body, this behavior may lead to vascular disease of emboli (blood clots) formation, which in turn may cause heart attacks and strokes. The combination of destabilized blood flow and pressure, in turn, may lead to aneurysms (weakening of the arterial vessel wall). The implications in arterial flow and blood behavior with the arterial system make understanding the non-Newtonian nature of blood most important in bloodstain pattern evidence.

The importance of non-Newtonian fluid behavior varies for the dynamic acts that distribute blood. For impact, blood does behave pretty much like other viscoelastic fluids. A force is applied that breaks the substance into drops and distributes them away along flight paths that can be estimated with math and physics. The composition of blood in terms of red cells will influence the size of drops formed, their holding a spherical shape in flight, and the distance they are able to travel. Because red cells are heavier than plasma and red cell count varies per individual and body part/organ location, it is illogical to expect uniformity of blood drop size for different sources (animal or human) during the variable dynamics of crimes. Variance between concentration of red blood cells considered with variation in impact degree of force may require too much additional information to be useful in providing investigative information at crime scenes. Understanding non-Newtonian behavior at this time is regarded as providing insignificant additional information to the criteria used to identify, interpret, and apply, specifically, to impact spatter patterns.

For castoffs, blood behavior is more complicated because of the adhesion between blood and different surfaces. Water may be absorbed, so it does not adhere to surfaces in the same manner as blood. The latter coats a weapon, depending on the attraction between plasma/red blood cells and a specific surface, with the behavior in coating and sloughing/casting off essential in interpretation of the patterns left at crime scenes. A metal ball bat may cast off smaller and more numerous drops than a worn wooden bat because the worn wooden surface absorbs the blood fluid substance, plasma, whereas metal fails to contain it. The easier blood leaves a surface, the more numerous the drops distributed. The size of drops is influenced by the type of surface in addition to the strength of the swing. In this situation, experimentation with a reasonable facsimile of the actual weapon can be beneficial. Still, the advantages of understanding non-Newtonian behavior are less important to bloodstain pattern identification than having a quality scheme in differentiating castoff patterns versus other dynamics. Most important in interpretation is that castoff patterns (a measure of assailant aggression) be differentiated from arterial damage patterns (the assailant need not even be present). Arterial patterns are definitely affected by non-Newtonian behavior.

For arterial damage, recognizing and interpreting bloodstain patterns require attention to non-Newtonian behavior if full benefit from the evidence is to be realized. The importance of this is emphasized by this author's frequent encounters with arterial patterns misidentified as castoff, when criteria should be clear. It is not advisable to rely on an autopsy to identify an artery before looking for such patterns at a crime scene. Not all pathologists will list arterial damage if the cause and/or manner of death does not directly relate to an arterial breach (Rooney, 1980). An autopsy report will list a gunshot wound to the temple only as GSW (gunshot wound) but may not include the fact that the bullet punctured an arterial blood vessel. The lack of reporting arterial involvement was confirmed during discussions at the AAFS pathology/biology section in New Orleans in 2005 (Wonder, 2005).

As previously stated, it is rheology that defines the dynamics of arterial distribution and provides investigative leads information. In other words, non-Newtonian fluid mechanics extends the information possible and application of bloodstain pattern evidence to quickly and economically resolve violent crimes, fatal accidents, and suicides where arterial damage has occurred. Arterial injury often figures in suicides mistaken as homicides and aggravated assaults misinterpreted as premeditated murder. Breaching a major artery, with massive blood loss, may be more quickly fatal than blunt force trauma, or may turn an assault into a homicide after the assailant is no longer present.

An example of the possibilities occurred with the bloodstain described on a sock linked to O. J. Simpson when he was accused of killing his wife and her acquaintance, a restaurant waiter. An expert at trial testified that the stain could have been staged by applying blood from a tube of blood, collected from the victim earlier, to a hand and then pressing the palm of the hand to a sock found at the scene (see Figure 2.1). The bloodstain on the sock was heaviest on the outside, but a small stain was left on the opposite inside surface as worn. A number of facts made the expert's claim unlikely. The sock was expensive and thick. Several students of a bloodstain pattern workshop attempted palm application (to mimic stepping on the sock or pressing blood from a palm to the sock). Not one of the attempts could force blood from a student's palm through the sock to the opposite side inside, especially in the pattern described (see Figure 2.2). Stepping on the sock after a spot of blood was deposited failed to transfer blood also, but was considered a possibility after the arterial deposit of blood, as illustrated in Figure 2.3A. What was successful in transferring blood as shown occurred with the sock worn, weave stretched, at the moment blood gushed from a carotid arterial injury (see Figure 2.3B). Such an event would be explained with arterial injury gushing against the ankle of a person wearing the sock.

More important than the possible methods by which the bloodstain could be recorded was the appearance of the stain as described. The pattern was described as a central core with small dots of spatters around it. This is a specific pattern consistent with arterial injury at the moment of great stress (Wonder, 2001, p. 76). When the body is under extreme stress, emotionally or physically, as much as

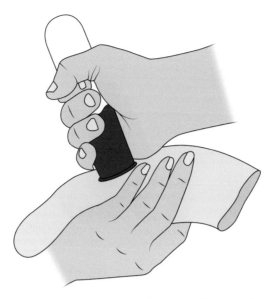

FIGURE 2.1   As explained in trial (no mention of presence of anticoagulant with blood on sock).

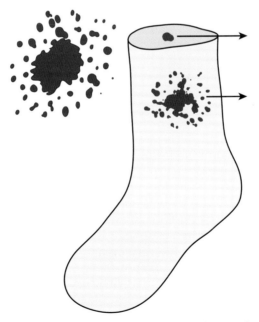

FIGURE 2.2   The description of the bloodstain found on a sock at the scene.

I. INTRODUCTION

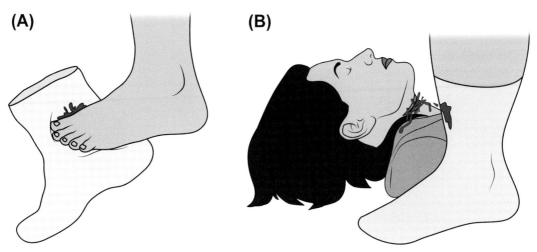

FIGURE 2.3   Two possible ways to deposit bloodstain pattern as allegedly observed: (A) step on sock after arterial spurt if sock on floor; (B) arterial spurt while sock was worn.

85%–90% of blood flow may be routed between the heart and the brain through the carotid arteries of the neck (Sohmer, 1979, p. 2.805). This accounts for the extreme pressure at the moment the neck was cut, and would be an explanation for the destabilized gush with dots around the central core of blood. Additionally, only Nicole Brown Simpson had arterial injuries that could distribute arterial blood externally. Ron Goldman's injuries were internal and would not project arterial spurts. It was Nicole's blood on the sock. If this was recognized as an arterial bloodstain pattern, the misdirection over Officer Mark Furhman allegedly faking the stain would have been discredited because he was unlikely to know that an arterial pattern existed, that it had to come from Nicole, and how to fake the appearance of this classification. Ignoring non-Newtonian fluid behavior of arterial damage patterns may prevent discoveries of applications that are valuable, cost efficacious, and essential for justice.

Perhaps the resistance to recognizing non-Newtonian fluid mechanics in bloodstain pattern evidence is the reliance on the concept of surface tension in describing why blood drops round up in flight. "Surface tension" is found in all fluids in various degrees of strength, although all are relatively weak forces. As the term implies, this force is limited to the surface of the fluid (Hunter, 1993, p. 132). The larger the drop of fluid, the weaker the force holding it to a rounded shape. Water is considered one of the strongest surface tensions recognized, yet it oscillates, wobbles, and may merge with other drops during flight. An illustration is shown in Figure 2.4. As shown in Figure 2.5, blood drops are seen to round up in tighter spheres with little motion after drop separation from the blood source. This photograph is of the very instant after an injury to an athlete's face. Blood has surface tension yet that alone cannot account for the tight rounding up to form drops. This topic was discussed in *Blood Dynamics* (Wonder, 2001, pp. 26–28) and again in *Bloodstain Pattern Evidence, Objective Approaches and Case Applications* (Wonder, 2007, pp. 29–31), yet criticism has occurred in regard to the statement that blood drops do not round up because of surface tension alone. In fact, blood drops do not round up because of surface tension alone. The internal cohesion created by red blood cells forms a much stronger bond to keep the blood drops in a tight spherical shape compared to the surface tension of water.

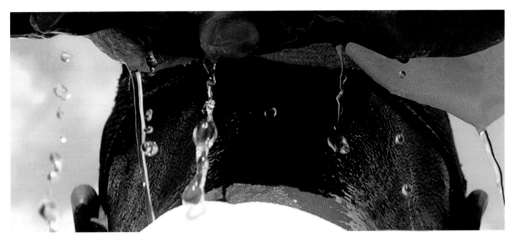

FIGURE 2.4   Water drops distortions in flight. *(Photograph by John Kim)*

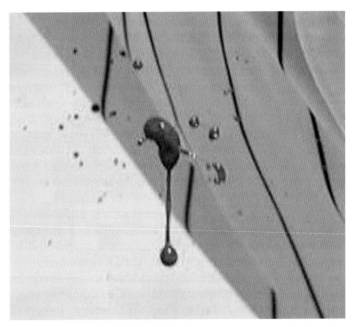

FIGURE 2.5   Blood drops from injury to the mouth (see also the cover photo of this book). *(Photograph by John Kim)*

The difference between water and blood rounding up is described in Epstein's book on physics as the difference between surface tension and internal cohesion (Epstein, 1993, pp. 190–191). An internal molecular attraction should, obviously, be stronger than a force solely on the surface. Less easy to explain but more telling in regard to the surface tension argument between

Newtonian and non-Newtonian fluids is the fact that all textbooks reviewed for information on non-Newtonian fluid mechanics for *Blood Dynamics* (2001), *Bloodstain Pattern Evidence, Objective Approaches and Case Applications* (2007), and *Bloodstain Patterns: Identification, Interpretation, and Applications* (2015) do not list surface tension in the indexes associated with the subject researched. Surface tension is listed in those indexes only when applied to Newtonian fluid behavior (Vennard and Street, 1982, p. 16) and in books on non-Newtonian behavior when Newtonian behavior is also mentioned. Early textbooks on hydraulics do not discuss non-Newtonian fluid mechanics. It follows, then, that surface tension is not a serious consideration when scientists who write the applicable textbooks are defining non-Newtonian fluid behavior. It is a major consideration with regard to Newtonian fluids such as water. It also follows that discussions of water behavior rounding up or not, oscillating/wobbling or not, and having influence on resultant stain measurements do not necessarily apply to blood spatter stains. Note that exceptions have been found after research experiments which are discussed in Chapter 14.

In the early history of physics (1687 and earlier), the science of motion relied on classical mechanics (Parker, 1998, p. 412). Fluid mechanics was viewed more as a stationary concept, not a flowing one. This is where the strider insect is shown balanced on a fluid surface from surface tension alone, but also applied as an explanation for liquid drops rounding up in flight. A sewing needle may be placed on a surface, especially if the needle has skin oil on it. If, however, the water is flowing, both the strider and needle will fall according to the displacement of the object. True, water drops form and can be distributed in flight paths. Drops that touch may flow together and subsequently form bigger drops because the surface tension is a weak force in repelling adjacent drops. Blood drops that touch, in marked contrast to water drops, tend to resist flowing together and, in fact, give rise to a unique pattern known as "blood dripping into blood." Blood drops bounce off a pool of blood initially, forming small satellite spatters around the pool circumference, rather than immediately merging together in the pool. Blood will form a rebounding drop but also merge with milk rather than bounce off the surface. Blood onto blood causes drops to bounce off the surface and away from the pool. This is contrary to reasoning in regard to surface tension. It is consistent with and explained by the additional strength of internal cohesion.

What is internal cohesion, and how does it influence bloodstain patterns? Blood is not a uniform fluid; therefore, the forces that influence behavior are not uniform. The composition of blood includes a liquid that may vary from clear and colorless to opaque and bright yellow. This is dependent on protein, fat, and bile in the liquid plasma. In a healthy body, particles are suspended in plasma. As seen after blood is removed by venipuncture it becomes settled red blood cells (the most numerous), white blood cells, and platelets. In various ailments, crystals and/or solid fat particles may also be found. Red blood cells consist of a protein coat with enclosed red pigmented hemoglobin molecules.

Although mature adult red cells do not contain a nucleus, such as found in tissue and white blood cells to provide DNA (please consult DNA textbooks for further information if required), their synthesis does involve identifying globulin characteristics (Stamatoyannopoulos et al., 1987, p. 67f). This composition provides surface cell attraction that contributes to the core type of flow in blood vessels. The attraction also tends to hold the cells together in flight. Blood drip experiments show that the lower the hematocrit (the ratio of red cells to plasma), the wider a bloodstain will be (Wonder, 1982). The difference in stain diameter occurs for variations in red cell content as has been seen in hundreds of experiments during bloodstain pattern workshops. The simplest explanation is that the internal cohesion of blood drops is influenced by the red cell concentration. The red cell concentration may contribute to surface tension but will be most effective as internal cohesion, not simply drop surface force. This verifies the statement that surface tension alone does not account for the tightness of a sphere for blood drops in flight.

Because red cell ratio influences the tightness of blood drops and the tightness of the sphere affects the spread of the blood drop on contact with a surface, the red blood cell to plasma ratio, expressed as a percent hematocrit, will influence a final bloodstain diameter. However, it has been proven repeatedly (Wonder, 2001, p. 29; Wonder, 2007, p. 367; Dailey, 1998, pp. 70–71, 284) that red cell ratio varies for injury location as well as between different victims. It should follow that all arguments and experimental design based on the theory that a blood drop size can be correlated with the distance the drop fell by measuring the resulting stain are irrelevant to actual crime scene application.

Despite these facts and the discounting of use in investigative methodology, the exercise is still often included in blood spatter workshops. The association between distances fallen and bloodstain diameter provides an easy illustration and reproducibility, with the single variable being surface texture of the target material. What instructors may not share with participants is that, for this experiment to provide predictable results, the blood sample and droppers must be uniform for the entire exercise. Change dropper size, amount of delivery (Wonder, 2001, pp. 19–20), or blood sample red cell composition (i.e., hematocrit) (Wonder, 2001, p. 21), and reproducibility and predictability are lost. If red cell ratio and/or dropper size can skewer a workshop exercise, an actual crime scene cannot possibly benefit from this information gleaned from a training workshop.

Another concept that has been studied is whether blood drops do or do not round up in flight. Again, the idea includes water drop behavior in which drops oscillate and elongate in flight. Yet, blood drops have repeatedly been photographed as nearly complete round spheres in free fall. A short length of fall may be associated with action/reaction, or bounce, after the elasticity of a blood drop breaks contact with the blood source. With continued fall, the lower edge of a blood drop may slightly flatten. The interpretation as an elongated shape may be based on photographs from the side showing contact and continued flow on a slant or the lack of speed in capturing the drop in free fall. What is essentially important in determining drop shape in flight is the initial footprint on contact. Note the cover photograph of a baseball hitting, and creating an injury at, a player's mouth. Drops distributed are predominantly round. Any contact with a surface will be initially round. The teardrop, oval, and exclamation mark shapes result from continued travel after the initial footprint.

Experiments were conducted to view the footprint, beneath the target surface, of a blood drop falling onto a slant. The results are discussed in Section V of this book. A result found during these experiments is applicable to the present discussion of the importance of blood hematocrit. Hemoglobin is also a measure of red cell volume and is a smaller value to deal with. The hematocrit is normally three times the hemoglobin value. Blood drops (0.05 cc) of different hemoglobin values were dropped from a Beral disposable pipette onto a tracing paper sheet at 60-degree slant. The drops, varied only by red blood cell ratios, did not flow the same distance down the slant (see Figure 2.6). Measurements and calculated angles are shown in Table 2.1.

This experiment was interesting because it may provide information to satisfy the NAS request for percentage of errors or error rates for bloodstain pattern techniques. Red blood cell ratio does influence the shape and appearance of blood spatters. A range of 6% to 18% hemoglobin (18%–54% hematocrit, respectively), however, provides only a plus or minus 2 degree variation in angle estimate. Supplying this information is far better in satisfying scientific application than ignoring the fact that it exists.

I. INTRODUCTION

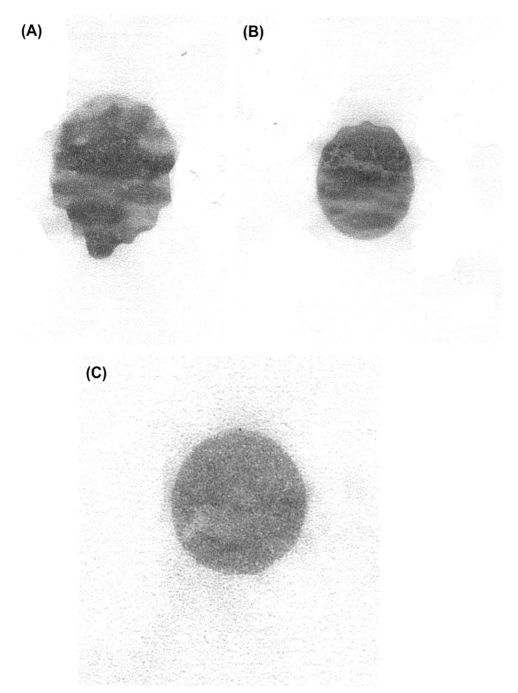

FIGURE 2.6   Variation of appearance and shape for different hemoglobin: (A) 18.1 mg%, (B) 13.4 mg%, and (C) 6.1 mg%.

TABLE 2.1   RBC Volume (as Hemoglobin) Relative to Measurements of Angled Stains

mg% Hgb	Width of Spatter	Height of Spatter	Calculated Angle
18.1	11.5	14.0	55
13.4	10.5	12.5	57
6.1	09.0	10.5	59

The next consideration must be how blood drops result and are distributed following specific events. It is uniformly accepted that some kind of event breaks up a blood source into drops and distributes them along flight paths. That event may be as simple as the force of gravity or as strong as a bullet penetrating tissue. What is desired from blood spatter analysis is the prediction of which type of event was responsible for which group of recorded spatters. Size and shape of individual spatters alone cannot provide that information. Shape of recorded spatters shows the angle of contact with a target and the velocity the drop of blood was traveling when contact and deflection occurred. Just the size of a resultant spatter provides information regarding the degree of the event in transferring energy to expose and break up the quantity of blood available but not necessarily which dynamic event occurred. Because firearms provide a stronger degree in a smaller area, thus possibly breaking a blood source into smaller predominance of drop sizes, experienced investigators soon learn and associate such distribution with gunshot wounds. It is essential, however, that all training include instruction that even mist-sized spatters are not exclusive of gunshot wounds. It is required that the event be identified from bloodstain pattern characteristics criteria before the size and shape of individual spatters within the arrangement are interpreted. This topic is addressed in Section II.

REFERENCES

Connes, P., Dufour, S., Pichon, A., Furet, F., 2013. Blood Rheology, Blood Flow, and Human Health. In: Bagchi, D., Nair, S., Sen, C. (Eds.), Nutrition and Enhanced Sports Performance. Academic Press, New York, NY, pp. 283–293.

Dailey, J.F., 1998. Blood. Medical Consulting Group, Arlington, MA. pp. 70–71, 284.

Epstein, L.C., 1993. Lessons in Thinking Physics. Insight Press, San Francisco, CA. pp. 190–191.

Hunter, R.J., 1993. Introduction to Modern Colloid Science. Oxford Science, Oxford. p. 132.

King, H.W., Wisler, C.O., Woodburn, J.G., 1949. Hydraulics, 5th ed. John Wiley & Sons, New York, NY. pp. 1, 7–13.

Lowe, G.D.O. (Ed.), 1988. Clinical Blood Rheology, vol. 1. CRC Press, Boca Raton, FL. p. 5.

Park, C.-S., Cho, N.-S., 2012. C1 Study on the Effects of Surface Roughness on Blood Patterns. Paper presented at the American Academy of Forensic Sciences, 64th Annual Meeting, Atlanta, GA. before the Engineering Section.

Parker, S.P., Ed., 1988. Concise Encyclopedia of Science and Technology, 4th ed. McGraw-Hill, New York, NY, p. 112.

Piotrowski, E., 1895. Ueber Entstehung, Form, Richtung und Ausbreitung der Blutsuren nach Hiebwunden des Kopfes. Vienna.

Raymond, M. E., Smith, L.C., Liesegang, J., 1996. Liesegang, Oscillating Blood Droplets - Implications for Crime Scene Reconstruction. Science & Justice. 36(3): p. 161–171.

Rooney, P., 1980. Personal communication. Sacramento Pathology Group.

Scientific Working Group on Bloodstain Pattern Analysis Response to the National Academy of Sciences Executive Summary for Strengthening Forensic Sciences in the United States Path Forward, 2009.

Sohmer, P.R., 1979. Hemotherapy in Trauma and Surgery. A Technical Workshop. American Association of Blood Banks, Washington, D.C. p. 2.

Stamatoyannopoulos, G., Nienhuis, A.W., Leder, P., Majerus, P.W., 1987. The Molecular Basis of Blood Diseases. W.B. Saunders Company, Philadelphia, PA. p. 67f.

Testimony of the inquiry held under section 475 of the Crimes Act of 1990 into the conviction of Alexander Lindsay (formerly Alexander MacLeod-Lindsay), 1991. pp. 820–821.

Tietz, N.W. (Ed.), 1983. Clinical Guide to Laboratory Testing. W.B. Saunders Company, Philadelphia, PA, p. 502.

Vennard, J.K., Street, R.L., 1982. Elementary Fluid Mechanics, 6th ed. John Wiley & Sons, New York, NY. p. 16.

Wonder, A.Y., 1982. Effects on Geometric Human Bloodstain Design by Hemoglobin Concentration and Time Sequence of Moisture Exposure. California State University, Sacramento, CA. Master's Thesis.

Wonder, A.Y., 2001. Blood Dynamics. Academic Press, London. pp. 10, 19–21, 26–29, 76.

Wonder, A.Y., 2005. An Expert Witness Requests Re-evaluation of SOP for Autopsy Reporting. Paper presented at the American Academy of Forensic Sciences, 57th Annual Meeting, New Orleans, LA. before the Pathology/Biology Section.

Wonder, A.Y., 2007. Bloodstain Pattern Evidence, Objective Approaches and Case Applications. Elsevier, San Diego, CA. pp. 2–4, 29–31, 367.

I. INTRODUCTION

Discussion on Terminology

Some terms related to bloodstain pattern analysis have been discussed and used in the preceding chapters, yet many more need consideration for future scientific justification. An essential approach to terminology in scientific disciplines is that terms not be written in stone. This contrasts markedly from legal professions where set terms and definitions are often kept consistent for decades, if not millennia. Although forensic scientists may defend keeping traditional semantics as being scientific. Advances in comparable research have shown a need for modification. These efforts favor legal precedents more than science. This is especially true with administrative positions, as seen with the reactions to the National Academy of Sciences (NAS) report. Because law, courts, and law enforcement are the primary as well as final users, they also set the justification for budgets. Administrators may focus on keeping terminology consistent with prior testimonies given at trial to avoid future challenges to previous convictions. Repeat trials may result in budget dilemmas that outweigh concerns for the field of science updating its semantics.

Terminology lists of the International Association of Bloodstain Pattern Analysts (IABPA), International Association for Identification (IAI), the Scientific Working Group on Bloodstain Pattern Analysis (SWGSTAIN), and those submitted to the ASTM International (prior to 2001 known as the American Society for Testing and Materials) have attempted to set standards for years. There are reports that complete agreement with experts in the discipline has not been established to date, although reported lists are published based on majority votes of committee members. The National Institute of Standards and Technology (NIST) could provide not only a framework for establishing terminology but a process for periodic updates based on information from its principal website (Methane).

The terms and, more importantly, definitions listed here are suggestions to achieve three considerations in future committee reviews: (1) to be technically correct based on updated scientific knowledge, (2) to relate to colloquial terms commonly accepted in the past, and (3) to bridge these two with simplified definitions for court. The terms are not now, and should never be, engraved in stone for a scientific discipline. The following sets of terms could provide information for updating for science recognition.

Scientific studies put less emphasis on using the exact words and definitions than the law does. Considerable emphasis, however, has been placed on creating a standardized terminology list for bloodstain pattern analysts from individuals who also put an emphasis on the use of bloodstain pattern

31

evidence in court, rather than as a scientific tool for initial investigation of crime. A problem with forcing conformity to a particular set of semantics in this discipline is the considerable diversity of individuals who firmly believe in their own expertise. Students of bloodstain pattern lectures, and the like, include detectives, law enforcement identification officers, commanders, pathologists, crime reporters, criminalists, college instructors, judges, and lawyers. Each area may have or develop its own vocabulary. This author has had students claim they had signed up for a workshop in "blood splatters" [sic] simply to learn the terminology. In other words, they wanted to learn to speak the language but felt they already knew how to perform the analysis. Performance in the workshops showed they all had more to learn than memorizing terminology lists.

In science, especially medical science, terms grow and change with discoveries. Different medical departments may recognize different terms and definitions of those terms for the same or similar procedures. These differences do not disqualify practitioners from the science of healing. Doctors and nurses often use the term "blood thinner" when there is no such thing. The term was applied before coagulation was fully understood. An early application was to name the concept of blood seeming to thin rather than thicken from clotting. The term is retained because patients accept it as an explanation for the tendency to continue to bleed when injured. The actual science is presently understood as biological prevention of coagulation rather than thinning of blood itself. The clinical lab scientist calls this process "anticoagulation," whereas the doctors who deal with the disorder call it "hemostasis inhibition." Blood thinning, anticoagulation, and hemostasis inhibition all describe the same event. Similar diverse understanding of terminology may occur with forensic science terms as understood by jurors from a variety of backgrounds.

Physics is often used to explain blood flight characteristics, and physicists understand the term "vector" to describe the direction and quantity of force. In contrast, pathologists who also work with microbiology and entomology departments might immediately think of a "vector" as being the agent carrying disease from one host to another. The same word has different meaning to different professions. Likewise, "bloodstain pattern evidence" applies to a wide range of professions involved with the investigation of violent crime.

There can be at least three ways to view a terminology list for the discipline: (1) to be able to communicate pattern identification at the scene to fellow investigative team members; (2) to understand and relate to information from other experts such as criminalists in trace evidence, DNA experts, and firearms, pathologists, and prosecuting attorneys; and (3) to communicate the evidence to members of the court.

Another way of looking at the subject of terminology is to ask what mental image the terms convey. If investigators receive the wrong image, this can lead to biased thinking and taking the wrong track in forming a scenario for the alleged crime. For example, because of the shift in meaning for terms related to velocity impact, the mental image has been altered. The original term "high velocity impact spatter" was a blood drop hitting a target surface at high speed. The shift to meaning an object causing impact to distribute blood drops may cause the crime scene investigator to initially create a mental image before determining the type of event. An example is to immediately say "that's HVIS" because the victim sustained a gunshot wound or "that's MVIS" because no gunshot is immediately determined. This way of thinking leads to immediate bias in concluding that a bloodstain pattern identifies a dynamic event based on assumptions other than the pattern characteristics.

Some of the following discussion is in regard to historical application and definitions that have been modified by applicable committees on bloodstain pattern evidence terminology. The discussions are offered as required from the SWGSTAIN regarding education and training (SWGSTAIN, 2008). A request is made here that future consideration of terminology also include semantics common to professionals who work in fields peripheral to bloodstain pattern evidence experts. The following discussions can be submitted for consideration of future revisions of a terminology list.

ABSENCE TRANSFER

Technical: The lack of blood spatters seen in an area of a recording surface (target) due to the angle from the distributing event to the target being such that none of the spatters are directed at that area of the target. This suggested definition is to separate two different kinds of template transfers included within the term "void."

Discussion: Although the term "void" is frequently used, it is a term that may be considered dated. In the 1940s, void was commonly used to denote a lack of something within an area. Present usage equates void with canceling out, as in "null and void"—for example, "voiding a check" or collecting a biological specimen, such as "voiding a urine." "Absence" is a suggested term for a bloodstain pattern where no spatters are seen in an area of the target for reasons other than a true blockage.

Court Use Suggestion: The absence of spatters on a surface because of the position relative to flight path of blood drops distributed.

AREA OF CONVERGENCE

Technical: The locus of points on a plane surface defining an area where accurately placed direction of travel lines intersect. This area should be proven to have resulted from a single impact event.

Discussion: The term "point of convergence" was used in the past instead of "area of convergence." That is considered to be the point to which a bloodstain pattern can be projected. This point is determined by tracing the long axis of well-defined bloodstains within the pattern back to a common point or source (Eckert and James, 1989, p. 330). The main issue that requires review is that there is no such thing as a *point* of convergence or a point of origin. Blood drops are distributed away from an impact area, but drops travel in a variety of paths that do not lead back to a single point. No two incompressible fluid drops can originate from a single point. Most substances, including blood, are incompressible; that is, they cannot be compressed to a smaller volume than exists. When an impact is applied, the breakup and distribution project drops away from the circumference of the impact area. The term "area of convergence" is now recognized, as indicated with omissions in the SWGSTAIN terminology list of terms such as "Point of Convergence", and coming into training and applications. A second problem with this definition is that bloodstains are influenced by the surface they contact. If the material has grain, weave, warp, differential absorbency, or is slanted, the spatter may be distorted (MacDonell and Bialousz, 1971, p. 7) so that the long axis is not necessarily the direction of travel. The definition lists well-defined spatters, but what is "well defined" is not always explained, which may allow subjective application.

Court Use Suggestion: The area on a recording surface used in a technique to locate an origin of a single impact in space. The convergence will be perpendicular to the determined origin of the impact.

ARTERIAL DAMAGE STAINS

Technical: Unique and identifiable bloodstain patterns that result from blood drops distributed by the pulsing, pressurized release from a breached arterial blood vessel. This type of pattern may continue to be recorded as long as the heart continues to beat. If the heart stops, the pressure drops, and the column of blood is no longer forced out as a recordable spatter pattern.

Discussion: The terms "arterial spurt" and "arterial gush" (described later, along with "spray") are sometimes used interchangeably. Clear distinction, however, may not be defined. This is seen in investigative reports showing a lack of identification of arterial damage patterns and/or misidentification as castoffs (defined later). Where blood originates from an artery should not be limited to predominantly large stains and volumes of blood. Arterial spurt (spray) may occur if minor arteries are involved, especially with pinhole breach. This latter occurs by way of a ruptured aneurysm, and blood projection continues as the victim moves rapidly to another location. More tools are necessary to extend the ability to label the variety of arterial patterns so that this valuable information may apply to crime investigation. The identification of specific patterns is essential before establishing a scenario and zeroing in on a person of interest. The patterns that identify the manner and location of an arterial breach aid in the determination of intent. For more discussion, see Section III and Section IV.

Court Use Suggestion: A group of recognized bloodstains forming a pattern as a result of injury to an arterial blood vessel.

ARTERIAL FOUNTAIN

Technical: The recording of blood drops, usually on an adjacent vertical surface, from fallout of a column during arterial projection. Arterial pressure may push a column of blood upward, while the drops that separate from the column fall in reverse by gravity. The downward directions may be recorded on adjacent surfaces in recognizable parabola-shaped patterns.

Discussion: This term is not commonly used although it is usually recognized by investigators. As previously pointed out, more terms and definitions are necessary for arterial injury distributed bloodstain patterns. Ideally, pathologists and/or other qualified professionals should confirm arterial behavior while the investigators define the resulting patterns. A team approach is favored.

Court Use Suggestion: An arrangement of spatters created when blood drops fall by gravity from an upward-projected breached artery.

ARTERIAL GUSH

Technical: A large bloodstain, more than a few overlapping drops, projected from a breached artery that remains in one position while the heart continues to beat.

Discussion: As presented later, this term is interchangeable with "arterial spurt," which may lead to subjectivity in application. Gush may be differentiated from spurt depending on the length of time an artery projects blood in one position (gush) or if it moves (spurts). Because a large volume of blood may be overlaid from a gush, the historic definition based on size of spatter has been applied. Size alone may lead to confusion between castoff patterns (defined later) and arterial damage.

Court Use Suggestion: A bloodstain pattern created when an artery projects blood from one place while the heart continues to beat.

ARTERIAL RAIN

Technical: The scattered spatters recorded on a horizontal surface that have resulted from the fallout of blood drops from an arterial fountain.

Discussion: The term has not been commonly used but, as with other suggestions, is understood by most. The pattern may be confused with drip castoffs and thus requires confirming evidence to define and identify.

Court Use Suggestion: A bloodstain pattern that confirms the possible presence of an arterial fountain, thus the possibility of arterial injury.

ARTERIAL SPURT

Technical: Blood exiting a breached arterial vessel as a column that separates into drops as the victim moves. The drops may be recorded in parallel arrangements of similar-sized and similar-shaped spatters.

Discussion: One definition suggests that this pattern is identified by appearance, but how that specific arrangement appears is not part of the definition. Such definition can be applied subjectively and leaves veracity to the resume of the investigator. That approach may, or may not, be accepted by courts but does not provide evidence derived from science. The lack of scientific basis can invalidate the testimony, thus leading to exclusion from testimony. Because bloodstain patterns of arterial injury provide much to benefit interpretation of the crime, mainly criminal intent versus premeditated homicide, accurate definition and identification are essential.

Court Use Suggestion: Blood exiting a pressurized blood vessel as the victim moves, leaving a recognizable arrangement on a recording surface (target).

ARTERIES

Technical: Muscular, pressurized blood vessels that carry oxygenated blood away from the heart to all parts of the body. A principle in medical science accepted from the 1980s states that at times of extreme stress and/or blood loss, 85%–90% of the body's blood flow may be routed through arteries from the heart to the brain and adrenals (head area) (Sohmer, 1979, p. 2).

Discussion: It is best to follow medical terminology with body physiology. The bloodstain pattern analyst, however, should understand the source of blood that may be expected to leave specific patterns. This requires one of three approaches during trial: (1) have medical background in addition to forensic science training, (2) work with the autopsy physician before testimony, or (3) list questions for laying the foundation with the autopsy pathologist (or medical doctor) for later arterial damage type patterns testimony.

Court Use Suggestion: Pressurized blood vessels that carry blood away from the heart.

BACK SPATTER

Technical: A bloodstain pattern that results from a dynamic act suggestive of Newton's Third Law of Motion.

Discussion: This principle derived from Newton during his lifetime states that for every action there will be an equal and opposite reaction. When a force is applied causing an impact to a blood source, blood drops are distributed away in the opposite direction to the applied force. Actually, drops are distributed in many directions, all away from the impact itself. Some of these drops will be back in the general direction of the wielder of the weapon causing impact. The semantics is often applied to patterns associated with gunshot injury. Application to gunshot-only assaults can be ambiguous because blood drops are not distributed directly back from the entrance wound, but rather in a cone shape away from the circumference of the bullet entrance. Bystanders close to the wielder of the weapon may receive blood characteristic of gunshot distribution. In fact, any impact, including gunshot, blunt force, and knife thrust, may direct blood drops in the opposite direction to the area of applied force to a blood source. Before conclusions of gunshot can be presented, respiratory and/or pinhole arterial pressure–distributed blood drops must be ruled out as possible. Size and shape of spatters by themselves cannot identify blood distributed from gunshot injury.

Court Use Suggestion: Blood drops directed away in an array from an impact which may include some drops back toward the wielder of the weapon causing the impact. This term may be applied to blunt force, knife thrust, or gunshot.

BLOCKAGE TRANSFER

Technical: The lack of blood spatters found in an area of a target due to the location of a blockage somewhere along the flight path between the blood source of distributed blood drops and the recording surface of those drops. The term is called "transfer," although no contact between surfaces occurred, because the distribution of spatters can outline an object, thus transferring the shape of the object to a recording surface. Template transfers terminology is sometimes applied to this pattern identification.

Discussion: See "absence transfer" earlier. The term "void" has been used, although current understanding may suggest updating to differentiate the pattern from others included with void. "Blockage" and absence transfers are suggested to replace the single group term "void" and to separate the different reasons blood spatters are not recorded in an area of a crime scene.

Court Use Suggestion: An absence of spatters due to a specific blockage to blood drops distributed toward a recording surface.

BLOOD

Technical: A non-Newtonian fluid that contains biological and biochemical particles in a fluid. Non-Newtonian means blood does not behave like water even though there is a predominance of water in blood. The composition, including particles, blood cells (red, white, and platelets), and protein contributes to behavior different from Newtonian fluids such as water.

Discussion: Although the principal substance for bloodstain pattern analysis is blood, a definition of this fluid is not always included in a submitted terminology list (SWGSTAIN Terminology list). A definition often submitted at the beginning of testimony states that blood is "a fluid like any other fluid which behaves according to the laws of physics" (MacDonell and Bialousz, 1971, p. 3). This usage was discussed in Chapter 2. The question is which laws of physics because this concept mixes ideas from different branches and theories from physics. Blood is not equated to aqueous (water-based) fluids in modern science.

Court Use Suggestion: A complex biological fluid that may be identified when injury occurs.

BLOOD INTO BLOOD

Technical: A pattern created when blood drips into a pool of blood. This may be recognized as a periphery of secondary smaller spatters seen around the circumference of the pool, a pattern created when the internal cohesion and non-Newtonian elasticity of blood drops cause them to break up and bounce off the pool, rather than immediately diffuse into it.

Discussion: Terminology lists tend to define application rather than the term. Some references claim the distance the associated blood drips fall determines the characteristics of blood (MacDonell and Bialousz, 1971, p. 15; James and Eckert, 1999, pp. 25–27). Experiments, however, show that the rate of bleed from the same heights causes markedly different final whole group of spatters patterns (Wonder, 2001, p. 135). For blood into blood pattern appearance, rate of bleed is more important than the height from which the drops fall.

Court Use Suggestion: A recognizable bloodstain pattern that results when blood drips into a pool of blood.

BLOOD SPATTER

Technical: A blood spot recorded on a surface after traveling from the source of the drop separation from a blood source.

Discussion: Confusion may result from earlier attempts to define spatter as resulting only from an impact to a blood source (Bevel and Gardner, 1997, p. 55; James and Eckert, 1999, p. 305). Definitions limiting the term "spatter" to impact or even forceful projection ignore drips, which are defined as not having force but resulting in patterns which are still composed of spots of the same size and shape as those resulting from true impact. Arterial spurts and castoff patterns would be excluded as spatter patterns in those definitions. Because there is a considerable overlap in size and shape for different dynamic acts, the term "spatter" is usually immediately applied to any spots seen. The limited definition may create a biased conclusion that the spots must be from some impact event. The definition of a spatter—as any spot of blood followed by analysis to define the dynamic act that distributed the blood drop—is more reliable.

Modifications of the term definition have been added to describe "a bloodstain resulting from a blood drop dispersed through air due to an external force applied to a source of liquid blood," which corrects earlier misconceptions but should include that gravity is also an external force (SWGSTAIN definition of Spatter Stain). Recognizing gravity as a force would include blood dripping to leave spatters at a crime scene.

Court Use Suggestion: A bloodstain recorded on a surface from a formed blood drop.

BLOODSTAIN

Technical: Substance found on a surface, identified and verified by specific tests, to be blood.

Discussion: The previously accepted definition—that a bloodstain is evidence that blood came into contact with a surface—suffices, as does the definition of "blood deposit on a surface." The only confusion could be when the discussion differentiates "whole" patterns from individual spatters. In other words, committees need to consider what constitutes a whole (or complete) bloodstain pattern. The SWGSTAIN terminology list does expand the definition to include whole patterns described as "A grouping or distribution of bloodstains that indicates through regular or repetitive form, order, or arrangement the manner in which the pattern was deposited."

Court Use Suggestion: Blood deposited on a recording surface.

BLUNT FORCE IMPACT

Technical: An act involving an object of some size and weight sufficient to cause bodily injury creating a blood source without specific penetration by knife or missile (bullet).

Discussion: This term is shared with the field of pathology and is not usually included with specific bloodstain pattern terminology. It is the suggestion here that such terms do have application to be shared with bloodstain pattern analysis. The objective is not to mix opinions but to share the same semantics for clarity in the whole case and between team members of the same investigation.

Court Use Suggestion: Assault with a weapon other than a gunshot or knifing.

BULLET CAPSULAR BLAST

Technical: The small amount of explosive gas from a discharged bullet that surrounds the bullet in flight (DiMaio, 1998, p. 40).

Discussion: Many bloodstain pattern experts are also firearms experts. The additional training and experience qualify them to understand and define the term. Again, this is a shared term that is usually excluded from specific lists. It is a suggestion for inclusion on future lists.

Court Use Suggestion: Suggest this be defined by a firearms expert if the bloodstain pattern expert does not also have that qualification, or questions be asked of other experts to lay the groundwork regarding its use.

CALIPERS

Technical: Device for measuring small stains.

Discussion: No different definition was found to be in use, but the term is widely understood. It is more important to understand how the device is used and what the measurements determined mean in an investigation. Because this is a device used in bloodstain pattern analysis, a definition should be included on the terminology list.

Court Use Suggestion: A measuring device used in bloodstain pattern evidence.

CASTOFF SPATTERS

Technical: Spatters resulting from blood drops distributed by centripetal force and/or gravity, when the adhesion and cohesion are broken between blood and the weapon, carrier, or blood source. Drops that are distributed have sufficient mass and momentum to overcome fluid elasticity and the adhesion between the blood substance and carrier.

Discussion: An accepted definition from history explains that castoffs are created when blood is flung or projected from an object in motion. More recent modifications shorten the definition, which in turn may be shortened further.

Court Use Suggestion: A bloodstain pattern resulting from blood drops released from an object in motion.

CESSATION CASTOFFS

Technical: Blood drops are formed when the motion of a blood carrier immediately stops or reverses in travel. Adhesion is broken between the blood and the moving object so that drops are formed and distributed. This event leads to continued travel of the drops formed in the relative direction the carrier was moving before motion was interrupted.

Discussion: Castoff bloodstain patterns have been recognized for some time (MacDonell and Bialousz, 1971, p. 59); however, recognition that they result from different kinds of events had not been labeled until more recent consideration. To not recognize, and define, this as a unique castoff category is regrettable because it may apply to investigative leads where self-defense actions may be identified and added to the scenario development for the crime events.

Court Use Suggestion: (The SWGSTAIN definition works very well here.) A bloodstain pattern resulting from drops released from a moving object due to its rapid deceleration (Scientific Working Group on Bloodstain Pattern Analysis: Recommended Terminology, 2009).

CLOT (COAGULATION)

Technical: The biochemical reaction within a quantity of blood where liquid fibrinogen molecules catalyzed by calcium cause a precipitation which forms in a semisolid fibrin matrix (Dailey, 1998, p. 191ff).

Discussion: Although terminology often used in training workshops for bloodstain pattern evidence may be technically correct, it may exceed the qualification of the law enforcement personnel being trained in bloodstain pattern evidence. Using the description "the gelatinous mass formed by the collection of blood cells in fibrin, this mass will usually exhibit separation of the liquid and solid materials" (James et al., 2005, p. 531) may be viewed as outside the expertise of the witness, if education, training, and experience have not been demonstrated. If "clot" is essential to the testimony, the groundwork should be laid with a pathologist or an expert with a qualified background if the bloodstain pattern analyst does not have that background. This is not to say the expert doesn't recognize the event but rather to prevent loss of the testimony if the judge questions the expert's background qualifications.

Court Use Suggestion: A biological process that changes fluid blood into semisolid and solid masses. (Laying the foundation with an expert with a medical background protects admissibility of the bloodstain pattern analyst's testimony where changes to blood are indicated in the bloodstain patterns.)

CONTAMINATION

Technical: Changes to the bloodstain patterns at a crime scene by assumed uninvolved persons after the crime events are over.

Discussion: Contamination is widely accepted by investigators but not specifically defined in most BPA terminology lists. This is another shared term and definition for communication among members of the crime scene investigation team. The suggested addition is to differentiate contamination of a crime scene by uninvolved persons versus changes to the scene resulting from investigative personnel. This is not to place blame but rather to deal with the issue of scene changes before it can become an embarrassment in court. Despite the occurrence of a contaminating event, often bloodstain patterns can show what happened before, during, or after that contamination and thus lead to what changed in stages of the crime. It is suggested that changes to the scene by investigation or rescue (paramedics, etc.) be classed as "investigative transfer," which could be important in developing a time line.

Court Use Suggestion: Changes to the crime scene that are regarded as not relative to the actual crime or rescue/investigation afterward.

DIRECTION OF TRAVEL

Technical: A line drawn from the smoothest side to the opposite most irregular edge of a blood spatter, which determines the direction the blood drop was traveling when it contacted the target. This is not necessarily the longest line through the stain because of differential absorption and/or texture of the target surface material.

Discussion: A possible explanation of the phrase involves the term "vector." That is, the direction of travel for a spatter is a vector drawn through the stain to indicate which direction the blood drop was traveling when it left the spatter stain. This is a correct and scientific expression. Stating that direction of travel is a vector of the blood drop in relation to a target suffices unless the investigator is not well versed in physics and/or the use of the term "vector." A simpler definition for communication with investigators and in court may avoid confusion and/or technical questions on cross-examination. Simply saying the longest axis of a stain ignores surface texture and absorbency.

Court Use Suggestion: A criterion applied to show directionality of blood drops from dynamic events to the location where they were recorded.

DRIP CASTOFF

Technical: A pattern resulting from blood drops that overcome adhesion to an object and fall by force of gravity to a target surface.

Discussion: The expression "passive bloodstains" was applied when the fact that low velocity impact spatters no longer fit the post-1970s definition of a low velocity force. This was discussed in

Chapter 2. The grouping of drips with the term "passive" confuses scientific nomenclature. The definition claims that no force is applied yet admits blood drops are acted on by gravitational *force*. This is a contradiction in terms. Recent modification has been simplified to call the occurrence a drip stain defined as a bloodstain resulting from a falling drop that formed due to gravity (Scientific Working Group on Bloodstain Pattern Analysis: Recommended Terminology, 2009). This is a good definition but might be further simplified for court applications.

Court Use Suggestion: A blood spatter formed by and falling from gravity.

ENTRANCE WOUND SPATTER

Technical: Blood drops distributed according to Newton's third law. This event occurs relative to the medically identified entrance wound of a victim, which is as an equal and opposite reaction to the impact of a bullet or missile. Newton's law applied to solid material rather than breaking up of a liquid but later was used long after his death to explain liquid behavior in the study of fluid mechanics. In reality, the result of a bullet penetrating flesh distributes blood drops away from the entrance of the bullet in an array suggestive of a cone shape.

Discussion: "Back spatter" is sometimes substituted to mean blood directed back toward the source of energy or force that caused the spatter (James et al., 2005, p. 136). Back spatter is often associated with gunshot wounds (James et al., 2005, pp. 135–137), yet blood drops are directed away from any impact, whether it is knife, bullet, fist, club, etc. When the term is applied to the blood deposited in the barrel of a firearm after discharge, another expression of the concept could be "draw back spatter." Scientists have disagreed with this latter concept and the label applied. (Personal discussion with a criminalist ...). The term definition is good if the interpretation is expanded to mean any event that distributes blood toward the source of the object delivering impact.

SWGSTAIN modification improved the definition but did not address the fact that back spatter can originate with various events: "a bloodstain pattern resulting from drops that travel in the opposite direction of the external force applied, associated with an entrance wound created by a projectile" (SWGSTAIN Terminology list). The request is that one consider that a fist or blunt weapon will project blood back toward the force also, but without an entrance wound from a projectile.

Court Use Suggestion: Blood drops distributed from a force of impact to open and expose, or encounter a previously exposed blood source on a victim.

EXIT WOUND SPATTER

Technical: Specifically associated with gunshot wounds (GSW), the pattern that may result from blood distributed after a bullet/missile exits a body.

Discussion: The commonly accepted label and definition has been "forward spatter: blood which travels in the same direction as the source of energy or force causing the spatter. Forward spatter is often associated with gunshot wounds of exit" (James and Eckert, 1999, p. 72). The term and definition can be limited. The blood drops distributed from an exit wound are not necessarily limited to the same path as the exiting bullet or fragments, especially if a head wound is involved. In fact, the drops are distributed away from the center of the bullet path. Blood from exit wounds fans out in much the same way as entrance wound spatter, but some differences between the two may be identified. This is discussed further in Section II and Section III.

Court Use Suggestion: A blood spatter pattern that may result from blood drops distributed after a firearms bullet exits the body.

GUNSHOT WOUND

Technical: A wound identified, usually by medical expertise, as resulting from a firearm-projected missile. Abbreviated on most autopsies as GSW.

Discussion: After a gunshot wound is identified, the bloodstain pattern analyst should be able to describe the dynamics of gases and projected missiles from a firearm in creating blood drop distribution. The bloodstain pattern analyst should anticipate excessive limitations of the scope for testimony in courts and deal with them in pretrial motions. It is unwise to delay descriptions of injuries as they relate to bloodstain pattern evidence until after an analyst testifies. This is discussed further in Section IV.

Court Use Suggestion: Identification and description of this term must follow medical testimony, or be brought out in examination/cross-examination of medical experts identifying the location of gunshot wounds.

HEMOLYZE

Technical: A biological event that may occur when red blood cells are exposed to a hypotonic (lower specific gravity) solution. Red pigment from free hemoglobin is seen in the clear solution following exposure to water or a like substance.

Discussion: This term is another example of a borderline issue in which some courts could question expertise. It is advisable to have a qualified background witness define the process of hemolysis before testimony by a bloodstain pattern expert, if sufficient background in science is lacking. Unfortunately, hemolyzed bloodstain patterns may not yet be required as part of basic training in bloodstain pattern analysis, although most courses include examples.

Court Use Suggestion: The result when blood is exposed to water or other low specific gravity liquid. The solutions may become clear with released red coloring.

HIGH VELOCITY IMPACT SPATTER (HVIS)

Technical: A term coined by Dr. Paul L. Kirk to explain the exclamation mark appearance of blood spatters. The designation was relative to how fast a blood drop was traveling when it made contact with the target. This affects the shape of the resultant stain. Refer to Figure 1.5 in Chapter 1.

Discussion: Velocity impact spatter terminology was developed by Dr. Kirk prior to his death in 1970. Shift in the terminology and definitions of the VIS terms occurred after Dr. Kirk's death. If used as an identification term, it is subjective. A claim has been made that the subjective applications in BPA are based on 100-year-old science. One notices an improvement in the omission from recent terminology lists, which show a shift of regard for velocity as a pattern identification (Scientific Working Group on Bloodstain Pattern Analysis: Recommended Terminology, 2009).

The difference in velocity of blood drops when they meet a recording surface follows the scientific principles going back hundreds of years, not the present equation of velocity with a force delivered to a blood source separate from where the spatters are recorded.

Court Use Suggestion: Not recommended in court because the term as modified after Dr. Kirk's death in 1970 is subjective.

INCIDENT ANGLE

Technical: The angle between the flight path of a blood drop and the target surface on which the blood spatter from the drop is recorded.

Discussion: Angle of impact may be defined as the acute angle as viewed from the side, created by the drop vector (Bevel and Gardner, 1997, p. 52). This is technically correct and applicable if the expert is comfortable describing vectors. As with some other terms, the person testifying as a bloodstain pattern analyst may not feel comfortable discussing mathematics and physics terms beyond those listed for bloodstain pattern analysts. In that case, it is best to keep the description simple. Lack of a math and physics background does not disqualify a bloodstain pattern analyst if he or she has applied specific criteria to identification of patterns and limited interpretation to the facts regarding the evidence.

Court Use Suggestion: An angle between a blood drop's flight and the surface it contacts.

INLINE BEADING

Technical: The in-tandem arrangement of spatters recorded on a target signifying blood drops from a column or single blood source as it moves. These may occur from castoff, arterial, or hair fiber transfer distribution.

Discussion: The term applies to the essential nature of an arrangement of spatters in perfect alignment. This must be with no deviations or offset in the line and is thus limited to only those events where blood drops can originate from the same source. The fact that drops are in line may provide evidence that the blood drops formed while in flight after distribution as with arterial-projected columns or were transferred along a single line from a hair strand. The definition, thus, needs to be extended to allow awareness of extended dynamics and interpretations.

Court Use Suggestion: An arrangement of blood spatters in a consistent line.

INSIDE ANGLE (INCIDENT ANGLE OR IMPACT ANGLE)

Technical: Angle within a calculated right angle triangle that is drawn between a recorded spatter and a theoretical blood drop in flight from a blood source.

Discussion: The term "angle of impact" is commonly used when describing a step in the process of locating the origin of a group of blood spatters defining an origin for a criminal impact to a blood source. The definition has been that this is the acute angle relative to the plane of the target at which a blood drop strikes the target (SWGSTAIN Terminology list). The angle being described, however,

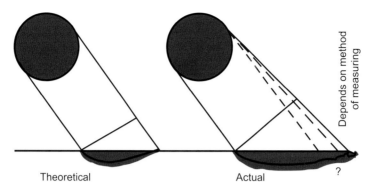

FIGURE 3.1   The right triangle drawn for a theoretical blood spatter to determine an angle of impact.

may not be the angle determined according to the technique. There are three angles to a triangle: one right angle and two acute angles. The initial contact of a blood drop with a target surface is the smooth end of a blood spatter. The right angle is drawn from the first contact point to the imaginary line from the drop to the farthest end of the spatter. The point of this imaginary line is the assumed impact angle. The second acute angle is at the irregular end of the spatter, which may be questioned depending on the method of measuring the stain (see Figure 3.1).

Obtaining a value for the inside angle, or angle of impact, requires the theorem that a line crossing parallel lines will create equal angles between the lines. For the lines to be parallel, this requires that the lines drawn from the blood drop in flight be the same width as the spatter formed from the drop. The blood drop is three-dimensional, whereas the stain is two-dimensional with *conservation of volume* from the drop. The theoretical lines drawn cannot be parallel. Thus, the angle of incidence is not the same as the inside angle, or angle of impact, when a right triangle is drawn. The most serious error is that speed of the drop of blood forming the spatter is ignored with regard to the effect on the resultant stain length and width. Considerable experimentation, however, has shown that although flawed, this technique can be reliable under some circumstances. It remains to be proven which circumstances these may be.

Court Use Suggestion: A term that identifies the angles within a theoretical triangle used in a reconstruction for the origin of an impact to a blood source.

INVESTIGATIVE TRANSFER (IT)

Technical: The transfer patterns, where blood is deposited on crime scene surfaces from foot, shoe, hand, or equipment used at a crime scene by investigative personnel. This transfer should be recognized for value in developing a time line and/or eliminating necessary rescue and investigative presence to a crime scene.

Discussion: An attitude of embarrassment exists regarding contamination during procedures after the crime scene is discovered. To recognize it, label it, and explain it saves time, face, and embarrassment later. Recognizing IT can be used to establish a time line for wet blood at a crime scene. Providing a term and including it in training also becomes an alert to investigators to be aware of actions that result in contamination and that if such contamination occurs, it should be admitted to other investigators. The occurrence of contamination may result in the absence of failure to follow protocol but be a necessary part of rescue and recovery, whether from investigators, EMTs/EMSs (rescue attempts), or involved persons prior to crime scene work-up.

Court Use Suggestion: Unfortunate but occasionally unavoidable changes in bloodstains at a crime scene resulting during discovery, rescue, and investigation techniques.

LOW VELOCITY IMPACT SPATTER (LVIS)

Technical: Defined by Dr. Paul L. Kirk as blood drops falling by gravitational pull alone, thus impacting a target at relatively low velocity. This affects the shape of the resultant spatter.

Discussion: The confusion over blood simply dripping from a victim, assailant, material, or object was previously discussed in Chapter 2 and with the drip castoff definition.

Court Use Suggestion: Not recommended for court use. "Drips," "drip castoffs," or "gravitational drops" are preferred terms. Using "passive stains" is not recommended.

MEDIUM VELOCITY IMPACT SPATTER (MVIS)

Technical: Based on Dr. Paul L. Kirk's classifications, medium velocity impact spatter is spatter resulting from blood drops traveling slower than distributed by events such as gunshot but faster than dripping by gravity alone. All of the dynamic classifications of events—castoff, blunt force impact, arterial spurts, and/or respiratory coughs—may distribute blood drops that can leave blood spatters of a size and shape included in those historically called MVIS.

Discussion: This term, as historically defined, depended on the opinion of an expert. At a crime scene, it cannot be known how fast a fist, blunt instrument, or assault was occurring without regard to the mass of the object making contact. An example is to question the difference in spatter size and shape for a long-haul diesel truck hitting a pedestrian versus a bicycle rider going the same velocity. Defining a term as something that cannot be stated changes the statement from scientific logic to something subjective that derives meaning based on the resume of the expert. More accurate scientific terms and definitions are available.

Court Use Suggestion: Not recommended for court use. Other terms are more descriptive and less subjective.

MIST SPATTER OR MISTING

Technical: When blood is atomized to form drops so small they ultimately leave stains of less than 0.1 mm in diameter. Detection of mist-sized drops may require microscopic examination.

Discussion: "...[A] mist-like appearance, which are generally associated with explosive force such as gunshot" (Bevel and Gardner, 2002, p. 74). This definition of mist-sized spatter misses the fact that events such as respiration, specifically wheeze, can result in depositing mist-size spatters on persons and surfaces during attempts to aid a living victim. Pinhole breach of an artery during high blood pressure phases can also project mist. Gunshot is not the only source and thus should not be applied as a definitive interpretation. If other events can be eliminated, such as respiration after injury and high pressure arterial breach, the presence of mist may act as one criterion to identify gunshot impact spatters. Examples of misapplications have been encountered in which the label was applied merely because the crime involved gunshot injury. The link between the gunshot and the bloodstain pattern may or may not exist at the location viewed. If the victim lived for a period of time, simple respiration may have been responsible for mist-sized spatters.

Court Use Suggestion: Blood spatters from very tiny blood drops signifying considerable breakup of the blood source. This may be by gunshot impact; high blood pressure with arterial breach; or respiration after injury to the nose, mouth, or lungs.

MOVING CONTACT BLOODSTAINS

Technical: Transfer of blood during the movement of an object, skin, or material across a recording surface while depositing or spreading blood substance.

Discussion: No specific definition is presently used with this term. Other terms applied—wipe, swipe, and smudge—are described later. During an investigation, it is not always immediately clear which action occurred during movement. Rather than label a pattern and then need to correct it later, it is suggested to label all patterns for contact with movement as moving contact stains and then classify as to how the movement occurred after further examination.

Court Use Suggestion: A transfer of blood during movement of something along a surface while spreading or depositing blood.

MUZZLE BLAST

Technical: The gases created when the charge that propels a bullet (missile) out of the barrel of a firearm explodes. This force can atomize a pre-opened bleeding injury to form mist-sized blood spatter deposited as directed toward a person holding the gun. See also "bullet capsular blast."

Discussion: Popular literature for bloodstain pattern evidence does not identify muzzle blasts specifically. Initially, descriptions listed the bullet at impact as a response for misting/mist spatter. Mist-sized spatters are defined as spots of less than 0.1 mm. Actually, mist may be microscopic, unseen by the naked eye, because the dynamics that cause mist result from the expansion of gases (an explosive force), not the impact of a bullet creating injury. The main argument is that dynamics are not limited to gunshot entrance wounds. Wheeze respiratory action may be similar and rarely pinhole puncture of a high pressure artery can produce mist-sized blood drops. Defining the results of muzzle blast, specifically from firearms, should be more specific than the size and shape of the spatters.

Court Use Suggestion: This term refers to gases that act to propel and follow a bullet out of the barrel when a gun is fired.

ORIGIN

Technical: The locus of points in space from which a group of blood drops originated at the time of a single injuring impact event.

Discussion: A historical definition equated the origin with a point in space. Some individuals misunderstand the use of the word "point" and apply it to any arrangement of several blood drops. The point in three-dimensional space is the place where a blood drop, which leaves a blood spatter, was created and distributed, as included in the updated SWGSTAIN definition (SWGSTAIN Terminology list). The distribution of several blood drops cannot be drawn to a single point for a true impact. No two drops of an incompressible fluid may originate from the same point. Blood, like most fluids, is incompressible; that is, several drops cannot be compressed into a single drop. Furthermore, drawing several stains to a "point" of conversion in order to locate the origin misses the size and shape of the impact origin itself. Using several spatters without an effort to find a point defines an area that may provide investigative information. The actual size and shape of injuries in a sequence of assaults may help to define the size and shape of the weapon used in the impact assault.

Court Use Suggestion: The location in space where a single injuring impact occurred.

PARENT DROP

Technical: The original blood drop that leaves a spatter stain after travel from the origin to the target. The term "parent" is used to differentiate the source of a spatter from secondary or wave castoffs that occur after the drop has impacted the target.

Discussion: The primary drop that was the source of blood for a small secondary or satellite spatter may cause confusion when viewed at a crime scene. Larger spatters may result in distribution of smaller drops after contact with specific target surface characteristics and/or impact angle.

Court Use Suggestion: The large drop that acts as the source of blood for a secondary spatter.

PASSIVE

Technical: A kinematic term denoting something resting but with potential energy should it become active.

Discussion: Historically, a group of bloodstain patterns were moved to this term classification after it was realized that the phrase low velocity impact spatter (LVIS) had became ambiguous with the shift of the velocity impact terminology. Other terms for the bloodstain patterns included here are suggested for scientific nomenclature.

Court Use Suggestion: Not recommended in court. Jurors may include engineers, teachers of math and physics, and others who are comfortable with scientific nomenclature. Out-of-context use of the term may cause them to disregard other essential information from an analysis.

PATTERN

Technical: An identifiable arrangement of several blood spatters recorded on a target from one dynamic event.

Discussion: The essential reason for defining what the analyst means by "a pattern" is to confirm that in order to recognize which dynamic events were part of a crime, one must have several blood stains. No single or pair of stains can identify a specific event. Confusion has been encountered in which the size of one blood spatter is immediately equated with an identification of the event. This application of size for identity is subjective and not based on modern scientific principles. Fortunately, sizes alone are not favored in recent scientific applications.

Court Use Suggestion: An arrangement of spatters that allows identification of the action that was recorded in blood.

PHYSIOLOGICALLY ALTERED BLOODSTAIN (PABS)

Technical: A bloodstain that is recorded after a physiological change occurred to the blood. This change may be drying, clotting, or mixing with another substance.

Discussion: "Altered stain" is now accepted, but the addition of "physiological" is suggested to avoid the misperceptions of calling it physically altered blood. Including the classification within passive stains is correct because the physiological changes are viewed as stationary with perhaps some potential to become active on a viewable basis.

Court Use Suggestion: A bloodstain recorded after drying, clotting, or mixing with another substance.

PLASMA

Technical: The clear to opaque and colorless to bright yellow liquid phase of blood that has not initiated coagulation.

Discussion: As with the term "clot," it is suggested that this definition be completed by those with some medical background or that background be laid with earlier medical testimony in trial.

Court Use Suggestion: The liquid part of fresh flowing blood.

POOL (VOLUME)

Technical: The term "volume" may be used for science purposes. A volume of blood is a quantity in excess of a few drops, which collects from bleeding injuries and lies undisturbed.

Discussion: "Pool" is often used in investigations and widely understood as being a relatively large amount of blood without a specific quantity understood.

Court Use Suggestion: A volume of blood in excess of a few drops.

PREBLAST

Technical: The small amount of gas that precedes the bullet in travel to a target. (See "bullet capsular blast" and "muzzle blast" for bloodstain patterns associated with this event.) With moving targets used in gunshot experiments, this stain is recorded when the blood source is exposed prior to a bullet impact.

Discussion: A good reference discussing the parts of a gunshot is recommended (DiMaio, 1998, p. 40).

Court Use Suggestion: An expert with qualifications in firearms should present this evidence with the terminology developed for the phenomenon.

PROTRACTOR

Technical: A mathematical tool used to draw or construct angles of known degree.

Discussion: Some experts use an instrument to construct angles for reconstruction of the origin of an impact.

Court Use Suggestion: A mathematical tool used in crime scene procedures.

RED BLOOD CELLS

Technical: Also called erythrocytes or RBC. The most numerous particles found in blood. These particles are what contain hemoglobin, the red pigmented substance that gives blood its characteristic red color. Mature red cells do not normally contain a cell nucleus and thus are not applicable to DNA identification at this time. The cells are encased in a protein coat that contributes to non-Newtonian fluid behavior.

Discussion: Unless the expert has medical or other applicable background, descriptions of blood and blood functions may be challenged as describing blood inside the body. Rather than risk the evidence not being admitted to trial, in those jurisdictions which specify that bloodstain pattern analysts do not deal with blood except outside the body, it is suggested that either the expert be qualified to define blood behavior during pretrial motions such as a motion in limne or groundwork be laid with other medical experts.

Court Use Suggestion: The predominant red-colored particles in blood.

RETRACTION (CLOT)

Technical: The stage in the coagulation process in which fibrin strands tighten the bundle of cells into a solid mass while extruding liquid serum. Retraction can contribute to a time line if identified and recorded soon after a crime scene is found.

Discussion: Definitions were not found in current terminology lists. Adding them to future lists could benefit those working with pathologists in a teamwork context.

Court Use Suggestion: It is recommended that only experts with a medical background or other medically qualified experts define this term, or background for BPA should be laid with prior medical testimony.

SATELLITE SPATTER

Technical: Usually, several small to tiny spatters formed from a primary event such as blood dripping into blood or arterial gushing on the target surface.

Discussion: A historical definition of "small stains when drops detach from a bigger drop as it impacts a target" (Bevel and Gardner, 2002, p. 66) may limit the description of impact events where satellites are more often encountered with blood into blood and arterial gush. Small stains resulting from impact are part of the distribution from impact spatters but can be distributed from other events.

Court Use Suggestion: Small drops formed around the circumference of a pool or large spatter.

SECONDARY SPATTER

Technical: The single small drop thrown ahead of a larger "parent" drop by the wave motion when the drop contacts a textured recording surface. The leading edge of contact breaks like an ocean wave with a small amount of the original drop thrown ahead of the final parent spatter.

Discussion: "Satellite" and "secondary" are often interchangeable, which may add to confusion. Separating the definitions could help prevent this confusion as well as provide additional identification material in an analysis.

Court Use Suggestion: A small drop that results from a wave motion after a larger blood drop contacts a surface.

SERUM

Technical: The clear to opaque liquid phase that results from settling of red cells after blood has coagulated.

Discussion: Recognition of serum at a crime scene should be verified by those with training and experience with blood physiological properties or those who have received training in the recognition of the specific stain characteristics.

Court Use Suggestion: A liquid that separates from the clotted lump of red cells after blood clots.

SERUM STAIN

Technical: A stain that may be separated from a clotted portion of blood but is seen as the colorless, shiny (reflective) edge, or spots. This pattern is sometimes seen in photographs later rather than when viewing the actual crime scene. Serum stains are associated with clot retraction, i.e., sometime after bloodshed, and occurr before the bloodstain dries.

Discussion: If the nature of clot and clot retraction is first established with a witness or a motion qualifying the bloodstain pattern analyst, the recognition of a serum stain should be acceptable when discussed by the bloodstain pattern analyst.

Court Use Suggestion: As with the terms "clot" and "retraction," defining the source for a serum stain may be challenged as being beyond the expertise of a bloodstain pattern analyst. Consideration should be given to pretrial establishment of qualifications, or an expert with medical background or training should be used to lay groundwork prior to testimony from a bloodstain pattern analyst.

SHADOWING

Technical: The effect seen on the edge of a blockage pattern by some of, but not all of, the blood drops from the distributing event outlining the object. The drops have been partially blocked or they touched a rounded surface, following paths of least resistance to form a shadow outline to the full blockage pattern.

Discussion: The term and definition have mixed meanings in common usage. In general, this term is taken as an area of a spatter pattern that has fewer stains than the rest of the group identified from one event. Care must be taken regarding measurements of an obstruction recorded by blocked blood drops. Shadowing decreases the dimensions, so the estimate of size may be too small.

Court Use Suggestion: Stains inside the true dimensions of a blocked pattern caused by drops curving from their flight path against an obstruction before contacting the target.

SIMPLE DIRECT TRANSFER PATTERNS

Technical: A pattern which results from two surfaces, one or both holding blood, coming into contact without movement, i.e., touch transfer only.

Discussion: Transfer patterns are defined in criminalistics and police work. The term presented here adds further clarification of being direct without horizontal movement. "Direct," "absence," and "blockage" all add much to investigative leads and thus should be a crucial part of initial crime scene examination, with characteristics to differentiate each type of bloodstain pattern transfer.

Court Use Suggestion: A bloodstain pattern recorded from direct contact between surfaces. This should not be confused with the term "direct transfer" used with DNA testimony. If DNA testimony is to be given during the same trial as the bloodstain pattern analysis, communication between experts or via attorney may be advisable.

SMEAR (SMUDGE)

Technical: A moving transfer pattern that cannot be limited to an identifiable direction of travel. Back-and-forth motions in cleaning may leave this type of stain.

Discussion: An earlier definition is a stain that has been distorted to such a degree that further classification is not possible. A smear is regarded as a large stain while a smudge is a smaller stain" More recent listings of the terms "smear" and "smudge" are lacking although "wipe" and "swipe" are (James and Eckert, 1999, p. 305). usually included. Unlike other terms that need separation and differentiation of definition, smear and smudge are both bloodstains that could feasibly describe the same appearance. Because no specific size ranges are listed or advised, separating the definition becomes subjective. Either term suffices for a bloodstain with multiple directions of travel overlapping.

Court Use Suggestion: A moving bloodstain that lacks apparent direction of action.

SPATTER

Technical: The individual bloodstain recorded when a distributed blood drop contacts a target surface.

Discussion: One historical definition includes "a dispersion of small blood drops due to the forceful projection of blood" (James and Eckert, 1999, p. 305). Although this definition focuses on just spots from impact-distributed bloodstain patterns, the modification by SWGSTAIN covers other dynamic events. This is an example of improving terminology with slight modifications: "A bloodstain resulting from a blood drop dispersed through the air due to an external force applied to a source of liquid blood" (SWGSTAIN Terminology list). Because some historical confusion may exist, it is good to add that the external force may be an impact, exit of a missile, or centrifugal momentum. The only problem may be that this does not include the internal pressure forcing out a blood column from a breached arterial vessel.

Court Use Suggestion: A spot recorded on a surface from a distributed blood drop.

SPINE

Technical: A pointed irregularity located at the circumference of a spatter.

Discussion: This has been described as "linear characteristics evident in both single-drop stains and volume stains" (Bevel and Gardner, 2002, p. 94). Scallops are also found as edge characteristics for spatters. The importance of describing the edge characteristics is in the forcefulness of projection behind the drop recorded as a spatter and possibly indication of the true direction of travel on differential absorbent surfaces. It should be noted that the red cell composition in blood also influences the production of scallops and spines. The fewer red cells, the lighter the internal cohesion and thus the less constrained spherical shape in flight.

Court Use Suggestion: Sharp projections along the outer edge of a spatter.

SPLASH

Technical: Spatters distributed from an impact to a volume (pool) of blood.

Discussion: An accepted definition has been "a stain created when a volume of blood impacts a target with minimal force; such a stain tends to have a consolidated appearance" (Bevel and Gardner, 2002, p. 95). "Minimal force" may make the definition subjective because what is minimal must be left to an expert. Splash could occur from heavy force, such as a heavy person stomping in a pool of blood. In general, the event is regarded as a large object hitting a blood pool. Although "large" is still subjective, it is a measurement that could be defined later.

Court Use Suggestion: A broad edge impact to a pool (or volume) of blood.

SPLATTER

Technical: A spatter resulting from a blood drop distributed from a splash.

Discussion: This term is not interchangeable with "spatter," and not commonly accepted by bloodstain pattern analysts, although it may be encountered with lawyers, news media, and those lacking specific training in bloodstain pattern analysis.

Court Use Suggestion: A term combining "splash" (see earlier definition) and the formed "spatters."

STRING RECONSTRUCTION

Technical: A technique used to approximate the location of the origin of an individual impact in space.

Discussion: The "method of determining the point of origin..." (James and Eckert, 1999, p. 35) promotes the misunderstanding that the origin is a point in space.

Court Use Suggestion: A technique used to approximate the location of the origin of an individual impact in space.

SWIPE MOVING TRANSFER PATTERN

Technical: A moving contact transfer where a bloodied material brushes against a target.

Discussion: The historical definition "the transfer of blood onto a target by a moving object that is bloodstained; the motion involved is generally considered as some type of lateral motion" (Bevel and Gardner, 2002, p. 102) has been modified and improved to delete the lateral reference but further clarify the dynamics as being a "blood bearing surface onto another surface with characteristics that indicate relative motion between the two surfaces" (SWGSTAIN Terminology list). Swipes and wipes are lateral motions differing by which surface is bloodied before the transfer. Smudge and smear are also lateral motions, although commonly accepted as being in more than one direction. Noting that the pattern requires wet blood is also a consideration for improving the definition.

Court Use Suggestion: A bloodstain pattern recorded when something wet with blood is brushed against a surface.

TARGET

Technical: The surface upon which blood is recorded during accidental, suicidal, and/or criminal injurious events.

Discussion: "A surface upon which blood has been deposited" (James and Eckert, 1999, p. 306) suffices between investigators.

Court Use Suggestion: The surface onto which blood has been deposited. (Using the word "target" in court may be associated with gunshots and have a negative connotation with jurors. This term can be explained to them as merely a surface that is the "target" of a distributed blood drop.)

TEMPLATE TRANSFERS

Technical: A description of a blockage pattern where the obstruction acts like a template or stencil blocking all distributed blood drops. The true shape and size of the obstruction may be seen.

Discussion: The term is not presently used in investigations but would benefit the description of transfer patterns from blockage. This can also lead to the explanation of shadowing on some template-type transfers. Transfer patterns may provide highly probative evidence in trial. The nature of template transfers depends on how close the obstruction is to the target when the blood drop event that is recorded occurs.

Court Use Suggestion: A pattern, in the shape of an obstruction, recorded where blood drops are blocked by an object placed between the blood source and the surface.

TRANSFER PATTERN

Technical: A bloodstain pattern on a target surface of an image, material, or object resulting from touch or blood drop distribution from a blood distributing event. This may either outline or transfer the image of an object present. Unlike transfer evidence in general forensic terminology, blood spatters may outline an object without direct contact between the object and the recording target.

Discussion: Pattern transfers my be defined as "any stain created when a wet bloody object comes in contact with another surface" (Bevel and Gardner, 2002, p. 97). This applies to direct contact, but with blood transfer, it is possible that an identifying pattern is transferred without contact. Blockage can form a template outline of the object when present during a spattering event.

Court Use Suggestion: The recognizable characteristics of one item that have been recorded by contact or blockage on a recording surface. (It must be noted that "contact" and "transfer" are terms used in DNA testimony. The definitions are applied in a different context; thus, each expert may need to explain his or her specific semantics.)

VOID

Technical: A term that is recognized in court but historically has shifted meaning with time. In the 1940s, it was used to identify a blank space, which fits this definition. In recent semantics, and for scientific application, the term has moved toward an emptying or canceling as null and void (voiding a check) or voiding (emptying out) the bladder for a urinary specimen.

Discussion: "Blockage" is a suggested replacement for some of the former void identifications, with the meaning to stop blood drops reaching a surface. This can be contrasted with "absence," which may be used to signify that blood drops didn't reach a surface due to the angle of distribution; that is, there was nothing there blocking blood drops from reaching the target, but the flight path of drops did not lead to the surface.

Court Use Suggestion: This term will probably continue to be used, but suggestions for future improvements to the terminology list are still included here.

VOLUME (POOL)

Technical: The accumulation of blood larger than a few drops.

Discussion: The term "pool" is used frequently and widely understood. Saying "volume bloodstain" may separate the observation from other pools of liquid at a crime scene and represent more scientific semantics.

Court Use Suggestion: An accumulation of a quantity of blood in excess of a few drops.

WHOLE PATTERN

Technical: An arrangement of enough individual spatters, or portion of blood staining, to allow identification of the dynamic event that distributed blood. In practice, at least three spatters are required to define a location in space, but it is better to have five to eight before attempting to classify a spattering event.

Discussion: Some confusion has resulted in using this term if a focus on size and shape of individual spatters occurred. The term may be assumed to refer to a *whole* individual spatter. When alignment criteria become the primary method of classification, the term "whole pattern" will be obvious.

Court Use Suggestion: A group of spatters, or portion of bloodstained surface, sufficient to identify a specific dynamic event.

WIPE MOVING TRANSFER PATTERN

Technical: A moving contact transfer where one material brushes across a bloodstained target.

Discussion: "A stain created when an object moves through a pre-existing wet bloodstain on another surface" (Bevel and Gardner, 2002, p. 102). This may be confusing with a more recent definition. The use of "wet bloodstain" (SWGSTAIN Terminology list) may conflict with (physiologically altered) blood stains. Wipe through water diluted, drying, and clotting blood (all part of PABS) can have probative value.

Court Use Suggestion: An action that spreads a prior existing bloodstain.

REFERENCES

Bevel, T., Gardner, R.M., 1997. Bloodstain Pattern Analysis with an Introduction to Crime Scene Reconstruction. CRC Press, Boca Raton, FL. pp. 52, 55.

Bevel, T., Gardner, R.M., 2002. Bloodstain Pattern Analysis with an Introduction to Crime Scene Reconstruction, 2nd ed. CRC Press, Boca Raton, FL. pp. 66, 74, 94, 95, 97, 102.

Dailey, J.F., 1998. Blood. Medical Consulting Group, Arlington, MA. p. 191ff.

DiMaio, V., 1998. Gunshot Wounds: Practical Aspects of Firearms Ballistics and Forensic Techniques. CRC Press, Boca Raton, FL. p. 40.

Eckert, W.G., James, S.H., 1989. Interpretation of Bloodstain Evidence at Crime Scenes. Elsevier, New York, NY. p. 330.

James, S.H., Eckert, W.G., 1999. Interpretation of Bloodstain Evidence at Crime Scenes, 2nd ed. CRC Press, Boca Raton, FL. pp. 25–27, 35, 72, 305, 306.

James, S.H., Kish, P.E., Sutton, T.P., 2005. Principles of Bloodstain Pattern Analysis. Taylor and Francis, Boca Raton, FL. pp. 135–137, 136, 531.

MacDonell, H.L., Bialousz, L.F., 1971. Flight Characteristics and Stain Patterns of Human Blood, LEAA. National Institute of Law Enforcement and Criminal Justice, Washington, D.C. pp. 3, 7, 15, 59.

Personal discussion with a criminalist with the California Department of Justice Laboratory in Sacramento, CA, 1988.

Scientific Working Group on Bloodstain Pattern Analysis: Recommended Terminology, 2009. Accepted for publication in Forensic Science Communications.

SWGSTAIN, 2008. Scientific Working Group on Bloodstain Pattern Analysis: Guidelines for the Minimum Educational and Training Requirements for Bloodstain Pattern Analysts. Forensic Science Communications. 10(1): p.1–10.

Sohmer, P.R., 1979. Hemotherapy in Trauma and Surgery: A Technical Workshop. American Association of Blood Banks, Washington, D.C. p. 2.

SWGSTAIN definition of Spatter Stain.

SWGSTAIN Terminology list.

Wonder, A.Y., 2001. Blood Dynamics. Academic Press, London. p. 135.

I. INTRODUCTION

IDENTIFICATION

Review of Historical Approaches to Bloodstain Pattern Identification

Back in the late 1960s, Dr. Paul L. Kirk presented the "Identification of Bloodstain Dynamics" to the annual California Trial Lawyers Meeting in San Francisco. His notes on historical precedents are available for review at the University of California, Berkeley, Bancroft Library. What was to be an outline for identifications, interpretations, and applications of bloodstain pattern evidence was presented in the lecture quoted here:

> Distribution and Character of Blood Spots
>
> One other type of information [from physical evidence] that is most helpful and greatly neglected is the analysis of blood distribution at the scene of violent crime. The Hydrodynamics [sic] of flying blood drops has received very little attention, although numerous discussions of angle and velocity of single drops are available. The general pattern is actually far more informative, and in favorable cases, is by far the most significant of both the assailant and the victim during the critical moments of the commission of the crime.
>
> Blood which is thrown during a crime shows definite regularities as to size and velocity, which will differ depending on whether they received their velocity from impact, from being thrown from a bloody weapon as it swings, or from spurting from a severed artery. These patterns are not only different, but show characteristic patterns that can often be recognized. Disregard of this rather obvious source of information has lessened the total information obtained by investigators of many serious crimes and is well worthy of more study and of greatly increased utilizations as an investigative function. It is expected that rather lengthy experiments already conducted in this area of research will reach the stage of publication shortly (Paul Kirk Papers).

The identification guidelines included in *Blood Dynamics* and reiterated in *Bloodstain Pattern Evidence, Objective Approaches and Case Applications* emphasized Dr. Kirk's concept of bloodstain pattern evidence. After his death in July 1970, attitudes toward the evidence shifted in a direction that was contrary to what was advocated in his notes and lectures. This included not accepting, specifically, expert witnesses who might claim opinions soley based on their experience. Dr. Kirk's papers suggest he was very academically inclined, which could satisfy the demands for scientific principles of the NAS Report and NSIC (National Institute of Standards and Technology).

Identifying the dynamic act that distributed blood drops is probably the simplest step in a bloodstain pattern analysis. Unfortunately, it is that step which is sometimes skipped or assumed from information other than the alignment and distribution characteristics of the bloodstains themselves. Too often in crime scene processing, an investigator may jump from verifying a substance

59

as blood to interpreting what the mere presence of blood spots (spatters) of certain size and shape means. Predominant size and shape of the spatters may then be used as justification for the conclusions regarding involvement and stated as consistent or inconsistent with a desired assumption. Whether impact, castoff, or arterial spurting was responsible for the group of spatters may be missed in favor of the size and angles of individual spatters lumped with an assumed relative velocity of a weapon. An example of this is to say, "That's high velocity impact spatter," when it is known, or assumed, that a victim sustained a gunshot injury. After this statement, conclusions are drawn that anyone with small bloodstains on his or her person was the shooter. Sadly, the case may not be that simple.

Another example is the case in which a neighbor came into an apartment because he heard moaning on the other side of the door. The badly injured victim was still alive and wheezing while propped against the door. The neighbor raised the victim's head and received respiratory-distributed blood spatters on his shirt. The responding law enforcement officer arrested the neighbor and claimed that the "suspect had medium velocity impact spatters on his shirt, which meant he did the beating." The facts were that the victim, beaten with a cricket bat found at the scene, lived for a period of time after the assault. The neighbor was just attempting to aid the victim and had fine spatters near the shoulder where the victim's head rested. By virtue of spatter size, the conclusion should have been high velocity impact spatter, but no gunshot was involved. No one else was even considered, despite evidence that the assailant walked, dripping the victim's blood, to a sink and washed up before leaving the scene. The neighbor showed no evidence of attempts to wash up and no connection to the blood drips leading to the sink before the police arrived.

An occurrence that is worse than misinterpretations made during investigation may happen if bloodstain pattern analysis is not considered until after an arrest is made, when the case is being prepared for trial against a specific accused. In this case, bloodstain patterns are not used in the investigation but rather brought in later to prove a specific point. Although one hopes these occurrences are rare, in some jurisdictions, a prosecutor may ask the crime lab to supply evidence against a specific suspect while ignoring exculpatory interpretations of the patterns identified. If bloodstains exist at a crime scene, confirmation information that may be vital to an investigation is available and free for the taking so that resulting charges are reliable and accurate, even if, or especially if, staging and contamination occurred. To ignore, or to use it only if other evidence is unavailable, i.e., as "instant evidence," is to not fully appreciate the probative benefits of this form of forensic evidence. The result could also be a waste of time, money, and possibly the quality of human lives. Though seldom acknowledged, embarrassment may result during trial if the opposing counsel puts on a better trained, more objective bloodstain pattern analyst (Reynolds, 2012).

It has been repeatedly emphasized that size and shape alone cannot be used to identify the dynamics that distributed blood drops forming a pattern on a recording surface. These criteria can, however, be useful in deciding the degree of force involved for each dynamic event after classification. For clarity, it must be stated that a spatter mentioned here refers to a single spot that has resulted from a single blood drop after travel from an event such as impact, castoff, arterial spurt, blood dripping into blood, or respiratory distribution. Whole patterns, on the other hand, are made up of a group of spatters, never one or two, and preferably more than a few, which represent a single dynamic event. Preoccupation with size and shape of individual spatters may influence development of a reliable scenario. It is beneficial to repeat the whole pattern identification criteria here.

Some primary observations that help in forming a criteria-based identification scheme of whole patterns was first presented in *Blood Dynamics,* (Wonder, 2001, pp. 33–34), and can include the memory device *SAADD* (may also be simplified to SAD (Shape, Alignment, and Distribution [or Density]):

Shape of a collective group of spatters believed to comprise a single event
Alignment of spatters
- With respect to the whole group of spatters
- With respect to adjacent individual spatters of the group
Distribution and/or Density
- Of the frequency of the number of spatters per area, forming a whole pattern
- Of the spatter sizes within areas of a whole pattern

IDENTIFYING THE WHOLE PATTERN

Before one attempts to classify a group of spatters, it is essential to locate the group that comprises a single event. Because this task is so important, to focus on spatter sizes may miss the correct identification of each evidential pattern, especially if crime scene evidence overlaps. One learns to recognize the arrangements to locate a group of spatters that represent a single dynamic event. During simple workshops, where exercises illustrate single pattern arrangements, recognizing these arrangements is relatively easy. At a crime scene where multiple events may overlap, doing so is much more complicated. Perhaps an important primary technique in learning to recognize separate dynamics is to look at the directions of travel of individuals as part of a group as well as how they relate to adjacent spatters within the whole group.

DIRECTIONS OF TRAVEL

The significance of direction of travel is twofold. The approximate line of travel from the blood source is shown for individual blood drops. Additionally, the directions of travel for groups of blood drops making up the whole pattern are indicated, thus leading back to the identity of the dynamic event which distributed blood. *Bloodstain Pattern Evidence, Objective Approaches and Case Applications* (Wonder, 2007, p. 356) showed a technique using a string held with both hands, as a hands-on technique, to associate relative grouping of several spatters. A caution is necessary, however, when one is determining the directions of travel for individual drops. Such a focus sometimes favors a shift to preoccupation with individual spatters. This is an area where experience is very much a part of the process. With experience from a case log of several crime scenes, one can become proficient in determining directions of travel for groups of spatters without applying the hands-on technique. Careful identification of the spatters comprising an individual event is essential when several different events overlap. At a crime scene, the investigator must become proficient in mentally separating events so that interpretation may be accurate.

Participants in workshops may be told that the direction of travel is the longest measurement to a spatter. Three cautions exist in determining directions of travel. First, there are two ends to a long spatter: the direction of travel and the point of first contact. Saying the longest length is the direction of travel may suggest two directions. The second reason is that surface characteristics of a target may cause the blood drop to be absorbed and/or spread in an uneven manner. Blood drops contacting this type of surface may appear wider at the cross-section of the drop than in the direction of travel. The third reason was pointed out in a Ph.D. dissertation study (Pizzola et al., 1986, p. 58). In that experiment, it was found that movement of the target at the moment a blood drop was recorded as a spatter not only could change the stain appearance, but under some conditions could show a reversed direction of travel. Crime scenes may have considerable movement; thus, attention to those actions which affect spatter shape must be considered. One is likely to be more accurate in regard to direction of travel if one considers the most irregular edge of the resultant bloodstain; i.e., the direction of travel of an individual spatter is toward the most irregular edge of the stain. Refer to Figure 4.1 for examples of directions of travel.

The location of the surface where the spatter is recorded is important in interpretation. If the spatters are found on the ceiling, wall, or on a wood/tile/linoleum floor, the directions of travel may be used in a reconstruction of the area of convergence, which should exist at a right angle to an origin of an impact event. Indications may be provided, although no reconstruction measurement techniques are used, for the manner of swings distributing castoffs or blood pressure at the moment an artery spurted. If the spatters are found on walls, the location becomes more complex. The question is this: Was the blood drop traveling up or down when it made contact with the wall? The tailing nature of a spatter does not necessarily answer this question. After a drop makes contact, gravity may draw liquid blood downward, suggesting the drop was traveling up to down. Large drops may travel up and then be overcome by gravity and either reverse travel or include a long tail of excess fluid blood by the time they reach a surface. The distance between the origin and the wall becomes a necessary consideration.

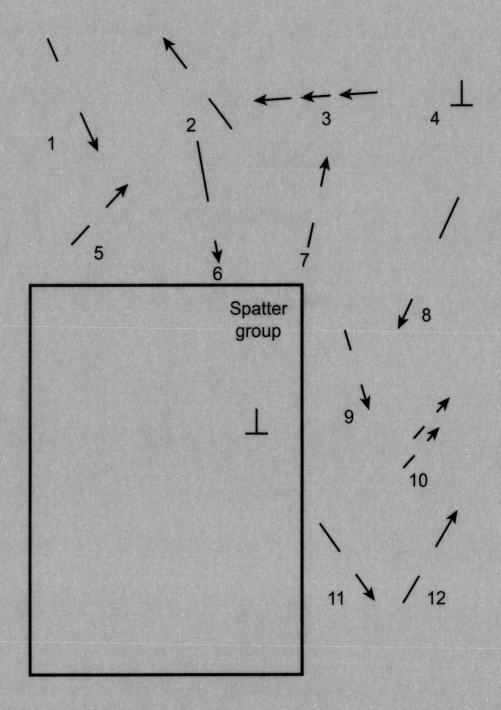

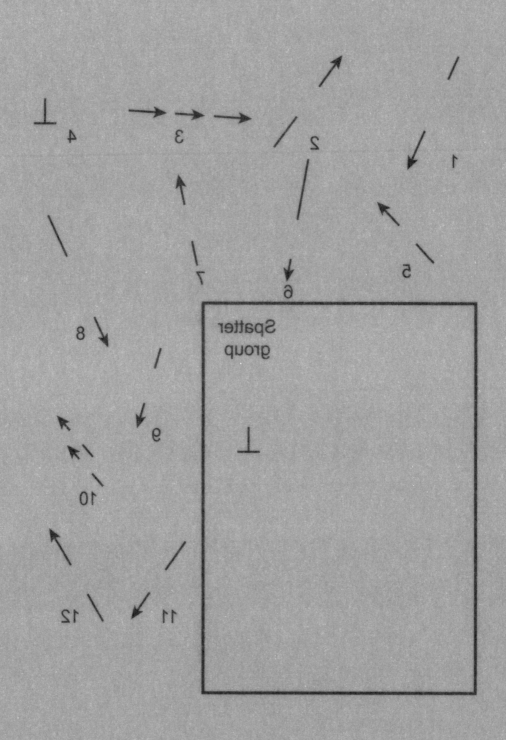

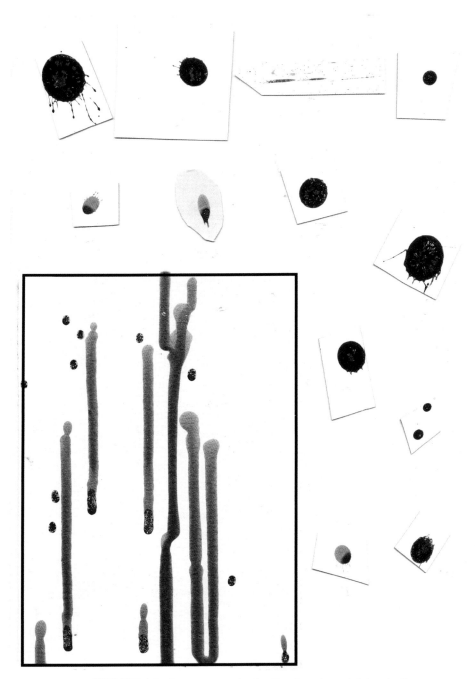

FIGURE 4.1   Practice examples for direction of travel determination.

FIGURE 4.1: EXPLANATIONS FOR DIRECTIONS OF TRAVEL PRACTICE BLOOD SPATTERS

In Spatter 1, the irregularities span almost 50% of the circumference of the stain, and the spikes are evenly balanced per sides of the stain. The direction of travel is drawn halfway between the spikes.

Spatters 2 and 9 have faint irregularities and almost round stains, but the direction of travel is indicated by the spines.

Spatter 3 could be two very small drops or one small drop skipping after making contact at a very low angle. The edges to the left show irregularities. This type of spatter may be misread as to direction of travel because of the belief that the wider part is the beginning, not the end of travel. The narrow angle and fast velocity mean the drop did not make a strong footprint but barely touched the target before travel moved on. This can be characteristic of gunshot. Respiratory distribution tends to be blood drops that are deposited on contact rather than streaking such as this.

In Spatter 4, no direction of travel is indicated. This is considered a direct-hit, 90-degree contact.

Spatters 5 and 11 are presented to show that the dense blood part of a stain must not be used as a direction of travel indicator. Blood drops hitting a vertical target at an angle can show blood draining due to gravity, which does not indicate a direction of travel from a distributing event.

Spatters 6, 8, and 12 are fairly straightforward. Spatter 12 has a little irregularity at the opposite end to travel due to hitting other blood marks on the target.

Spatter 7 is very subtle, but a few scallops on one edge show slight direction of travel in that direction.

Spatter 10 requires very close observation, perhaps with magnification. Very small scallops show directions of travel.

The group exhibit shows many runs down the target that do not indicate directions of travel (see Figure 4.2). A simulated artery with a recirculating pump was angled directly at a target positioned vertically. The runs were from either very large drops and/or multiple drops hitting in tandem. This is a double clue that one is dealing with arterial damage because impact cannot have drops distributed from the same point in time and castoffs do not have the random arrangement and uniform size to the scattered round stains. An exception to this, however, is with cessation castoffs, which are described later.

As with anything being studied, the shape of spatters that will be used to determine direction of travel requires that one examines the factors that affect final shape of a blood spatter. In relative order of importance, parameters that affect blood drop shape include the following:

1. The speed of the blood drop when it contacts a recording surface (target) is the most important parameter. This was Dr. Kirk's primary division of blood drop behavior as described in Chapter 1. The values of velocity were relative rather than absolute numerical values. Efforts to identify the numerical values for drop distribution speeds may be seen as consistent with the motor with paddle fan workshop device (MacDonell and Bialousz, 1979, p. 13). This device involves an enclosed motor in a box with a drive shaft to which rotating paddles are attached. A hole in the top of the box set above the paddles allows an aliquot of blood to be dropped onto the rotating paddles. The aliquot, usually about 1–2 cubic

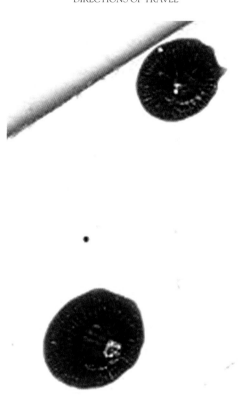

FIGURE 4.2 Detail of stain 10 from Figure 4.1. Sometimes the direction of travel is a subtle blip at the leading edge. Small stains may be secondary to larger "parent" stains, so one needs to be cautious in interpretation.

centimeters, of blood is broken up on impact with the spinning blades and then projected out the front opening of the box as a castoff array of blood drops. A tachometer can be applied to determine the speed of rotation of the drive shaft turning the paddles. The reading is used to estimate the speed of rotation of the paddles. Review of the correspondence in the Kirk Papers at the Bancroft Library of the University of California shows that Dr. Kirk anticipated something of this sort to help determine the velocity impact of blood drops as correlated with their size and distance traveled. Dr. Kirk died before the shift occurred in terminology, as later presented in papers, regarding the site velocity as considered for impact spatters.

The paddle fan device is interesting and useful for workshop experiments if the limitations are understood and stated. The process involves a blood source introduced above spinning paddles. The blood source is broken up at contact and distributed as groups of drops out of an opening at 90 degrees from the input. The individual drops distributed out of the box may leave the opening at a different velocity than that measured on the drive shaft. The reason for this is that mass of the drops and wind sheer affect the velocity of the drops over the distance they travel before falling to the target surface. The main caution is that the interpretation of the dynamic act measured by the location and size of distributed spatters outside the box is not from an impact. The impact is inside the box when a paddle meets part of the aliquot of blood. The fact that the aliquot is impacted with more than one blade can be seen by examining the blades after a blood drop. The dynamic event that distributes blood drops out of the opening of the box is castoff, which is a centripetal motion event, i.e., angular momentum. Castoff dynamic distribution is seen on all sides inside the box after the motor is turned off. The research method to identify the effects of impact would be with use of a force tensor at the site of the impact with a blood source. Unfortunately, interpretation also requires information regarding the composition of the blood sample used in the experiments. This information would not be known at crime scenes.

Some authors mention that the shape of spatters depends on angle of impact and surface texture but omit the speed of the drop as essential in determining blood spatter shape (James et al., 2005, p. 103). The speed of blood drops at contact cannot be ignored in defining spatter shape. Different dynamic events—impact, castoff, arterial spurt, or blood dripping into blood— distribute blood drops at different velocities. However, there is variation of drop velocity within each category with considerable overlap in variation of size and shape of spatters. In crime scene work-up, one must recognize that events other than those immediately considered may be responsible for sizes found. There is an alternative approach to identification of spatter groupings that is historically taken from Dr. Kirk's original applications.

2. The angle at which the blood drop encounters the target surface will influence the leading edge of a spatter; thus, a group of spatters contributes to the shape of a whole bloodstain pattern. The effect on the shape, however, depends on whether the drop volume is large enough to continue travel after contact. Small, tiny, and mist-sized drops may be projected so that their forward momentum is overcome by air resistance before they encounter a target. After forward motion stops for a blood drop, it may dry and be dispersed in the air currents or may settle straight down with no apparent direction of travel. This is often seen with gunshot and respiratory-distributed blood drops as a result of the explosive nature of the shot or sneeze. Mist and tiny drops are initially accelerated but lack sufficient mass (weight per volume) to continue travel against wind sheer and air friction.

3. The composition of blood in the blood drop is often ignored in research experimental design (Adam, 2012, pp. 76–87), yet is crucial for the appearance of the blood spatters formed (Wonder, 2001, pp. 20–21). It is required that characteristics of the blood sample used in any project be stated, including source (animal or human) and the hemoglobin/hematocrit (abbreviated Hgb/Hct) values listed. Red blood cells will contain more mass (weight per volume of blood in the drop). This information applies to how far a blood drop is able to travel after distribution from a dynamic event. The composition also influences the size of the drops formed because the greater the number of red blood cells, the greater the internal cohesion in drops. High Hgb/Hct drops may be smaller but have higher mass and thus travel farther but leave smaller stains. Low Hgb/Hct will form bigger drops with less cohesion and possibly less stability; i.e., they are capable of oscillation. Stains may be larger but with more irregular edges.

The changes in appearance of the resultant spatter affected by Hgb/Hct are shown in Figure 2.6 in Chapter 2 and with angle of impact as considered in Figure 4.3. One can study the effects of higher mass for blood higher in red blood cells by using the paddle fan device. The mistaken belief that blood is a uniform substance has contributed to acceptance of projects in which the composition of blood was ignored. Blood composition not only varies from person to person, but more importantly also varies for different organ systems in the body for a single victim (Albert et al., 1965, pp. 20–21).

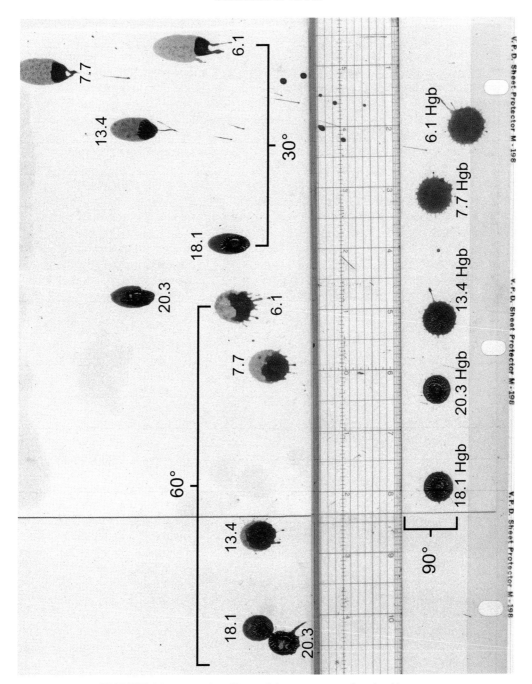

FIGURE 4.3 Examples of hemoglobin variation and angle of impact.

II. IDENTIFICATION

4. The importance of volume in a drop can be demonstrated with drops from different-sized droppers. Big drops will have slightly different shapes simply because there is more blood to continue travel before forward momentum ceases. Very large drops recorded on vertical surfaces may have spillover with a long tail running down the surface. The stain recorded for spatters that "run" after being recorded may provide confusion if it is concluded that such a tail indicates direction of travel. Large drops may be projected from arterial damage, splash, or swing castoffs, but the direction of travel could result from upward or sideways actions to contact. If the drop, which is deposited on a vertical surface, has so much volume that all the blood cannot remain deposited on contact, the remainder after the drop stops travel will flow downward by the pull of gravity alone.

Workshops usually provide uniform droppers and a consistent blood source. The effects of drop composition of blood may not be stated. However, workshop often include experiments using different sized droppers. This can lead to misunderstanding when conclusions are drawn in casework. Refer to Figure 4.4 for a view of workshop humor.

5. The importance of the angle at which a drop contacts a target is useful in determining where an impact occurred, yet large drops are less likely to be distributed from blunt force or missile (bullet) impact. Castoff and arterial spurts occur over a range of time and space, not from a specific area at a point in time for a specific dynamic event. It follows that locating an area of

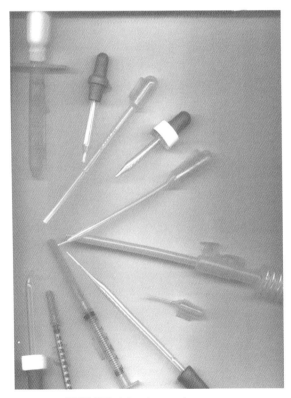

FIGURE 4.4   The usual suspects.

convergence is not advisable for any spatters not identified with an impact because a group of drops from other than impact dynamics would not have originated from a single area. The importance of volume affecting spatter shape is used to eliminate those large spatters from any reconstruction of an impact. Be aware that spatters from large drops from subsequent events, such as blood dripping, may be found at or near the convergence of impact-distributed spatters. Crimes of violence are very active, with blood dripping, being cast off during struggles, and/or exiting a breached artery after an assailant is no longer present. All may exist as overlapping bloodstain patterns at a crime scene. If an array of droppers can result in noticeable variation in drop size and behavior, crime events should not be solely evaluated on the basis of a concept that there is a standard, or typical, drop size.

6. The surface characteristic of the target where the spatter is recorded has been stated as one of two significant factors in spatter shapes (MacDonell, 1982, pp. 5–6; James et al., 2005, pp. 106–107). This is frequently illustrated with drips at different heights on materials in question. The problem, however, is that in casework very large blood stains, such as those resulting from a medicine dropper or a wounded victim, are not measured in work-ups. The measured shapes of blood spatters are only used for reconstructing the origin, i.e., where in space an alleged impact occurred. Drips, by definition, receive no additional force input besides gravity and thus are not associated with impacts and are not used for those reconstructions. Blood drips located along a trail leading away from an apparent area of convergence are best analyzed for directions of travel to or from blood-distributing events at the convergence. The amount of elongation, not absolute value, can indicate that the person bleeding, or carrying something dripping blood, was moving slow or fast. Efforts to use bloodstain shape to determine the specific velocity a person was moving are unreliable in providing investigative information because of the small difference in shapes for different speeds of walking versus running. A slow walk, staggering (from side to side in the directions of travel), or running with jostling may suggest actions of benefit to investigations more so than attempting to assign a specific velocity to movement.

ALIGNMENTS

After one identifies a group of spatters associated with one dynamic event and notes the direction of travel for individuals as they relate to the group, the next step should include descriptions of alignments. This will also help to confirm that the correct classification for the whole pattern, or group of spatters, was chosen. There are five basic alignments of spatters with respect to each other and with respect to the whole pattern (see Figure 4.5):

1. aligned at angles to each other, apparently all from a central area, which *may be* an area of convergence;
2. aligned at an angle to each consecutive spatter but with a consistent shift in the angle;
3. parallel arrangement of spatters with groups of three or more spatters per arrangement;
4. random distribution, with no discernible order to the alignments; and
5. "direct hit," stains most or all show no direction of travel (i.e., 90-degree contact between drop and target).

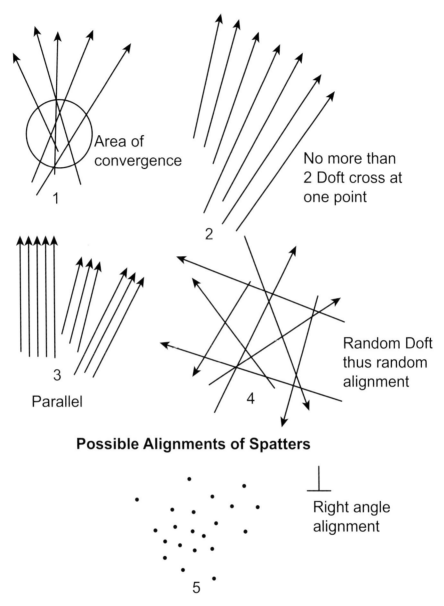

FIGURE 4.5   Schematic arrows showing alignment alternatives for pattern identification.

DISTRIBUTION/DENSITY

Mentioned as early as 1895 (Piotrowski, 1895, p. 33f), sketches of whole pattern shapes with approximations regarding how arrays of blood drops are distributed away from an impact were available to investigators of crime in Europe. Experiments were conducted to show the distribution and densities from impacts of blood spatters resulting from various blows to the heads of live rabbits. Prior to 1970, this same type of reconstruction was used to support testimonies in the United States. Over time, emphasis shifted toward recognition that different events and degrees of force created predominance of different size ranges of spatters. Arrangement of the stains resulting from impact is still considered but may not be given the same weight in interpretation and conclusions as the predominance of sizes within groups of spatters. This shift in emphasis may result in experimental design for reconstruction based on re-creating spatters of a predominant size rather than on how the sizes were arranged to form the whole patterns (Wonder, 2007, pp. 66–67).

Reliance may be focused on distribution and density of predominant size ranges rather than the absolute measurements of some of the available spatters. This would be considered consistent with the early research of Piotrowski. His sketches, however, favored whole arrangement distribution rather than relationships between adjacent spatters. There are basically three groupings with regard to spatter distribution density:

1. The size ranges and number of spatters decrease away from a central area, which may contain an area of convergence.
2. The size ranges and number of spatters remain roughly the same over the range of the whole pattern.
3. The size ranges are randomly distributed over a set area with regard to the group of spatters.

With impact spatters, there is a recognized involvement of multiple-sized spatters, especially with smaller stains from gunshot. Some other events predominately show smaller stains and may identify respiratory-distributed spatters and pinhole breach of a high-pressure artery. Blunt force may cause a large range of sizes, from small to large, as may blood dripping into blood and arterial spurts under a variety of blood pressure, source of artery, and type of injury. The distribution of the size ranges, i.e., how many different-sized spatters result from an event, may be more important than the actual sizes themselves.

Criteria identification involves the use of specific guidelines to classify bloodstain patterns. The following series of pattern examples with overlays are presented to show how criteria may be used for identification and the clarification of the criteria concept. Scales have been intentionally left off of the exhibits to focus identification on group arrangements rather than size of individual spatters. After pattern identification, size of spatters can provide an indication of the degree of force per dynamic event.

Words describing the criteria are necessary for lawyers and court. Investigators, however, tend to be more visual and appreciate demonstrations of the points made in words. Figures 4.6 through 4.6 show examples of the main bloodstain pattern classifications with overlays to illustrate how criteria can be applied to identify the dynamic events involved. It will be beneficial to the reader to study the picture first before folding over the overlay and seeing the answers to criteria use.

Detailed descriptions of criteria identification follow.

IDENTIFICATION FOR FIGURE 4.6: A BLOODSTAIN PATTERN FOUND ON A FLOOR (FOLLOWING THE SAADD CRITERIA)

Shape: The whole arrangement is in a starburst type pattern.

Alignment: Directions of travel for the spatters making up the pattern are outward in all directions from a central region located at the top of the page if viewed vertically and to the left if viewed horizontally.

Alignment: Each spatter is at an angle to its neighbors. No two spatters of equal size are in tandem. A caution is applied here that secondary spatters cast ahead of parent drops may appear as drops in tandem, but the sizes of the two drops vary, with the smaller one being in front of a larger one.

Distribution/Density: The number of spatters recorded decreases from a central area as noted in the alignment above.

Distribution/Density: The number of different sizes in spatters decreases away from a central area that we now call the "area of convergence." The small-sized spatters resulted from blood drops that lack enough mass to carry over a distance from the impact and thus settle or are dispersed in the air and not recorded. Large drops have too much mass and are slowed and stopped by wind sheer/air resistance. Thus, those drops with just enough mass to carry but not too much mass to be stopped by wind sheer are recorded on the target. The result is a decrease in the number of different sizes observed as one proceeds away from the area of convergence. Remember that the area of convergence is located at right angles to the impact origin somewhere in space.

Classification: The pattern shown in Figure 4.6 is classified as an "impact spatter pattern." Spatters are very small but lack the characteristic misting identified with gunshot at close range. Thus, this could be any impact including gunshot from a distance or very forceful blunt force impact with a heavy object on an exposed blood source, i.e., prior injury. It could also be respiratory distribution projected in an impact-like arrangement.

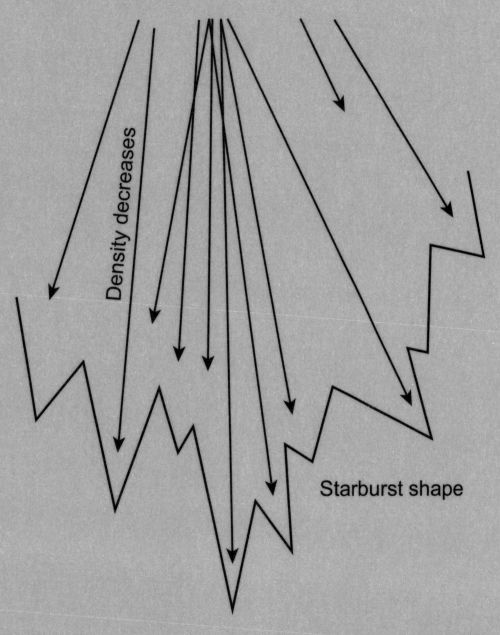

Density decreases

Starburst shape

FLOOR

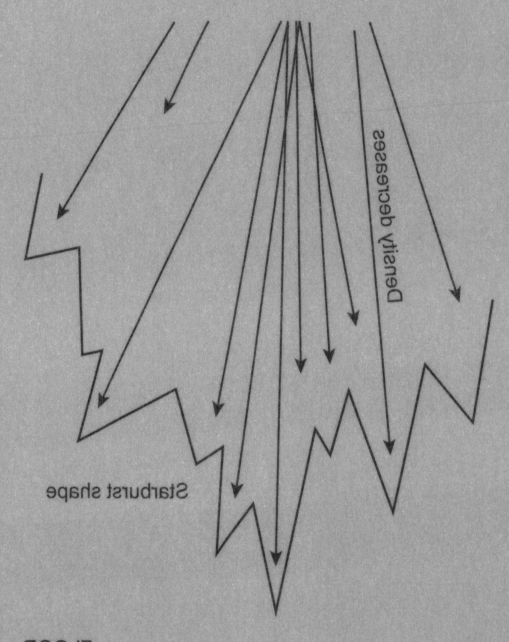

FIGURE 4.6   Bloodstain pattern found on floor.

II. IDENTIFICATION

IDENTIFICATION FOR FIGURE 4.7: A BLOODSTAIN PATTERN FOUND ON A WALL

Shape: Groups of spatters with directions of travel noted form two apparent boxed arrangements.

Alignment: Alignments based on directions of travel tell two things: The boxes show opposing directions of travel (A1 and A2), and the target appears to have been rotated 90 degrees before blood dried within the spatters. If this was truly a wall section, it would be contradictory. If it were a movable article such as a wall mirror, glass panel, or sheet of paneling, it would indicate that the position during the event changed soon afterward. With respect to the whole pattern, the spatters are aligned adjacent to each other with some subtle changes in angle. Some in-tandem alignment is indicated.

Alignment: Rotating the exhibit 90 degrees to the left positions the spatters so that the two directions of travel define forward and backward motions. The smaller box arrangement suggests a back swing, whereas the larger box suggests a more forceful swing, possibly toward a victim.

Distribution/Density: The number of spatters in each box does not show decrease over the length of each array.

Distribution/Density: The number of different-sized spatters seems consistent over the range of each box's dimensions.

Classification: A single spatter located to the left of center if the page is viewed vertically or to the right if viewed at 90 degrees rotated to the left shows direction of travel aligned with box A2. This could have been the place where the swings reversed; i.e., it could identify where the victim was located when the blows were delivered. The composition of patterns comprises swing castoffs showing both legs of a complete swing to and away from a victim.

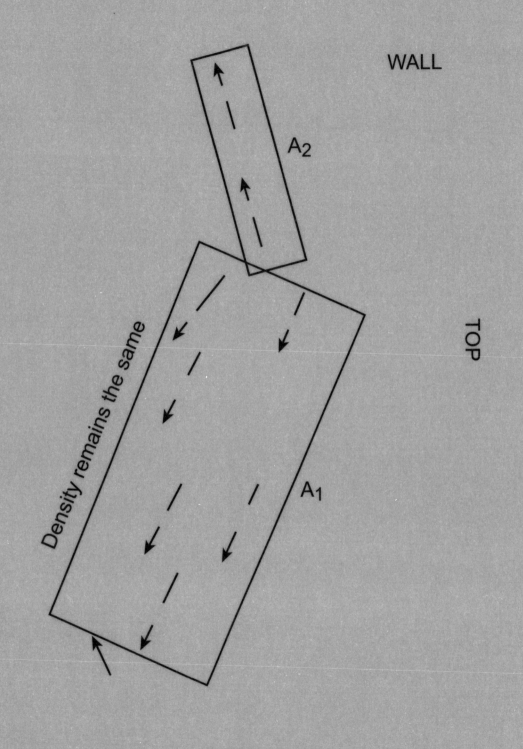

WALL

TOP

Density remains the same

A_2

A_1

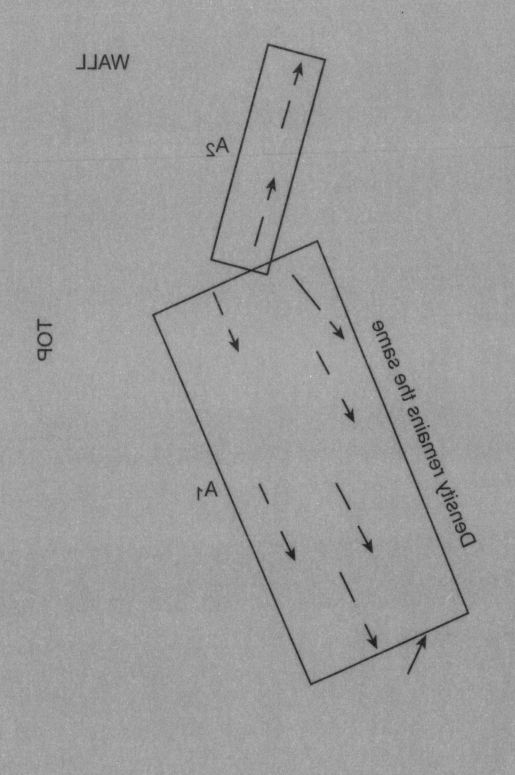

WALL

TOP

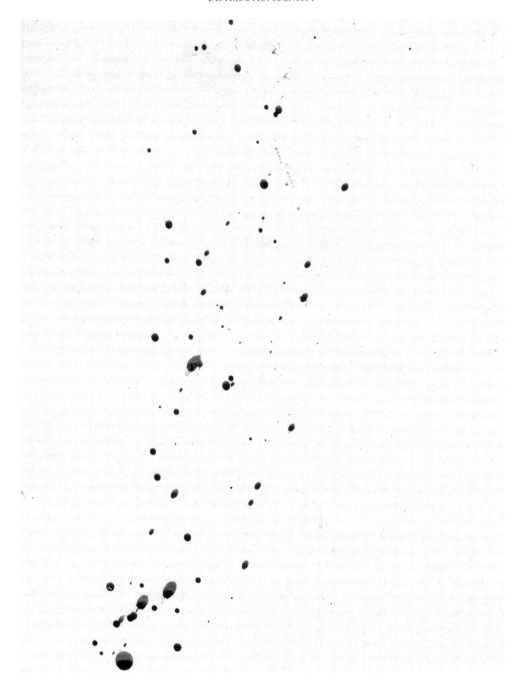

FIGURE 4.7 Bloodstain pattern found on a wall.

II. IDENTIFICATION

IDENTIFICATION FOR FIGURE 4.8: A BLOODSTAIN PATTERN FOUND ON A FLOOR OR ON A WALL

Shape: Care must be taken when apparent composite arrangements are found. This type of combination could be found on a floor or on a wall. Two possible arrangements are noted that indicate a single event. One can see a scattered moon/half moon/pie wedge arrangement combined with linear or rectangular columns.

Alignment: All of the spatters in both arrangements are at or close to perpendicular impact alignment. In other words, there are no or very slight directions of travel indicated for the individual spatters.

Alignment: With the lack of direction of travel for individual spatters, their relationship with adjoining spatters is indeterminant or is consistent with all coming from a near 90-degree impact.

Distribution/Density: It becomes apparent that with this composite of patterns, the distribution of spatters is more important than the alignment. The scatter at the top of the page, if viewed vertically, or at left if rotated 90 degrees to the left, indicates something broad carrying blood, whereas the linear extensions with the same density of spatters indicate something narrow holding blood until it was released by the event creating the whole pattern.

Distribution/Density: There is an abrupt decrease in sizes and number of spatters at the end (right or bottom as viewed) of the columns.

Classification: The columns show that this was a castoff event, but the scatter and different shapes help to fine-tune the classification. The definite end of the columns show that blood was released from a narrow object at once. This is in contrast to blood drop release over a range, as with swings. The action that results in the immediate cessation of the pattern is a cessation castoff. The object carrying blood abruptly stopped, or ceased, motion. Blood adhering to the surface of the object continued traveling in the same general direction as the object was moving prior to cessation. The scatter at the beginning of the columns shows that the object was narrow but had depth, like an axe perhaps. Because cessation castoffs result from blood continuing to travel after the object stops, the direction in which it was being delivered can be interpreted, i.e., the manner in which an assailant was delivering blows. Right- versus left-handed swings may be seen.

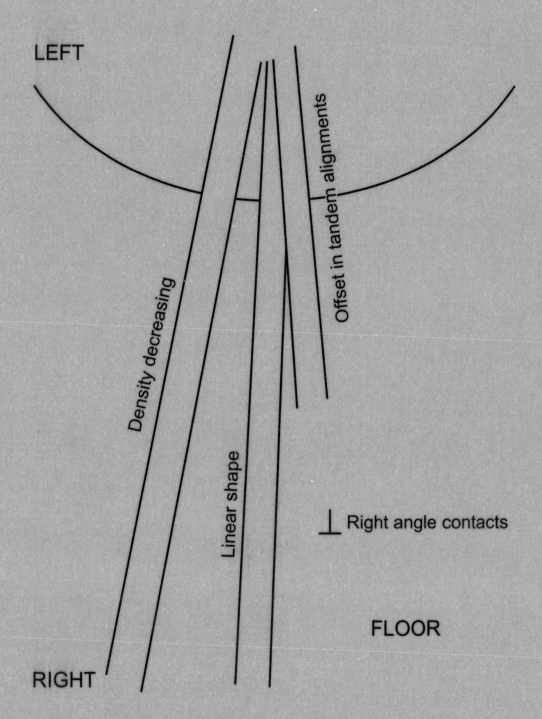

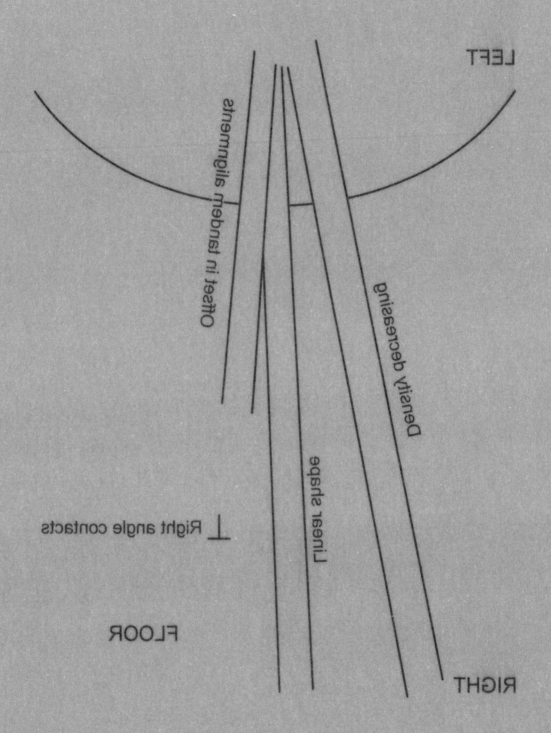

FIGURE 4.8   A bloodstain pattern that could be found on either a floor or a wall.

II. IDENTIFICATION

IDENTIFICATION FOR FIGURE 4.9: A BLOODSTAIN PATTERN FOUND ON A WALL

Shape: Again, a composite of patterns results from a single dynamic event or, in this situation, a series of events. The top of the page as viewed shows repeating curves of direct-hit (right-angle contact) blood drops recorded. A cascade of spatters follows below the curves. The curves can also be called waves; undulations; or upside-down Us, Ms, or Ns.

Alignment: The curves consist of blood drops hitting so close together that separation for appearance is not possible. This shows the blood source was a column of inline drops, separated or not when contact was made at the target. The cascading spatters below, however, show in-tandem arrangement in columns, confirming that the curves were from blood drops distributed in columns.

Alignment: The most remarkable characteristic is the parallel arrangement of the in-tandem spatters. Groups of spatters shift slightly, but each group has three or more spatters that can be considered parallel to each other.

Distribution/Density: The consistency of spatter numbers throughout the whole arrangement shows a blood source that is continually providing more blood drops; i.e., the amount of blood is not a specific amount adhering to an object.

Distribution/Density: There is a more diverse number of spatter sizes than can be expected from this type of dynamic event. The reason could have been that the event was simulated and not an actual crime scene occurrence. In this case, a recirculating pump with a bulb to add periodic pulses was used to mimic an arterial spurt sequence. An actual artery spurting would be expected to project similar-sized drops of a consistency of spatter sizes over the range of the pattern. It must be accepted that the spatter size alone cannot identify arterial damage. Everything from mist to extremely large spatters can depend on the type of artery and the nature of the injury/breach.

Classification: The pattern was reconstructed as an example of arterial spurting. The consistency of spatter density, sizes, and parallel arrangement showing the distribution as columns of drops is definitive of arterial damage–type patterns.

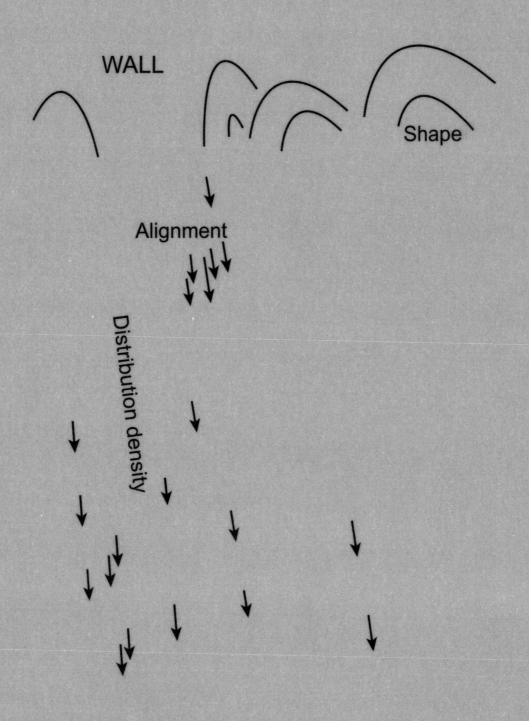

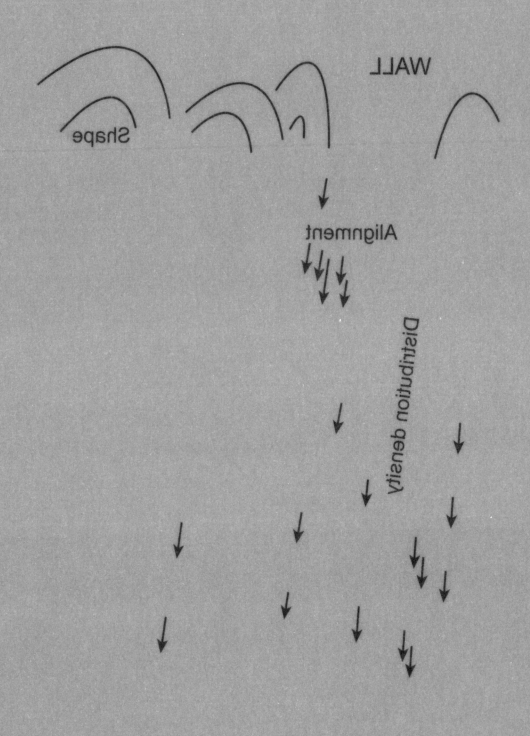

FIGURE 4.9 Arterial damage patterns: An example of arterial spurting is shown. Contrasting appearances with castoff patterns is essential.

II. IDENTIFICATION

If the question for Figure 4.10 was which of the three examples is from gunshot, the answer would be all of them. See the placement of bullet holes in Figure 4.11. Interestingly, exhibits A and B are from the same gunshot, a 9 mm handgun. The difference in appearance occurred from one, A, being an "entrance wound" and the other, B, being an "exit wound." Why was the entrance wound so much more staining with the characteristic mist and fine spatters? The reason is that the blood source produced by the bullet and the muzzle blasts that preceded and followed the bullet encountered a previously exposed blood source. When a bloody sponge is used as a blood source, one should consider the additional interpretation necessary for the experimental results—that is, that the blood source was available for drop distribution before the muzzle blast and bullet impacted the source. The mist and fine spatter result from the explosive muzzle blast, not necessarily the high-velocity bullet.

Recognizing entrance versus exit wound arrangements co-relates to the pathology reports better than the terms "forward spatter" and "back spatter," especially when one considers that the distribution need not be in a direct line forward or backward. Note the offset of the bullet hole in Figure 4.11C. The bullet bent the target so that spatters from the muzzle blast were recorded offset from the bullet penetration hole.

Something that could be more important to investigative leads information is shown in Figure 4.12. Hair was carried with the bullet and/or muzzle blast as the bullet passed through a human hair wig. This composite would locate a specific shot to the head. The small number of spatters overall resulted

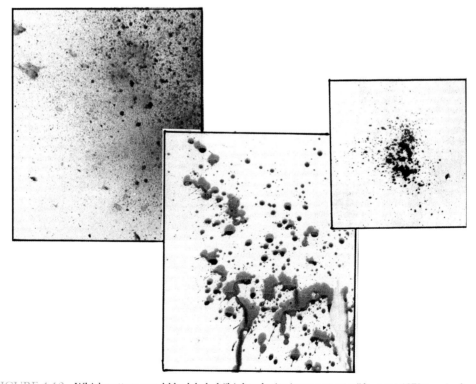

FIGURE 4.10   Which pattern would be labeled "high velocity impact spatter" by post-1970 terminology?

from blockage by the wig, but breakup of the blood source by the muzzle gases carried the hair forward. The presence of hair may also explain the lack of bloodstains distributed in the direction of the shooter by a gunshot. Making assumptions about the presence and absence of blood spatters is not advisable for initial investigative leads because it may send the reconstruction of a scenario in the wrong direction.

Of course, having a bullet hole in a target near spatters is helpful in labeling the pattern as gunshot for workshop exercises. Not all firearm injuries in actual casework, however, result in the bullet exiting. One still needs to consider the association between spatters and a bullet hole at a crime scene for crime dynamics. If lung, throat, or facial injury occurs without immediate death, respiratory distribution becomes a concern (see Figure 4.13). If the victim is alive when found, any person attempting to assist may receive mist and fine spatter on his or her person. Such evidence becomes significant only if the person claims no contact or encounter with the victim. Conclusions as to identification of the pattern must take into account where spatters were found, what the person of interest claimed to have done when in contact with the victim, and what injuries were involved. The autopsy findings of blood in the respiratory system could provide information that respiratory distribution may have been possible.

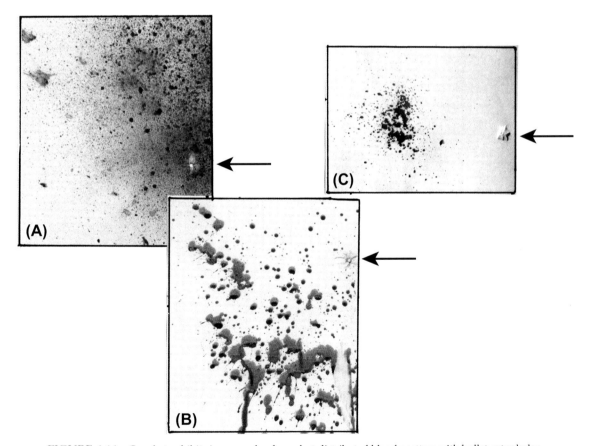

FIGURE 4.11 Gunshot exhibit: An example of gunshot-distributed blood spatters with bullet entry holes.

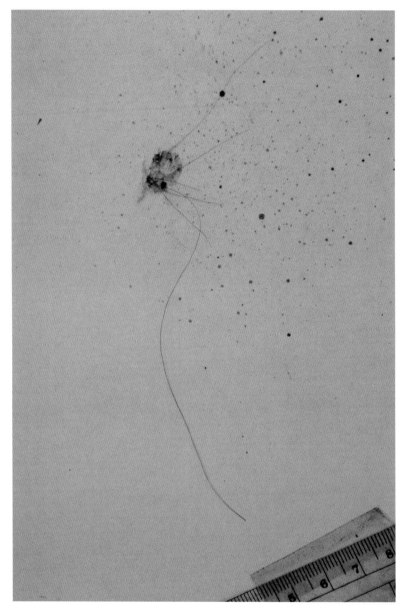

FIGURE 4.12   Hair carried with the bullet and muzzle blast.

Confusion may occur when differentiating between castoffs and arterial damage patterns and identifying gunshot-distributed spatters versus respiratory projection. These similar whole patterns bring into consideration the challenge of classification solely based on similar predominant size ranges of whole groups of spatters. This is discussed further in Chapter 5.

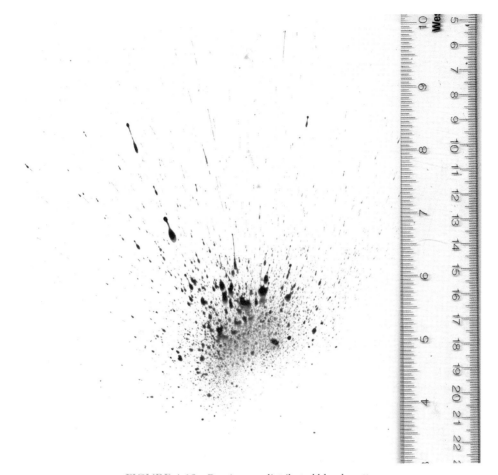

FIGURE 4.13   Respiratory-distributed blood spatter.

FURTHER DISCUSSIONS REGARDING EXAMPLES OF SPATTER PATTERNS

Blunt Force Impact: Floor

Directions of travel are first drawn for widely spaced spatters (refer to Figure 4.6). It is important that measurable spatters be found and used to locate other spatters comprising a single impact. It is essential that directions of travel be drawn through a spatter in the exact direction it was traveling when contact with the surface occurred. The reason for this is to help identify the size and shape of the area of convergence. Trying to wrap directions of travel so that they meet in a point is not only unrealistic of the actual crime event but misses the information possible from the shape of the area of convergence. No two drops of an incompressible fluid can originate from the same point.

When a blunt weapon is used, the area of the origin will be larger than for a bullet impact, and blood drops will be distributed from the circumference of the contact area between weapon and blood source. Because of this effect from a blunt force impact, one may use the size and shape of the area of convergence to show the approximate size and shape of the origin for that impact. If more than one impact exists, the size and amount of blood may show the sequence to an assault. The sequence of an assault may be correlated to the autopsy or medical reports to identify the weapon and characteristics of the assailant.

From the directions of travel, the shape of the whole pattern becomes apparent. The spatters forming the pattern show an outward orientation from a central area of the overall pattern that resembles a pie wedge, starburst, or even a pyramid shape. If employing an abbreviated approach using only the size of spatters, one might jump to the conclusion that this was gunshot or a sneeze. The tiny stains within the angled ones suggest drops so small that their forward movement was blocked by wind sheer, and they settled straight down. At a crime scene, they would indicate a strong force but probably not gunshot if the area of convergence was over an inch wide. Bullet impacts of smaller caliber handgun have smaller areas of convergence, whereas large calibers, as well as narrow blunt force weapons, may have multiple areas of convergence from fragmenting of projectiles or bone of the victim. Exceptions to every criterion exist, so nothing should be "written in stone" until the entire analysis has been completed.

The next part of the identification is to evaluate the distribution and density of spatters and their size ranges. Most bloodstain spatter workshops advocate measuring spatters, yet graduates of the programs seldom apply measurements later in casework. It is sad if the evidence is ignored because of the work-intensive requirement of hands-on measurements. Information can be gleaned without measuring spatters initially. The heavier density is assumed to be closer to the origin, but this may not be as the pattern is recorded. Impacts may distribute blood drops away in a cone-shaped alignment from the origin. An area close to the origin but located at 90 degrees from it may show fewer spatters than the area at an increased angle from the origin. As stated in the previous paragraph, one must take care not to jump to conclusions prematurely.

Swing Castoff: Wall

In Figure 4.7, directions of travel are drawn. The positions are often downward unless the strikes occurred close to the wall. Although the stains, at a quick glance, may appear to all be part of one event, identifying the directions of travel shows different blocks of spatter groups. The offset alignment suggests swing castoff, and two swings or more are often indicated for the event. This is investigative information because any pairs of swings can be used to place the assailant during an assault. One could argue that there is parallel alignment, but such is not seen if alignment is slightly off and/or stains are not in tandem. This alignment also excludes impact dynamics as the distributing event. Both arterial distribution and castoffs can have in-line arrangement of spatters because the drops are distributed from the same position in space of a blood source.

From the directions of travel and the alignment, one can see a whole pattern shape as linear, boxed, or rectangular. This is characteristic of swing castoffs because they are distributed in roughly linear, rectangular, or boxed arrangements. The pattern may be curved if recorded on a wall or vertical surface. The next step would be to place the victim, not the assailant, during the swings. The weapon will pick up blood from the victim. Actions of assault involve the back swing, which is less important to the assailant and thus not as forceful as the forward swing. The back swing merely positions the blow for the next assault to the victim. To cause injury to the victim, the forward swing is delivered with greater input of force. Because the weapon picks up more blood from the victim on impact, the density of large drops will be closer to the victim's position.

The important consideration for placing victim and assailant is to understand the difference in bloodstain pattern workshops. The objective in workshops is to create bloodstains for the class to examine. When one is swinging a weapon to and from a blood-soaked sponge, the objective is not to cause injury to a victim. On the back swing, students will frequently snap the weapon, like flicking a wet towel in locker-room play. This clears the weapon of blood much like play clears water from a towel. At a crime scene, the weapon is being used to cause bodily injury. The back swing has less force because it is merely being positioned for the next forceful forward swing. The best way to learn about castoffs in a bloodstain pattern workshop is to visualize someone that the participant would like to beat to a bloody pulp, figuratively. Keeping this in mind, one should be very careful about drawing conclusions from swing patterns at crime scenes. More important is seeing whether one can identify the weapon. Was it a tire iron or a two-by-four board?

In the example presented in this chapter, the weapon was a board. The "victim" was at right, and the small rectangle represented a short back swing. The length of swing can help position the victim, whereas the arcs, if they are seen, can indicate handedness of the assailant.

Arterial Damage Spurts and Gush: Wall

When drawing directions of travel with such patterns, one sometimes finds that the alignment defines different shapes: a heavy/dense group with overlapping spatters and a "rain," or cascade, of many individual spatters aligned across columns (refer to Figure 4.8). More important are the spatters of the same size and shape positioned in tandem. For tandem arrangements, there are two possibilities: castoffs or arterial spurting. Both castoffs and arterial spurting can result in the fallout that is also called an "arterial fountain arrangement" or a "castoff upside-down U."

Here, it is essential to understand how blood drops are distributed by each dynamic event. Arterial damage begins with blood inside arterial blood vessels. Some jurisdictions attempt to limit bloodstain pattern testimony to blood behavior outside the body only. This assumes that any blood behavior with regard to arterial blood vessels will be addressed by medical experts or an autopsy physician. As of the present time, it is not required to list arterial vessel injury on autopsies if it is not directly associated with the cause of death. Emergency rooms are good at mentioning arterial damage because of the seriousness of blood loss from arteries. Some investigators may be less inclined to read medical reports, if available, and if the victim survives. In those jurisdictions where testimony is later limited to outside the body, the bloodstain pattern analyst must either gain qualification to explain the source of arterial injury bloodstain patterns, possibly through a pretrial motion in limne (discussed in Chapter 12), or by the presenting attorney establishing the background with prior examination/cross-examination of medical witnesses.

How does one know whether one is dealing with arterial distribution or castoff? Castoff bloodstain patterns result from blood drops being sloughed off, or cast off, a moving blood carrier over a range of time and space. As drops are released, the amount of blood still adhering and available to be released is reduced. The act of swinging a bloody object is rarely as a straight line. This may be a limitation to experiments in which a reproducible fling is created to study castoffs. The action may or may not reproduce the way an assailant used the weapon. The shift in how a swing is delivered will offset alignments, which may appear in tandem but will have size and shape variations as a result of slightly different angles and force applied during the swing. The changes may affect the release of blood drops from the object and thus affect the arrangement of the resultant whole pattern.

Arterial-projected blood drops form as a column of blood that separates into drops after exit from the blood vessel. The separation occurs as a result of the viscoelasticity of blood. Viscoelasticity is part of the definition of non-Newtonian fluid behavior. Because the spatters recorded are from a column that separates into equal drops, the pattern from arterial damage is made up of substantially similar drops resulting in drop contact at similar angles in tandem. The spatters will have distribution of the same size and shape density in recognizable parallel arrangements. As the artery moves during spurting, directions may shift but usually will include three or more spatters per position aligned as parallel.

In the author's experience, castoffs versus arterial damage patterns and gunshot versus respiratory patterns are more likely to be mistaken in casework than other pattern identifications. Bloodstain workshops may focus on castoff and impact patterns with less emphasis on recognition of arterial damage identification. Yet casework often shows that arteries are involved in the death or serious injury of the victim. One must remember that arterial injury can occur from assault, with death following after the assailant has left the scene; i.e., the perpetrator truly believes claims that the assailant left the victim alive. It must be emphasized that autopsy reports may not include mention of arterial injury, thus requiring identification at the scene by those processing the information prior to autopsy. A clue that an analyst is dealing with arterial distribution and not castoffs is the reproducibility of the pattern. Multiple arcs or rows of spatters that appear to re-create the same lines of travel are more likely to be arterial in origin. When these are seen, the analyst needs to consult the autopsy physician or medical records to determine whether an artery could have been involved and which one it could have been. It is essential that the basis for suspecting arterial involvement not be delayed until review of the autopsy. Not all autopsies include such material if arterial involvement is not included in the manner or cause of death.

REFERENCES

Adam, C.D., 2012. Fundamental Studies of Bloodstain Formation and Characteristics. Forensic Science International 219 (1-3), 76–87.

Albert, S.N., Jain, S.C., Shibula, J.A., Albert, C.A., 1965. The Hematocrit in Clinical Practice. Charles C. Thomas, Springfield, IL. 20–21.

James, S.H., Kish, P.E., Sutton, T.P., 2005. Principles of Bloodstain Pattern Analysis. Taylor and Francis, Boca Raton, FL. pp. 103, 106–107.

MacDonell, H.L., 1982. Bloodstain Pattern Interpretation, Revision. Painted Post Press, Corning, NY. pp. 5–6.

MacDonell, H.L., Bialousz, L.F., 1979. Laboratory Manual for the Geometric Interpretation of Human Bloodstain Evidence. Painted Post Press, Corning, NY. p. 13 (Experiment 11).

Paul Kirk Papers, Bancroft Library, found in the file of The Credibility of Physical Evidence Testimony presented at a Criminal Law Seminar, December 15, 1968.

Piotrowski, E., 1895. Origin, Shape, Direction, and Distribution Following Head Wounds Caused by Blows. Translated from the German presentation at the Institute of Forensic Medicine of the K.K. University, Vienna.

Pizzola, P.A., Roth, S., DeForest, P.R., 1986. Blood Droplet Dynamics II. Journal of Forensic Science 31 (1), 58.

Reynolds, M.E., 2012. An Expert for the Court: Testimony in the Magdalena Dzubia Case. Presented at the AAFS Meeting, Atlanta, GA.

Wonder, A.Y., 2001. Blood Dynamics. Academic Press, London. pp. 20–21, 33-34.

Wonder, A.Y., 2007. Bloodstain Pattern Evidence, Objective Approaches and Case Applications. Elsevier, San Diego, CA. pp. 66–67, 356.

Differentiations Between Similar Patterns

The examples in Chapter 4 illustrate how unreliable simple size and shape of spatters may be in identifying the dynamics that distributed blood drops. Experienced investigators may look at the patterns, the overlays, and the explanation and then immediately begin disagreeing with the identifications even though the examples were manufactured for the purpose of workshops. The first cry will be for scales, but would scales help? Not necessarily. Dr. Paul L. Kirk pointed out that grouping was more important, and that doesn't really require a scale. Exceptions will always be a consideration to what was presented in Chapter 4. For example, cessation castoffs may be found when the blood source is no longer present. Gunshot may have involved fine and mist-sized spatters not seen on the exhibits shown. Respiratory patterns may be found on paramedics, responding law enforcement officers, and innocent bystanders but are never mentioned when the spatters are found on persons of interest. Size and shape are not enough to identify the dynamics of a crime, but the criteria known as SAD (Shape, Alignment, Distribution and/or Density) also may not be enough. If the information is to be used to solve violent crimes that may result in the loss of freedom for persons of interest, more criteria than suggested, even with sizes and shapes added, are necessary before one can make solid conclusions.

ADDITIONS TO GUIDELINES FOR IDENTIFICATION

Following are some additional guidelines to bear in mind when reviewing cases and evidence related to bloodstain patterns.
1. Accept that there will be situations in which a final identification based on scientific principles is not possible.
2. Identification should be *confirmed* with other evidence, not *based* on it. Because a victim is beaten does not automatically lead to the identification of spatters as medium velocity impact spatter, nor does the fact that a gunshot occurred lead to identification of high velocity impact spatter. Beatings as well as knifings may involve arterial damage. Castoffs may often be found with impact; thus, one should pay attention to the different kinds of castoffs when attempting to identify impact patterns.

87

3. Most important is that scenarios be formed from the various bloodstain patterns found based on reasonable knowledge of crime. Interpretation, to be discussed in Section III, will depend on the accurate identification of the dynamics involved before outlining the sequences of violent crime. Pattern match approaches assume reconstructed patterns will look like crime scene evidence when the reconstruction is not substantially similar to the way criminal assaults are perpetrated. One person claiming expertise in "blood splatters" [sic] demonstrated the way a hammer was used as a weapon in a baseball bat–type swing. The suspect was a carpenter. It was later found that the suspect had used his childhood ball bat to kill his parents. The ball bat, not a hammer, was used in that baseball bat–type swing.

4. It is essential that patterns which resemble each other be separated and identified as the true dynamics they represent before conclusions about scenarios are reached and charges are formed. Reconstruction to re-create the size and shape of spatters alone does not represent the true dynamics that left physical evidence.

5. There are too many permutations of dynamics for one to re-create and memorize all the possible arrangements. Pattern match and/or size and shape spatter identifications are doomed to be subjective. The predominant belief is that the identification is correct based on other evidence, such as eyewitnesses, trace evidence, fingerprints, and/or perceived confessions. Bloodstain patterns should be used to *confirm* or *refute* other evidence, and not be based on it.

Because of the considerable complexity and variation in how crime events may injure and cause the distribution of blood, the task of identifying patterns appears to be nearly impossible. Many otherwise knowledgeable forensic scientists believe that the examination of evidence is not a science but must apply it at the requirement of administrators. There is a better way, but to truly understand the evidence, one must keep it simple. One way to improve on the science is to find ways to separate identification patterns that resemble each other but are the result of different dynamics. This is as Dr. Kirk suggested back in 1968.

Bloodstain patterns that resemble each other are not limited to but may include

1. gunshot and respiratory-distributed patterns (refer to Figures 4.9 through 4.11 compared to Figure 4.12);
2. arterial spurting and swing castoffs;
3. various scattered spatters on the floor; and
4. moving contact transfer patterns.

The first step in making comparisons between these pattern groups is to see how they relate to each other in a flow diagram (see Table 5.1). This table shows how blood spatter patterns, formed from blood drops from dynamic acts, relate to their initial distribution.

Impact is a direct application of physical force to a blood source. The form of the force may be a blunt weapon, a footfall, a bullet, or the exhalation of air from the lungs. Because the principle of force application is relative, the final patterns will bear some resemblance to each other.

Castoff patterns result from blood drops sloughing, or being thrown or cast off, some type of carrier. The carrier may be stationary, may be swinging, may abruptly stop moving, or may be flicked like a bath towel in locker-room play. The latter example has been related to a snap when a swing reverses to change direction. Because the dynamics are similar, the patterns that are formed may have some characteristics in common.

TABLE 5.1   Flow Diagram Showing Relationships between Blood Drop Distributing Events

Impact	Castoff	Arterial
Blunt Force	Drip	Breach
Splash	Swing	Spurt
Gunshot	Cessation	Gush
Respiratory	Flick	Rain

Arterial damage occurs as a direct result of injury to an arterial blood vessel. These muscular vessels are under constant pressure with rhythmic pulses in response to the beating of the heart. The strength of distribution originates from blood pressure; thus, patterns formed will all relate to the variations possible with heart function while the victim of such injury lives.

Bloodstain pattern workshops focus primarily on isolated individual patterns. Rarely can such purity of evidence be found at crime scenes. It is essential, therefore, to learn to recognize patterns that overlap with other dynamic groups of bloodstains and that may be similar but are very different in interpretation. For each of the following groups, one should ask two questions: how would you classify each of the patterns shown, and how would you know that they are another similar-shaped identification?

Respiratory versus Handgun

Yes, handgun bullet impact may distribute smaller-sized blood drops, thus leaving mist and fine-sized spatters. The key word is "may." Not all firearms injuries will show the characteristic mist, and mist is possible from events other than firearms. Some of the bloodstain patterns from injuries with gunshot may require microscopic examination. Very few law enforcement officers would be willing to devote the time and trouble to do microscopic examination of bloodstain patterns, even if they had access to a microscope. One such expert testified in court that there was mist involved, but the jury couldn't see it. The witness, however, did not provide any indication for the examination that magnification was used to verify the presence of mist. Supposedly, the witness just knew it was there because it was from gunshot.

The point is that mist may not occur with gunshot, especially if hair or clothing blocks the spatter, or the victim moves at the moment of the gunshot. Also, if the shot is located at a distance, a few feet even, from any recording surface, mist-sized spatters may not be seen. The part of the handgun discharge that causes mist and fine-sized spatters is more likely to be the muzzle blast that follows the bullet out of the barrel, not the bullet itself. Note that Figure 5.1 shows a bullet hole and offset distribution of spatter from a spinning target; i.e., the target moved between bullet entrance and muzzle blast contact. The bullet entered, but the muzzle blast carrying the blood drops from the blood source impacted the target at a different position on the target. This brings up another point of concern in regard to Figure 4.9: whether or not the blood source was exposed at the time of a shot or it was necessary for the bullet to open a wound before blood drops would be distributed. The muzzle blast that follows the bullet is a more likely source of mist-size spatters because the blood source is then available.

So with the various parameters of concern over gunshot being identified from the size of spatters, one also must consider the fact that respiratory-distributed blood drops can also be mist and fine

FIGURE 5.1   Muzzle blast separated from bullet entrance.

sized. The patterns shown in Figure 4.12 and Figure 5.2 are caused by strong pants, not a sneeze, cough, or gentle wheeze. This pattern could occur from a struggle between combatants if one of them exhales explosively near a recording surface. Size and shape of the whole pattern resembles that of gunshot. How does one determine whether or not it is gunshot? The first consideration is the simplest and not necessary to be learned from training. There must be a blood source or there will be no bloodstains. If it is important to determine whether a gunshot occurred, or if the pattern resembling gunshot is actually respiratory, the investigator first must look at autopsy and medical reports. This is especially applicable when a victim is found at a location other than the scene of the initial crime. The simple lack of any blood in the mouth, throat, nose, nares, or trachea suggests that the pattern is probably not respiratory.

Some experts state that the investigator should look for bubbles and mucus. Some mucus is seen in Figure 5.2. However, the assumption of defects from mucus comes from re-creating respiratory bloodstain patterns for demonstration. Crime scenes involve a different mechanism. In emotional and physical trauma, the respiratory organs become very dry. If blood is drawn during assault, any respiratory distribution may be devoid of saliva, mucus, or normal mouth and nose fluids. Using normal situations to induce saliva and mucus flow for sneezing and coughing will not duplicate the same bloodstain defects produced from an aggravated assault.

If blood exists in the respiratory organs, or there is nobody to determine the presence of a blood source, the pattern can still provide information to suggest a more likely dynamic event—gunshot or respiratory. In Figure 5.2, there is an apparent area of convergence but no bullet hole. Bullet holes may be offset so that they are not positioned at the location of an area of convergence, yet blood was distributed. Again, there must be blood to have bloodstain patterns. The next consideration is where the pattern is located in regard to a possible blood source. If the pattern is on the clothes of a person

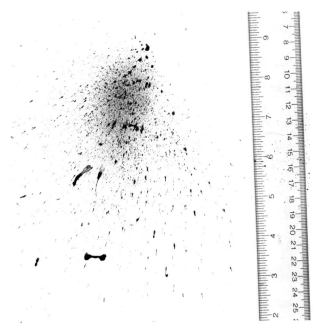

FIGURE 5.2   Strong wheeze/pant from a bloody nose.

of interest who claims to have tried to assist the victim while that person still lived, extreme caution is indicated before one calls the pattern gunshot.

Both Figure 4.12 and Figure 5.2 show fairly small areas of misting, with shapes more oval or round than a pie wedge or star burst. The reason is that the source of the blood drops is from the nostril (oval) and/or mouth (round). Both gunshot and respiratory patterns are directional, showing definite directions of travel for any stains farther from the area of convergence.

An example of this type of pattern was found on the left forearm and chest of a shirt worn by the suspected assailant of a woman who was beaten in the face (Figure 5.3). The question was whether the stains on the shirt were from the beating, from the victim's respiring after she was beaten, or possibly both. Blows to the victim's face as the assailant held her head in the crook of his arm would direct blood away from the victim but be recorded on the right arm and sleeve of the assailant, assuming blows were right-handed. If the assailant cradled the victim's head in his armpit as she breathed, that would account for the blood on the shirt's left side. The attention should shift to whether the assailant was left- or right-handed, whether the injuries suggest blows to the right or left side of the face, and how the bloodstains indicated cradling the victim. Blood on the right side of the shirt—the sleeve, arm, and shoulder—could indicate blows to the victim, not respiratory patterns. The main point is that simple presence or absence of bloodstains cannot be concluded when the victim lives and wheezes blood.

Castoff versus Arterial Spurting

Although the difference between gunshot and respiratory patterns can be essential for interpretation, casework involving these patterns has encountered fewer missed identifications than for arterial

FIGURE 5.3 Examination of bloodstained T-shirt.

spurts being called castoffs. With gunshot versus respiratory patterns, an innocent person could be charged, whereas with castoff and arterial patterns, the wrong charge may be brought against the accused person. Correcting a wrongful conviction is difficult, but correcting the wrong sentence is close to impossible. The primary error in identification is with swing castoffs, although cessation and even drip castoffs may be identified in error as actual arterial spurt and rain patterns (Figure 5.4).

In most patterns from arterial injury, the amount of blood provides a strong clue as to the blood source. Unfortunately, this may lead to viewing the autopsy before identifying the patterns, and if no mention of an artery is found, one may think that the bloodstains could not be arterial in origin. The guidelines suggested by the Scientific Working Group for Medicolegal Death Investigation (SWGMDI) list bite mark evidence collection but do not mention specific identification of arterial injury nor how that injury was inflicted (SWGMDI, 2013). Although support for the addition of the requirement was expressed during discussions following the presentation of a paper before the Pathology section of the AAFS in New Orleans, LA in 2005 (Wonder, 2005), the addition has not made it into requirements for autopsy. The fact remains that the bloodstain patterns suggestive of arterial injury are seen first before the pathologist identifies the location of a blood source. It is then necessary to ask the pathologist to specifically examine for arterial injury.

It is especially important that investigators understand that arterial injury is not limited to knifing. A prosecutor once said to the author that she knew there was no arterial injury because she saw the autopsy photographs and there were no cuts on blood vessels shown. Arteries may be injured during blunt force blows to the temples. This occurs where the exterior carotids are located, without fat padding, against the hard skull. Injury first causes weakening of the arterial vessel with the formation of a balloon aneurism. Subsequent blows tear skin and pop the bulb. The injury to the artery is a pinhole tear, not a cut. The small size of the breach and the possibility of high blood pressure when the victim is fighting for life may create tiny blood drops capable of leaving mist-sized spatters. Because of the constriction and muscular walls of the artery, one may not see a hole during autopsy unless expressly examining to find it. Fortunately, emergency rooms are very good at listing arterial injury because of the potential for rapid, possibly fatal, blood loss. If a homicide

FIGURE 5.4   Heavy arterial spurting on a vertical surface.

victim is seen in an emergency room prior to death, the medical reports may be more enlightening than the autopsy. See Figure 5.5 for a sketch showing how arterial injury occurs from blunt force trauma and/or gunshot to the temple or eyebrow area of the face.

With arterial injury, the victim may not necessarily die immediately. Movement away from the site of arterial rupture can leave separated arterial spurts that resemble castoffs. This becomes a major issue at trial because castoffs would indicate a vicious, continued beating by an assailant, whereas arterial spurting could have occurred after the assailant in a beating was long gone from the scene. The jury would view one situation as intended vicious murder, but could view the other as just a fight in which the assailant left while still thinking the victim would live. It is also possible for arterial spurting to be recorded on innocent bystanders. One such case happened in a police department (Wonder, 2001, p. 72) where the victim of a fight spurted blood over a detective's desk during an interview. In this case, there was a pinhole breach to the artery above the eyebrow (see Figure 5.6).

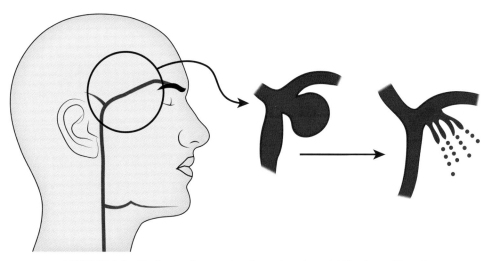

FIGURE 5.5   Mechanism for aneurism formation of arterial blood vessel breach.

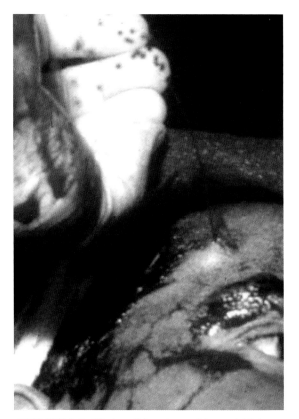

FIGURE 5.6   Victim of blunt force with arterial injury.

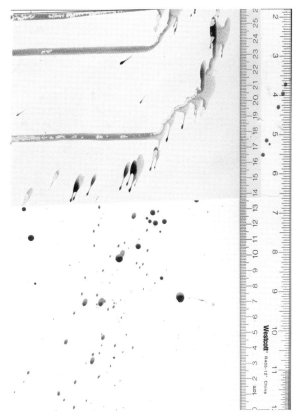

FIGURE 5.7   Comparison of castoff versus arterial spurting, arterial to the left with castoff to the right.

Blood drops traveling from an artery are broken off the column and distributed in tandem arrangements that appear as parallel rows of similar size and shape. The size of the spatters depends on the size of the injury to the artery and the blood pressure behind the distribution of drops. In contrast, swing castoffs depend on the amount of blood on the carrier, the strength of adhesion between blood and the carrier, and the way the carrier is moved while casting off drops. Drops may be in tandem but are not usually of the same size and shape, and they are seldom arranged as adjacent spatters. The offset arrangement is more pronounced. Blood is continually added from an artery, but there is a finite amount of blood on a carrier. Thus, drops continue in the same, or close to the same, density for arterial patterns, whereas castoff numbers decrease along the length of the whole pattern (see Figure 5.7).

As a carrier of blood swings, the angle between the blood source and the contact of drops with a surface may remain close to the same. Only at the ends of the swing will drops be cast off to form elongated spatters. Arterial spurts, by contrast, may originate from a stationary source and thus leave more elongated spatters as the spurts move away from the origin of the artery.

An interesting phenomenon occurs with arterial spurt patterns. There are actually two directions of travel to consider: first, the direction the artery is spurting, thus the direction that blood drops separating from the arterial stream travel, and second, the direction the victim having an arterial breach

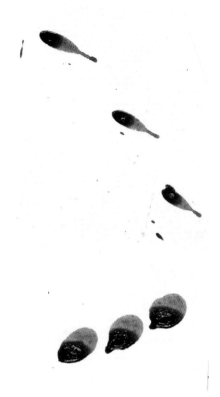

FIGURE 5.8   Directions of travel combinations for arterial damage.

is moving at the time of spurting (see Figure 5.8). In these cases, there are two possible appearances to the spatters from arterial spurting that show the combinations: egg-shaped with little direction of travel indicated and teardrop with marked direction of travel indicated. Explanations of why these patterns happen seem insufficient. The egg shape occurs when the victim with arterial damage is moving in the same direction as the artery is spurting, whereas the teardrop shape means that the victim was moving in the opposite direction to arterial spurting.

The problem with identifying arterial damage bloodstain patterns starts with training. In workshops, castoff patterns are numerous and entertaining to participants. These patterns set the memory so that later casework is immediately classified without eliminating the possibility of arterial injury being involved. There is also the reliance on pathology, which must change in time. Two essential examples are included here to illustrate the importance of correct identification from initial crime scene work-up.

Case A: A confrontation between a man and woman ended up with the woman dead from knife injuries over various parts of her body. Individual stab wounds were identified during autopsy as left back, left thigh, front right breast, and right side. Blunt force trauma was identified on the upper right eyebrow. No mention of any arterial injury was included in the autopsy report. The assault was located predominantly in the kitchen and a short hall leading to the living room and front door. Bloodstains on the wall between the kitchen and living room were labeled as castoffs (see Figure 5.9).

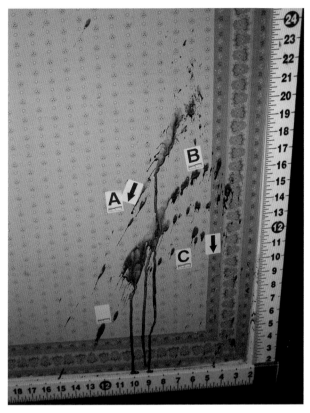

FIGURE 5.9   Wall with alleged castoffs.

Why would one consider arterial injury? There are a number of alerts here that one should consider before concluding that the patterns on the wall were castoffs. The main ones include

1. The amount of blood is inconsistent with the ability of a knife to hold blood long enough to provide the amount of staining seen on the wall.
2. The victim had numerous stab wounds located separately, on opposite sides of the body. For castoffs in uniform arc rows, as seen, the victim would have to have been positioned in alignment for each stab.
3. The number of rows identified was three, perhaps because that number matched the major stab wounds listed on the autopsy. There were five trails on the wall. Two were apparently ignored, possibly because they would disagree with the autopsy.
4. The action of stabbing does not usually cast off blood on an adjacent surface. Swinging with a blunt force weapon may leave blood spatters on adjacent surfaces, but rarely would stab thrusts. The action expected would be more up and down so that castoffs would be more likely arranged as parallel to the wall, not recorded on it. Sideways thrusts to the victim would not be toward the wall.
5. Interestingly enough, there were also no castoffs on the floor by the wall, which indicates that the pattern recorded was solely directed toward the wall. This indicates a force directing blood that way, not a reaction to an event which should involve dripping blood.

FIGURE 5.10   Kitchen area showing struggle.

Clearly, the rhythmic arrangement of spatter rows of similar size and shape, arranged in parallel adjacent spatters, identifies arterial spurting. At trial, the main problem was identifying the fact that an artery was breached. How and where was proof other than the patterns on the wall? The victim was hit in the face at the corner of the eyebrow. Second or more blows would have created and ruptured an aneurysm. The accused claimed to have left and was unaware that the victim had died. This could have been true. The pattern on the wall with lack of bloodstains from struggle suggests the victim was moving into the living room after the artery was breached in the kitchen, perhaps trying to reach the front door (see Figure 5.10). There is no indication that anyone else was present or absent at that time. The jury believed the bloodstains were from arterial injury but convicted the accused as a violent intentional murderer.

Indications are that the assault started in the kitchen area. Numerous knives were available. It's possible that both the victim and assailant were using knives and struggling. The assailant was cut and left blood at the scene. The victim apparently sat down on the kitchen floor at one point. This was definitely not a case of innocence, but was it a case of premeditated murder? That issue was not put before the jury as it should have been.

Case B: This example is presented to show how arterial injury can, or probably should, enter into charges filed in a case. There was a confrontation between two brothers. They were known to fight with each other all their lives. The older brother was living, without paying rent, in a house bequeathed to him and his younger brother by their mother. He was alleged to be manufacturing drugs in his mother's home, which angered the younger brother. The younger brother kept his bike in the garage, which angered the older brother. One day, the younger brother arrived with his bike, putting it in the garage. The older brother picked up a baseball bat to confront his much stronger younger brother. Apparently, the younger brother took the bat away from the older brother and beat him with it. What led to the death of the older brother started in the garage with the man falling against a freezer.

FIGURE 5.11   Side of freezer located in garage.

The bloodstain patterns on the freezer side (see Figure 5.11) were ignored by prosecution experts because the charges were formed based on the younger brother having a key to the front door, and the crime was alleged to be initiated and completed there. No mention of the garage was included before defense brought it out at trial. Again, no mention of arterial injury was found in the autopsy report, but under cross-examination, the autopsy physician admitted that death was in part due to the victim "bleeding out." The victim died from massive blood loss and blunt force trauma to the head. All injury to the head was stated as associated with a baseball bat found later at the scene.

It was an obvious error to ignore the bloodstains on the freezer, but why would one suspect arterial injury? Again, there are suggestions in addition to recognition of the many spatters of a similar size and shape arranged in parallel rows. Investigators should have considered the following alarms for arterial damage before drawing conclusions:

1. The victim bled out. Copious quantities of blood were identified in the living room. True, head wounds do bleed a lot, but the body was almost devoid of blood when found. That much blood loss would not be expected to exit the head alone unless under pressure from arterial damage.
2. Blood loss occurred over a range from the garage to an adjacent bedroom, down a hall, and across draperies in the living room. The victim apparently sat down on a couch in the living room, where he bled out onto the living room carpet. No associated impact spatter patterns were identified as the victim progressed from the garage to the living room.

II. IDENTIFICATION

FIGURE 5.12   Bedroom wall with bright red spatter.

3. The bright red color of spatters seen in the bedroom, a room located near the door to the garage, was also an indicator (see Figure 5.12). The spatters on the wall were inconsistent with swings with a ball bat with the victim facing the wall. No position for an assailant to swing a weapon aimed at the victim was possible between the victim and the wall. The bright red color is usually recognized as oxygenated blood from an artery; this color would have been enough in and of itself to ask the pathologist if there could have been specific arterial involvement.

The last point mentioned here could be rationalized as occurring at any time, not necessarily following the assault. The bright red color, however, is widely recognized as oxygenated arterial blood and unlikely to be the result of any simple prior injury.

How does the accurate identification of the stains on the freezer door affect the case? The two brothers were known to fight. The younger brother was considerably stronger. If confronted with a ball bat, he would have had no trouble taking it away and, because he had anger management issues, using it on his brother. Was it premeditated murder? Probably not, but that was the charge

FIGURE 5.13   Typical flick arrangement of castoffs.

and conviction. If the jury knew the alternative of blood loss from accidental arterial injury, would they have found the same? That is the question which was never answered.

One final comment must be made in regard to identification of arterial damage bloodstain patterns. For any injury involving the temples, jaw, eyebrow ridge, neck, arms, and legs, the investigator should ask the autopsy physician whether injury to an artery was possible. Injury to the collar bone, heart, top of the head, and under fat and muscle mass will more likely be unproductive of external bleeding sufficient to produce specific arterial damage bloodstain patterns. One should not wait for an autopsy to mention arterial damage, and one should not assume knifings are necessary to eliminate them from consideration.

In the flow diagram shown in Table 5.1, there is a listing for "flick" under "castoffs." This pattern may or may not be mistaken for arterial spurts. The importance of the pattern is that it shows up in cases of staging. The person staging a crime scene may draw something through a pool of blood and flick it at a surface. The cane-shaped dots are a giveaway that the action was flicking at the surface, not necessarily associated with a crime event (see Figure 5.13).

VARIOUS BLOODSTAIN PATTERNS FOUND ON THE FLOOR

The previous sets of similar pattern appearances are predominantly seen on vertical surfaces. As such, the patterns may be visually separated from other events so that differentiation is possible. Nothing is more frustrating to a thorough bloodstain pattern analyst than viewing photographs of a crime scene where first responders have tracked and contaminated bloodstains on the floor around, near, or leading away from the victims of crime. Blood is frequently distributed by criminal assault, but also by a number of people during the aftermath and discovery of the crime. This is more likely to be recorded on the floors around and leaving the scene. This is also where contamination by investigators, paramedics, innocent bystanders, the victims, and assailants may occur to confuse events of the actual crime. Putting emphasis on recognizing the evidential value of various patterns found on the floor of assaults may help first responders to be aware and to make preliminary observations before the confusion of investigation and/or rescue of crime victims.

The scatter of bloodstains on the floor may result from several events

1. drip castoffs,
2. cessation castoffs,
3. swing castoffs,
4. blood into blood,
5. splash,
6. arterial rain, and/or
7. struggle composite.

Each of the preceding items suggests a different kind of involvement in the perpetration of an assault. Drips may occur without direct criminal actions; for example, a body is removed later, the assailant was injured in the assault and drips blood, or innocent persons at the scene acquire and distribute blood. In contrast, cessation and swing castoffs are, or at least can be, part of the assault that distributed blood drops to begin with. Blood into blood may result from drip castoffs during and after the crime, and splash may result from the assailant, victim, or rescue personnel stepping into pools of still-wet blood. Arterial rain may occur with a breached artery aimed vertically after the assailant is gone, and a struggle composite would include two or more of the preceding, all possible during and after an assault.

So how does one differentiate and identify these bloodstain patterns for investigative information? A whole pattern or group of blood spatters that show organization as a group may be totally lacking. The alignment of spatters may be difficult to establish due to overlapping of several events happening together or as a sequence of events. Directions of travel may or may not be part of the pattern. If inline arrangements are seen, it is suggested that one is dealing with one or more castoff group dynamics. If the line of large drops moves away from an area with direction of travel indicated, an identification of drip castoff is suggested, which may show someone wounded or carrying something dripping blood away from the area. Most drip castoff patterns are recognized even without training in bloodstain pattern analysis.

One fact is essential in reading bloodstains on the floor. The first observation should be whether the spatters show tracking from shoe, foot, or drag patterns through the blood patterns. If none exists, spatters are seen as separate and not stepped in or part of moving contact patterns; this fact can provide simple and available information. Transfers of shoe prints and/or sliding shoe prints (moving transfers) should be seen with the spatters on the floor if the stains are from the assault

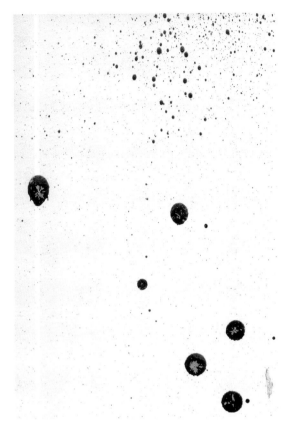

FIGURE 5.14   Cessation castoffs on the floor.

and/or struggle with the assailant. If there are no overlapping prints on the bloodstains, it is suggested that the distributing event projected blood drops to the recording surface rather than falling by gravity alone while a victim, assailant, or bystander stood in the area. Staged crime scenes may have this type of bloodstain near an inside door or window to imply an assailant entered from outside.

Some patterns are readily identifiable, such as shown in Figure 5.14. Notice the small spatters scattered at the top of the view. These are from the impact as the weapon stopped. The bigger drops were thrown ahead of the contact between the weapon and objective of the blow with a weapon. Bloodstains such as those in Figure 5.15 are not as identifiable because of the strong similarity with those in Figure 5.16, which involves totally different dynamics.

Both Figures 5.15 and 5.16 were products of a bloodstain pattern workshop. When unexpected results occur during workshops, the benefit from observations is in understanding dynamics of events and possible variations seen later in casework. Exceptions to the expected results should never be ignored. Possible differences between the two results were the number of different-sized spatters and the distribution of spatter sizes. Arterial patterns had a greater variation of sizes and densities than castoffs. Arterial patterns also involved a greater amount of blood. An analyst would ask what was on the walls adjacent to each floor pattern, which would assist in identification.

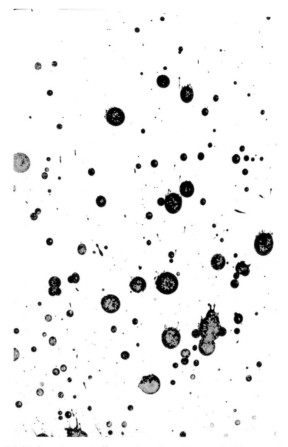

FIGURE 5.15   Multiple swing castoffs on a target position under the experiment, on the floor.

FIGURE 5.16   Simulated arterial rain in shower stall.

Another pattern that may be confused with arterial gush is the splash, as shown in Figure 5.17. Stabs to the chest such that the lungs may be opened could be the source of large amounts of blood flowing toward the floor as a victim gasps for breath. Large amounts of blood would splash when hitting the floor. However, stepping into a pool of blood on the floor would also create splash. The difference would be the shoe print seen stepping into and possibly tracking away from the splash, whereas volumes of blood falling from a chest wound would not necessarily involve shoe tracks. Another indication would be the presence or absence of the bright red oxygenated blood color for an arterial blood source.

Blood into blood is often encountered on floors of crime scenes. Because of the number of spatters distributed with rapid bleeding over a pool of blood, the key information is whether any blockage or absences occur that could indicate a rug or carpeting removed to hide the amount of blood loss. The transfer of something that blocked recording of blood into blood might be more important than the actual event of blood dripping. In Figure 5.18, what would the smaller, directional spatters be labeled?

FIGURE 5.17   Splash from a footfall into a pool of blood.

FIGURE 5.18　Combination large and small spatters.

If the identification of medium velocity impact spatter was attached, the information could be directed toward the wrong reconstruction of the crime. The large drops are from drips, but the smaller drops are from blood dripping into blood. The source of these drops can be traced back to the circumference of a pool of blood, as shown in Figure 5.19. The results of blood dripping into blood depend on the speed of drip, not the height from which each drop falls. Because of the strong interface of blood layers, each drop hits a surface rather than a liquid. Drops bounce off the surface. With rapid drips, the bouncing drops can cover a wide area with spatters that have directions of travel, but the directions are away from the circumference, not the center of the pool.

II. IDENTIFICATION

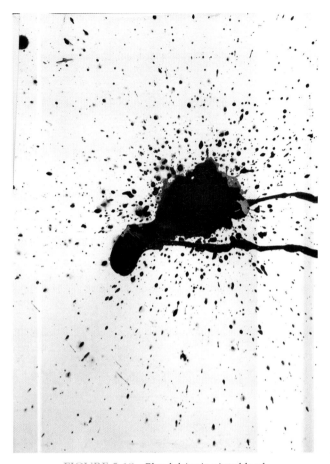

FIGURE 5.19   Blood dripping into blood.

MOVING TRANSFER PATTERNS

For the most part, after training, workshop participants can appreciate and apply transfers in bloodstain pattern evidence. Instruction is usually good and entertaining, so graduates are well aware of the probative value of pattern matches from transfer of images in blood. There is one area where additional mention may be beneficial. Moving transfer patterns show up in many crime scenes and also in staged crimes. These patterns may be ignored because they can be treated as contamination, and may be such from discovery of the crime, attempts at rescue, and preliminary investigation. If the action is only one way, identification of whether it is a wipe or swipe can provide investigative leads. One—a swipe, or the depositing of blood from a moving material or object—can be an unintentional contact with blood deposited during the crime, whereas the other—a wipe, or the moving through the exiting blood deposited earlier—may indicate a deliberate attempt to clean up the scene. Further, one can sometimes identify whether the swipe or wipe was made with cloth or skin.

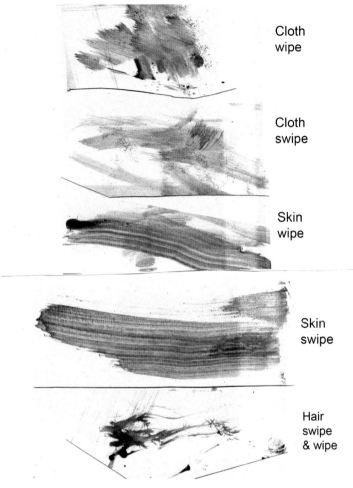

Cloth
wipe

Cloth
swipe

Skin
wipe

Skin
swipe

Hair
swipe
& wipe

FIGURE 5.20   Wipes and swipes.

Wipe versus Swipe with Cloth and Skin

The clue to which bloodstain pattern one is seeing lies in the fact that blood is composed of particles, the most numerous being red blood cells, more or less suspended in a liquid. The red cells are not absorbed, whereas the liquid may be. A moving action will spread red cells but may absorb liquid if the material moving across or depositing blood is capable of absorption.

Skin is not capable of absorption and is, by nature, a smooth surface. A swipe with cloth will deposit blood as it moves from the beginning touch to the lift-off edge. Because there is less blood as the swipe progresses and leaves a trail of blood, the lift-off edge may be lighter and more irregular than the beginning edge. A swipe with skin, however, will push blood along so that the lift-off edge is more concentrated in red blood cells, thus darker and smooth (see Figure 5.20). A wipe will

TABLE 5.2   Comparisons of moving transfers

	WIPE	SWIPE
Material (Terry cloth)	Beginning - Texture	Texture of cloth
	Stain - Mottled	Streaked
	Lift Off - Feathered	Lighter
Skin	Beginning - Smooth	Dark smooth
	Stain - Smooth uniform	Smooth darker
	Lift Off - Regular smooth	Regular darkest
Hair	Beginning - Streaks	Streaks
	Stain - Separated locks	Inline beading
	Lift Off - Feathered separated	Feathered lighter

pick up some red cells as it moves but will predominantly push extra red cells along (see Figure 5.20). The lift-off edge is darker, with some of the pattern from the material wiping. Skin wiping pushes red cells along and is thus darker and smooth at lift-off. The clue to reading moving transfer stains is to note three things: the beginning touch, the smoothness of the stain, and the lift-off edge (see Table 5.2).

An additional swipe pattern that is often seen at crime scenes but usually provides no problem in identification occurs when hair brushes against a surface. This pattern often shows a light touch, with strands indicating separation of hair fibers. The feather lift-off edge permits a conclusion of hair. This evidence does not automatically lead to a conclusion of head injury, but it does indicate the hair came into contact with blood. As such, it means the hair could be from the victim or assailant or even an uninvolved person.

In differentiating similar patterns, one needs to include interpretation to understand how the dynamics distribute blood. It is important to realize that interpretation does not precede identification but only assists in conclusions of identity. Section III presents formats to achieve the most information from interpretation.

REFERENCES

Scientific Working Group for Medicolegal Death Investigation, 2013. SWGMDI Autopsy Performance Criteria (DRAFT): Standards, Guidelines and Best Practices.

Wonder, A.Y., 2001. Blood Dynamics. Academic Press, London, p. 72.

Wonder, A.Y., 2005. An Expert Witness Requests Re-evaluation of SOP for Autopsy Reporting. Paper presented at the American Academy of Forensic Sciences, 57th Annual Meeting, New Orleans, LA, before the Pathology/Biology Section.

How Many Pieces of Evidence?

Identification of bloodstain patterns requires understanding the behavior of blood both outside the body and, with gunshot and arterial damage, inside the body. Physiology is taught in secondary schools, and not limited to medical schools; thus, it should not be excluded from testimony by qualified bloodstain pattern analysts. The previous chapters touched on interpretation so that the reader may better understand how bloodstain patterns may be identified. Before we can move on to a more detailed look at interpretation, there is one more process that helps in confirming the correct identification from a base of scientific principles.

When one is viewing a crime scene there are usually several different patterns, and some may be overlapping. Fixating on the size and shape of spatter and then labeling them with velocity impact spatter terminology may shortchange the information available from an investigation and possibly lead to a biased and/or subjective approach in developing a scenario of the crime. One technique that can help both to broaden the initial view of the scene and to start off an investigation with as much leads information as possible is to ask this: How many different pieces of bloodstain pattern evidence do I have?

The following scenario targets were manufactured for an advanced course presented as a workshop for the American Academy of Forensic Sciences meeting in Atlanta, Georgia. For each target, the first question was: How many pieces of evidence are seen? This question was followed by discussion regarding identifications based on criteria as presented in Chapters 4 and 5.

General information regarding the figures: A 24-inch ruler is placed so that no bloodstains are hidden. Detail views precede the photograph of each 4 feet-by-6 feet white fiberboard. The blood used is human, packed red blood cells. The hematocrit for such blood is higher than normal blood drawn for laboratory testing, usually in the neighborhood of 20.0 mg%. The concentration of red blood cells provides a darker bloodstain, which is easier to see on a scanned photograph. Each of the targets is classed as a wall or a floor. For walls, the top is labeled. The reader should assume each full target is a crime scene where there may or may not be a body found. The reader should answer how many pieces of evidence are seen, what the various patterns suggest, and what other questions he or she would ask to gain more information for investigative leads. The purpose for the questions listed in the discussions is examined in Section III.

Caution is necessary regarding the questions suggested, as these are provided as a possible list for everyone involved with a case, including pathologists, witnesses, persons of interest, first responders, paramedics, and surviving victims. They are suggestions, not conclusions.

Bloodstain Patterns
http://dx.doi.org/10.1016/B978-0-12-415930-3.00006-8

111

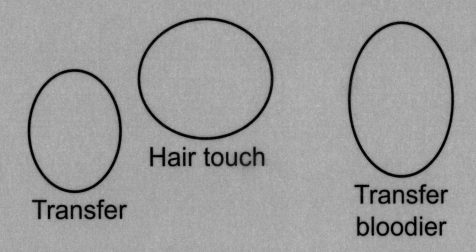

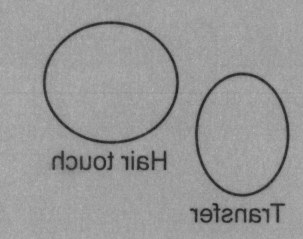
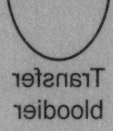

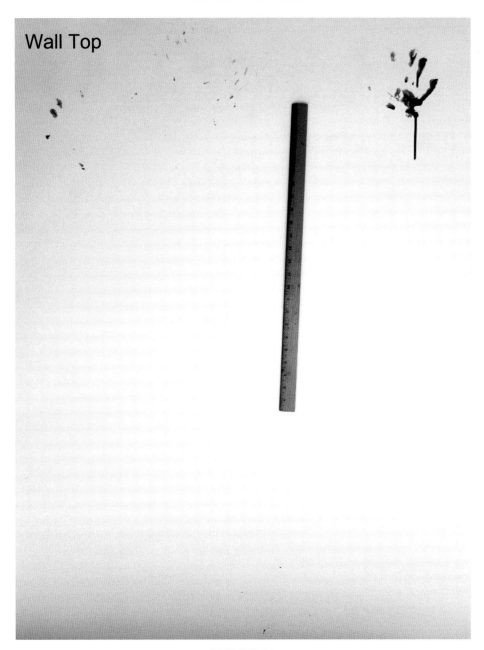

Wall Top

FIGURE 6.1

II. IDENTIFICATION

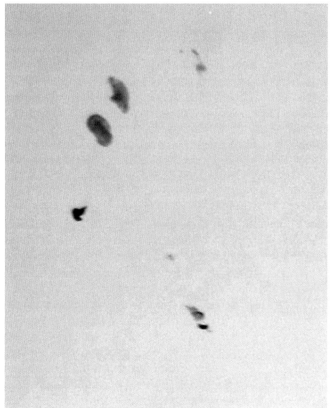

FIGURE 6.1—Cont'd

II. IDENTIFICATION

DISCUSSION OF FIGURE 6.1

How many pieces of evidence do we have? There are five pieces of evidence, although there are only two (or three) bloodstain patterns.

1. The first piece of evidence with all the targets is that blood was shed. This may require one or more events before blood begins to flow.
2. There are two handprints, but the right handprint is bloodier than the left. This suggests the right hand came into contact with a blood source. The left hand may have also touched something bloody or may have just received transfers from the right.
3. Between the two bloodstained hands is a hair swipe. This is not heavy in blood; therefore, it's unlikely the blood source is an injury to the head. Blood stained the hair, perhaps from the hand.
4. Given the two hands and the hair, the victim was facing the wall, not back to the wall.
5. At the bottom of the exhibit are a few random spatters that could suggest the victim fell to the floor after contact with the wall. What the random spatters resulted from is not known but can provide some questions.
6. The hair transfer is just a touch. It is not clear if movement is to one side or the other.

What questions would help develop a scenario?

1. If a body is found, where is the bloodshed? The hair got bloodied, but not heavily like the hand.
2. Were there drips and more blood on the floor by the wall? If there are no drips on the floor near this wall, it suggests the person leaning against the wall may not be the injured person.
3. If a victim is found or suspected, was that person right-handed? A possible reflex to being injured is to place the hand most used over the injury, i.e., acquire blood with the appropriate handedness hand. An alternative would be the hand closest to the injury. This can be used with medical information.
4. Could handprints be from an assailant? An assailant could have acquired blood during the assault and then fell or leaned against the wall.
5. If the assailant was the one who leaned against the wall, was the injury to the victim a knifing? Heavy blood is seen on the hand, but there is no indication of impact spatters.
6. If the assault was a knifing, was the assailant right-handed? Knifing with the right hand could be the source of blood on the hand.
7. Could the victim have fallen to the floor and wheezed against the wall? Did the victim live for a time after the assault?
8. DNA and latent print examination of the handprints would add to bloodstain pattern analysis.

II. IDENTIFICATION

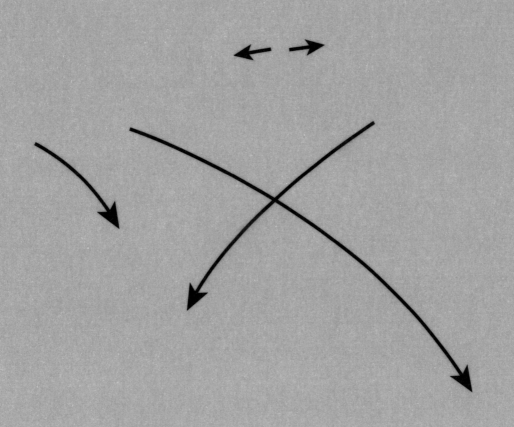

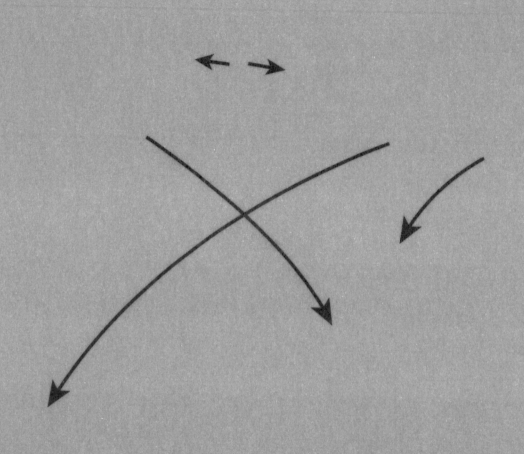

FIGURE 6.2

II. IDENTIFICATION

FIGURE 6.2—Cont'd

DISCUSSION OF FIGURE 6.2

How many pieces of evidence do we have? There are at least four things to note, perhaps more.

1. Blood was shed.
2. There are at least three swing castoffs identified. Two additional short ones could be return swings or additional swings. The important point is that the swings come from two directions. This could be two assailants, an ambidextrous assailant, or two separate attacks.
3. All the swings were with a narrow weapon that doesn't seem to hold blood well.
4. Between the swings is a moving hair swipe that may have occurred in two directions. It could be from receiving blows from both the right and the left. Again, this could be two assailants, but they used the same kind of weapon.
5. Confirmation of multiple blows is that with castoffs, blood must be exposed before the weapon becomes bloody enough to distribute drops. Therefore, we know we have at least four swings.

Questions that could be asked:

1. Was there injury to the victim's head?
2. Was there a person of interest who was ambidextrous?
3. Could there have been two or more assailants?
4. Was there something like a crowbar, tire iron, or iron rod at the scene?
5. Does the autopsy confirm the number of blows as two to four?
6. Were the blows from different sides of the head?
7. Were there drips on the floor showing directions of travel away from the wall?
8. Which way is the entrance and exit to the room with the wall?
9. What was the cause of death, as there is not enough blood in the stains seen to account for death unless severe head trauma led to death? Such trauma might not have caused instant death.

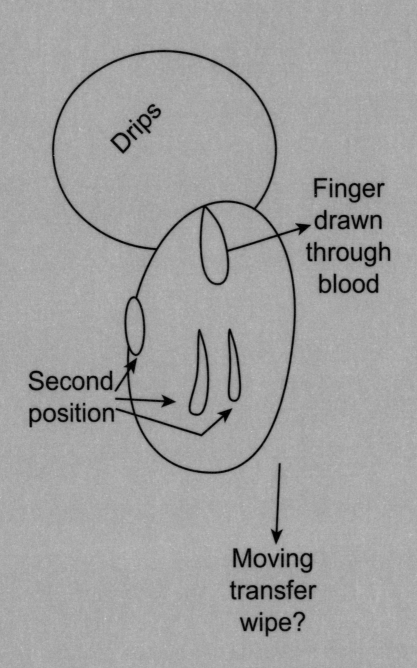

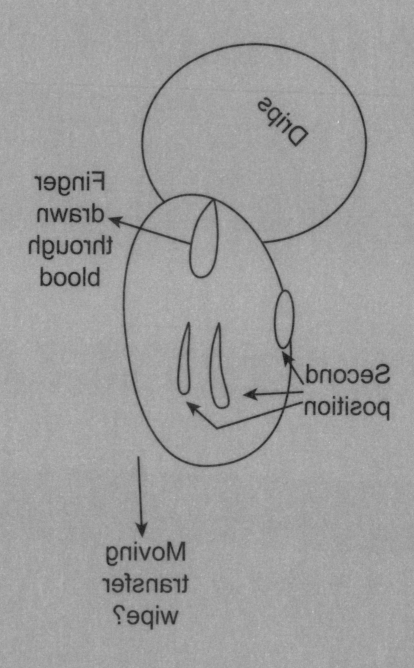

Drips

Finger
drawn
through
blood

Second
position

Moving
transfer
wipe?

FIGURE 6.3

II. IDENTIFICATION

FIGURE 6.3—Cont'd

II. IDENTIFICATION

DISCUSSION OF FIGURE 6.3

How many pieces of evidence do we have? At least four items are available.

1. Blood was shed…a lot of blood.
2. Blood dripped off the victim, which means the body was lifted while actively bleeding, blood was still wet under the body, and/or the victim was able to lift himself or herself up.
3. The body was dragged a short way back from the pool of blood, while the blood was still very wet, which might be contradictory to the victim rising on his or her own.
4. Finger marks are seen in the pool, which requires some clotting before an attempt to lift the body.
5. Moving transfer appears to be two layers. This could be two layers of clothing, two bodies, two positions of one body, or the victim bled and rolled and returned to position.

Questions that may be asked to provide more information:

1. Was the blood clotted and/or dried when found?
2. Is there a body? Or was there a hospital admission associated with the place where the bloodstains were found?
3. Is there another area with impact spatters, because there is no evidence here of the initial attack?
4. Are there two DNA phenotypes in the finger marks in the pool? Is this an indication of more than one DNA profile within the finger marks in the pool?
5. Is there a person of interest strong enough to lift the victim's body?
6. Where is the entrance and exit to the room where the blood was found?
7. Would the drag marks be toward an exit or an entrance?
8. Is there a left-handed person of interest?

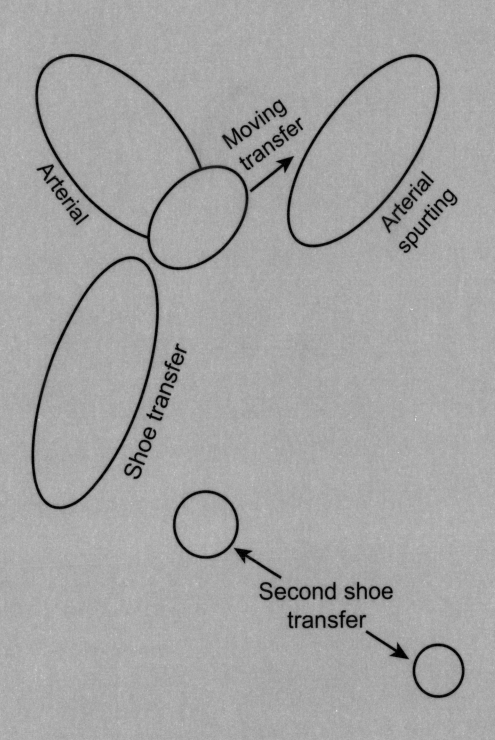

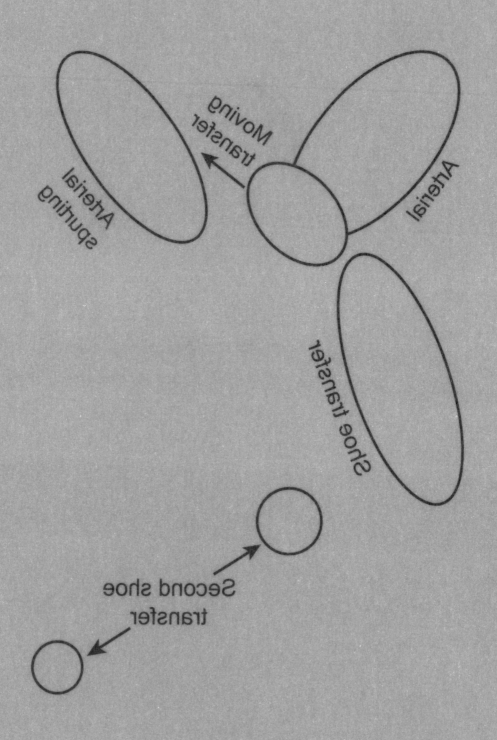

FIGURE 6.4

II. IDENTIFICATION

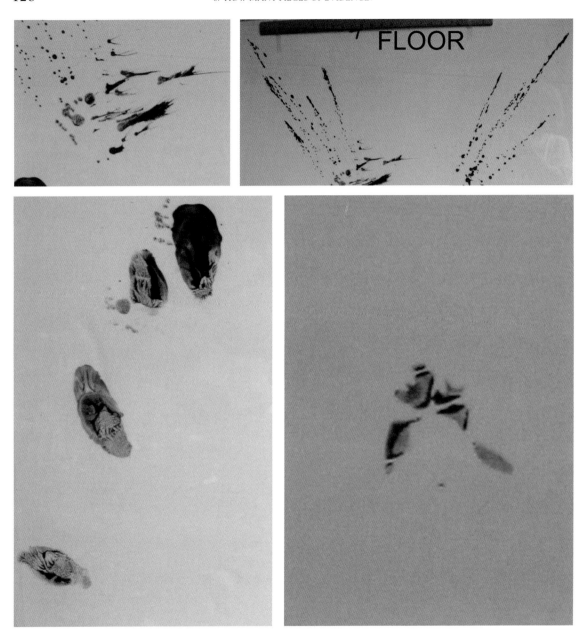

FIGURE 6.4—Cont'd

DISCUSSION OF FIGURE 6.4

How many pieces of evidence do we have? At least six points are available.

1. Blood was shed and was probably a fatal loss if loss was rapid, as from arterial gushing.
2. Shoe prints in blood are to the left, but there is no pool at this position to act as a blood source.
3. The victim shifted positions slightly after the throat was cut. No signs of a struggle.
4. There is bilateral arterial spurting suggestive of both carotid arteries being cut, i.e., rapid, fatal blood loss.
5. A second shoe print is located to the right, but again no blood source is associated with the prints.
6. The victim was on the floor face down when the throat was slit.

Questions that could provide more information with the bloodstains seen:

1. Where is the body located? There is no pool of blood at this location.
2. Are there drips or shoe prints leading to another area and a pool blood source?
3. Are there persons of interest wearing shoes consistent with either of the patterns seen?
4. Is there a person of interest who is left-handed?
5. Was something placed over the victim's throat to prevent a quantity of blood loss in this position?

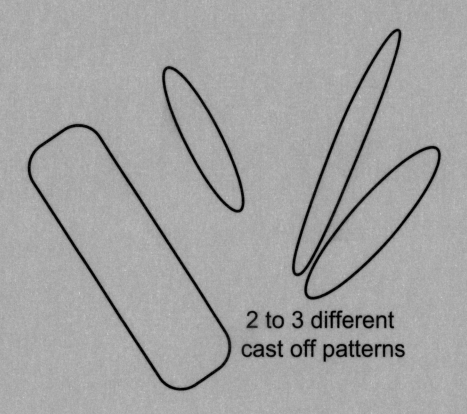

2 to 3 different
cast off patterns

Impact or Respiratory?

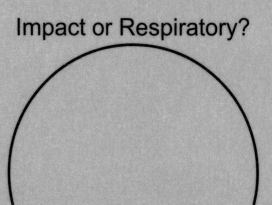

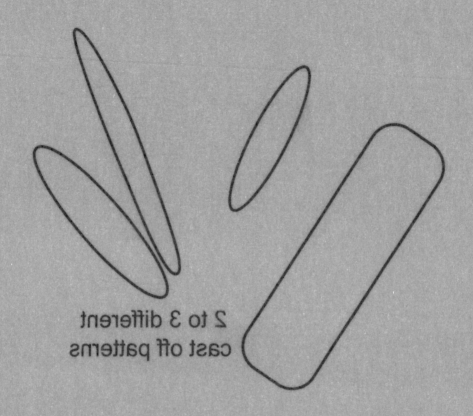

Impact or Respiratory?

FIGURE 6.5

II. IDENTIFICATION

FIGURE 6.5—Cont'd

II. IDENTIFICATION

DISCUSSION OF FIGURE 6.5

How many pieces of evidence do we have? There are at least five items of interest on this wall.

1. Blood was shed, but not a lot of blood. If a body is present, the cause of death cannot be assumed. True, a pathologist is required to provide the information, but law enforcement officers are generally eager to begin their investigation. Jumping to a premature conclusion is not good practice.
2. At least three swing castoff patterns are present. The fact that castoffs are present, however, is less important than the fact that two to three different weapons are suggested.
3. A gang approach is possible from the different castoff patterns.
4. One weapon is narrow, like a crowbar, tire iron, iron bar, etc., while another is broader. A second narrow weapon is suggested, but it appears to hold blood better than the other narrow one.
5. The attack comes from each side of the victim.
6. Small spatters near the floor could be either impact or respiratory.

Questions that may supply more information:

1. If a body was found, was it found at a different location?
2. Were weapons found at the scene? Specifically, were there two or more possibilities?
3. Were persons of interest involved who were right- and/or left-handed?
4. Was blood seen in the mouth and/or nose of the victim?
5. Was the face of the victim found facing the wall?

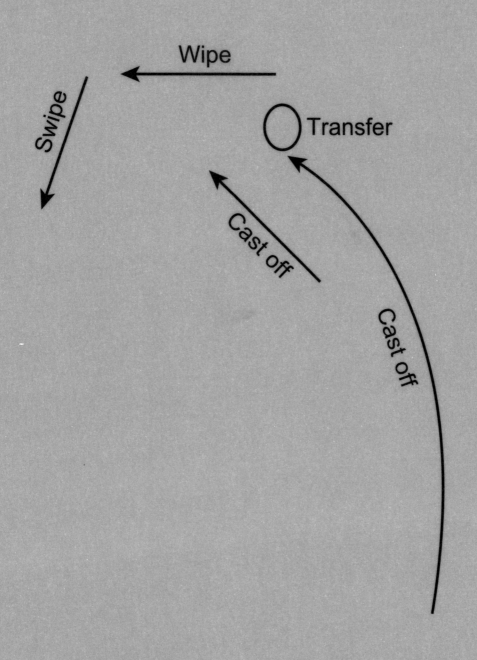

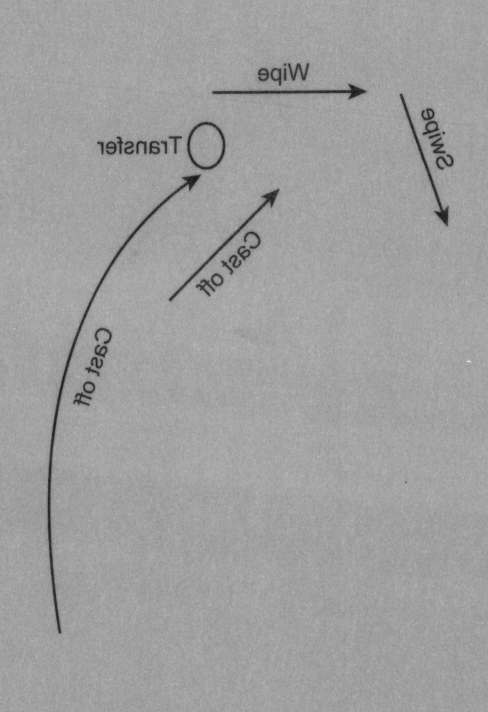

Wall Top

FIGURE 6.6

II. IDENTIFICATION

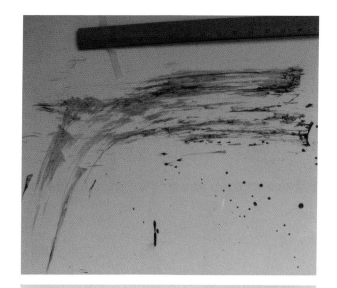

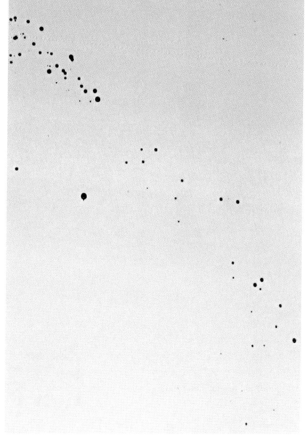

FIGURE 6.6—Cont'd

II. IDENTIFICATION

DISCUSSION OF FIGURE 6.6

How many pieces of evidence do we have? There are at least six items to consider.

1. Blood was shed.
2. Two castoff bloodstain patterns were distributed from what appears to be the same weapon, from the same general direction.
3. The weapon is not narrow but also not wide. Something like a ball bat is suggested. It holds blood but not a lot; thus, it could be a metal bat or one with a new finish.
4. The victim shifted to the left, which means the blows were struck from the right, consistent with where the castoffs are seen.
5. After a shift to the left, the victim fell.
6. There might be a transfer from the weapon at about the 2 o'clock position, the end of the castoff series of spatters.

Questions that may provide additional information:

1. Was there a head injury?
2. Is the person of interest right-handed?
3. Is the person of interest shorter than the victim? The castoff pattern seems to come from low to the blood source.
4. Are there self-defense injuries on the victim's arms?
5. Are there drips leading away from the wall?
6. Where is the entrance and exit to the room of the wall?

PUTTING THE SECTIONS TOGETHER FOR A CRIME SCENE INVESTIGATION

Sometimes a case seems straightforward, and nothing can be gained from examining the bloodstain patterns. Sadly, it is not economically beneficial to dispense with an analysis on that assumption. Such was the example that follows. The story provided by law enforcement investigators was that a couple was in their kitchen talking. They were legally married, but the husband did not live with his wife and daughter. During the parents' visit, two young males broke in from the front door and pistol whipped the husband yelling, "Where's D's shit?" When the husband and wife repeatedly yelled back, "We don't know; we don't have it," the two intruders left.

Supposedly the husband was dazed from being hit in the head, but he ran after the two assailants. He got in his pickup truck and drove until he found one of the males walking along the sidewalk. The husband drove his truck over the curb and pinned the male against a fence, cracking two ribs, puncturing a lung, and seriously injuring him.

Afterward the husband and wife told the story to the police. The law enforcement officers then arrested the male in the hospital where he had been admitted. The husband refused to see a doctor or go to the hospital himself but allowed officers to photograph the injury he claimed was from the butt of a handgun. No weapon was found either at the scene or on the male pinned against the fence.

A public defender was given the case, which he felt was hopeless; however, the defender wanted to give the male as good of a defense as legally possible. Because there was blood

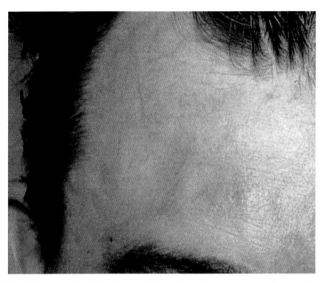

FIGURE 6.7   Photograph of bruise on victim alleged to have come from a handgun butt.

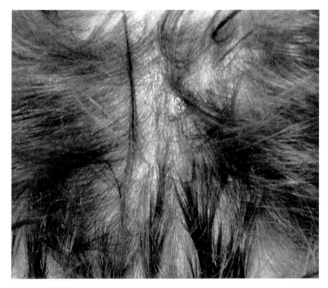

FIGURE 6.8   Photograph of the victim's cut scalp.

staining at the residence where the situation supposedly started, a bloodstain pattern analyst was consulted. The following photographs were taken of the victim and the residence.

The injury to the victim's head is seen in two places: the forehead (Figure 6.7) and the scalp (Figure 6.8). Unfortunately, the photograph was taken after the face and scalp were washed. It would have been good to see how the flow marks were recorded.

FIGURE 6.9   The outside glass panel of the entrance door.

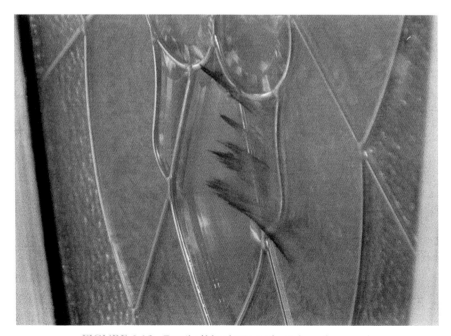

FIGURE 6.10   Detail of bloodstain on front door glass panel.

II. IDENTIFICATION

FIGURE 6.11   Outlined outside front door latch.

Although the husband and wife alleged the assault occurred in the kitchen, no bloodstains were found there. Blood was seen on the outside of the front door (Figures 6.9 and 6.10). It was claimed that the two assailants broke in the front door, but no signs of break-in were seen. Inside the entry were many drips around the floor, but only one shoe print type (photograph not available).

The husband claimed to identify the one male whom he had pinned against the fence with his pickup truck but could not identify any other person of interest from the police logs. When asked regarding identification, both the husband and wife claimed that the intruders were wearing pantyhose masks. When asked how the husband could identify the one male, the answer was that the pantyhose came off in a struggle inside the front door. No pantyhose were found initially, but a pair was found next to the front door one week after the incident. No testing for DNA was done on the pantyhose found.

Although the attorneys involved and the bloodstain pattern analyst felt this was a clear case of drug dealing, the original photographs were reviewed for information. When the photos were viewed on consecutive pages, the resemblance between the injury to the husband and the front door latch of the residence was noted (see Figures 6.11 and 6.12).

At first, the assistant DA trying the case refused to reconsider the charges against the male in the hospital. The DA replaced the ADA, and the new trial attorney dropped all charges against the male. The following points were reported:

1. No blood in the kitchen as alleged.
2. No break-in as alleged.

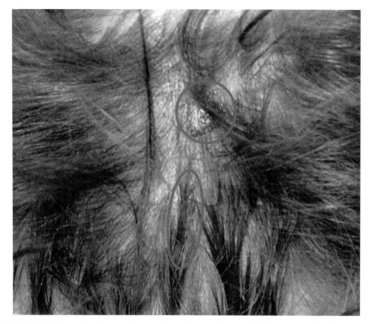

FIGURE 6.12   Outline to show mirror image of outside front door latch pattern.

3. Moving contact bloodstain classed as a skin swipe on the glass panel outside the front door.
4. Pattern match of injury to the forehead and the door latch.
5. Scattered drip castoffs at the front door entry, but only one shoe print.
6. No handgun found, but also injury not consistent with gun butt.

The couple's 14-year-old daughter was interviewed by law enforcement. All she would say was "The cops don't have a clue." Later, it was found that the name the alleged assailants yelled regarding drugs was that of the daughter's 20-year-old boyfriend, whom the parents very much wanted to stop dating their daughter. It was suggested that the husband was on drugs. His eyes in the photograph showed narrowed pupils, from drugs or from the light flash of the camera. His refusal to submit to a medical examination raised some questions. He apparently fell into the door latch. Whether he deliberately ran down the male or was dazed from drugs is unknown. He could have accidently ran off the street and used the story both to get out of a charge of DUI and to provide a dig at his daughter's boyfriend.

None of the examples shown in this chapter involved clear patterns from impacts. It is unfortunate that sometimes investigators drop the analysis of bloodstain patterns when a velocity impact spatter label cannot be applied. It should be clear from the information supplied so far that whether or not impact spatters exist at a crime scene does not end an analysis. Considerable investigative leads are available from identification and the complete interpretation of bloodstain pattern evidence available. Sections III and IV provide additional approaches to interpretation and applications for investigative leads of the bloodstain patterns identified.

INTERPRETATION

7

Information for Interpretation

Any bloodstain pattern analysis must begin with identification and preferably be completed before finalizing an interpretation. The previous section on identification, however, included some interpretations as they assisted in, and related to, classification of bloodstain patterns in categories. It is wrong, though, to leap from recognition that spots found on evidence are blood to an interpretation of what the spots must mean. Small spots and mist are not automatically called gunshot (or high velocity impact spatters). Medium-sized spots are not immediately indicative of blunt force trauma. Size and shape of spots have considerable overlap between different dynamic events, leading to considerably different interpretations. In actual crime situations, one must understand the type of event before developing a scenario of the crime as a whole. This advice is repeated ad nauseam because the approach of leaping from identification of a blood substance to conclusions of what occurred in a crime has resulted in considerable injustice as well as a bad reputation for bloodstain pattern evidence as a true scientific discipline.

One frequently encounters the subjective approach to interpretation in television episodes of cop shows. The "expert" will look at a bloodstain and comment, "That means he/she/it did ____." Using only one pattern while ignoring others can create problems, especially later in court. In some cases, an expert explains one pattern at the scene but ignores another that is contradictory. This type of approach to interpretation has been taught to hundreds of students. The best approach is not to ignore any of the patterns initially. An objective approach helps to avoid embarrassment and/or injustice later.

The process of applying bloodstain patterns in a scientific methodology involves several specific steps:

1. verifying the material being analyzed is blood (preliminary CSI work);
2. classifying as to the category of dynamic events responsible (identification);
3. confirming and verifying the classifications (identification);
4. sequencing events (identification/interpretation);
5. interpreting the combination and sequences (interpretation);
6. defining a scenario that may fit the sequence of crime events (interpretation); and
7. determining which events can be concluded, reported, and testified to (application).

Unfortunately, the whole process requires time, effort, acquired experience, and knowledge. It is easier to leap to a conclusion based on size and shape of patterns, but such approaches are subjective. Time- and funds-strapped agencies may feel the conclusion would be justified for cost savings; because doing so is not based on scientific principles, shortcutting interpretation may be more expensive in the long run as a result of prolonged trials and appeals.

Other books on police investigative work present various methodologies of approach to crime scene investigation, so they are not repeated here. A list of preliminary information specifically for bloodstain pattern evidence is, however, helpful in the steps that follow identification. In an initial approach to a crime scene, investigators may start with these facts immediately:

1. If bloodstain patterns are verified at a scene, injuries must have occurred.
2. If human blood exists, that blood was available for a bloodstain pattern.
3. Relative amounts of blood at different locations of an area believed to be the crime scene provide preliminary sequences of an alleged crime. More blood equals later stages of an assault, whereas less blood more likely indicates the beginning stages. A caution is necessary here that different areas of blood staining be verified as to source. More than one individual, i.e., another victim or an assailant, could have sustained injury.
4. Checking door frames and window blinds, inside drawers, beneath furniture, in room corners, etc., might provide blockages that may be used to determine and/or confirm location and angles to/from blood distributing events during the crime.
5. Transfer patterns always indicate a sequence; thus, subsequent as well as primary sources for the blood and the transferred patterns need to be found.
6. Drip castoffs show directions of movement during and following crime sequences.
7. Volumes of blood (pools) represent where a bleeding person or a very bloody object remained for a period of time.

The logical sequence for events proceeds from these preliminary facts. Investigators must keep an open mind no matter what they think they see immediately—especially in the present time when staged crime scenes are frequently encountered but not always recognized initially. If there is blood, there was an injury. The injury may have occurred from homicide, suicide, or accident. Injury and blood distribution during a homicide may involve accidental additional injury; therefore, the objective approach is to view the scene as open to interpretation regarding the events that distributed blood. Quantity of blood, of course, can be in and of itself a manner of death in exsanguination. Information from medical and autopsy reports can narrow down whether the quantity of blood resulted from bleeding for a long period of time or from a rapid bleed. Was the injury arterial, i.e., a rapid bleed, or was the bleeding for a long duration exacerbated by drugs and/or alcohol so that clotting did not stop it? Verification during autopsy is thus required.

An injury means some preliminary event occurred to open a blood source. This may be by cutting, gunshot, blunt force, or internal health issue. Gunshot and blunt force that breaks skin should involve spatters, but if the event happens in a space away from recording surfaces, the evidence of distributed spatters that could identify the event may not be available. Blunt force and cutting may not show blood distribution initially until blood accumulates enough to flow and be distributed. Blood spatters on floors should be regarded with caution due to subsequent events such as blood dripping into blood, drip castoffs, and/or splash.

The two possible limits of the beginning and the final resting place of a victim may encompass the crime: beginning events to provide a blood source and the ending sequence where blood accumulates. In between these limits are the direct transfers, moving transfers, subsequent blood spatter events, and physiologically altered events such as clotting, drying, and mixing with other substances. The one thing to look for after establishing the ending is the area with the least amount of blood. Some place with a few isolated spatters may be the beginning of the blood distribution events. If the victim was able to move after assault, moving transfers become important to the whole interpretation. Contacts between clothing, hands, feet, shoes, and head hair all show how the victim moved after an assault. Was the claim self-defense? If so, why would the victim move as such if acting as an aggressor?

The sequences of bloodstain patterns are

1. injuring events: stabbing, cutting, hitting, gunshot, falling against an object that injures, heavy object crushing, or machinery-imposed injury;
2. transfers, moving, direct contact, smudge;
3. drip castoffs, subsequent spattering;
4. PABS (physiologically altered bloodstains);
5. volume blood (pooling); and
6. staging?

Each pattern classification provides information for investigative leads. Too often the prosecution team may wait until a trial strategy is being developed before exploring the application of bloodstain pattern evidence. This can be a serious waste of time and information. Not only is ignoring bloodstain pattern evidence until after an arrest a waste, but it also can lead to missed information, leading to inaccurate charges, perhaps even of the wrong suspect. Leaping to conclusions from assumed pattern identity, usually after knowing the manner of death or assault, often occurs after a suspect is identified from other investigative techniques, not necessarily those with scientific foundations. This may result from the prosecution's request to "find anything you can" on a specific subject. The bloodstain pattern evidence is sometimes shoe-horned into the format without identification or interpretation of the evidence itself.

Applying bloodstain pattern analysis to gain investigative leads initially helps prevent biased thinking and provides information, corroboration, and suggestions for finding additional evidence. Thus, an objective approach is highly cost efficacious and can help streamline an investigation, saving time and money, which is extremely important in the investigation of violent crime. To begin, one needs to be aware of what each pattern identification may provide.

A general sequence of bloodstain pattern evidence may be associated with interpretation:

- **Impact spatter patterns:** These patterns indicate the beginning of the assault; they bring assailant and victim together at one segment in time and space.
- **Castoff patterns:** These patterns must occur after a blood source is exposed. The actions show spatial relationships between assailant and victim.
- **Drips:** These patterns show movement of either the victim or assailant after a blood source is exposed and flowing.
- **Swings:** These patterns provide information regarding the assailant during an assault. They indicate use of a weapon and self-defense gestures by a victim. They also confirm spacial relationships between the victim and assailant and may show the presence or absence of other persons of interest.
- **Cessation:** Self-defense gestures of a victim may be illustrated. Also, for each cessation, there should be swing castoffs. The reason is that if cessation causes blood drops to continue to travel, there should have been enough blood available to be distributed by a swing prior to

stopping. Impact might result from the bloodied object stopping when blocked if the stoppage also resulted in contact between it and the swinging object. If neither swing castoffs nor impact spatters are associated with a cessation castoff pattern, one should eliminate staging before listing interpretations.

- **Arterial damage:** These patterns may denote the beginning of an assault or the event that changed an assault to a homicide. Only the victim's actions are identified after a specific injury breaches an arterial blood vessel. There is no such thing as a nonarterial pressurized blood vessel. Veins, even large veins, are not under pressure once their connection to an arterial system behind them is broken. The major veins do provide blood for pooling, but the pressurized distribution is absent.
- **Transfers:** First, for these patterns, one must identify a blood source. Finding the source can lead to additional important information. Direct patterns link contacts between the victim and the scene and may also link the victim's injuries to the assailant. One also should remember that assailants may be injured at the scene.
- **Physiologically altered bloodstains (coagulation):** These patterns indicate either a crime of long duration, separate visits to the crime scene, or events that occurred later. One must rule out contamination before concluding the scene was staged or the assailant returned to the scene.
- **PABS (mix):** These patterns indicate conditions, location, and follow-ups of a crime. Blood mixed with cerebral spinal fluid (CSF) indicates a specific injury to the head, while blood mixed with semen is a direct link to aggressive sexual contact. Blood mixed with saliva may indicate a blow to the face, and blood mixed with water may indicate cleanup attempts. It's unfortunate that such evidence is often ignored.

INTERPRETATIONS BASED ON COMMON WORKSHOP EXPERIMENTS

Students of workshops assume the experiments they conduct illustrate what the instructors have told them. Instructors often ignore criticisms of standard workshop exercises as they may believe that there is an answer even if, at the moment, it is unknown. Defenses and explanations for historical significance of out-of-date experiments are not always offered at the time of workshops. The argument in favor of voted-on exercises for workshops is that "we have to do it this way because this is the way we've always done it." Subconsciously, the approach to interpretation follows legal reasoning and the adherence to set principles and precedents in law that may have been established by popular vote, not scientific applications. The science claimed to apply is sometimes based on principles that are out of date, since modified, or completely abandoned.

Paddle Fan Device

One of the exercises commonly included in workshops involves using a paddle fan device (see Figure 7.1). This device consists of a fan with paddle blades inside a box. A hole in the top cover located over the leading edge of the fan blades allows blood to be dropped, while an opening in front of the box lateral to the blades allows distribution of blood drops from the spinning fan. Fan motors lend themselves to measurement of blade speeds, and these measurements permit the assumption of speed versus size and distance blood drops travel. Interestingly enough, this experiment relates to the original terminology of Dr. Paul L. Kirk. Dr. Kirk coined the term "velocity impact spatter" on the basis of the speed of

FIGURE 7.1   Paddle fan device.

blood drops distributed from an event to impact with a recording surface. The term thus could apply to any type of event, impact, castoff, or arterial damage distribution. MacDonell changed the terminology to apply only to impacts between an object (bullet, fist, weapon, etc.) and a blood source (MacDonell, 1971). This change in definition confuses the interpretation of the results from the paddle fan device.

The usual instruction for using the device is to measure the speed of the blades and then locate and measure spatters distributed from an aliquot of blood. Blood is dropped into a hole at the top, which results in blood being deposited on the spinning blades at the velocity measured previously. Blood is allegedly broken up by the impact and distributed out the front opening. Students are told that the size and distance that the drops which form stains on the target surface travel represent the size and distance traveled from impacts of that velocity. Although the quantity of blood dropped into the hole will impact the blades, the drops distributed do not originate from an impact. Blood coats the blades and is cast off, or thrown out, as the blades rotate. One can confirm this by looking inside the box after a drop. Blood coats the sides from the spinning blades, i.e., castoffs, not impact. Thus, interpreting the size and distance traveled as relating to impact spatter distribution is erroneous. To testify that one can recognize individual spatters from a specific impact, such as gunshot, based on experience with the fan exercise is saying "It must be impact based on results from a castoff experiment." This experiment also illustrates that one cannot limit identification of an event to just the size and distance that blood drops travel based on experiments with a castoff methodology. It is a good experiment to show the distance traveled based on size of the drops distributed, as Dr. Kirk advocated. The problem is overextending the interpretation.

III. INTERPRETATION

The factors influencing size and distance traveled include, but may not be limited to, the following:

- **Blade composition:** Glass will slough drops sooner, thus smaller, than unfinished wood, etc., will.
- **Blood composition:** A higher ratio of red cells will slough smaller drops due to higher mass sooner than larger drops with less mass.
- **Length of time the fan runs:** Each revolution distributes blood with the chance a drop will go farther. Instructors learn to turn off the fan soon after blood is dropped into the opening to the blades.
- **Height over target surface the fan box is placed:** Greater height permits forward travel longer before being overcome with wind sheer and falling to the target surface.
- **Speed of the fan:** Centripetal force projects farther. Please note the term is "centripetal," not "centrifugal." These are two different concepts in physics.

The way most instructors handle this experiment is to turn off the fan immediately after the aliquot of blood is dropped. This action influences the results because the slowing fan blades are still casting off drops as the fan stops. Measuring spatters close to the front aperture represents a different velocity than the measured fan speed when the fan is running at full rotation speed. The author found that students in workshops were more confused than informed with the fan results. For research purposes, this experiment has applications, but for workshops, it must be further explained regarding interpretation of results in relation to actual crime scenes.

Sadly, the usual interpretation of the fan device results is in terms of "impact" spatter size and distance traveled. This, of course, can be true, but it isn't that simple. Drops of different sizes are more common to impact, whereas similar sizes are more common to castoffs. The distance the drops travel depends on drop mass and amount of initial speed imparted. The initial aliquot of blood coats the blades, providing a different surface than after blood has been thrown off. This accounts for apparent drop size variation, while the reason for impact-imparted velocity is that the surfaces making impact contact exert a varying amount of force over the area of contact. The results are interesting, but presently with the parameters commonly included, they provide little if anything of use for investigative leads in actual casework.

For research purposes, some modifications were made to the device. Holes were added to show that the place where the blood was dropped could affect the distribution. Note the spatter size cast back at the box top and enclosure for the blades in Figures 7.2 and 7.3. The outer part of the blade surfaces broke up the blood into small drops because the circumference of rotation affected the speed of the rotating fans.

Another modification was to make it possible to exchange blades so that different surfaces such as rubber, glass, plastic, and cardboard could be tested. This relates to the surface of an object casting off, not impacting at a measurable speed of blood drops. More work in this area needs to be done. Such projects would benefit investigations more than attempts to prove drops falling by gravity have variations that affect diameter. Red blood cell composition affects diameter more than concepts of flattening or oscillations of drops in free fall.

Castoff Interpretations

One of the most popular exercises used in bloodstain pattern workshops is creating hands-on swing castoff examples. These were described in *Blood Dynamics* (Wonder, 2001, pp. 63-64) and *Bloodstain Pattern Evidence, Objective Approaches and Case Applications* (Wonder, 2007, p. 72). The

FIGURE 7.2   Inside the fan device box.

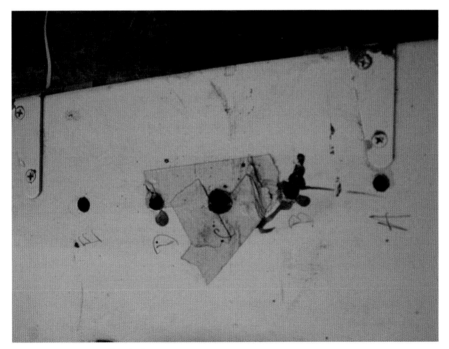

FIGURE 7.3   Modification holes for the fan device.

III. INTERPRETATION

purpose of this workshop exercise is to create bloodstains. Students mash the chosen weapon in blood, usually a bloodied sponge, and then swing back forcefully. This action does a good job of casting blood onto a paper-constructed ceiling and walls. Interpretations are suggested for crime scene evidence. Some items of interpretation lead to confusion because of the different dynamics between a bloodstain pattern workshop and a violent crime: which leg of the swing distributes the most blood, the meaning of direction of travel in castoffs, and drop separation dynamics.

Alleged scientific studies of castoffs have been designed to explain the dynamics of actions. Some of these confuse concepts of physics: the stopping angular momentum (cessation castoffs) and the continual change in centripetal direction (swing castoffs). Research projects to study castoffs may focus on centripetal motion alone. Blood drops are distributed during a blunt force beating because of a combination of the centripetal arc *and* the constant change in direction as the swing is directed to a victim. Applying two-dimensional reconstruction to study swing castoffs ignores the force interplay of the changing of direction applied in beating with a blunt weapon. Researchers who say this doesn't matter miss the point that such changes in direction help identify how an assailant used a weapon. Right-handed, left-handed, back swing, and forward swing all reflect how the weapon changed direction while being used to beat a victim.

In addition to providing information on how a weapon was used, the changes in swing direction during casting off blood drops help differentiate castoffs from arterial damage events. Both arterial damage patterns and castoffs involve chains of blood drops forming and being distributed over a range of time and space. This is contrasted with impact spatters, which are distributed from one segment of space for one discrete unit of time. Chains of spatters resulting from either castoffs or arterial damage patterns may be arranged in either an inline or a shifting-line arrangement. Either can be castoffs or arterial damage in origin. Check a section of an inline pattern for additional characteristics to differentiate castoffs from arterial damage. As stated earlier, the importance of correctly identifying these two pattern categories is that the castoffs are interpreted as the actions of an assailant, whereas the arterial pattern is all about the victim. The assailant may be long gone when the blood drops for arterial damage are being distributed.

String Reconstruction

It is inherent in crime labs to seek scientific justification for bloodstain pattern evidence. There is security in being able to say "that is the result from the instrument." Many otherwise knowledgeable criminalists feel that bloodstain pattern evidence lacks a scientific basis and should be limited to police work. Government crime labs, however, may be required by their legal representatives to provide the expertise, if only as guidance for law enforcement CSI personnel.

One technique that is supposedly based on trigonometry—mathematics being one of the undisputed scientific qualifications—is the reconstruction of the origin of an impact. The initial technique was performed manually with strings and a compass. This technique now can be computerized and any error blamed on instrumentation. String reconstructions can be very useful, but only if certain limitations to interpretation are considered before expending the time and energy to conduct one:

1. Stains to be used must be correctly identified as impact-distributed blood before starting. Castoffs and arterial damage patterns do not originate from one origin; thus, they should not be traced back to a hypothetical one.

2. Stains selected must represent only one event, not multiple impacts or overlapping separate events, perhaps including other acts than impacts.
3. The purpose of locating an origin for the impact must have a clear, justified objective. Just doing a string reconstruction to show a person was murdered wastes time, money, and effort if nothing is proven.
4. Stains used must not be too big or too small to actually represent an angular contact. Blows to the head may involve explosive rupture of blood and cerebral spinal fluid. In Dr. Kirk's instructions, this type of rupture involves high velocity stains, which are elongated too much for measurement of angular impact.
5. A true area of convergence must be constructed that does not involve drawing a group of strings to a theoretical point. No two incompressible fluid drops can occupy the same point. Blood is an incompressible fluid. Drawing several spatters to a point is either a fabrication of the true area of convergence, or the spatters used are not from a single impact. Arterial damage patterns and castoffs can appear as if they have come from the same point because blood is continually added from the source as movement progresses; i.e., blood drops may originate from the same source over an area of space.

Too often, identification is skipped, and interpretation is consistent with other information rather than from bloodstain patterns themselves. This situation is encountered when an investigator identifies blood spatters in terms of *assumed* velocity alone and then states the conclusion of what that identification means in the investigation, i.e. "That's medium velocity impact spatter, which means the perp was the one who beat the victim." Based on size and shape of individual spatters alone, the stains found could be from respiration (cough, sneeze, wheeze, breathing), artery breach with high blood pressure, cloth contact with prior recorded wet impact spatters, abraded injury, or rapid bleeding blood into blood. Leaping to conclusions is a waste of the information provided by bloodstain pattern analysis. Sadly, an expert can show the string reconstruction as a science in court to justify using the evidence, rather than to provide interpretation. Jurors assume that because the expert appears for one side, he or she is offering proof of that opinion. Since the primary value of a string reconstruction is to position the individual/blood source at the instant of an impact, doing a string reconstruction may be useless without an arrest and a specific statement offered to be confirmed or refuted. Section IV further describes the technique of applying string reconstructions to casework.

The size of blood spatters has been mentioned repeatedly. Because many well-qualified criminalists want a scientific basis with which they feel comfortable, math and physics applications are favorites because they seem to provide the security of science, even if applied out of context. The problem is that instructions for measuring blood spatters are not simple. The rationale is greatly flawed (Wonder, 2007, pp. 33–38). This point should be obvious, but it is sometimes shrugged off as "there must be an explanation" and ignored. The main error in logic is that a spherical blood drop will flatten out as a two-dimensional shape on a recording surface yet supposedly retain the same diameter as the three-dimensional blood drop recorded.

In Figure 7.4, the equal symbol with the diagonal line through it is the mathematic expression for "not equal to." It should be obvious that a two-dimensional blood stain cannot have the same diameter as a three-dimensional blood drop. This thinking has, however, been accepted by many experts without argument. Experts use the answer that the proportionality remains the same, but no experimental evidence has been published to support that claim. It is more likely that the places where measurements are made on spatters are adjusted to fit angles, thus giving the appearance of being proportional to assumed dimensions of a blood drop in flight.

III. INTERPRETATION

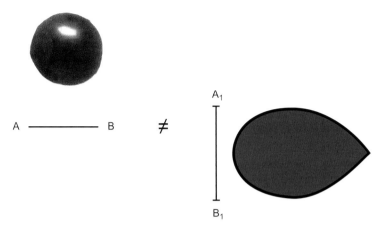

FIGURE 7.4   Blood drop diameter not equal to blood spatter diameter.

The second error is that a spherical drop will make an oval footprint stain on contact. With a recording target, there is no way to draw a cross-section of a sphere that will result in an oval shape. Efforts to prove that blood drops in flight are distorted may be offered as the rationale for oval shapes resulting from round drops. However, the principles for such experiments lie with water and other Newtonian substances, not with non-Newtonian blood. The greater the concentration of red blood cells in a blood drop, the more stable and spherical drops will form. Distortions will be more likely to occur in flight for anemic blood drops. Contacts with these drops are still not in the shape of ovals. Contact will be a circle; then continued travel will develop into the elongated shape recognized with spatters. The speed of the drop at contact will influence the shape more than any oscillation or flattening of the lower edge of the drop (see Figure 7.5).

The third error in reasoning is to believe that the speed of the drop at contact has no effect on the shape of the drop; i.e., a drop contacting a recording surface at medium velocity will not vary from a drop hitting a recording surface at high velocity. This thinking is totally illogical but accepted by those without adequate knowledge of current science.

However, with hundreds of workshops, perhaps thousands, including all instructors and classes where the technique is offered, many examples of the string reconstruction have proven very informative. The object must be to understand the limitations, not discard the technique altogether. Why does the string reconstruction work if it is so flawed?

1. Most workshop examples where the string reconstruction is shown to be good information were constructed using simulated blunt force assault. Blunt force–distributed blood spatters of a medium size range are easier to measure than those from gunshot-recorded bloodstains. Velocity of the drop does matter. High speed makes measuring more difficult and leads to erroneous interpretation. The slower drops can be included with more accuracy.
2. The author's workshops strenuously advocated the time and accuracy of constructing an area of convergence rather than assuming a "point" of convergence and starting the construction from stains measured without an established area of convergence. This approach eliminated overlapping patterns better than drawing stains close to a point and focused students' attention on identifying the size and shape of the impact that distributed

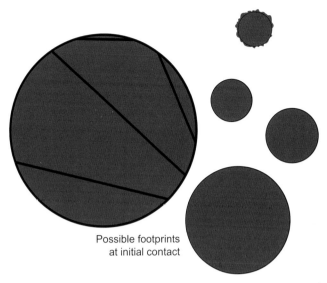

Possible footprints
at initial contact

FIGURE 7.5   Chords (cross-sections) of a sphere are always round.

the blood drops forming the pattern in the first place. This approach can also be used to test and confirm the interpretation of a finished string reconstruction.

3. Measuring the stains made an extreme difference in the interpretation.

This last point is a major criterion of either the hands-on string reconstruction or the computerization efforts for locating the origin of an impact. There are basically three ways to measure stains that are not at all consistent with each other. The three major techniques also could be used in any automated or computerized technique so that instrumentation would not correct and/or prevent errors. These three major techniques include the following:

1. The whole stain, including overflow and run, is measured. Although this technique may still be encountered, it has mostly been discarded from updated protocols. The reason for not applying this cut-off is that a blood drop traveling and adding to the stain length for longer distances will leave tails that are not representative of the angle that a drop made contact with a recording surface. Velocity of a drop will definitely affect the final dimensions. The error of measurement will be to make the stain longer than would represent the angle and thus position the origin too low (see Figure 7.6, view A). A statement such as "the victim could not have been standing because the origin was 4 feet off the floor and the victim is 6 feet tall" could be wrong because the injury could be at 5 feet with 1 foot error due to stain measurements. See Figure 7.7 for effect on interpretation.

2. Because of concern over where to cut off the tail on stains, a technique was suggested such that the oval of first contact would be used to complete cut-off at the opposite end, i.e., the end in the direction of travel (refer to Figure 7.6, view B). This approach seems ideal because this set technique can be applied easily and with computer programming. In fact, the author presented this technique in initial workshops and found later that it has been repeated by former students. Unfortunately, this technique ignores one of the original errors with the reconstruction of an origin: the assumption that a sphere makes an oval footprint at contact with a recording surface. Remember that the initial footprint must be a circle, but the velocity of the blood drop will

III. INTERPRETATION

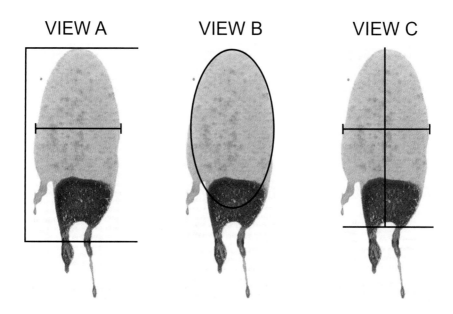

FIGURE 7.6   Techniques to cut off blood spatter length.

FIGURE 7.7   Cutting off stain too long.

III. INTERPRETATION

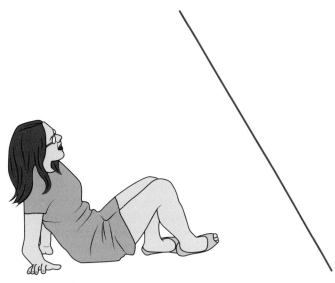

FIGURE 7.8   Cutting off stain too short.

determine the shape of the oval following initial contact. Cutting off the stain as a perfect oval will cut it too short because blood is lost at the initial contact with less spread as the drop travels (see Figure 7.8). The ratio of height to width will change with velocity. The shape of first contact is not necessarily applicable to the angle calculated from the stain measurements.

3. The third method of measurement has been used the longest and may have been wrongly abandoned when the technique for completing the oval was introduced. This technique involves dropping blood on slanted boards at known angles. The place for cut-off is calculated to give the angle of the drop. With this exercise, training was presented to show how to measure bloodstains. This approach was used predominantly in the author's workshops and some other programs visited. The problem is obvious: it requires thought and training specifically in how to adjust the cut-off line to measure impact spatters (see Figure 7.6, view C). It is also a problem when workshop participants interpret the exercise as measuring drips. Drips are not measured because the angle interpretation is not the same as drops distributed from impacts. A solution is to provide adequate practice with true impact spatter–distributed blood spatters so that workshop participants understand where to cut off spatter stains in measurements. Additionally, including a specified error will keep statements accurate. In the examples shown in Figure 7.6, the variation of calculated degrees was between 6 and 7 degrees. Using an average of plus or minus 4 degrees would include the true angle.

There will be those cases where the error in measurement is small enough not to matter. The major concern is that more importance is placed on the area of convergence. If the location of origin is not correct, the importance of the measured blood spatters increases in degree of error. See the example in Figure 7.9.

The solution is not to give up on locating the origin by reconstruction, but to conduct the reconstruction with considerable forethought and confirmation. The most important part of any reconstruction is the measurements. Events considered "high velocity" will present problems that may

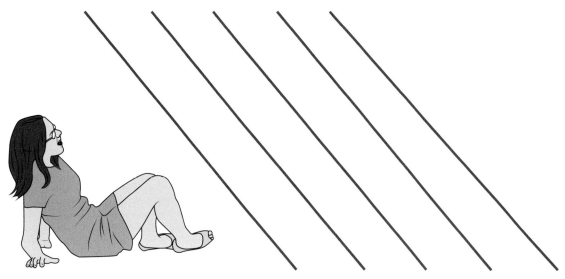

FIGURE 7.9   Increases in error from wrongly placing victim.

not be overcome by any reconstruction of the origin by using strings or computer. The preliminary considerations were given previously; the confirmations should include finding other bloodstain patterns that are consistent with the estimate of origin:

1. blockage and the angles between the reconstruction and the blockages (voids);
2. drip castoffs on the floor or ground beneath the origin location;
3. termination of swing castoff patterns at or in the direction of the origin estimation;
4. transfer patterns of struggle or position of victim at the suggested origin;
5. drip castoff trails leading from a calculated origin; and
6. reconstructions based on surfaces at 90 degrees to each other, as with walls and ceilings and floors and furniture.

Amount of Blood Estimate

One more commonly encountered misinterpretation involves estimations of how much blood would be distributed from an assault. In watching true detective–style television programs, one commonly encounters cases in which detectives claim "the suspects must have had a lot of blood on them." This is not always true. The author has conducted hundreds of experiments with blood, without any drops reaching clothing. Some reasons for not acquiring blood during a dynamic event are planned, and some may be the accidental conditions of distribution. Such conditions, planned or accidental, may involve the following:

1. Assault is to the head, with hair blocking projection away from the injury.
2. The angle of assault projects blood further on rather than back at the assailant.
3. There is a blunt force assault to a clothed area of the body with the cloth blocking drops.
4. The length of a blunt force weapon can limit the amount of blood that reaches back toward the user of the weapon.

5. The distance between a shooter and the victim can involve drops not carrying to the shooter.
6. A very broad weapon is used and therefore blocks blood from being thrown directly back.
7. A gunshot will usually cause distribution on the sides in an extended cone arrangement and thus may not be recorded on the assailant. Caution is advised here because anyone standing near the victim could acquire blood spatters yet not be the assailant.
8. The angle of blows from the weapon may direct blood to the sides rather than back at the assailant. Here, recorded patterns on vertical surfaces may help identify why blood would not be directed back toward an assailant.
9. The victim may grab at the weapon and block distribution of blood toward the assailant.

The biggest challenge to interpretation occurs when several events overlap. Workshops that present only isolated dynamics do not adequately represent actual crime scenes. In the confusion of overlapping patterns, investigators may fall back on trying to remember a pattern match and become confused by the quantity of bloodstain patterns at an actual crime scene. Either the evidence is not used beyond a designation of general velocity impact spatter designation, or it is shoe-horned into the events learned from other information. A way to practice using bloodstain pattern evidence for investigative leads is to examine targets and photographs for the number of patterns present. Because each pattern provides evidence, one can say he or she is counting the number of pieces of evidence present. Chapter 5 provides a format for this type of interpretation by focusing on the possible number of pieces of evidence rather than developing an initial scenario from information other than bloodstains and fitting the stains to it.

REFERENCES

Wonder, A.Y., 2001. Blood Dynamics. Academic Press, London, pp. 63–64.

Wonder A.Y., 2007. Bloodstain Pattern Evidence, Objective Approaches and Case Applications. Elsevier, San Diego, CA, pp. 33–38, 72.

MacDonell, H.L., 1971. Flight Characteristics and Stain Patterns of Human Blood. Law Enforcement Assistance Administration, National Institute of Law Enforcement and Criminal Justice, p. 1–77.

Investigative Leads: Suggested Questions and Answers

Each bloodstain pattern identification suggests evidential leads information. Investigators who have learned to use bloodstain pattern evidence in their initial interviews have found confirmations and/or contradictions in statements that speed solutions to violent crimes. Using such information is in contrast to waiting until after a person of interest is identified before analyzing bloodstains from photographs or finding questions after interviews are completed. The following lists provide questions from bloodstain patterns that may be answered if they are known at the time of interviews. They are arranged by category of bloodstain and are followed by explanations detailing how bloodstain patterns may be used to answer specific questions. The essential approach is that bloodstain patterns are analyzed before interviews, not after. The presentation here is in words without pictures to show how explanations can be applied later to court testimony. A picture may be worth a thousand words, but lawyers prefer the words.

THE MAJOR CATEGORIES, SUBCATEGORIES, AND A CONTINUOUS LIST OF QUESTIONS FOR INTERPRETATION OF BLOODSTAIN PATTERN EVIDENCE

I. Impact Spatters

Patterns from impacts bring a victim and an assailant together in one instant in time and space. It has been emphasized repeatedly in this book that one must not leap to identifications in terms of velocity of an alleged impact. To do so confuses the information available when the bloodstains are not, in fact, from impact events.

In the following questions, the concept is that bloodstains should be identified per category before applying velocity gradients. In that way, the patterns help answer questions, and recognizing the degree may assist in fine-tuning information from those answers. For example, a castoff pattern may show how a weapon is used. Recognizing the velocity at which the blood drops were distributed from a swing castoff then might tell how violent the swing may have been and, in turn, what kind of perpetrator would be capable of swinging a weapon that way. Questions with regard to identified impact spatter patterns provide investigative leads information that may include the following:

1. Where did the assault begin or terminate?
2. How many blows were struck if a blunt force attack is identified?
3. If separated events (for example, a fight or beating followed by a gunshot) were involved, where and how (directions of delivery of blows, gun alignment) did each happen?
4. From the location of a fatal event, was the victim upright or supine; that is, was the event self-defense or possibly homicide with intent to deliver assault to an immobile victim?
5. If more than one victim was present, where was each victim possibly located?
6. When no body is present, what type of event (shooting, fistfight, blunt force, accident) is suggested?

II. Castoffs

Patterns from castoffs are all about movement by the victim, the assailant, or bloodied material after blood begins to flow. The main interpretation is that castoffs must occur after another event exposes a blood source; thus, this is never the beginning of a violent crime. For the first few assaults, there will not be sufficient blood distributed to identify the action. Castoffs provide information after initiation of attack and with regard to the sequences of events. This can be part of the investigative leads but must be recognized as dependent on other bloodstain pattern evidence for interpretation. Questions that may be answered from interpretation of castoff patterns include, but are not limited to, the following:

A. Drip Castoffs

7. Was the victim moved or moving after injury caused blood to flow?
8. Did the assailant have sufficient injury to drip blood (possible DNA sampling)?
9. Was the trail from a bleeding victim, suspect, or a carried bloody object?
10. Was the bleeding person walking or running?
11. Did the person carrying the victim struggle with the heavy weight?

B. Swing Castoffs

12. How many blunt force swings with the weapon were delivered?
13. Where approximately did the assailant stand during the assault?
14. Was the assailant using his or her right hand, left hand, or both hands?
15. How were the swings performed: overhand, horizontal, or backhand?
16. What kind of weapon was used in the assault?

C. Cessation Castoffs

17. Was the victim defensive or incapacitated?
18. Were there one or more assailants involved in a beating?
19. Does the scene appear staged to confuse the manner of death?

III. Arterial Damage

Identifying arterial distributed spatter provides valuable information, but this evidence is often mistaken for castoffs. Correct identification and interpretation provides information regarding the victim's movements after an artery is breached. Arterial damage bloodstain patterns should not be used to explain or suggest the assailant's actions. The evidence is all about the victim, whereas castoffs are predominantly about the assailant. At the point in time that arterial breach occurred, copious blood loss may follow, with the assailant departed or insignificant at the scene. Although four types of patterns result from arterial injury, these patterns are often mistaken for other events that arterial distributions may resemble. It is therefore essential for the interpretation and acquisition of investigative leads that correct identification occur before interpretation. It is here that size and shape are the least beneficial to classification of dynamic events. *Spurt* and *gush* have been noted as a matter of terminology rather than separate events. In this book, the term *spurt* is used to signify that the artery is moving at the moment drops are being projected, and *gush* is used when the artery remains stationary with overlapping drop contact with a recording surface. Separating the terminology helps identification and interpretation, such as what the victim was doing while the artery projected blood.

A. Arterial Breach

20. If blood loss is the cause of death, which breached the artery change the outcome to homicide?
21. Where is the most likely point that the artery was breached?

B. Arterial Gush

22. How can arterial damage patterns help justify bloodstain pattern analysis as science based?
23. Can one determine whether arterial injury occurred before the autopsy is available?
24. Can one provide information regarding manner of death before autopsy? This point must be confirmed by autopsy, but advance notice is good for investigations. It also can be a reminder for the pathologist to list arterial damage in the autopsy. Is suicide, accidental injury, or homicide suggested? This information also provides questions the attending officer can ask of the autopsy physician while viewing the autopsy.

C. Arterial Spurt

25. Which direction did the victim move after arterial injury?
26. If arterial injury occurred, can it be verified as to which artery was injured before autopsy?

D. Arterial Rain

27. Was there contact between the assailant and victim after arterial breach?
28. After it is established that an artery was breached, are there areas on the victim's clothing that should have received blood from an arterial fountain?
29. Do folds in the victim's clothing contradict the arrangement of the body at the moment of arterial spurting?

IV. Transfer Patterns

All transfer patterns provide investigative leads information as well as essential trial testimony, yet they are often ignored in favor of spatter patterns. In forensic parlance, *spatters* are class characteristics, which may resemble various nonspecific events, and as shown in Section II may involve similarities that overlap between major categories. Transfer patterns may be individualizing and thus unique for a specific event at a crime scene. Information provided may include the following:

A. Blockage

30. Can the location of an impact origin be confirmed?
31. Were any objects moved or removed from the scene? If so, can any investigative information be gleaned from the objects suggested by the blockage?
32. Where was the assailant at the moment of blood drop distribution?
33. Where was the victim during the blood drop distribution?
34. Were bystanders or more than one assailant present?

B. Absence Pattern

35. Can spatial positions at the time of the assault be reconstructed?
36. Was the door opened or closed during the assault?
37. Do folds in the victim's clothes show lack or presence of bloodstains out of context with the position of the body?

C. Simple Direct Transfers

38. Is there a fabric impression that links the scene with the victim or assailant?
39. Can fingerprint impressions be identified within blood?
40. Is a weapon match to the assault suggested? This is especially important with knives because assailants will often wipe a knife on clothing after an assault.
41. Was an item moved or removed from the scene?

D. Moving Transfers (Swipe and Wipe)

42. Which items or victims were dragged within or out of the crime scene?
43. Was the person doing the dragging dealing with a heavyweight or easy-to-move object?
44. Did the assailant or another person attempt to clean up the crime scene?
45. Was the victim able to crawl after the assault?

V. Physiologically Altered Bloodstains (PABS)

A. Mixing with Other Substances, Water, Mucus, or Dry Particles

46. Were there any attempts to change or alter the crime scene?
47. Did the assault occur before or after rainfall, dew point, or water sprinklers went off? Was the victim water-boarded?
48. Was the victim vomiting and/or wetting his or her head in any way after or during the assault?
49. Did the assailant attempt to clean himself or herself up before leaving?

B. Drying

50. Did the assault cover a longer period of time or was it completed in one continuous stage?
51. Did subsequent bystanders or first line officers contaminate the scene?

C. Clotting

52. Was this a crime of long duration?
53. Can the time span be suggested?

54. Was the scene contaminated?
55. Can an estimate for time of death be suggested? (This information must be confirmed by the pathologist.)
56. Is there impression evidence to be used?

VI. Volume

57. When was the body moved?
58. Was the assault immediately fatal or prolonged? (Confirmation from medical experts is needed.)
59. Could the victim have survived blood loss with or without transfusion? (Pathologist confirmation is needed.)

VII. Miscellaneous

60. Was the witness telling the truth or supplying a false statement?
61. Are there items that would provide some additional characteristics of the assailant?
62. Are there any bloodstain patterns that are contrary to other patterns? For example, were there any swing castoffs without any impact or drips showing the termination of the swing?
63. Is the person claiming to be a bloodstain pattern expert truly knowledgeable or merely speaking memorized terminology?

HOW BLOODSTAIN PATTERN EVIDENCE MAY BE USED TO ANSWER THE PRECEDING QUESTIONS

Most books available on bloodstain pattern evidence provide lists of some of the items in the preceding sections. They do not usually provide instructions on how to arrive at the information using analysis of the bloodstain patterns. Instructors may omit investigative leads approaches from training programs for economic reasons or because the instructors themselves have not received that training. The following sections provide approaches to obtaining the interpretations to the preceding questions, which may assist initial investigations. Multiple interpretations from pattern categories may confirm each individual suggested conclusion. A good rule of thumb is to have three or more different patterns with the same interpretation before claiming bloodstain pattern evidence as proof of a scenario.

I. Impact Spatters

Impacts occur in one place in time and space. It is wrong to interpret an impact spatter pattern as occurring at a point because no two drops of an incompressible fluid can originate from the same point. It is good news if this fact is recognized because the arrangement of spatters extending away from an area of convergence will show the size and shape of the impact. The size and shape of the impact will provide investigative leads to the size and shape of the weapon.

Traditionally, impact patterns are divided into velocity assumptions of low, medium, and high velocity impact spatter patterns. The problem is that sizes overlap with all the major categories. Size alone cannot be used to identify the dynamics involved in an impact pattern. Shape of spatters depends on the speed of the blood drop at impact, yet different speeds may be encountered with different degrees of force within each category. The best approach is to first identify the dynamics and then apply speed only as an interpretation regarding degree of force within the category—i.e., *x* velocity impact, *x* velocity castoff, or *x* velocity arterial distribution. If the use confuses members of the investigative team who have been trained to use velocity terms as identification, it is strongly suggested to omit the terms altogether. Say instead *low, medium,* or *high degree of force* (impact, castoff, or arterial spurt).

Bloodstain pattern interpretation that may provide answers to at least 63 investigative leads questions include, but may not be limited to, the following:

1. Where did the assault begin or terminate? At a crime scene, look for impact spatter patterns with less blood involved and then locate impact distributions with more blood. As the assault proceeds, the impact patterns will draw forth more blood. In the case of blunt force trauma, it usually takes several blows before enough blood is distributed to identify an impact. This helps indicate the sequence of blows. No blood drops will be distributed from the initial impact because a source has not been opened. Start with heavy impact patterns and move backward to the fewest spatters that can be identified as impact distributed.

2. How many blows were struck if a blunt force attack is identified? Blows struck in blunt force assaults may be suggested when one counts the impact spatter patterns when they are recognized as separate events. The number determined is a minimum number because seldom does the first strike (or first few strikes) draw enough blood to create the impact pattern. At least one or more impacts may be delivered before the wound becomes bloody enough to provide a blood source for impact distribution. If the patterns are separated, noting the amount of blood in each pattern helps to estimate the location of earlier assaults and place them in a sequence. This information gives the investigator an idea of where the assault began and how victims and assailants moved during the attack.

An important variation of this is that a series of broad impacts are aligned along a hard edge. If the assault was predominantly to the victim's head, this evidence can suggest the assailant repeatedly hit or kicked the victim.

3. If separated events (for example, a fight or beating followed by a gunshot) were involved, where and how (delivery of blow, gun alignment) did each happen? After identifying patterns as impact, note if there is a marked difference between the stain sizes. Specifically, note whether exclamation mark–shaped stains are present because they identify blood drops accelerated at contact with a recording surface. If there are more oval-shaped stains separated from the exclamation mark ones, a separation of blunt force versus gunshot is suggested. The alignment of spatters with direction of travel away from an area of convergence shows how the event or events took place. Gunshot will likely have a smaller area of convergence than blunt force trauma. Horizontal blows to the victim distribute spatters from side to side, whereas overhand blows distribute drops that become spatters down to up. For blunt force assault, this distribution may be important in showing how an assailant used a weapon.

When one is determining locations where a victim was beaten versus where he or she was shot, care must be paid to blood around the face. Blood around the nose and mouth—confirmed with autopsy of blood in the nares, trachea, larynx, or lungs—could indicate respiratory-distributed spatter, which may be confused with mist-sized spatter often associated with gunshot. Follow up with questions to the autopsy physician if there was blood in the respiratory organs but not mentioned on the autopsy report.

Although many investigators prefer an autopsy be performed before interpretation of other evidence, if they don't have it and instead form some preliminary questions to ask when the autopsy is performed, those questions can provide valuable investigative leads. This is especially true in determining whether a bloodstain pattern is from gunshot or is respiratory distributed and whether a beating occurred before a gunshot.

Criminalists who prefer confirmation from an instrumental test may depend on using amylase determination as a means of differentiating respiratory-distributed spatter from gunshot. There is a problem with this concept. Amylase is an inducible enzyme found in the blood and normally found in much higher quantity in the saliva (Quintana et al., 2009, pp. 822–830). This means that the amount of amylase will be influenced by stimulation. To create a control for experiments, one stimulates saliva production in volunteers. This increases the amount of amylase in the saliva. The key word is *normally*. People under extreme stress, such as fear of bodily harm, death threats, public speaking, excessive exercise, and/or emotional confrontation may produce so little saliva that their mouth is extremely dry. If injury occurs to the face, the mouth will have very little saliva. The amylase determination, even though distribution is from respiration, will be borderline concentration rather than characteristically elevated concentration for saliva, especially if compared to experimentation where amylase is elevated from stimulation.

A second issue may make amylase determination invalid for distinguishing blood from respiratory sources versus blood from gunshot injury. Amylase is inactivated by the stomach acidity and enzymes. A victim's vomiting will decrease the amount of amylase that would be attributed to respiratory distribution (Tietz, 1986, pp. 725–730).

Labeling any blood spatters seen as velocity impact spatters because they are associated with a known beating or gunshot wound, and determined from sources other than analysis of bloodstains, provides nothing for investigative leads. Beatings may happen before gunshot, and respiratory distribution may happen before or after gunshot. Accurately identifying patterns may help sequence events. The more accurate the scenario presented to suspects and reluctant witnesses, the better the chance of truthful admissions.

4. From the location of a fatal event, was the victim upright or supine; that is, was the event self-defense or possibly homicide with intent to deliver assault to an immobile victim? This information is better obtained by performing a *string reconstruction* or a computer model. With computer applications, it is essential that the area of convergence is not determined from averaged points, i.e., a complete locus of points of convergence. Such forming points of convergence fail to acknowledge that the impact is not a point in space. When the reconstruction identifies the impact event, it can be shown that the victim was or was not standing or approaching in a threatening manner to justify self-defense, or lack thereof, by the person of interest.

5. If more than one victim was present, where was each victim possibly located? Identifying the impact patterns associated with each victim provides a basis for collecting blood samples for DNA testing. Patterns directly related to the victim obviously locate the victim, but blood spatters found at a distance or out of context with those from the victim should be tested to verify identity. When one is sampling for DNA in a violent scene, it is impossible to test every spot. Identifying patterns and spatters that can be shown to be part of a whole makes sampling easier and more effective. If victims do not die, their movement can be established by locating two or more impact spatter patterns.

6. When no body is present, what type of event (shooting, fistfight, blunt force, accident) is suggested? Impact spatter patterns suggest violence more than castoff patterns. Finding them at a

III. INTERPRETATION

bloody scene suggests assault where a victim was injured. The amount of spatters, amount of blood loss, and sequence of patterns can provide information that a crime might have occurred. Constructing an area of convergence for the impact pattern can suggest firearms or blunt force attack. Depending on the missile size, the entrance could approximate a near point, although not exact, whereas large, odd-shaped areas of convergence suggest blunt force attack with a broad weapon. This evidence may help connect a body found elsewhere with a specific scene.

II. Castoffs

All castoff patterns provide classifications predominantly based on the directions of travel of the individual stains comprising the pattern group. This also helps differentiate castoffs from arterial damage patterns. Both categories predominantly involve medium-sized blood spatters with lesser quantities of mist, small and large, associated with impact events. Exceptions occur, so size alone cannot be definitive. Casework has shown a predominance of arterial spurt patterns mistaken as castoff actions; therefore, locating as many points to differentiation as possible is advisable before concluding a pattern is indeed castoff.

A. Drip Castoffs

When a blood source becomes available yet there is not enough blood to create a recognizable impact spatter pattern, drips from an injury may be found on a horizontal surface under the location of the event. Several investigative leads interpretations are possible.

7. Was the victim moved or moving after injury caused blood to flow? Drips are usually large in size, with irregular edges showing direction of travel (which may be abbreviated as DT for convenience). If the edges of some of the stains do not show irregularity, movement is probably slow. The shapes of spatters do not necessarily show speed of movement, however. Large blood drops from a victim or a bloodied object being carried slowly can be affected by the surface characteristics to an extent that direction of travel is not reliable.

It is especially noteworthy to determine direction of travel relative to doors. If drips lead to a door, a victim may have been attempting to flee, whereas drips from a door into a room may indicate the assault started at the doorway with the victim fleeing back into the room.

If a beating does not include enough blood for impact spatters at the beginning of the assault, drip castoffs may still leave a few drops on a horizontal surface under the location of the first few blows from the weapon.

8. Did the assailant have sufficient injury to drip blood (possible DNA sampling)? More than one separated line of drip spatters with only one body present should be evaluated as either a missing victim or that the assailant was also injured. Additional trails should be tested separately for DNA. This is especially true if one trail remains within the scene, whereas additional trails lead out of the area.

If two victims are involved, there may be drip trails between the bodies, suggesting one assailant dealing with two victims. Samples of the trails require DNA testing to rule out injury to the assailant or one assailant carrying a bloody object between the two bodies. Either identification to blood source may indicate one assailant working between victims. If there is no trail between victims, the evidence suggests more than one assailant dealing with the victims separately. If changes to blood drips between bodies show time lapse, that can also mean a second victim arrived after the assault on the first victim. This evidence indicates which was the intended victim and which might have been an accidental witness.

9. Was the trail from a bleeding victim, suspect, or a carried bloody object? When a victim has been carried to another location either within or outside the original crime scene, drip castoffs may be seen as two overlapping trails. One might have uniform-sized and linear spatters leading in the direction of travel, and the second trail may be broader, with the direction of travel at a right angle to the straight path. If the body is carried, there may be a sideways swing to movement, with drips flicked side to side across the linear path.

Spatters in a drip castoff pattern can suggest whether the drip trail is from a bleeding person or a carried bloody object. In addition to determining whether a victim was bleeding while moving, one also needs to determine whether the assailant was also injured or just carrying something dripping blood. Note the directions of travel and the frequency of drips. A drip trail that starts with many drips but decreases in frequency as the pattern progresses suggests that something bloody was being carried; i.e., as blood drips are deposited, there is less blood available to drip. By contrast, an injury will continually supply more blood, and the frequency will either remain relatively steady or may even increase in the direction of travel.

Interpretation may be based on three factors: (1) the spacing of the spatters; (2) uniformity in (or lack of) size and shape; and (3) presence of, or lack of, distortion in the pattern, such as footprints and/or changes in direction of travel, etc. for the spatters in the trail. Equal size and shape over the range of the drips suggest uniform bleeding from a source of blood. Changes in size and shape may indicate struggle, especially if moving transfers are also seen with the drips.

10. Was the bleeding person walking or running? Although some training workshops suggest the shapes of the drips determine the speed of travel for someone bleeding or carrying something bloody, the spacing between spatters is more reliable. Surface texture and movement while walking can influence the shapes of recorded drips. Spacing over the range of drips can show changes in gait as well as relative speed. Scattered drips along the path may indicate struggle, whereas wide spacing with smaller stains in between may show a victim running with body jostle. If no body was found with the scene, the spacing of spatters with size and shape and any additional characteristics may help identify what happened at the scene.

11. Did the person carrying the victim struggle with the heavy weight? Scattering of drips and a greater variety of drop size suggest struggle or that a heavy weight was being moved. Multiple drips hitting a surface together may be found within a random group of drips. Whether the person carrying the victim was struggling with a weight (such as a victim's body) may be suggested by examining small, scattered spatters associated with the main trail. The body will have some movement as a blood source is walking or running. Some drops will not be in line. If the assailant is walking while carrying something heavy, the scattered small drops will occur and leave stains sporadically, rather than consistently in a linear arrangement. Swaying while carrying a bleeding object may dislodge blood drops flicked at right angles to the main trail of castoff spatters.

B. Swing Castoffs

Swing castoffs are very dynamic events and should be viewed as such. Two-dimensional considerations ignore facts necessary for interpretation of the pattern. Workshop experiments are designed to show bloodstain patterns. Blunt force assaults are performed to create bodily injury.

The different student viewpoints affect the way blood drops are distributed. Unfortunately, statements and interpretations of evidence are often derived from results obtained from workshop experiments. Noting the directions of travel, size of spatters, and frequency of spatters can show which direction the weapon was moving in respect to the victim. Because the weapon is moving and the swings start away from the assailant's actual position, stating that the swings identify where an assailant stood is not necessarily fact. It is better to interpret how the assailant used the weapon. This latter approach is applied based on the size and shape of the impact spatter area of convergence to indicate the nature of the weapon itself. Castoffs add to investigative leads by including the following information:

12. How many blunt force swings with the weapon were delivered? The number of blunt force blows involved in an assault is commonly determined from the number of linear or broad linear patterns identified. Two cautions exist with this interpretation. (1) Many more than one blow are usually delivered before the weapon is sufficiently covered with blood to provide distributed drops that identify a castoff pattern. (2) Castoffs must be differentiated from arterial damage patterns before interpretation is attempted. Therefore, if analyzing a suspected castoff series, also check identification and possible need for interpretation of arterial damage patterns. Ask the autopsy physician if any breach of an artery was found, including pinhole tears that could indicate a breach by way of an aneurysm.

The direction of travel is essential with swing castoffs. Note whether there are tracks leading in opposite directions. These are combinations of forward and backward swings. There may be larger and more numerous stains leading away from the victim because the weapon will pick up blood. However, swings toward the victim will be more elliptical because the swings are more forceful and can actually distribute more blood drops. A lot depends on the weapon used, which is investigative leads information. Interpretation of swing castoffs helps position the victim with respect to the swings of a bloody weapon. If only one track is found, the pattern is either arterial damage or swing castoff with a weapon that does not hold blood well so that blood is cast off only with the extra force of the forward swing.

13. Where approximately did the assailant stand during the assault? Determining where an assailant stood during an assault depends on how the assailant used a weapon. Using the information possible from castoffs to determine how someone would use a weapon against a victim is more important than stating where the assailant stood. Bloodstain pattern workshops often create confusion with castoff interpretation because they offer exercises that are predominantly conducted with overhand blows to a blood source. The objective is to create spatter patterns on the ceiling of an enclosed area to notice where the spatters are recorded. In homicides, the goal is to beat a victim, creating bodily injury. The power behind the overhead swings is different. With workshop experiments, emphasis is on the back swing away from the blood source. When the swing reverses, the weapon snaps and is returned to the blood source just to pick up more blood, i.e., with less force. In actual beatings, the weapon is drawn back with less force, and may completely lack the snap, with returns to the victim with the greater force in order to deliver a damaging blow. Because there is more force toward the victim, more blood may be cast off, and the snap occurs at the victim. When one is determining location, it is acceptable to position the assailant within the castoff trail but not necessarily at either end.

14. Was the assailant using his or her right hand, left hand, or both hands? A better interpretation from overhand swing castoffs is to determine which hand the assailant was using during the assault—right hand, left hand—or whether he or she was behaving ambidextrously. Overhand swings tend to arc. If the arc swings to the right, a right-handed swing is indicated. If the arc swings to the left, a left-handed swing is indicated. No arc at all is very rare but may be from backhanded delivery or two-handed swings.

If castoffs are recorded on vertical surfaces, handedness of the assailant should be reliable because the assailant is positioned in the direction he or she was facing when swinging the weapon. Care must be given to note those scenes where swings are recorded on both the right and left sides of the victim. These blows may be from more than one assailant, from someone swinging the weapon in an ambidextrous manner, or from separate attacks. Older assailants may have been forced to use their right hand when young and thus during action may shift between left and right hand. This may also be true of younger people today because most items are manufactured for right-handedness. Left-handed people are thus more likely to adapt to right-handedness out of necessity. There are additionally many situations in which injury or limited function to the dominant hand makes use difficult. If handedness is indicated in a swing castoff pattern, more investigation is required before drawing conclusions.

15. How were the swings performed: overhand, horizontal, or backhand? The same castoff patterns that help determine handedness also help determine how a weapon was used. In case-work, this author has encountered situations in which CSIs assumed a weapon was used in a manner consistent with their favorite suspect. One case involved a suspect who was a carpenter, so the assumption was that the weapon was a hammer, but to match castoffs, the hammer had to be used like a ball bat. This reasoning is unfortunate because, after the investigation started, the bloodstain pattern evidence was ignored in favor of experience, not necessarily investigative experience. In another case, the prime suspect was a tennis player, but the CSI was a baseball fan. In a reconstruction, the swing castoffs were placed as ball bat swings although the crime was more likely performed with shorter and forceful backhand swings. Because the arm is brought back in a shorter arc for a backhand swing, the swing castoffs start higher and are shorter than for a bat swing.

Confusion may result if the assailant uses a backhanded approach. This can be suggested if the swings are shortened. There is less freedom of swing with a backhand blow than with a complete swing on the same side as the hand holding the weapon. In backhanded blows, there also may be an upswing at the beginning of the swing, farthest away from the victim.

A final caution is that right-handed individuals may use their left hand and vice versa. Statements should not indicate the assailant's handedness but rather that the assault was predominantly or wholly delivered as a such-handed assault. Left-handed individuals may use both hands, shifting the weapon back and forth during a beating. This behavior is rarely seen with right-handed individuals. Perhaps age comes into play because older left-handed people may have been forced to use their right hand when raised. Younger lefties have been more accepted with their natural instincts.

16. What kind of weapon was used in the assault? The width of a swing castoff pattern will indicate the type of weapon involved. Broad weapons such as boards, ball bats, and wood logs will show broad castoff bloodstain patterns. Narrow weapons such as tire irons, golf clubs, crowbars, and fireplace pokers will show narrow castoff patterns. Objects such as lamps, ceramics dishes, vases, and bottles may involve swings of such low force that they do not produce identifiable castoff patterns. It is essential that castoffs be recognized and differentiated from arterial damage patterns for the investigative leads information possible.

III. INTERPRETATION

C. Cessation Castoffs

The term *cessation castoff* is a relatively new term used to identify those bloodstain patterns resulting from the abrupt termination of a swing with a bloodied object. The event identifies the abrupt cessation of motion. Theoretically, blood drops are dislodged and continue in the same general direction as the weapon was moving before motion ceased. In actual practice, there may be some random vibration at the moment motion stops, which will scatter drops rather than permit steady forward travel in the same direction. Information may be important relative to cessation because these scatter drops originate from swings with a weapon delivered to a victim.

17. Was the victim defensive or incapacitated? Perhaps the most important interpretation of cessation castoffs is when the pattern occurs from self-defense gestures (or lack thereof) by the victim. The weapon being used in a beating stops when it contacts a raised arm or other blocking object. Recognizing the pattern before attending an autopsy provides an opportunity to verify the self-defense gestures. Ask the pathologist if there are bruises and/or abrasions on the victim's arms, legs, and/or body that would be consistent with the cessation pattern seen at the scene.

18. Were there one or more assailants involved in a beating? When one victim was assaulted from two directions, or two or more victims were assaulted in different areas, more than one assailant should be considered.

Cessation castoffs are blocked blows from a weapon; therefore, the pattern can show how a weapon was being used against a victim in self-defense. Confirmation of the bloodstain pattern should be found on the victim's body at autopsy.

19. Does the scene appear staged to confuse the manner of death? Before cessation castoffs are distributed, the weapon in a beating must abruptly stop motion. This is often an impact to the victim's person, or object in the vicinity of the victim, during a beating. Cessation castoff blood drops, in contrast to impact spatter drops, usually occur from perpendicular contact with the recording surface. The whole picture should include swing castoffs, bruises, or scrapes on the victim's person. If there are swing castoffs terminating but no cessation castoffs, that pattern suggests the swing was made without making contact with the victim, i.e., possible staging of a beating.

The whole picture of swing and cessation castoffs may indicate that the victim moved or was moved after sustaining injury. A question that provides investigative information is whether a drip trail indicates a bleeding individual or someone carrying something bloody away after the swing and cessation castoffs.

III. Arterial Damage

Arterial injury, although it possibly projects copious amounts of blood, is insignificant regarding the information about the assailant and/or an assault. Patterns identified as occurring after one determines the manner of the arterial breach are all about the movements of the victim alone and not directly associated with the assailant. The most investigative importance is that arterial damage bloodstain patterns be recognized rather than confused with other pattern categories, especially castoffs. Castoffs are linked to the crime and the behavior of the assailant, whereas arterial damage occurs after the crime and is linked to the movement and behavior of the victim. The assailant may have merely observed the victim bleeding or may even have fled the scene while the true cause of death, blood loss, was occurring.

The initial breach can be estimated, but it usually more closely resembles either impact or respiratory-distributed bloodstain patterns to the extent that care must be taken in interpretation. The size of spatters from initial breach of a ruptured artery may be as small as mist, which may encourage erroneous classification as gunshot. This is one of the reasons size alone cannot define the type of dynamic act which distributed the blood drops that became spatter. The point where an assault opened an artery, however, can be the point in time when an aggravated assault changed to homicide. This is essential information for charging a suspect. Finding valuable investigative leads information from arterial injury is possible. Examples of the use of the various patterns from arterial injury include those described next.

A. Arterial Breach

If the beginning of arterial exposure can be suggested by identification of any combination of gush, spurt, or suggested breach, sequencing an assault with arterial damage may proceed from those identifications. It may be possible to identify the location where assault turned into homicide. Certain areas of the body involve an artery located against bone, particularly the head. Blunt force trauma to these areas weakens the artery so that a bulb is formed in the cell wall. Pressure from the artery pushes out a balloon in the arterial wall. Subsequent blows tear the skin and pop the balloon. Although head injury may lead to death if not properly treated, breaching the artery makes death more likely. This manner of death may qualify as accidental during an assault rather than homicide, which would justify charging a person in a fistfight with manslaughter without the intent necessary for first degree.

20. If blood loss is the cause of death, when did an assault change to homicide? Because arterial injury is in and of itself life threatening, identifying and correctly interpreting how the artery was distributing blood drops can be useful in determining the manner of death. The essential information here is to recognize the nature and area of injury to the victim. Arteries are protected by two things: their location behind bone and muscle mass and being contained in thick-muscled vessels. Arterial damage patterns can be explained with scientific principles even if the investigator does not have medical knowledge. These patterns provide essential investigative leads as soon as they are recognized, i.e., saving time waiting for an autopsy. Further, arterial damage bloodstain patterns are the result of a specific scientific process that helps justify the scientific validity of bloodstain pattern analysis. It has been stated that bloodstain pattern analysis deals solely with blood outside the body, but this is not necessarily true with arterial damage patterns. These patterns are unique because of the way blood leaves the blood source to create bloodstain patterns. Understanding this is within the expertise of the bloodstain pattern analyst and can be enhanced with one of two qualifying characteristics: (1) a background in a clinical lab or medical science and/or (2) groundwork for the analysis previously established with a pathologist. These additions to the experts background qualifications should be recognized before evidence is presented at trial.

Because information from a pathologist should be included at trial whether or not the primary expert has a medical background, methods for dealing with arterial damage identification in trial testimony are dealt with further in Section IV, "Application."

21. Where is the most likely point that the artery was breached? Arterial breach is identified by observing gush and spurting and then backtracking to the point *occurring near* the first of the recognizable patterns. A convergence and/or direct hit group of spatters at what appears to be the beginning of a group of spurts may represent the actual point where arterial injury occurred.

B. Arterial Gush

The terms *arterial gush* and *spurt* are often used interchangeably because of lack of understanding and training in recognizing arterial injury. A worse approach is to wait for the autopsy to determine if the pathologist identifies arterial damage before assuming arterial patterns are present. In this text, arterial damage patterns are suggested from bloodstain pattern analysis before autopsy. Confirmation is requested during autopsy or, if not found in the report, brought out in trial during the autopsy physician's testimony. This approach prevents loss of essential information from identification of arterial bloodstain patterns. To date, pathologists are not required to list arterial injury unless it is the direct cause of death. This occurs when the cause or manner of death is exsanguination from direct injury, i.e., blood loss. If blood loss is secondary from gunshot to a temple, or exterior carotid artery via aneurysm, no mention may be made of the source of arterial blood distribution. It is essential that such information be included with the identification of arterial bloodstain patterns.

22. How can one justify bloodstain pattern analysis as science based? Arterial gush is explained as a recognizable bloodstain pattern because of the science behind blood distribution from the specific type of blood vessel. To limit explanation to blood outside the body assumes blood inside the body exits the same way, no matter which blood vessels are involved. This is not true and thus a limitation that does not follow scientific application. High blood pressure results in destabilization of flow so that blood exiting the arteries will behave as a Newtonian fluid rather than normal flow as non-Newtonian. The shift in flow, seen as a central flow with destabilized dots (satellite spatters) around the center column, identifies not only a specific bloodstain pattern but also a pattern possible from a specific injury. This is justified by recognition of non-Newtonian shift to Newtonian distribution. Because such scientific facts regarding bloodstain pattern analysis were not known prior to the 1950s, assumptions in explanations originating from science of the 1940s or earlier are not sufficiently updated to justify scientific application.

23. Can one determine whether arterial injury occurred before the autopsy is available? As previously stated, the usual procedure must begin with recognition of arterial bloodstain patterns at the crime scene before autopsy. This procedure provides information to be verified at autopsy. A clue to arterial damage includes copious quantities of bright red blood in large ovals that form trails and flows that may run down vertical surfaces. Arterial gush is the result of an artery held in one location, which will resemble a column of drops overlapping in one spot. Castoffs move across a surface, thus showing chains of drops/spatters as the weapon moves, whereas the arterial gush shows the chains hitting in the same spot as blood is projected out of the injured artery.

24. Can one provide information regarding manner of death before autopsy? No, such testimony is reserved for autopsy physicians or in some places an elected coroner. However, advanced notice is good for investigation and provides a basis for questions from investigators while viewing the autopsy. Some pathologists take bloodstain pattern workshops that will enhance the team approach to investigation of violent crime.

Explaining arterial injury and how blood from a breached artery distributes drops provides scientific justification for the application of bloodstain pattern analysis as a true scientific discipline. The fact that blood behaves according to non-Newtonian flow rather than Newtonian, like water, comes from many fields of science, not specifically medicine. As shown in the section on identification, this behavior has a well-defined scientific foundation. A caution, however, must be stated with regard to who is qualified to describe the science behind the formation of arterial damage bloodstain patterns. Anyone may learn to recognize the patterns, but testimony from experts regarding the identity of the artery requires that a foundation be laid with the autopsy physician, either in advance or on cross-examination at trial. After the artery is identified, explanations regarding the identity of the bloodstain patterns will be up to the discretion of the court.

Such explanations need not, and should not, invalidate the identification of arterial damage bloodstain patterns.

C. Arterial Spurt

Although an artery may project blood in a column that separates into rows of drops, it may remain stationary or move in any direction. This means that with arterial spurt patterns, there are two directions of travel to include in an interpretation: the direction the column is projecting and the direction the victim who has a breached artery is moving. Because these are independent of each other and may show distinctive differences in pattern alignments, and thus shapes, victim movement may provide answers to investigative questions.

25. Which direction did the victim move after arterial injury? There is an observed phenomenon that occurs when a victim with an arterial injury moves while an artery is spurting blood. This can indicate which direction the victim moved in relation to the direction the artery was projecting a blood stream. First, as mentioned above, be aware that there are two directions of travel to interpret: (1) the direction blood is being projected out of an arterial breach and (2) the direction the victim is moving while the artery is projecting blood. The combination of these two actions appears to influence the shapes of the recorded spatters. If the victim and artery both have the same direction of travel, spatters will be oval or egg-shaped. If the victim is moving in the opposite direction to the artery projection, spatters will more likely be teardrop-shaped. The size of the drops determines how much influence gravity will have on the individual blood drops. Because arterial blood is projected as a stream that separates into drops, due to the elasticity of blood after leaving the blood vessel, it is possible to have spatters made up of more than a single drop hitting together. This may result in extremely large stains, which have given rise to the identity based on spatter size. Arterial patterns may have anything from mist-sized spots to stains several times the size seen from impact or swing castoffs.

The unusually large spatters will have flows toward gravity after being recorded on a vertical surface. This results from too much blood in a single spatter or combination of spatters, which, in turn, create excess that cannot remain within the primary recorded stain. The excess flows toward gravity. Because death may not be instantaneous, arterial damage patterns may show the victim's movement after arterial breach.

Arterial damage results in categories of patterns, each with its own information. The first observation may help indicate homicide, suicide, or accidental death. Establishing which artery was breached and possibly how the injury occurred can help sequence the different arterial-distributed patterns. Whether this involves a rapid major loss of blood may provide information regarding homicide, suicide, or accidental injury. Too often prosecutors assume that arterial damage requires knifing or cutting when the mechanism is as described in Section II, via blunt force trauma to the arterial cell wall, followed by a second blow that causes rupture. The injury may be as small as a pinhole tear. Routine overviews of arterial involvement during autopsy may not show the pinhole, and/or the pathologist may omit listing the injury if it is perceived as not involving the cause of death. This is why such patterns must be recognized at the scene so that the autopsy physician can identify, confirm, and verify the artery for his or her report.

An excellent example of how this evidence may determine whether the death was homicide or accidental was found in the bloodstain pattern shown in Chapter 5, Figure 5.9 and discussed further in Chapter 9. The first question is related to what dynamic event was involved. Impact is eliminated because the pattern is linear or rectangular with spatters in line. Only one blood drop can originate from one point in an impact. Inline beading requires a dynamic event that distributes blood drops in chains directly from the injury or from the same blood source (object) over the range of movement.

III. INTERPRETATION

This author defines arterial gush as when the artery stays in one position while distributing blood from a column. Because of the viscosity and non-Newtonian behavior of arterial blood, it is projected as a stream that separates after it leaves the blood vessel. The size of the injury and the pressure in the vessel when injury occurs determine the size of the drops that form from the stream. For gunshot and knifings, the blood drops may be so large that huge ovals are recorded; they may contain so much blood that not all of it can be contained in a single spatter. These drops have overflow running from the bloodstain toward gravity. The overflow is not a direction of travel.

Castoffs and arterial spurts both may distribute a column of blood that separates into drops in flight or leaves stains in rows on a surface. If the pattern is castoff, it would require many swings, with little or no changes of the swing angle, to produce the lines of parallel spatters seen in arterial spurts. If they are castoffs from a broad weapon, they might achieve the parallel rows, but they would show variation of the spatter sizes. The rows of same-shaped and same-size spatters in line, parallel with each other and arranged as parallel rows, should be identified as arterial spurting.

Castoffs from very bloody objects, material, or hair may have large amounts of blood that will run. Another clue that helps differentiate castoffs from arterial gush is the bright red color of arterial blood. Be aware that victims of carbon monoxide poisoning may have bright red blood from veins in addition to arteries. If a crime scene is observed over days, the red of arterial blood should darken because red blood cells respire and lose the oxygen being carried, whereas blood with carbon monoxide will remain the same bright red because red cells cannot release it.

Autopsies are not always completed at the time a scene is being processed. Thus, reports may not be available in time for the initial investigation. Also, it is not yet universally accepted among physicians conducting autopsies to mention arterial injury. Being able to identify bloodstain patterns makes that information available before autopsy results are available, and alerts any law enforcement officer attending autopsy to ask for the identity of the most likely artery involved.

Most bloodstain patterns may be identified and applied to investigative leads without concern for which blood vessels were involved. This is not true of arterial damage. Because some courts insist on separating medical testimony from testimony regarding bloodstain patterns, it is essential that arterial blood vessel injury be confirmed with the autopsy pathologist.

26. If arterial injury occurred, can it be verified as to which artery was injured before autopsy? We now consider where the blood source is located and possible types of injury exposing it. Consider whether the victim suffered a blunt force injury to the eyebrow area. Further, if the body is found to have bled out, lacking blood volume, an arterial injury is strongly suggested. Next, consider whether the victim was a drug and/or alcohol abuser; in that case, bleeding may have occurred over a long period of time, and thus need not be arterial. With the latter situation, there could be considerable movement with drip castoffs and dried bloodstains from separated bleeding. On the other hand, if this state of health occurs with arterial breach injury, blood loss could occur rapidly without much movement of the victim. Liver damage from drug and alcohol abuse causes a decrease in production of those biochemicals which act to provide blood clotting and blood vessel constriction. Injury may lead to accidental death following an aggravated assault without intention to murder or following accidental injury while under the influence.

D. Arterial Rain

Depending on which artery is injured, the pressure behind the blood stream may cause blood to exit as a column reaching several inches to several feet. Over the range of the projected column, gravitational pull will be exerted on the blood drops formed. If the column is directed upward, the fallout will resemble a fountain. When drops from the arterial projection reach a recording surface, they will provide answers to some investigative leads questions.

27. Was there contact between the assailant and victim after arterial breach? Part of the reason that it is essential to identify arterial damage and determine with the pathologist which artery was involved is that arterial injury close to the ground or floor may be mistaken for drip or cessation castoffs. If the pattern is arterial rain, the distribution resulted from a fountain-like vertical projection from the artery. If the arterial rain bloodstains lack smearing and transfer of foot/shoeprints, it suggests that no one was standing near the victim during arterial distribution. Thus, the assailant could be absent at this time. Cessation and drip castoffs, on the other hand, would suggest the assault continued after arterial breach. Smearing of stains shows an assailant or another person was still present. Care must be taken, however, to rule out attempts at rescue.

28. After it is established that an artery was breached, are there areas on the victim's clothing that should have received blood from an arterial fountain? A victim lying on the ground or floor may have an arterial fountain spewing blood upward. The fallout will be arterial rain. If such a situation occurred, there should be spatters on the victim's clothing consistent with the fallout from the fountain. In the absence of rain spatters on the clothing with arterial rain on the floor around the victim, one could conclude that the victim remained standing until his or her heart stopped and then fell on top of the arterial rain fallout.

29. Do folds in the victim's clothing contradict the arrangement of the body at the moment of arterial spurting? This is the reverse of question 28. If blockages on the victim's clothing are exposed, or spatters within folds of clothing are hidden at the moment of arterial spurting, this suggests rearranging the body after the victim no longer had an artery spurting, i.e., possible staging.

IV. Transfer Patterns

All transfer patterns provide investigative leads information as well as essential trial testimony, yet they are often ignored in favor of spatter patterns. In forensic parlance, *spatters* are class characteristics and, as shown in Section II, may involve similarities between major categories. Transfer patterns are considered individualizing, and thus unique for a specific event at a crime scene. Transfers as they relate to bloodstain patterns differ from transfers in the division of forensic science known as *trace evidence* by the addition of a method through which the transfer is achieved. In trace evidence, this transfer is defined as a contact between two surfaces as assumed with the identity of what was transferred favored. In bloodstain pattern evidence, two types of transfer may not involve contact between surfaces: blockage and absence. In addition, in the patterns that do involve contact, two different actions may be involved: simple direct and moving. In the moving transfer category, two ways that the bloodstain patterns may occur are recognized: swipe and wipe. This suggests five different pattern types that may provide investigative leads in excess of the simple statement regarding "transfer" simple direct, moving Wipe, moving Swipe, texture of contact material smooth or rough.

A. Blockage

Most textbooks on bloodstain pattern evidence concentrate on a memorized terminology that was compiled in the 1940s to 1950. This terminology served well until modern science was incorporated to extend the applications for bloodstain pattern evidence. One term that may be out of date, although it is commonly used, is *void*. In modern semantics, *void* means "to empty out," such as used in clinics to instruct patients to "void a urine specimen," i.e., empty out the bladder and collect a sample of urine for analysis. With bloodstain pattern evidence, *void* means an area devoid of blood. Basically, this pattern may happen in two ways that can provide investigative leads information: (1) the blank space was blocked by some object so that blood didn't reach it or (2) blood distribution was at an angle so that drops did not reach the surface. In this latter situation, blood is absent although not blocked. The terms *blockage* and *absence* permit differentiation of why blood didn't reach a surface as might be expected with the dynamics of the crime. This can also apply to clothing and the assailant. Folds in a shirt or presence of an over layer can explain why blood was blocked from being recorded on the assailant, victim, or bystander during an assault.

30. Can the location of an impact origin be confirmed? String reconstruction is often used to locate origins of impacts. Unfortunately, there are problems with interpretation of the string and computer origin locations. Confirmations are both desirable and necessary to prevent misinterpretations. Blockage patterns help determine angles between an impact origin and the recording surface on furniture, doors, and persons standing near the victim. Absence patterns in room corners, angles between the impact and surface, and the nature of impact distribution can confirm the determination of origin. These should coincide with the origin located by computer and/or string-reconstructed locations. If not, then more than one impact is suggested, or the bloodstains used for the string reconstruction were not from an impact. Possible errors may exist and must be determined before conclusions are based on the reconstructed origin.

31. Were any objects moved or removed from the scene? If so, can any investigative information be gleaned from the objects suggested by the blockage? When a spatter pattern exists on two or more sides of a spatter-free area, the whole area lacking blood spatters should be examined. If possible, a clear plastic sleeve (those used to protect sheets of paper can work) should be laid over the spatter-free area and the outline drawn. The size and shape may suggest something not found or found elsewhere in the scene.

32. Where was the assailant at the moment of blood drop distribution? The same consideration used to identify objects removed from the scene applies to outlines of the assailant. Outlines to shoes, especially, locate an assailant, second assailant, or bystander attempting to intervene in the assault. One should also consider that not finding any blockage could indicate no assailant was present; i.e., injuries were accidental or self-inflicted.

33. Where was the victim during the blood drop distribution? Spatters should be blocked beneath and around the victim's body and the assailant if the assault was carried out in place. If cessation castoffs occurred from self-defense gestures, blockage outlines should illustrate where the victim was located within the impact blow, thus blocking motion. Self-defense to blows from a beating may show the outline of an arm in a blockage pattern. One should take care not to equate the measurement of the blockage with the object doing the blockage. Blood drops distributed at the surface may be deflected by the object to provide a shadow within the measured area of blockage. Claims of self-defense but lack of evidence indicating blockage should be considered a possible contradiction. There should also be evidence of the assailant standing near the victim during assault.

34. Were bystanders or more than one assailant present? Where a person stood during an assault is often presented as blocked outlines, at least partially suggesting shoes, and sometimes silhouettes of legs or heads. Where a person stood can be an indication of whether that person was a bystander or was involved in the assault. Again, be aware of shadow blockage patterns. At the edge of a blockage, there are fewer spatters than farther outside the blocked image. Dr. Kirk presented presence of this type of pattern in the Sam Sheppard case, where Dr. Kirk identified a blockage from the assailant over Marilyn Sheppard.

III. INTERPRETATION

B. Absence Patterns

Although the absence of bloodstains in most cases can be considered of no significance, in this scenario there are a few questions that can be answered. It is essential that these questions and the use of absence patterns be understood when first approaching a crime scene. Movement and investigation can confuse what was and what was not changed in the scene during the investigation. If doors are opened or closed, it is essential that the wall behind the door and the door jamb be examined.

35. Can spatial positions at the time of the assault be reconstructed? Combining patterns that answer questions 28 though 34 can help reposition people, objects, and doorways for reconstruction of the crime scene. This type of reconstruction is also advocated in other books on bloodstain pattern evidence. What is advocated here, however, is that the bloodstain pattern analysis begins the reconstruction, not ends it. The common approach is to reconstruct the scene, spatter blood by hitting a bloody sponge or firing a gunshot into a bullet trap, and then announce that the reconstruction matched the crime scene, thus proving the scenario established without identification of the different patterns overlapping. Here, it is suggested that one first identify the pattern categories present and use them to reconstruct the scene. Construction of spatter patterns can never be exactly like the crime because it is against the law to kill someone.

36. Was the door opened or closed during the assault? When spatters are found by a door, always open the door and view behind it and inside the door jamb. If the door was open during the distribution of blood drops, the edge would provide blockage to the door jamb. If the door was partially open, the angle between the event and the area where spatters were recorded would show an absence pattern to be used to position the door at the moment of blood drop distribution. If the door was closed and there are spatters inside the door jamb, an impact is suggested at the crack between the door and door frame. Note that if spatters reached the door jamb while closed, the shape of the spatters should be very elongated because they must have hit the surface at a very narrow angle.

37. Do folds in the victim's clothes show lack or presence of bloodstains out of context to the position of the body? Again, one should examine the body before it is moved or removed from the scene. Too often the body is ignored or simply photographed and not given attention until after transport in a body bag. Bodies provide the best probative (proof in trial) evidence because they can be portrayed as the victim reaching out from the grave pointing at his or her killer. Folds in clothes show positions of bodies, but the information is lost as soon as those bodies are moved, especially if blood is still leaking and in contact with the body bag. Was the victim standing and fell, or fell and then was assaulted? Did the victim attempt to move, crawl, or roll over after assault? Many permutations of questions may be answered through observations of blood on the victim as found before the body is moved and placed in a body bag for transfer to the morgue.

C. Simple Direct Transfers

The direct transfer of a print in blood has been recognized since the beginning of crime scene investigation. Sadly, such evidence is sometimes ignored in favor of linking spatters to the perceived solutions of what happens in cases of violent assault. Ignoring any bloodstain patterns that can be identified to source is a waste of valuable information.

38. Is there a fabric impression that links the scene with the victim or assailant? Direct match transfers are individualizing evidence of far more importance than any interpretation of spatters. In every crime scene that is worth analyzing, one must pay attention to the possibility of direct transfers that show clothing contact; finger, foot, or weapon transfers; body part contact; or objects at the scene or on the assailants or additional persons present in blood that can be a direct link between the victim and the crime. Spatters on surfaces around the victim may record foot- and fingerprints of the assailant but, more important, may carry those imprints onto other surfaces at the scene. These spatters identify not only those individuals present at the scene but also the sequence where evidence of their presence was transferred.

A foot/shoe contact with blood will grow lighter away from the initial contact. If the initial contact with blood is followed by more contacts, such as someone walking over a spattered area, the imprints increase to show the direction the person took walking through the area. It has been found that faint prints on the edge of volume stains (pools) may provide little transfer. This light transfer must be examined with alternative light systems and developed because often it will provide better detail of the print than a heavily stained transfer.

39. Can fingerprint impressions be identified within blood? Any impression within an existing blood spot on a surface should be photographed and examined before dusting for a print. The depth of the print is important in interpretation because blood that had initiated clot formation will hold a print better than freshly shed blood. This evidence provides not only the presence of the print but a time consideration and sequence in which the print was left. Blood on the figure itself provides a good print, but the depth is less of an issue.

As with shoeprints in question 38, light prints that are not clearly visible to the naked eye may be developed with alternative light systems. They may show greater detail for identification than heavy prints.

40. Is a weapon match to the assault suggested? Numerous actions leave recognizable prints on materials at the scene and on the body and clothing of the victim. As with castoffs and arterial bloodstains, they may be ignored in favor of concentrating on impact spatters alone. In beatings with weapons, often at least part of the weapon is imprinted in blood on the clothing of a victim. If patterns are seen on clothing, they should be brought to the attention of the pathologist at autopsy to identify specific injury possible from the suggested weapon. Weapons laid on fabric upholstered furniture or beds may leave identifiable imprints, especially if staging follows assault.

As with questions 38 and 39, light prints may provide good identification of what was transferred. It is essential that they be considered before autopsy so that such transfers to clothing and the link to injuries can be examined during autopsy.

41. Was an item moved or removed from the scene? Transfer patterns around a violent crime area may show that moveable objects fell, rolled, or were used as weapons and then laid down. The direct transfers may be used to sequence the events of the crime. In addition, how a weapon was used may be determined from a series of direct transfers.

D. Moving Transfers (Swipe or Wipe?)

Streaks and drag marks in blood have long been recognized as someone having moved objects around the scene, but the full interpretation is seldom found in review of casework. How the streaks and drags occurred provides investigative leads information. Section II showed how to differentiate between swipe and wipe, although even experienced analysts may find interpretation tedious. The simplest approach is to first call the patterns "moving transfers" and later decide whether they are swipe or wipe.

42. Which items or victims were dragged within or out of the crime scene? Streaks and drag marks are easily associated with a victim or object when the pattern ends with a body or object. The interpretation becomes more difficult when there is nothing present at the end or beginning of the identified pattern. DNA testing of the blood provides final identification for a victim; however, that may be available too late to provide initial investigative leads. To gain information, one needs an accurate interpretation of whether the marks are swipe or wipe. Swipe would suggest removal of the object, whereas wipe would suggest changing the scene.

43. Was the person doing the dragging dealing with a heavyweight or easy-to-move object? Drag marks indicate something too heavy to lift and carry. Drag marks that terminate within the scene without ending in a body or object suggest that a second person was available to help lift a body or object.

44. Did the assailant or another person attempt to clean up the crime scene? Moving transfers that are combinations of both swipe and wipe suggest the action was an attempt to remove stains or clean up the crime scene. The swipe leaves blood as it moves to the edge, leaving a lighter feathered edge, whereas a wipe picks up blood, shoving it toward the final edge, creating a darker liftoff area. Some blood may be removed but not all. The patterns created by a combination of swipe and wipe result in a smudge, blurring directions of travel with the rubbing back and forth. The investigative leads information from a wipe becomes a question of who would attempt to hide blood and why. A swipe usually leaves blood evidence unknown to the assailant.

45. Was the victim able to crawl after the assault? Wipe stains leading to a body can easily be interpreted as the victim attempting to crawl. Note whether impact spatters are seen along the crawl mark. Be aware that respiratory-distributed spatters may have occurred. These spatters will repeat along the path of the crawl at measured intervals. Impact spatters and/or castoffs from continued beating will be at irregular intervals and consist of large-sized spatters apparently lacking direction of travel because they are directed upward and fall by gravity. If the victim crawls over blood that has clotted or is in the process of clotting, fragments and smears with clot lumps may be seen along the path and on the victim's clothes.

V. Physiologically Altered Bloodstains (PABS)

PABS is a category of bloodstain patterns that was created to encompass changes to blood after it was shed but before an investigation was started. The main emphasis is on time and sequence for events. All PABS patterns occurr after the initial assault. The investigative leads information includes what happened after one or more violent events. Each question to be answered from interpretation depends on which change occurred to the blood. The categories of change were described in Section II.

A. *Mixing with Other Substances*

The most common substances that blood may mix with at a crime scene are water or watery fluids such as salt water, soft drinks, liquor, tears, cerebral spinal fluids, and urine. Water itself may be encountered in various ways that provide investigative leads information. Tap water; commode water; bottled drinking water; water in pet dishes, aquariums, and swimming pools; and garden watering systems serve to name some possibilities. The difference between water and watery substances may depend on the saltiness of the liquid. Salt concentrations are tolerated by red blood cells, whereas lack of salt is not. Red cells rupture and free hemoglobin pigment into the fluid. This is beneficial to investigative leads because different-appearing bloodstains are left when the red cells rupture.

46. Were there any attempts to change or alter the crime scene? Water will immediately rupture red blood cells and free pigment, which diffuses more readily than when cells remain intact. Soap, bleach, and other cleaning agents may also delete or decrease the red color. Something not often recognized when cleaning is that red hemoglobin complex may be destroyed, but the protein coat of the red cells remains attached or imbedded on the surface or in the fabric. This may confuse an investigation because the stain may test negative for blood if the test is based on detecting hemoglobin, whereas a test of the stroma (the protein coat of the red cell) may be detectable. Tests for the presence of blood may be better performed using a two-way approach: using a protein test (alternative light source methods) *and* a hemoglobin test. If protein is present but hemoglobin is negative, an absorption test for the red cell protein coat may provide some identity to the blood source that was being cleaned away. There is a serology test that identifies blood type from the stroma alone.

47. Did the assault occur before or after rainfall, dew point, or water sprinklers went off? Was the victim water-boarded? Characteristically, water and blood mix before a second event, which may show the sequence of exposure to water. After blood dries and then is subjected to water, the stain may be recognized. Free red pigment from ruptured red blood cells migrates away from the more dense, dried red cell mass at the center of the stain.

48. Was the victim vomiting and/or wetting his or her head in any way after or during the assault? Drug addicts and alcoholics, especially, may dunk their heads in a sink, bathtub, toilet, outside faucet, etc., in an effort to cool and clear their mind and vision. Bloodstains from a mixture of water and blood with pink water or lighter-colored flows through the blood can suggest an assault and the victim trying to recover with water at or near the scene.

For example, one homicide followed a fight between roommates. The injured roommate tried to apply ice to his nose and left telltale bloodstains in the kitchen sink. He was later shot near his nose. The autopsy established that he could not have been mobile after the shot; therefore, the nose bleed and exposure to the ice and water happened before the shot. Neighbors heard the fight, didn't hear anything for a lag time of half an hour, and then heard the shot.

49. Did the assailant attempt to clean himself or herself up before leaving? Blood-and-water mixed stains around sinks, showers, garden hoses, and tubs may be from an injury near the location of water or more likely the result of someone's attempts to clean up before leaving the crime scene. The occurrence with ice as mentioned in question 48 is an example of changes to the scene around water exposure.

B. Drying

Bloodstains dry beginning at the thin outer edge and move in toward the thicker center of the stain. Depending on temperature, air currents, and humidity, this process may take some time. During the drying phase, disturbing the bloodstain may move the fluid part, which is still wet. What kind of movement and how wet the stain remains when a disturbance happens provide sequence and time information for investigative leads.

50. Did the assault cover a longer period of time or was it completed in one continuous stage? Shoeprints across bloodstains that show major drying before the tracking occurred suggest either a crime of long duration; the assailant returned to the scene before the blood dried; or a bystander, rescue worker, or law enforcement officer arrived at the scene after the assault.

51. Did subsequent bystanders or first line officers contaminate the scene? With prior disturbance of the bloodstains, it is necessary to answer this question. If blood dries without any disturbance, one doesn't know if an overlapping event occurred or if the blood dried before subsequent arrivals. If blood was completely dry before someone stepped in or moved across the area, chips and fragments of dried stains may be seen. They can also show up on clothes and within the tread of shoe soles.

52. Was this a crime of long duration? It may be determined that the crime occurred and then the scene was left undisturbed for a period of time. The assailant could have left, was dealing with other matters such as another assault, or was attempting to clean up evidence. This situation may be seen with bloodstains in different degrees of drying before some sort of moving transfer spreads the stain. Multiple drying times, rather than a single period of undisturbed drying, shows continued presence at the scene or a second person of interest present before the stains dried completely. Also, if some spots were undisturbed but the centers of other spots were smeared, two events are represented. The arrangement of each determines whether the crime was of long duration and the full stains were avoided or if secondary events occurred after a time lag.

C. *Clotting*

Coagulation is a natural response for blood when trauma triggers a reaction from particles called platelets. Circulating through blood, platelets are triggered to form plugs in blood vessels that serve to prevent further blood loss. They also facilitate formation of a scab to seal and protect the injury from infection. Clotting may occur either inside blood vessels during life or outside the body after bloodshed. Strokes and heart attacks involve clots forming within blood vessels. Distinct stages to the biological process are described in Section II. First line personnel must recognize the stages; thus, they must be included in training. Investigative information will be available only if the stage of clotting is noticed as soon as possible after a crime scene is discovered.

53. Can the time span be suggested? Disturbance of clot material also prolongs clotting. To recognize when a clot has been disturbed, note blobs of solid-looking material offset from round or oval pools of lighter-colored staining. Different stages of clots before being disturbed indicate continued events. If the crime scene is found within a time span after the assault but before blood dries, testing for clots may provide part of a time line.

54. Was the scene contaminated? Moving the body when blood has been protected underneath may show secondary clots. This can provide information regarding contamination by bystanders, paramedics, or investigators. Again, the thing to look for at the scene is the solid, or three-dimensional appearance, of material with lighter material offset.

55. Can an estimate for time of death be suggested? (This information must be confirmed by the autopsy pathologist.) Clot material may be found in the body either from strokes and heart attacks or as part of lividity. Recording the stage of blood coagulation as soon as the scene is discovered contributes to estimates of time of bloodshed. Bloodshed can lead to specific injuries and estimations of how long a victim could live after such an injury. This information provides questions to ask the autopsy physician.

56. Is there impression evidence to be used? Prints and transfers may be seen and photographed with clot material that is in the firmed but not retracted stage. There is much debate surrounding times for stages of coagulation. Recorded times from workshops are influenced by disturbing the clot during testing, whereas clinical data may not apply to crime scene evidence. Rough estimates of times for clot initiation, completion, and clot retraction may be obtained from a local clinical lab, perhaps via the autopsy physician. These times should be considered rough estimates, not timelines that are written in stone.

III. INTERPRETATION

VI. Volume

The term *pools* is commonly used and understood. Volume is more than 10 to 20 cubic centimeters of blood. Less blood may be called a *pool,* and estimates of volume cannot be based on linear measurements on carpets or soft dirt. Depths and diffusion under carpets or into soil add significantly to the amount of bloodshed preceding.

57. When was the body moved? Blood pools are uniformly recognized by investigators even if they don't have any training in bloodstain pattern evidence. The main interpretation is usually to note that if the body is separated from a large pool, the body was moved. If a large pool is found but there is no body, it is understood that the victim left or was taken from the scene to another location. The lack of a pool of blood around and under the body when injury would suggest major bloodshed is also interpreted as the victim being assaulted elsewhere and moved to the place where found. A few words of caution here: if the injury primarily occurred internally, no quantity of bloodshed may be indicated. The latter condition may be found with internal arteries, such as the subclavian under the collar bone (usually a gunshot) or with blood filling the thoracic (chest) and abdominal (stomach) cavities (usually a knifing) instead of bleeding externally.

58. Was the assault immediately fatal or prolonged? (Confirmation from medical experts is needed.) It should be noted, however, that the amount of blood does not provide a good estimate of mortality or time of assault. The rate of bleed will determine degree of injury and a chance of fatality to consequences more than the final amount. Pools with even borders and rounded appearance suggest a slow bleed, whereas satellite spatters with spines or streaks along the edges suggest a rapid bleed, perhaps from an artery. This information should provide questions to be discussed with a pathologist.

59. Could the victim have survived blood loss with or without transfusion? (Pathologist confirmation is needed.) Females specifically can lose a large quantity of blood and survive. Estimates of blood volume are flawed because of blood's hygroscopic tendencies (ability to attract moisture) and the need to consider the addition of depth of the pool. If the linear area of a pool suggests major blood loss and that the loss was rapid, then searching in hospitals for possible admitted patients with major, rapid blood loss is essential to the investigation. Slow versus rapid loss is the key.

VII. Miscellaneous

60. Was the witness telling the truth or supplying a false statement? Here is the most important benefit to conducting a bloodstain pattern analysis in the beginning of an investigation. Too often the analysis is done after all other investigative work is applied or, worse, only done prior to trial after a scenario has been established for the crime. Witnesses lie or are mistaken even when there is no need or intention to lie. Street- and prison-wise criminals lie when they are innocent. First line investigators may form a bias from interviews and the first appearance of the crime scene. Once bias is introduced, it is difficult to move beyond and examine other scenarios. If the bloodstain patterns are identified and interpreted before interviews, it becomes immediately clear whether the witness is reliable, is lying, or shows too much knowledge of the events to not have been present.

Interpretations as to where people were standing, what their positions were, whether the door was opened or closed, where objects were around the scene, etc., may seem harmless to the interviewee but provide the investigator knowledge of the witness. All interviewees should be asked if they are right-handed or left-handed. This latter information is encountered too often in casework to ignore, yet it is sadly missing from interviews.

61. Are there items that would supply additional characteristics of an assailant? Using pathology information, one can estimate angles for injuries as a foundation for determining height and aspects of the assailant to fit angles of blockage and absence patterns. Where the assailant stood can suggest which hand was used to deliver the assault. The amount of force necessary for parts of an assault may be suggested from the impact and castoff patterns.

62. Are there any bloodstain patterns that are contrary to other patterns? This question must be answered before any scenario the investigator develops is set in stone. After analyzing and classifying as many of the bloodstain patterns as possible, the investigator must ask if there are any contradictions. Spatters where no impact event is suspected should be considered for respiratory distribution. Castoffs inconsistent with the handedness of the suspect should be noted. Each of the questions answered with bloodstain pattern evidence should be examined as to why it may be wrong as well as why it is concluded as correct. To help with this, many of the questions listed here have more than one pattern to answer the same or similar question. If a pattern is lacking, a caution is advised.

63. Is the person claiming to be a bloodstain pattern expert truly knowledgeable or merely speaking memorized terminology? Asking an expert how he or she arrived at the interpretation is very informative. If the expert is truly knowledgeable in bloodstain pattern physical evidence, initially he or she should be able to identify patterns and interpret them without bringing in other information such as witness statements, fingerprints, and firearms evidence. If preliminary analysis consists of all spots labeled as velocity impact spatters that match the weapon used in a crime—i.e., high velocity impact spatter if a firearm was involved or medium velocity impact spatter if death was by blunt force—the expertise should be questioned further. There are several questions for an expert that are best asked and answered before allowing the person or group to supply conclusions that will be used at trial in a case. Refer to Section IV.

REFERENCES

Quintana, M., Palicki, O., Lucchi, G., Ducoroy, P., Chambon, C., Salles, C., Morzel, M., 2009. Inter-individual Variability of Protein Patterns in Saliva of Healthy Adults. Journal of Proteomics 72 (5), 822–830.

Tietz, N.W., 1986. Textbook of Clinical Chemistry. W.B. Saunders Company, Philadelphia, PA, pp. 725–730.

Staging

Members of the court and science experts often lament a situation labeled "the CSI Effect" that occurs with jurors. This situation occurs when jurors believe television programs are reliable examples of crimes solved within an hour or so using DNA, bloodstain patterns, chemical tests, and futuristic instrumentation. The assumption these jurors hold is that in the absence of such evidence, there are insufficient grounds for conviction. Investigators, CSI personnel, criminalists, and attorneys are aware that TV dramas are rarely accurate and cannot portray the time lines in investigations realistically. Jurors who expect "TV CSI results" may ignore adequate circumstantial evidence presented at trial. They may find insufficient evidence for conviction or, worse for the economy, end in a hung jury. To the author, a far more dangerous situation exists and seems to be increasing in casework. Violent criminals also watch CSI-format television programs. All but the most naive, unintelligent, and/or confused criminals will be aware that they may leave behind evidence in the form of fingerprints, DNA, trace evidence, and possibly bloodstain pattern evidence. After realizing that these types of evidence are used to solve the crimes portrayed on TV, criminals may attempt to stage the scene of their own crimes to eliminate evidence. Reasons for staging may include

1. to hide the identity of the assailant or the fact that the assailant was known to the victim;
2. to make a homicide look like an accident or a suicide, especially if the homicide was, in fact, accidental; or
3. to make a suicide look like a homicide or accident for religious or insurance purposes.

Most investigative courses in bloodstain pattern evidence focus on straightforward interpretation such that what one sees is the facts to be interpreted using the simplicity of logic. In reality, if staging is done to implicate someone who was not the perpetrator, a great injustice may result. Bloodstain pattern evidence may assist in ruling out staging or confirming that staging of some degree occurred. The main observation is that staging must be considered before one develops a crime sequence scenario. The purpose of this chapter is to encourage investigators to constantly be aware of the possibility of staging and to eliminate this possibility before attempting to define a scenario for the crime.

TV portrayals of bloodstain pattern analysis are so inaccurate that staging based on such plots can usually be readily identified. Alerts to the possibility of staging exist at the beginning of an investigation when one observes the inconsistencies in the bloodstain pattern evidence. This gives investigators a heads-up near the beginning that may shorten the time necessary for the identification of the correct person or persons of interest. These preliminary observations may include, but are not limited to, the following:

1. Witness statements contradicting interpretations from bloodstain patterns.
2. Witnesses appearing to know more than is seen from the evidence, i.e., explanations volunteered which answer questions not asked.
3. Persons of interest claiming expertise in interpretation of evidence at the scene and emphasizing that skill to investigative officers. For example, one man claimed to know about body temperature in determining time of death. He was later a person of interest in the murder of a victim who had been positioned in a warm water bed.
4. Persons in numbers 2 and 3 above, with statements as in number 1.
5. Attempts by witnesses or persons of interest to focus the investigation on someone else, who may have items at the scene suggestive of involvement but out of context with other information.

The main issue is not to ignore inconsistencies, especially if a witness is emphatic that he or she be believed. Fortunately, bloodstain patterns shown on television provide so little factual application information that staging of this evidence is often obvious. It follows that the first indication of staging may be recognized by a routine analysis of bloodstain patterns early in the investigation before interviews are conducted.

A preliminary observation, which may also be included in workshops to focus investigators on eliminating staging, involves door frames. Investigators are advised to open doors and observe the door jambs to see whether impact spatters or castoff reached these hidden spaces. If castoffs are seen on a closed door, the assumption follows that the crime occurred inside an area with a closed door. If staging was done to indicate an intruder, this evidence provides a contradiction. If two residents are present, and a closed door separates them while one is assaulted, this evidence indicates an effort to conceal the assault from the other resident, contradicting statements that the resident committing the assault. Workshops can use either a mock door and frame or an actual door leading to another room or closet to reconstruct assaults with respect to doors.

When would staging occur if it was involved? The answer to that question may be obvious. The actual attempts at staging will occur after a crime. If the crime was premeditated, staging was probably planned in advance but carried out afterward. If the crime occurred after an unplanned sequence of confrontations, staging may be considered as a spur-of-the-moment cleanup. In this latter situation, the staging may be sloppy and incomplete. Because these two approaches can have different types of evidence with interpretations in the bloodstain patterns, the evidence may also assist investigators in identifying premeditation versus a crime of passion and steps in between. Regardless of criminal intent, if staging is involved, it was most likely applied after the assault was completed.

Impacts to a victim who is already down may be performed for the purpose of bloodying an object. In bloodstain pattern workshops, a bloody sponge is used to provide a blood source for a weapon used to demonstrate castoffs. In staging a crime scene, an assailant may use the victim, pools, and/or prior injury to the victim to provide blood on a weapon to fabricate castoffs. This may be done either in a different location from where stains were deposited during the crime or to fake a different handedness. If a different person of interest from the true assailant is being framed, and it is known that person is right- or left-handed, bloodstain patterns from castoffs with the opposite hand may be applied. Impacts to a victim who is dead or incapacitated may be interpreted as a vicious attack when they are, in fact, simply intended to bloody a weapon for the purpose of staging. The key to recognizing this is the association between the impacts and the castoffs.

Castoffs from a weapon being swung at random, not at a victim, may end in cessation castoffs, but no impact spatters are seen. A lack of drips, transfers, and so on is noted at the end of a swing castoff arrangement. If the assault on the victim was from blunt force trauma, it is important to note how the injury was delivered, i.e., right hand or left hand. This information is then compared to the swing castoffs to see if the pattern and injury are consistent or contradictory. It cannot be overemphasized that one must view the crime scene as three-dimensional. Too often an approach to the evidence is to view a scene as two-dimensional exhibits to be matched to two-dimensional designs from training, thus ignoring some of the evidence that would clarify the whole crime sequence.

The presence of arterial damage bloodstain patterns is unlikely to be staged. In the first place, an artery must be breached, and in the second place, it is unlikely that someone staging a crime scene would know how to fake an arterial pattern. This was an argument that was missed for lack of understanding in the O. J. Simpson trial. It was suggested that Officer Mark Fuhrman could have faked the pattern on Mr. Simpson's sock. The pattern described to fellow consultants was that of a central core of blood surrounded by secondary small dots. That was an example of Newtonian distribution from an artery with high blood pressure. When the sock was found at the scene, the autopsy was not yet been completed, and arterial injury had not been identified to Officer Fuhrman. Even if he had had knowledge that the injury was to Nicole Brown Simpson, and arterial in nature, it is unlikely that he would have known how to fabricate an arterial damage bloodstain pattern. It follows then that arterial damage patterns may be more reliable than castoff or impact patterns in interpretation of staging.

The application of bloodstain pattern evidence, seen in crime solving on television, occasionally involves "stringing." This process involves using strings to re-create the angles from impacts. TV programs have shown this technique used in applications for arterial injury, which cannot be identified and do not provide investigative information from that procedure. It is unfortunate that some actual crime lab workers feel that if they do a string reconstruction at a crime scene, they validate the science of bloodstain pattern analysis. Although the procedure involves math and trigonometry, the reconstruction of angles to an impact involves flawed logic. The alleged application for scientific validity may, in fact, show the opposite of that intended. Before one jumps to reconstruct the origin of an impact, it is essential to determine that a single impact is the source of the spatters being used to construct the origin. Even more important is to ensure that the reason time and effort are spent doing a string reconstruction is to answer questions for the investigation. It is a waste of time and funds to do one just because one feels he or she is trained how to do it and, perhaps, it will impress law enforcement officers.

Transfer patterns are excellent sources of information regarding staging because they are seldom featured in the TV crime solutions. Moving transfers show how objects are moved around a crime scene. If efforts were made to clean up, and the victim and/or assailant moved after injury, transfers may show the action. Brushing against furniture, walls, doors, and drapes may leave blood swipes, which may be missed in cleanup and staging later.

Direct transfers show sequence, or lack thereof, better than spatter evidence. If an object impression is recognized, it is essential to examine the scene for indication that the pattern was repeated as well as to seek the source of the blood for the observed print. This type of evidence has been seen in hit-and-run traffic accidents as well as staged scenes of homicides. Cloth imprints on auto bumpers may or may not include blood from victims. Note that very light prints may show detail better than heavy ones. Light prints may be missed during cleanup while heavy prints are cleaned.

PHYSIOLOGICALLY ALTERED BLOODSTAINS

Because staging is regarded as occurring after the completion of crimes, the pattern category with the best indication is probably physiologically altered bloodstains (PABS). The categories under PABS include drying of blood between events, blood coagulating before subsequent events, and blood mixing with other fluids and substances at the crime scene. Because of the importance of interpreting this type of evidence in investigative leads, each is discussed separately.

PABS: Drying as Indications of Staging

Blood begins to dry as soon as it is deposited on a recording surface or material. The event starts at the outer edge and progresses inward. If the recording surface changes direction, flows of blood will shift, and again the outer edge will begin to dry in the new position. One must always observe bodies of victims for blood flows before any moving occurs. For example, a blood flow down a cheek that abruptly changes direction and flows across the mouth indicates the body moved or was moved before the blood completely dried. One must ask whether the victim lived for a period of time after the assault and if he or she was capable of movement. Injuries can result in incapacitation although death does not occur immediately. If the bloodstain is wiped after a time period, the dried outer edge remains while the liquid center portion will smear. The transfer of the liquid portion can be used to find sequences of transfer as well as to show that staging may be involved.

Staging is one reason for flows to shift, but there are others: the victim moved to a new position before death, a paramedic or bystander tried to assist the victim and moved the body, and/or an injury could occur to a standing victim who stayed upright for a few minutes and then fell.

PABS: Coagulation as Indications of Staging

Blood begins to clot at a time interval following injury. There must be enough blood available for coagulation to occur before the bloodstain dries. After a bloodstain is dry, coagulation cannot occur. Another requirement for coagulation is that the pool of blood must not be disturbed during clotting. Agitation will delay clotting, not speed it up, as has been alleged by some attempting to explain time lines. This delay is also seen in workshop exercises where the students test the blood pool to determine when clotting occurs. The best way to illustrate the progress is to form three separate pools of freshly drawn blood. Test the first pool with wooden applicator sticks. When the pool shows some forming of clot strands, the test is moved to the second pool. A glass stirring rod is used to test the second pool. When the clot forming in the second pool begins to hold shape as the stirring rod is drawn through it, the test is moved to the third pool. The same stirring rod may be used on the third pool. Clot formation is complete when the clot moves as one lump when pushed by the rod. If the clot is then left untouched and is on a nonporous surface, the solid portion will retract (that is, shrink), and clear liquid will be expressed. This is the serum stain around the clot.

Serum lacks the cohesion of whole blood, because the red cells have been removed, and therefore will flow off the clot. Serum stains are refractile to light and may only show up as clear shiny areas in photographs of the scene. The yellow pigments sometimes seen result from the victim having liver damage, such as for an alcoholic or drug addict.

The importance of clotting in recognition of staging is that fragments of a clot may be broken off and distributed when someone attempts to change the scene. These fragments are irregular in shape and three-dimensional in nature. They are also very sticky and may adhere to some surfaces and clothing easily. Finding clot fragments away from evidence of fresh blood can indicate that changes occurred at a time period after a crime. One needs to consider whether they were from investigation, rescue, accidental, or staging actions.

PABS: Mixing as Indications of Staging

The obvious indication of staging should be physiologically altered bloodstains mixed with water. This indicates an attempt to clean up a crime scene, unless the event occurs where water from sources such as sinks, commodes, rain, sprinklers, or a swimming pool is likely to be present. Determining whether water is part of a scene becomes a CSI procedure if blood has been greatly diluted. When blood is in contact with aqueous (water-like) liquid, the red cells rupture, spilling red pigment. The pigment can be washed away so it is not visible to the unaided eye. However, the protein coat of red blood cells does not dissolve. This coat may remain on cloth after attempts to wash the blood away. Alternative tests, not dependent on hemoglobin molecules, may be applied to develop blood presence if mixing is suspected.

One interesting twist occurred in a case involving PABS-mix. An accused individual became adamant that a crime lab had falsified evidence when lab staff found a victim's blood on his trousers. His defense team contacted a bloodstain pattern analyst to determine the accuracy of interpreting the fresh bloodstains the crime lab claimed to have found. When a report was presented that there were two kinds of stains identified on the pants, one fresh and one denatured in some way, it was suggested that the pants had been exposed to water at some time after the crime. Because the suspect had not considered these two situations, he accused the crime lab of falsifying their finding of the victim's fresh blood on his clothes. Refer to Figure 9.1.

The finding of two types of bloodstains excited the suspect to the point that he insisted the expert testify to the presence at trial. Because the report was based on a few photographs, the expert requested the opportunity to view the evidence itself before agreeing to testify. When the evidence was examined, a T-shirt was found to include bloodstains that were very characteristic of the beating alleged to the victim. Still, the accused zeroed in on the two types of stains and felt this was enough to disqualify the crime lab work. The lab received a request to explain how the fresh blood could occur when the pants had been placed in a washing machine with bleach.

The explanation worked both ways, satisfying the accused that the expert was not a good choice and explaining why the expert strongly advised the client not to have the expert testify at trial. The pants had been placed in a washing machine. They were packed tight with other clothing, including the sneakers worn during the crime. Water was added and then bleach. Law enforcement investigators arrived at the scene and removed the pants from the washer before the cycle agitated. Bloodstains on the sneakers were visible due to the nature of the material. Folds in the pants protected some stains but not others, leading to the recognition of two types of stains.

III. INTERPRETATION

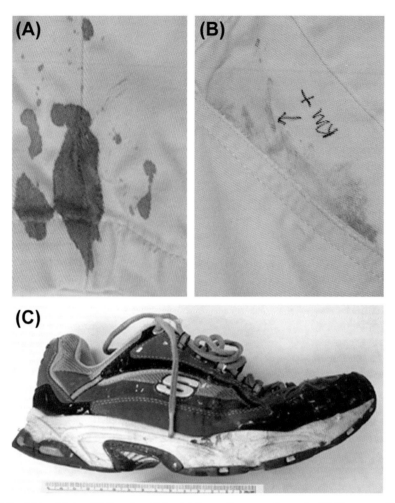

FIGURE 9.1   (A) Fresh bloodstains. (B) Denatured bloodstains on the suspect's pants. (C) The suspect's shoes were added to a laundry load.

VOLUME STAINS (POOLING OF BLOOD)

TV CSI programs frequently mention the presence or absence of a pool of blood as an indication that the body was moved. Little needs to be added to this statement. The only comment is that expecting a blood pool where it is not seen requires attention to the type of injury. Chest wounds can bleed internally and not have pooling. Arterial, heart, and head injuries should involve enough of a pool to show the final resting place of a body.

CASE EXAMPLES WHERE STAGING SHOULD HAVE BEEN ELIMINATED

Not all changes to a crime scene are the result of deliberate staging. It may also be possible to determine if staging was deliberate with forethought or if it was a spur-of-the-moment event. It is, of course, necessary to recognize what changes may occur from contamination, staging, or any other reasons. The following cases provide examples for study of the range of possible staging that may be found.

Chapter 5 described a case involving suspected arterial injury in a garage. Figure 9.2 repeats the view on the freezer corner. This case involved two brothers who had a long history of fighting. The older brother took drugs and was thin. The younger brother was healthy, muscular, and recently out on parole from an armed robbery conviction. The objections between them were that (1) the older brother was producing drugs in the house inherited from their mother, (2) the younger brother was storing his bike in the garage to the objection of the older brother, and (3) the home was bequeathed to both brothers but not equally shared. As described in Chapter 5, the older brother confronted the younger one in the garage with a baseball bat. The stronger, younger brother took the bat away and beat the older one. It was known that the bat belonged to the older brother and had been kept in the home.

Although the autopsy did not list arterial injury, questions to the pathologist later achieved admission that the victim bled out "possibly" from arterial injury. The most likely source, given the position of breach from the dent in the freezer corner, would be the victim's temple region. A major artery, the right exterior carotid, is located in this area with thin skin exterior to and skull bone behind it. Also, in periods of anxiety, blood increases flow between the head and brain via the carotid arteries of the neck.

FIGURE 9.2   Freezer door corner located in garage (Figure 5.11 repeated).

The older brother's body was found in a shallow grave in an abandoned home lot back-yard. The body began to give off foul odors that alerted residents to the presence of something dead, and they, in turn, notified law enforcement. Officers responded and found the body, which was identified soon afterward. Scratch marks and blood drips led back to the last known residence of the victim. Crime scene investigators examined the residence and noted bloodstains in the living room. Unfortunately, the bloodstains were not used as investigative evidence but were shoe-horned into a scenario that fit the case decided upon by those involved in the investigation. After the victim was identified, emphasis was placed on statements of friends and relatives of the victim regarding the bad relationship between the brothers. The younger brother became the person of interest, and the investigation centered on finding evidence against him.

Within statements collected was the incidence of friction regarding the younger brother storing his bike in the garage. The arterial spray on the side of the freezer in the garage was ignored because the scenario decided upon involved the entire assault occurring in the living room. The reason for that scenario was based on the fact that there was no breaking and entering, and the front door was locked with the younger brother having a key. The front door led directly into the living room. If the garage had been acknowledged as the beginning of the assault, one possibility that could have been considered was that a person or persons unknown entered from the garage. This, of course, would have confused the accepted scenario.

In addition to the freezer-side bloodstains and bright red stains in a bedroom opposite the door between the garage and hall leading to the living room, there were stains along the wall connecting the garage inside door to the living room (see Figure 9.3).

FIGURE 9.3   Wall between door to garage and living room.

III. INTERPRETATION

The direction of travel indicated is from the garage door to the living room, with no pattern present indicating the reversed travel of the victim after assault. This pattern shows the direction the victim moved was from the garage to the bedroom and then toward the living room. Although the pattern on the freezer is clearly arterial, the pattern on the connecting wall is not obviously so. The spacing and similar size with directions of travel suggest parallel distribution of individual drops met the wall. The spatters are separated so that they could be mistaken for castoff, but the direction of travel does not indicate an assault coming from the living room. This contradicts the claim that the crime was committed entirely near the front door entrance to the living room.

A note here is that if the stains on the wall were castoffs and were alleged to be from blunt force blows to the victim, they would identify a left-handed swing. The bloodstains are directed from the door to the garage toward the living room on the left as the victim moved. It would be a very awkward swing from the right arm of the assailant.

In the living room, there were stains on the drapes. These are probably from arterial damage but definitely not clear as to what dynamic act distributed them. They were assumed to be castoffs. Because the assault was made with a baseball bat, castoffs would be consistent with the events that led to the victim's death. The CSI offered no interpretation regarding which hand or arm would swing to dislodge castoffs as seen. The fact that arterial damage was noted in the garage, back bedroom, and possibly hall would normally suggest caution in labeling the drape bloodstains (see Figure 9.4).

The obvious attempt to alter the crime scene can be seen in the orange paint dumped on the stain in front of the living room couch (see Figure 9.5). An attempt to hide a volume blood stain where the victim bled out shows a very sloppy attempt at staging (see Figure 9.6). This is also consistent with other stains, suggesting the perpetrator had attempted other ways to clean up the blood before dumping the paint. The better suggestion is that attempts to hide the crime were probably not thought out before the assault.

All in all, the whole crime scene and the history of the brothers indicate a fight that got out of hand. The younger brother had beaten up his older brother throughout their childhood. The bat belonged to the older brother. It is suggested that the older brother was trying to use the bat as an equalizer in confronting the younger brother as he was storing his bike in the garage. Because the older brother fell against the freezer, he sustained arterial injury as he hit the freezer corner. From the location on the freezer, and given the older brother's height and the fact that he bled out before he died, injury to the exterior carotid artery at the temple is suggested. There is no blood in the dent in the freezer corner, which shows the artery was not breached before he hit the corner. After the artery was opened, he bled rapidly from a crucial arterial vessel while moving into the house, to the bedroom, to the hall, and finally to the living room couch, where he bled onto the carpet and died.

The prosecution had the right defendant, but the charges were for premeditated first-degree murder. If the crime was premeditated, surely the younger brother would have planned in advance how to dispose of the body. The sloppy attempts to stage the scene were directed at separating the occurrence of the offense from the mother's home, not necessarily from the garage. Failing to wrap the body for transport, using a leaking garbage can, attempting to wipe stains, and then pouring paint on one stain too big to clean up show panicked attempts to stage the scene. The garbage can used had a defective wheel that left scratch marks leading from the home to the vacant lot burial.

FIGURE 9.4   Drapes at living room front window.

FIGURE 9.5   Orange paint poured over a volume blood stain in front of the living room couch.

III. INTERPRETATION

FIGURE 9.6   Smears and wipes suggestive of different times and attempts to clean up the bloodstains.

It's possible that overcharging was part of the department's policies. Many years ago a former New York City prosecutor mentioned contrary policies in lectures before a California State University Advanced Criminal Legal Process class. That office refused plea bargaining, and its conviction rate was as high as other jurisdictions using pleas. However, the charges brought were as accurate as possible. In this case, there was a trial. Had the true nature of the homicide been brought out in initial interviews with the suspect, it's possible a confession and deal could have resulted without the cost of trial.

The important point is that bloodstain pattern evidence is the most cost-efficacious evidence available for reconstructing the sequences of a crime. Merely shoe-horning testimony as instant evidence to gain a conviction later is a waste and may be an injustice.

CLEVER STAGING?

One of the cleverest staging cases was described in *Bloodstain Pattern Evidence, Objective Approaches and Case Applications* (Wonder, 2007, pp. 172–180). The person of interest had been a coroner's deputy and admitted to law enforcement that he was aware of body temperature as a means of determining the time of death. Unfortunately for him, and fortunately for the prosecution, it was pointed out that he got too creative in his posing of both of his victims. Because bloodstain pattern evidence wasn't applied, the first murder was not recognized as such and was labeled a suicide. The preliminary hearing on the second homicide was flawed by indicating the murder was an interrupted burglary. At trial, an embarrassment resulted when the expert was required to explain the erroneous first call after he had been shown the importance of bloodstain pattern evidence. The explanation was that the case had been seen in a new light. The second murder was identified as murder, not an interrupted burglary, and led to reopening the first "suicide" case as a murder.

Sometimes staging is so well planned that it may not be accepted as an act of staging when presented to jurors. This means that the investigation must be very thorough and clear before going to trial. An example occurred some years ago. Because the question of whether or not this case involved staging may continue to be debated for years, no background details can be provided. The victim was a healthy middle-aged man who was found in the upstairs bedroom of his condominium in an upscale subdivision. He was found on the carpeted floor with his head bashed in. The person who claimed to find the victim was a coworker, later found to be lover, of his estranged wife. The coworker had experience with crime scenes in a previous profession as a paramedic. Law enforcement investigators appreciated bloodstain pattern evidence but were required to rely on a government crime lab to provide the analysis. The expert who responded claimed to have been trained and to have testified in trials on the subject previously. Figure 9.7 shows the "string reconstruction" the expert compiled.

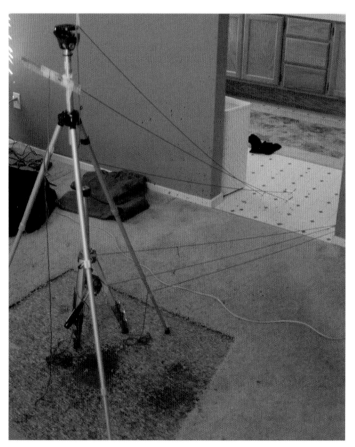

FIGURE 9.7   Misconstructed stringing.

No area of convergence was determined. The camera tripods were placed over patches of volume blood where the investigating officers told the expert that the victim's very bloody head had been found. Very narrow, elongated spatters were located, measured, and angles reconstructed with strings to the camera tripods. The report that was offered with the photos of this work stated that no one was in the bathroom because there were no smeared stains. The confusion between the statement and the strings is obvious. The origin indicated by the strings is on the bathroom floor, where the interpretation says no one was present. The errors here are many: (1) no area of convergence was constructed; (2) the reconstruction was basically made from statements by officers, not the knowledge of the expert; and (3) spatters selected for the reconstruction were too close together, on one surface, and too elongated to provide accurate angular interpretation. Most important is the fact that the stains on the bathroom floor showed parallel alignment and explosive-like distribution. The array was most likely the result of the spinal pressure building from assault to the head and explosion when the skull was breached. The victim was on the floor at the time, while the temple region of the victim's head was being bashed by up-and-down stamping of a ball bat.

All of this is useless information because there was no reason to construct an origin for what was already known to be a vicious beating, but it does add to the suggestion that the crime scene was probably staged. No other information regarding bloodstain pattern analysis was provided by the alleged expert.

The autopsy report listed the massive injury to the side of the head with fractures consistent with vertical stamping (like a rubber stamp but with a ball bat). This assault was achieved as the victim lay on the floor. A determination could have been made with the information available, without the time and expense of constructing a location for impacts. Saying that the impacts occurred at these locations (two camera tripods over two blood pools) raises (or should have raised) a question regarding inconsistency with the swing castoffs seen around the room (see Figures 9.8 and 9.9).

FIGURE 9.8   Castoffs over bed.

III. INTERPRETATION

FIGURE 9.9   Castoffs near window.

III. INTERPRETATION

Examination of the bedding showed considerable blood, but no area that indicated impact spatters was seen. Castoffs under the window did not show a blockage where the victim would have been positioned for the swing to have been part of the assault. In addition, there were no impact spatters showing a blow delivered at the end of a swing. The spatters were consistent with cessation castoffs at a right angle to the wall. Standing in the middle of the room and looking at the arrays of castoffs, one can see the swings were at random rather than directed toward an impact distribution that would suggest the presence of a victim.

On the sheer curtains near the castoff pattern for the window and bench seat is a fragment of clot. This suggests that the swing distributing castoffs was delivered at a time period after blood was clotting. The victim was not a drug addict or alcoholic, so normal clotting would be expected. No impact at the end of the swing to dislodge cessation castoffs that contained a fragment of clot strongly suggests staging after the victim had bled (see Figure 9.10).

The most interesting series of castoffs were on the ceiling and the back of the bedroom door (see Figures 9.11 and 9.12). These patterns show that the door was closed during the assault, yet the alleged attack was from one person staying at the residence with the victim alone. There was no apparent reason to close the door during the assault, as the door was found open when the body was found. The suggestion is that the assault was kept separated from another person at the residence at the time of the murder. A stepson was thought to be sleeping downstairs. Fortunately—or unfortunately—the stepson had left and was not where he was thought to be. The jury could not understand the significance of this information. It was pointed out in trial.

The subtlety of the evidence is that the castoffs suggested left-handed swings, yet the autopsy suggested the assault itself to be right-handed. This information could not be presented as evidence because left-handed people may shift hands, especially during emotional events. It should have been an alert to law enforcement or at least to the alleged crime lab "expert."

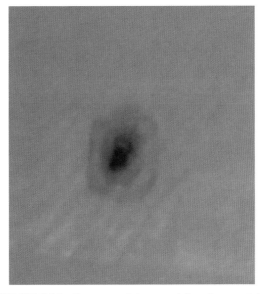

FIGURE 9.10   Fragment of clot material on sheer curtains.

III. INTERPRETATION

FIGURE 9.11   Ceiling castoffs.

FIGURE 9.12   Door cast spatters.

A third example of suspected staging occurred many years ago, with the true nature of the crime not recognized until recently. A woman was confronted in her upstairs bedroom by a would-be burglar/ known rapist. There was a struggle, and the woman was shot in the back. The body was later found outside the bedroom on a landing with legs extended down a few steps of a staircase (see Figure 9.13).

It was established that the gunshot occurred when the woman was facing away from her attacker with her head bent backward (see Figure 9.14). The scenario strongly suggested was that the attacker approached with a knife (admitted by the accused) and that the woman, who had self-defense training, grabbed the wrist holding the knife and pulled it over her shoulder to disarm him. It is suggested that he pulled a gun from his waistband and shot her in the back.

FIGURE 9.13   Victim position on the landing.

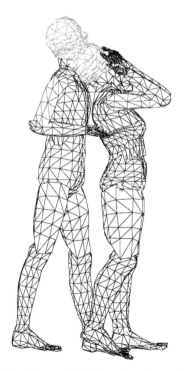

FIGURE 9.14   Human CAD illustration of gunshot to victim.

III. INTERPRETATION

The bullet hole in the woman's nightgown was much lower than the bullet entrance wound, and her hair was found in the wound, although the length of her hair was shorter than would fall over the entrance wound (see Figure 9.15). This pattern shows her head was bent back, and the gun bunched up the gown. The unstained area around the wound suggests close contact at the moment of the shot, verified at autopsy. Tracking of the injury was from back to front, directed up through vital organs. A unique pattern was seen on the nightgown with a rough pattern match to a stain on the bed sheet located at an angle to the stain on the nightgown (see Figures 9.16 and 9.17).

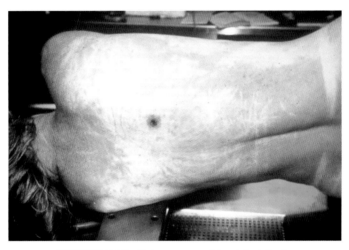

FIGURE 9.15   Entrance wound to victim's back.

FIGURE 9.16   Bloodstain on victim's nightgown.

III. INTERPRETATION

FIGURE 9.17   Bloodstain on bed sheet.

No blood drips or moving transfer stains were seen from the bed to the landing. A throw rug that was usually kept next to the bed was found under the body on the landing. The scene seemed to be staged because the body was not located where she was shot, and after the shot, she was incapable of moving to the landing by herself. The question that arises is why move the body to the landing? There are at least two possible suggestions: one is that the body was to be removed and a kidnap scenario followed, and the other is so that the body would be found sooner than waiting for someone to enter the bedroom. It was not until a great deal of time later that a possible third reason emerged.

The assailant had a history of rape and burglary, not murder. It is possible that he accosted the victim with the knife for the purpose of rape. When she grabbed his arm and was in the process of disarming him, he panicked and shot her. Afterward, although she was dead, he may have tried to complete the rape. The position on the bed suggests she was laid there at right angles to the bed, but the position was not acceptable so she was moved to the landing. He lost control of the body, which slid down three stairs of the staircase. Children sleeping downstairs heard three thumps. The body was pulled back up to the landing, but apparently the noise and time canceled that objective for the assailant, and he left the scene.

Each of these cases shows the degree of variation to staging considerations: the sloppy, spur-of-the-moment actions; the possibly cleverly planned; and the changes made by the perpetrator that were not specifically intended as staging. The important issue with staging is that it must be ruled out. A straightforward "interpret exactly as you see it" approach is not wise or good investigation in the face of the "CSI Effect" today. Bloodstain pattern evidence can be extremely important to initial investigations in ruling out staging, shortening the investigation, saving money, and bringing the proper charges for violent offenses.

REFERENCE

Wonder, A.Y., 2007. Bloodstain Pattern Evidence, Objective Approaches and Case Applications. Elsevier, San Diego, CA, pp. 172–180.

APPLICATION

10

Expanding Applications in Bloodstain Pattern Evidence

The process for bloodstain pattern analysis has been outlined, from identifying the various pattern categories to interpreting possible dynamic events that leave bloodstain records. This is not, however, the total involvement of the discipline. Consideration now must turn to applications of the information gleaned from the analysis thus far. Contrary to what one sees in the televised CSI programs, there is more than one way in which the information can be beneficial to crime resolution. After accurate and confirmed identification and suggested interpretations of patterns, various applications are available—from initial investigative leads to ideas for appeals when the resolution is perceived as unjust and/or a wrongful conviction. Even in cases of acquittal, the desire to prevent release of a perceived guilty person may require continued review of evidence, i.e., so the crime doesn't happen again.

The chapters presented thus far have shown that bloodstain pattern evidence is considerably more complex than is often represented in CSI television programs and even in textbooks on forensic science in general. Sadly, applications are often based on the limited view of information available. Historically, in the United States application of bloodstain pattern evidence has focused on expert testimony at trial. This unnecessarily limits application of a good solution to the present-day economic concerns with processing violent crime. This section is designed to expand applications that, one hopes, will also expand the regard for the importance and economy of providing training for all parts of the investigative teams. A list showing the expanse of investigative applications may include

1. interviews of individuals claiming knowledge of the evidence;
2. investigations of vandalism;
3. determination of suicide, accident, or homicide;
4. CSI general work-up for violent events;
5. recognition of staged crime scenes;
6. trial strategy for both prosecution and defense;
7. openings for appeals;
8. evidence for parole considerations;
9. cold case and historical considerations;

Bloodstain Patterns
http://dx.doi.org/10.1016/B978-0-12-415930-3.00010-X

10. child abuse and animal cruelty;

11. internal affairs investigations into officer-involved shootings; and

12. incarcerated population interrogation.

Each of these applications deserves discussion in greater detail than is usually found in forensic science books.

1. INTERVIEWS OF INDIVIDUALS CLAIMING KNOWLEDGE OF THE EVIDENCE

Law enforcement and prosecution departments, bureaus, and offices vary in how they handle examination of bloodstain pattern evidence. This is shown in the frequent application of the term "blood splatters" to the discipline. Blood spatters are but a small part of an analysis and are a broad-class characteristic that provides no immediate information. Bloodstain pattern analysis involves considerably more thought, knowledge, and training than just recognition that there are spots of blood at a possible crime scene. It follows that individuals claiming expertise may or may not be qualified to provide identification of the various patterns and then suggest interpretations as they relate to violent crimes. Some proclaim to be qualified simply because they have learned terminology.

Even if—in fact, especially if—a person claims qualification based on completion of a 40-hour workshop in the evidence, it is advised that questions be asked to establish that the training was adequate and that the participant actually learned how to approach the evidence in an objective manner. This author noticed in various workshops by different trainers that some individuals attend programs simply to learn terminology. This means the students felt they already knew how to interpret blood found at crime scenes but wanted to learn how to speak the language in court. Personal experience with training has shown most, if not all, attendees who felt they already knew it all before training had much more yet to learn. Some used the terms memorized to provide instant evidence where no other evidence was found. This means that cases were assumed solved before bloodstain patterns were identified and that identification was added simply as consistent with the proposed scenario.

It follows that one of the best questions to ask first is this: When was training in respect to the individuals' years of experience? Individuals claiming many years of experience but having received training within a few months of the need for analysis are likely to be among those who did not take advantage of all of the information available in a workshop. It should be remembered that experience begins to accumulate after training, not before. One cannot count as experience what one has not yet learned, i.e. what that experience means in terms of interpretation of bloodstain patterns at crime scenes.

Alternative answers may include "by size and shape." This phrase can be memorized without being able to identify different dynamic events from spatter measurements. Size is determined more by the degree of force than the type of force. Shape is greatly affected by velocity of individual drops, but that is the velocity of drops contacting a target surface, not the velocity of an object hitting a blood source. If this confuses the alleged expert it would be advisable to search elsewhere for a person to supply investigative needs.

The next question for a person who will provide analysis of bloodstain pattern evidence is: What did you learn in the program? Those who express caution are better at viewing the evidence objectively than those who feel they learned everything they need to know in a 40-hour workshop. If an oral or written report using the term "velocity impact spatter" has already been provided, the individual should be questioned as to how he or she knew what velocity the blood drops were traveling at impact with a surface. If the velocity is measured as an object making impact with a blood source, the question becomes, "How do you know an impact occurred, rather than a sneeze, castoff, or arterial spurt?"

When asked how the individual knows that a pattern is impact, castoff, or arterial damage, if the person states, "because of experience and training," especially if offered in that order, there is cause for caution. The most important point is that the answer is ambiguous. There is no fact offered unless the nature of the experience and training is also provided. Answers should be in terms of how the patterns of spots were arranged to help identify them as an impact, castoffs respiration, arterial damage, or a secondary event such as blood dripping into blood or a splash. The memory device SAADD (**S**hape of a group of spatters, **A**lignment of individual spatters, **A**lignment of groups of spatters, **D**istribution of spatters, and **D**ensity of number of spatters) has been presented to show a factual method of identification. This is not the only way, but it shows that identification may be stated as based on the bloodstain pattern characteristics, not an assumption that an individual will automatically know what dynamic act was involved by looking at the blood spots.

Alternative answers may include "by size and shape." One can memorize this phrase without being able to identify different dynamic events from spatter measurements. Size is determined more by the degree of force than the type of force. Shape is greatly affected by velocity of individual drops, but that is the velocity of drops contacting a target surface, not the velocity of an object hitting a blood source. If this distinction confuses the alleged expert, it would be advisable to search elsewhere for a person to supply investigative needs.

Perhaps the simplest way to determine whether an expert is knowledgeable in bloodstain pattern evidence is to ask if he or she believes the evidence is a pattern match procedure like fingerprints and tool marks. If the answer is yes, it means the person claiming expertise has approached training and experience by attempting to memorize simplified exercises as two-dimensional pictures. An impact is much more like a bomb blast than a fingerprint. Size and shape of the entire group of spatters matter, but only after the actual event—gunshot, fist blow, respiration, arterial projection, or blood dripping into blood—is identified. Because an impact occurs in a three-dimensional context with several variables, it is unreasonable to expect an analyst to have seen and memorized the exact same pattern in a 40-hour workshop or a previously viewed crime scene.

2. INVESTIGATIONS OF VANDALISM

The worst misconception regarding applications of bloodstain pattern evidence is to assume that it is used in court only for homicides. The previous chapters showed many uses of this evidence before a trial can be considered. Violent crimes that result in bloodshed provide the base applications because society demands resolution and such investigations provide the maximum in cost. In areas where violent crimes are uncommon, officials may feel it is not worth the budget to have personnel trained.

The author used such information in solving a crime of teenage malicious mischief many years ago. Two boys were left alone while the mother of one boy was out with a new friend. The friend had left a tennis ball launcher in the garage where the woman and her son lived. There was a carton of eggs in the refrigerator. Either out of spite toward the mother's new friend, boredom, or curiosity, the boys decided to use the eggs in the launcher. The result was a dozen eggs deposited after flight paths over two condominiums across a driveway from the launch site. Directions of travel were demonstrated to law enforcement officers responding. The boys were made to clean up the experiment. The point, of course, is that bloodstain pattern training can be applied to cases of vandalism and malicious mischief in addition to violent crime. Eggs, paint, feces, and mud can be viewed as to directionality.

3. DETERMINATION OF SUICIDE, ACCIDENT, OR HOMICIDE

When we speak of violent crimes, we usually are referring to assault and homicide. Unfortunately, which call is appropriate for first responders may not be immediately apparent. Calling a suicide a homicide will lead to considerable, perhaps unnecessary, cost outlay in investigation. Unfortunately, calling a homicide a suicide can be more costly the other way. There is always the danger that if a murderer gets away with killing, there will be temptation to commit the crime again. Lawsuits may follow deaths that would have been prevented had a perpetrator been identified from an earlier crime. This is in addition to the loss of human life should have considerable value in monetary terms. Both of these situations become questionable in some accidental events that lead to blood loss. The fact that bloodstain pattern evidence can provide immediate information to resolve the question of accident, suicide, or homicide, in addition to aggravated assaults that become homicides versus premeditated crimes, justifies good training of officers from patrol through detectives.

4. CSI GENERAL WORK-UP FOR VIOLENT EVENTS

The members of the investigative teams who commonly receive training are the crime scene investigation (CSI) identification technicians.

If there is a bureau of this kind within a service, the personnel must be trained in bloodstain pattern analysis. Historically, those working in fingerprinting disciplines were considered right for performing bloody crime scene work-ups. Fingerprint specialists, however, tend to regard the subject as pattern match physical evidence. Instead, bloodstain patterns must be considered as three-dimensional dynamics. This dynamic is more comparable to bomb blasts than to fingerprints and tool marks. Because bomb blasts can also cause injuries that act as blood sources for patterns, it makes sense that bomb investigators would be good at interpreting very bloody crime scenes even if no bomb was involved. With the present emphasis on terrorism and economy of law enforcement agencies, training bomb inspectors and investigators could be beneficial to departments.

5. RECOGNITION OF STAGED CRIME SCENES

Chapter 9 dealt with the complexity and current need for recognition of staging at scenes of bloodshed. Because violent criminals watch CSI programs, and such programs are common on television, staging may prove to be a growing danger. A principle paraphrased from Blackstone's formulation (http://en.wikipedia.org/wiki/Blackstone%27s_formulation) is that it is better to let a guilty person go free than to incarcerate an innocent person. Sadly, prosecutors and juries may lose sight of the damage to innocent lives when the wrong person is sent to prison. Extremely violent crime scenes beg for someone to pay for the deed. A double wrong results from convicting an innocent person: the life of an innocent person and the freedom of a guilty one. Staging is a major consideration that can lead to the wrong suspect being charged and convicted.

Another application that requires recognition of staging is insurance claims. Accidental injury with contributory negligence and suicide both require ruling out staging of the scene for payment of some claims to be made. Those with religious beliefs who feel suicide is a sin may try to change a scene to make it look like a homicide to protect the memory and afterlife of the deceased.

6. TRIAL STRATEGY FOR BOTH PROSECUTION AND DEFENSE

Of course, trial preparation may be considered by some the main application of bloodstain pattern analysis. The historical origin of this discipline in the United States was by individuals appearing as experts in the evidence of blood dynamics. Techniques, testimonies, demonstrations, and finally training of others were developed as a source of income. This led to some training being a "dog and pony show," without providing the tricks of the trade that would help resolve investigation before trial. It is the objective of this book to supply as much information as possible for the speedy and economical investigation of crime. A lot more needs to be said regarding trial preparation, which is discussed in Chapter 11.

7. OPENINGS FOR APPEALS

Much more information is possible with bloodstain pattern evidence than trial strategy. Discussions have been held in regard to detecting blood mixed with cerebral spinal fluid (CSF) in cases of assault to the head. This technique has not been examined in research, which would qualify as new evidence should new methods of determining such mixtures be found. Injuries to the head may have blood mixed with spinal fluid, providing stains that are crucial to interpretation of the crime. Spinal fluid contains all, or most, of the substances found in blood because it is a filtrate of blood. If blood is also present, then differentiating CSF from a mixture becomes complex, and at the present time, no chemical test is reliable in identifying the mixture. A suggestion for developing research to justify CSF mixtures with blood as new evidence in investigations could be the application of alternate light sources. One project completed for this book is presented in Section V.

There is considerable debate regarding the accuracy of time lines as applied in the use of drying times and coagulation. Some projects have been completed, but there is disagreement regarding times derived from clinical standards, bloodstain pattern workshops, and research projects. Should new, more reliable data be acquired, this could be offered as new evidence upon appeal. Research into and possible use of these subjects are discussed in Section V.

Failure to use bloodstain pattern evidence at trial has not shown success in obtaining appeals in the United States. Claims by trial lawyers to have not given adequate defense are also not usually successful with regard to not offering or offering poor expertise in Bloodstain Pattern. The courts still view bloodstain pattern evidence with a cautious eye and do not feel it is justification for reconsidering or changing previous adjudication. It is better to consider the applications at trial than to fall back on them for appeals. If the state puts a specialist in bloodstain patterns on the witness stand, it is essential that the defense seek its own interpretation of the evidence.

8. EVIDENCE FOR PAROLE CONSIDERATIONS

Staging a crime scene may continue to be significant long after a trial is over. Consultation requests have been received on behalf of a convicted murderer, for example, because the crime was allegedly staged, thus showing premeditation. Efforts to keep the individual in prison were based on premeditation of the original crime. Continued denial of parole was based on a fear that the individual would repeat the violent association with an abusive relationship. This was based upon interpretation of the crime scene as staged to look like self-defense. Review by someone qualified in bloodstain pattern evidence may be necessary to support or to refute such claims for parole hearings, even though the original conviction did not address the claim.

9. COLD CASE AND HISTORICAL CONSIDERATIONS

If quality photographs are taken of a scene, victim, and evidence, it is possible to resolve questions years or even decades afterward. In the absence of such photographs, the truth may never be known. The Lizzy Borden case is an example in which bloodstains were not specifically used but were described in detail. Years later, those studying bloodstain pattern analysis have had the information to review.

10. CHILD ABUSE AND ANIMAL CRUELTY

Many years ago, photographs from homes involving suspected child abuse were reviewed with the suggestion that child abuse investigations include bloodstain pattern training. In one case, for example, bloodstain patterns were consistent with a child being thrown against a wall at too high of a level to have resulted from the child running into the wall during play. Having physical evidence of abuse and danger to a child may speed removal of the child or children from dangerous and abusive environments.

Animal cruelty has gained importance in the hearts of people around the world. Some attorneys in America now specialize in claims against abusive owners, neighbors, and kennels. A situation was recently encountered in which a boarding kennel caused injury to a dog. The injury was blamed upon two dogs fighting, yet the injured dog's position when bloodstains were recorded on a fence was inconsistent with the claim that the dog was alone when it made contact with the fence, as shown in Figure 10.1. Figure 10.2 shows the gate with the dog's blood. Note the position of claw marks and fur on the lower edge of the smudges. The liquid causing runs down the post, shown in Figure 10.3, are probably submissive urination by the dog as it was held.

11. INTERNAL AFFAIRS INVESTIGATIONS INTO OFFICER-INVOLVED SHOOTINGS

In Sacramento, California, International Association of Identification (IAI) officers who signed up for workshop training showed satisfactory acceptance of the importance of including this evidence. Every officer-involved shooting must have bloodstain pattern analysis to provide factual background to the incident. Statements of fellow officers and/or eyewitnesses can be in error for many reasons. Bloodstain pattern analysis can take the emotions out of the equation for a speedy and cost-efficacious resolution to the investigation.

12. INCARCERATED POPULATION INTERROGATION

When investigating assault, suicide, and homicide within jail and prison populations, investigators face individuals who are conditioned not to be truthful. Whether or not an interviewed witness is providing accurate information needs to be checked against physical evidence. CSI work-ups in jails and

FIGURE 10.1   Bloody paw prints on a gate.

prisons are more complex than for crime scenes on the outside. When applied as a quick and economical source of information, bloodstain pattern analysis will benefit speedy resolution of the occurrences.

HOW TO APPLY BLOODSTAIN PATTERN ANALYSIS

As listed in the preceding sections, bloodstain pattern analysis has many applications, although not all are presently utilized. Discussion now shifts to how to apply an objective analysis of the bloodstain patterns identified. Several books describe bloodstain patterns as part of the forensic disciplines. These books usually suggest investigative formats. By necessity, one must examine approaches to violent crime scenes because that is the most widely recognized application of bloodstain pattern analysis. There are,

FIGURE 10.2   Detail of gate post.

however, as many different ways to approach the analysis of bloodstains at a suspected crime scene as there are different protocols for law enforcement and defense investigating agencies. This is to say, every group will have its own standard procedure, and that procedure must be followed for consistency of case work-up. In all situations, improvements to the way bloodstain pattern analysis is applied will be beneficial. The approaches to analysis that presently exist may include but are not limited to the following:

1. Ignore bloodstain pattern evidence unless case supervisors instruct to examine for it.
2. Collect many samples and photographs and then pass them on to someone else for interpretation.
3. Observe and tender an oral scenario to cover what is seen.
4. Write up a brief report.
5. Include an external review of the body only with the autopsy report.
6. Observe and collect but wait until after a meeting with and instruction from a prosecutor to write up a report.

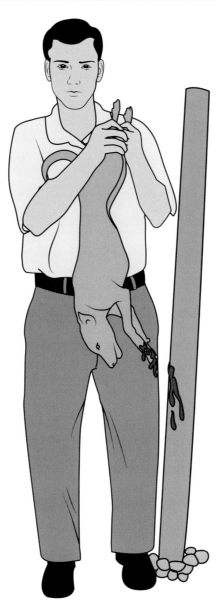

FIGURE 10.3   Example of how dog could be held to leave paw prints as seen.

7. Call an outside expert after the scene is routinely processed.
8. Call an outside expert for court testimony only.

All of the preceding permutations have been encountered in casework, although most books mentioning bloodstain pattern analysis do suggest its importance in the initial investigation. Bloodstains may be processed as an afterthought as a result of the historical regard to the discipline, in that it was an area for expert witnesses reserved for trial. If the general policy is to ignore bloodstain patterns unless instructed to process them, detectives must be trained to appreciate investigative leads applications so that they may instruct CSI staff to supply that information. CSI/evidence technicians may be cautious in stating their interpretations of the pattern arrangements seen and fall back on the path of least resistance, i.e., observe but say nothing unless requested to supply comments.

The least committed approach is to take many photographs of the scene but supply no identification or interpretation. In this author's experience, this approach often neglects to include all pertinent locations for interpretation of the evidence later. Most noteworthy are the absences and blockages of stains that help position events in a three-dimensional context. If the CSI personnel have not been trained or have not been adequately trained, they may photograph different parts of individual patterns separated. Most photographers of crime scenes are well aware that they must photograph both with and without a scale. Patrol officers, who take preliminary pictures of the scene as found, may not include their photographs of the evidence in the package for the prosecutor. Omissions can present problems with interpretation later, especially if paramedics and/or coroner's deputies change the position of the body before CSI personnel record the scene.

After collecting photographs, identification technicians/CSI personnel may hazard guesses at what the photographed bloodstains mean. This has advantages in focusing photography on whole arrangements rather than cutting them up based on areas of the scene. It is essential that the guesses be made after patterns have been identified. If a scenario is suggested based on other information—witness statements, fingerprints, evidence of breaking and entering or lack thereof—the bloodstains will not be applied to obtain investigative leads. Also, if the other evidence on which the scenario is based falls apart later—i.e., witnesses are found to have lied or there is a reasonable explanation for fingerprints—the bloodstain pattern interpretation becomes a liability in no longer being accurate. Contradictions may become embarrassing, rather than informational. Initially, reports are discussed before a write-up. This is the way it is done, although such can and has led to bias and influence from evidence other than the bloodstain patterns. For example, a CSI identified arterial damage bloodstains as three rows of castoffs probably because the autopsy found three stab wounds. In addition to the incorrect identification of the dynamics in that case, the fact was and could be demonstrated to the jury that there were five arterial spurts.

The photographs and report are then sent to a supervisor, crime lab technician, or prosecutor. The photographs may or may not show all the bloodstain pattern evidence and may not be immediately examined by the reviewer. Reports may be written up to interpret patterns as consistent with a desired scenario, which, in turn, may be based on other evidence such as fingerprints, witness statements, and/or DNA. Note that DNA identifies the presence of people, not necessarily what they did while there. The increased sensitivity of DNA testing, however, does provide valuable information that can be used with bloodstain patterns to confirm actions during the crime. For example, a blunt force beating could be followed by strangulation by an assailant identified from DNA.

Feedback from trained detectives has endorsed using preliminary bloodstain pattern identification and interpretation in interviews with witnesses as well as persons of interest. The rationale behind this approach is that the interviewer appears to know too much about the crime to accept lies. This can lead to statements that are closer to the truth and to confessions. If, instead, the scenario presented to a person being interviewed shows lack of knowledge of the crime or a scenario that is completely different from what happened, the temptation to lie is greater. Once a lie is told, it becomes more difficult to take it back and admit a lack of truthfulness in earlier statements. Obviously, knowing what happened in a crime at the beginning or early stages of an investigation will be beneficial to speedy resolution. Time is also money.

It is sad to find that many prosecutors do not make use of accurate bloodstain pattern evidence when forming charges. This may result from attempts to overcharge in hope that even if the jury finds the party guilty to a lesser degree, the accused will still be sent to prison. Another reason, however, is the mistaken identification of bloodstain patterns. This is more likely to happen if arterial damage bloodstains exist at a homicide scene but are labeled as castoffs. Castoffs can be interpreted as resulting from a vicious assault by the accused on a victim. Arterial spurting, on the other hand, may create rows of bloodstains even if the accused is no longer present. Such mistaken identification has also contributed to claims that a scene was staged and the crime was therefore premeditated. The first degree charge in this latter situation was pursued instead of second degree or manslaughter. Defense attorneys must be aware of the possibility of arterial damage and that autopsies do not necessarily list arterial injury involvement in the cause of death. Castoffs are all about the assault, whereas arterial injuries are only about the victim.

Bringing objective approaches together with comprehensive applications, we can list our format for handling bloodstain pattern evidence. *Applications after identification and interpretation of bloodstain pattern evidence should progress as follows:*

1. Use bloodstain patterns to suggest accident, suicide, or homicide immediately.
2. Process the scene and identify bloodstain patterns.
3. Use bloodstain patterns to eliminate the possibility of a staged crime scene.
4. List questions for the pathologist at autopsy to cover possible arterial injury, bruises, and defense injuries to confirm cessation castoffs and blood in the respiratory organs.
5. Develop investigative leads.
6. Use as suggestions for finding other evidence (such as collecting samples for DNA testing and impression evidence)
   and/or confirmation when other evidence
   is developed.
7. Use information to interview witnesses and persons of interest.
8. Consider for specific charging after an arrest is made.
9. Use in trial as separate physical evidence, not confirmation of other evidence.
10. Evaluate for appeals after trial.

The main argument against simply dumping the bloodstain pattern report on the attorneys is the history of underutilization of the discipline. Attorneys may have no idea how to apply the probative evidence available to them. For example, this author pointed out to one defense attorney that a homeless alcoholic victim died as a result of fungal toxemia, not from the beating he received by the accused. The lawyer obtained agreement from the pathologist that such toxemia is common among homeless alcoholics, yet no mention was made of this as exculpatory information at closing arguments. The accused was convicted of second degree murder. Instructions for report writing of bloodstain pattern evidence may include identification and conclusions, but complete interpretation, although essential, is often abbreviated or omitted. Demonstrating the importance of interpretation and pointing out the direct link between specific violence or the absence of such, as with arterial damage patterns, and other circumstantial evidence convinces attorneys of the timeliness and economy much better than a formal written report. This area is discussed further in Chapter 12.

The end use for bloodstain pattern evidence will always be the legal system. The accuracy, economy of the investigation, and speed of resolution will depend on the efficient application of definitive investigative tools. The most cost-efficacious and yet often grossly underutilized forensic tool is bloodstain pattern evidence. The most effective application is a full analysis in the initial approach to the scene. To not have the information from bloodstain pattern analysis later during the investigation is a waste of time and economy. The best initial application is done before interviews, fingerprinting, trace evidence collection, and DNA sampling. An initial approach used by trained examiners has several additional advantages:

1. Training first-line officers to appreciate bloodstain patterns helps to focus on sealing and recording the scene before investigative transfer (contamination by first response officers) can occur.
2. Recognizing the importance of bloodstain patterns as initial investigative leads helps establish a scene seal that encompasses all the blood evidence, including blood trails leading away from the main area of violence and blockage of spatters where they would be expected.
3. Identifying the bloodstain patterns before interviews helps identify witnesses who are lying or who know too much about the scene to not have been present during the assault.
4. Applying bloodstain pattern analysis to a crime scene can identify staging of the crime scene before the wrong scenario is established.
5. Evaluating the evidence can bring together an investigative team because bloodstain patterns apply to multiple areas of an investigation (responding law enforcement officers, detectives, identification officers, crime lab, pathology, and prosecution).

Some training courses in bloodstain pattern evidence are directed more at impressing students than making them self-reliant. Those programs may be designed to whet the appetite, emphasize terminology, and illustrate fluid (not necessarily blood) behavior in simplified exercises that may not represent actual crime events. Graduates of such classes are encouraged to "memorize" the appearance of the results from simple experiments and then recognize them in their own casework, or better yet, call the instructors to gain information for prosecution after an assailant is charged. This is not to say involving a professional bloodstain pattern analyst is unnecessary. Rather, involving a professional to verify and extend quantity of information for quality preliminary work will shorten the time and expense necessary for case resolution, even if in-house expertise is available. It should not be necessary to wait for an outside expert before gaining investigative leads from the bloodstain pattern evidence present at a crime scene.

Applying analysis to determine if and how extensive staging has occurred aims the investigation in the right direction. First-line officers may jump to conclusions about an obvious scenario, especially if receiving input from alleged witnesses and misguided initial interviews. A standard concept in law enforcement is that violence comes from individuals close to and known to victims. Unfortunately, the first statements provided are usually from those known to and close to the victim. If such an individual is the assailant, setting up an investigation can be delayed and misguided. It is commonly stated among workshop participants, and endorsed here for interviewers, to believe no one, no matter how reliable that person may seem at first encounter.

The two essential steps before application of the information are to confirm whether patterns are castoffs or arterial damage patterns and to eliminate indications of staging. Swing castoffs are investigative information primarily regarding the way an assailant assaulted the victim, whereas arterial damage patterns are only about the victim after the assault. Failure to recognize arterial damage, calling such patterns castoffs instead, provides a train of thought on the wrong track. Staging of the crime scene directs an investigation toward the wrong person of interest. These two cautions more than any other aspect of bloodstain pattern evidence are crucial to both accuracy and economy of time and attention initially applied in investigations. Refer to Section II for identification and confirmation of arterial damage patterns versus swing castoffs. If arterial damage patterns are suggested, one should ask the autopsy physician to specifically identify possible arterial damage. Inform him or her that the damage may be as small as a pinhole if the manner of breach was via an aneurysm. This occurs, more often than is recognized, from blunt force trauma and/or small caliber bullets to the temple area of the head.

Protocols should be established to include respect and recognition of bloodstain patterns from the first observation of a death investigation. Emphasis must be placed on recognition of arterial damage patterns so that verification may be obtained during autopsy. All parts of the investigative team should be instructed to work with the bloodstain pattern analysis and vice versa. A super sleuth or bloodhound mentality is too limited to obtain full benefit from this discipline of evidence. The more input and viewpoints, the better the collection of information early in the investigation.

IV. APPLICATION

11

Applications of Bloodstain Pattern Evidence to Crime Scene Investigation

INTRODUCTION

It has been emphasized throughout this book that bloodstain pattern evidence benefits an investigation if it is applied from the first discovery of a crime scene that involves blood distribution. Training, however, has been predominately directed at homicide-oriented investigators. First responders, paramedics, firefighters, coroner's deputies, local physicians, and so on may arrive first and direct later review toward suicide or accidental death, or misdirect toward homicide when the event was one of the former. Funds-strapped departments may breathe a sigh of relief if the call isn't in favor of a high-cost homicide investigation, unless the perpetrator is seen by several reliable witnesses. As has been previously pointed out, the wrong call can end up being more expensive than a perceived quick and easy call. Murderers who get away with murder may kill again, which may then require opening old cases for review along with the new. There is also the loss of freedom for innocent people and ruined lives over wrong convictions.

Obviously, something better than a brief review of a crime scene is necessary to provide a level of comfort in labeling a case as suicide, accident, or homicide. No one wants to shelve a suspected homicide for lack of immediate evidence, allowing it to become a cold case. If the people involved in the investigation are properly trained, this need not occur when bloodstain pattern evidence can provide free and readily available physical evidence. Obtaining the information may also be possible without applying chemicals, instrumentation, and/or lab time beyond verifying a blood substance. Thus, the evidence can be used both to determine the classification of the crime and to provide essential preliminary evidence toward a solution. The main consideration regarding bloodstain pattern evidence is: Who is properly trained to provide the information?

Some departments go with a "super sleuth" approach in which they employ one person or two people who enjoyed a 40-hour workshop or read a book they believe to be sufficient to make them experts in the subject. Unfortunately, these individuals are not called to examine every crime scene reported to the dispatch. Only after homicide detectives or the assigned prosecutor requests "blood spatter analysis" will these alleged experts review the crime scene. Sometimes the scene itself is not viewed, but a work-up proceeds using photographs of the scene, which may not necessarily have been taken by photographers trained in bloodstain pattern evidence collection.

Unfortunately, this also occurs most often after a specific person of interest is identified. Sadly, initial investigative leads information is not used enough early in the application to casework.

Another approach may be to use a team of individuals who have been trained at various workshops and then process the crime scenes together. This approach has definite advantages in including multiple viewpoints, which enhance interpretation. Good news and bad: the good news is that these agencies usually assign the team to a crime lab where scientific principles can be advocated over finding evidence against a specific accused person. The bad news is that, again, the team is not called out unless a member of law enforcement or the assigned prosecutor makes the call. In this case, if a review is completed after the initial approach to the scene, it is even more likely to be worked up only from photographs. This latter situation assumes all pertinent photographs were available for review. If the photographers have not received any bloodstain pattern training, it is not uncommon for crucial photographs to be missing. Images of bloodstains may be collected, but they may be missing the context in which the pattern is seen; i.e., there is a lack of windows, doors, furniture, or other reference items. As with law enforcement experts, the main issue with these alleged experts is who trained the individuals and what that training included.

Because graduating from training is the starting line for gaining experience, one must consider details of the instruction. The question that this author has asked for years, after trying various methods of training, is how will the graduates of our classes apply what we believe we have taught? Some experiments in 40-hour workshops train participants in techniques that may be essential to actual casework application later. Some planned objectives, however, are ambiguous to the workshop participants, especially law enforcement officers who may be unfamiliar with experimentation conclusions. These individuals may participate but promptly forget the lessons. With the unsatisfactory exercises, changes were made to adjust the training methods or delete and substitute a different experiment. Throughout the years of training, the objective has been to teach those in the classes how to do the work themselves. Earlier workshops in the United States tended to be "dog and pony shows" to "whet the appetite" and make contact with future clients for court testimony. Although very egocentric, this method of training still achieved a wide awareness of the evidence throughout the United States and overseas. Now the recognition of the evidence is so firm that there is no longer a need for showmanship, but there is still a need to provide applicable information to make departments self-sufficient in using bloodstain pattern evidence as economical physical evidence. Such training can also provide a framework for determining the need and/or role of an outside expert should an investigation and/or trial require one.

APPLYING WORKSHOPS AND LECTURES TO CASE WORK-UP

The first basic experiment in many programs is dripping blood from a dropper onto white cardboard targets. After the stains are allowed to dry, their widths are measured. The height of fall for each blood drop is recorded versus the diameter of the stains which fell that distance, and results are plotted on a graph. Participants are told that this experiment is consistent with crime scene evidence to determine how far a blood drop fell during and following a crime. Comments are added to show that different target material will influence the diameter of the bloodstains. It is not common to point out the effects of blood composition on the spread of the drop at contact. In fact, details regarding the composition of the blood used in these exercises are often lacking in these programs. Safety concerns in regard to handling blood are more important than the behavior of the blood substance itself.

Refer to Chapter 2 of this book, which described an experiment in which blood drops of different ratios of red blood cells were dropped onto white tracing paper. The point is that the spread of a blood drop depends on the ratio, expressed as a hematocrit in percent of packed red blood cell volume, in the drop or the equivalent measures as hemoglobin content expressed in grams (abbreviated as gm) per 100 cubic centimeters (decaliter abbreviated as dl). This is illustrated and discussed in *Blood Dynamics* (Wonder, 2001, pp. 20–21) and again in *Bloodstain Pattern Evidence, Objective Approaches and Case Applications* (Wonder, 2007, p. 348). Recall that distance fallen and bloodstain diameter experiments are predictable and reproducible only if the blood used has the same properties, hematocrit/hemoglobin, and the same dropper size. Some instructors do mention and include exercises that show differences in drop size effects but retain the assumption that this information can be applied to crime scenes. Because of the influence of blood composition and the fact that it varies throughout the individual body as well as between donors, there can be no application to crime scene situations. Some instructors admit the lack of validity to a standard drop size but claim to include the exercise simply for historical reasons. The fact remains that it confuses the participants of the workshop who feel they should be able to use it and fail to see how in their casework later.

There is no such thing as a standard-sized blood drop. The term *droplet* is derived from an assumed breakup of the fictitious standard drop. Blood drop size to address the claim of a standard size could be suggested by using a Burette pipette (which is glassware that produces a uniform drop size per blood sample) to measure volume. Although claims have been made that such a determination used blood from a wide range of ages, we must assume that the blood was taken without trauma and that the donors were not in serious difficulties because of the blood loss. Clinical standards of blood composition change for age ranges, so the statement that a set single standard could be determined from a wide range of ages is suspect. Despite the erroneous claims regarding the uniformity of blood, the conditions for stating a standard-sized blood drop are not equivalent to those for blood loss from victims of homicide, accidental volume blood loss, lengthy bleeds in alcoholics/drug addicts, or suicide by cutting, to name a few occurrences. A scientific phrase is applicable here: "for all practical purposes," the distance a blood drop falls and the diameter of the resultant bloodstain have no application to crime scene situations.

Another exercise that is commonly performed is dropping blood on a slant. This experiment does a good job of showing participants that blood hitting at an angle will form an alternate shape to the round shape seen from direct fall by gravity. There is confusion of interpretation, however. Two misconceptions arise among participants of the workshops that feature this experiment: (1) the sizes of the stains are large so that students tend to believe they can measure any bloodstain, including castoffs and arterial damage stains; and (2) the drips on slants represent only drips on slants, not blood drops distributed by impact to a horizontal surface.

Falling by gravity does not duplicate a blood drop traveling at some velocity, hitting a surface, and losing forward momentum. It is possible that this shift in focus required the shift in where the velocity of impact was noted. Velocity causes the drop distributed by force to elongate as the content is left on the target. By contrast, a drip falling onto a slant will form a larger oval because the footprint and collapse of the drop are from larger volumes of blood in the drops. This gives an oval shape, but excess blood will flow toward gravity, giving the stain a teardrop shape. In other words, the velocities of the drops forming each stain, whether they were propelled by impact or dripping by force of gravity onto a slanted target, are from different dynamics and not comparable.

IV. APPLICATION

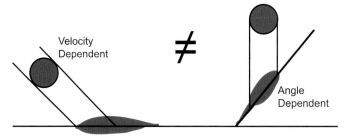

FIGURE 11.1   Application of drips on slants experiment versus impact spatter projected onto target.

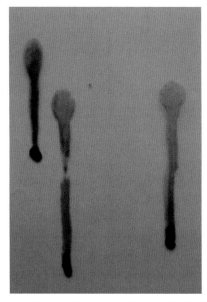

FIGURE 11.2   Blood dripping from a nose bleed with 10 gram/dl hemoglobin/hematocrit 30% ratio packed cell volume blood at 30-, 45-, and 60-degree angles from 24 inches height of fall, onto a sheet of frosted glass.

In the workshops held in Sacramento, California, these common exercises were bundled to show variations as well as the original intended concepts of height of fall, behavior on different surfaces, and slanted bloodstains (see Figure 11.1). Exercises included use of a scaffold to elevate a person with freedom of movement to drip blood from several feet up. Blood samples with various ratios of red blood cell volume to plasma were supplied. The same was done for 90-degree drop impacts as well as with slants from 10 to 80 degrees and different target materials. Participants were told they could learn to measure the big stains but would need to downsize the measurement technique to deal with impact spatters. Impact spatters are the only bloodstains that should be measured at a crime scene and only after verifying they are from a single impact. Measuring other blood spatters, before it is known what action distributed them, can be misleading. After students examined these exercises using large drips, they were given a handout sheet with known impact blood spatters (Wonder, 2007, p. 363 [Appendix D]) so that they could see that the smaller stains are actually what is measured at crime scenes, not the drips, castoffs, or arterial pattern stains (see Figures 11.2 and 11.3).

IV. APPLICATION

FIGURE 11.3 Blood with composition of 6.1 gm/dl (1,2,3) and 18.1gm/dl (4,5,6) hemoglobin, respectively, dropped from 6 (1 and 4), 3 (2 and 5), and 1 (3 and 6) foot heights onto newspaper at an approximate 45-degree angle.

Along the same vein (excuse the pun) is the drip-and-walk/run experiment. In this exercise, a participant holds a dropper and walks or runs along a strip of butcher paper or a series of white cardboard sheets. The idea is that one can determine how fast a person is moving from the bloodstains recorded. The same problem with interpretation exists as with two previously discussed exercises. First, the shape of the drips at contact will depend on other parameters than the speed of forward movement. The ratio of red cells influences the overall size and mass of the blood drips. The mass, in turn, affects the forward momentum of blood drops after release from the carrier. Second, the drop size will depend on the injury or blood adhering to something being carried. The size of the drops will be affected. A third observation is essential when translating this experiment to actual crime scenes. Someone moving while bleeding, or carrying something that is dripping blood, will probably not move at a steady rate. Any jostling, bouncing, swinging, or jiggling will involve distributing a variety of drop sizes with a resultant variety of shaped blood spots. The observation of drop size variations over the range of drips is more important than any individual measurement.

All of the comments relate to the instruction to measure the drips to determine a velocity of movement for the blood source. That type of determination cannot be applied to an actual crime scene. There is, however, a definite application for this exercise. In the Sacramento workshop, butcher paper was used to extend out 20 feet of travel length. Play acting was encouraged. Participants understood that walking or staggering as if drunk, carrying various bloody weapons and cloth, and/or carrying a heavy weight (crash dummy or willing fellow participant) could be applicable to casework later. They were instructed to note the variation of spatter sizes and directionalities, more than a single or predominant size. Areas of scattered spatters for smaller or larger stains were more important than a steady, uniform drip of blood. These situations and role playing prepared the participants for the types of situations they will encounter at actual crime scenes.

The direction of travel is the most important aspect for observing drips of different sizes scattered over the length of a path. Whether or not the stain is round will depend on the movement and the surface the blood drop contacts. One thing that is constant is that the leading edge, the direction of travel, will be slightly to markedly irregular, whereas the first contact edge, back toward the beginning of the trail, will be relatively smooth. Refer to Chapter 5 for examples illustrating direction of travel.

An addition to the experiment was essential in the ease with which it was performed. A transfusion two-way drip line was used to vent a blood pouch instead of trying to regulate the blood from a dropper. With the dropper, it was found that participants would squeeze the bulb too much and discharge a large amount of blood with little covering the rest of the recording target. The drip line could be adjusted for flow so that a uniform drip rate was possible, and the acting events compared with each other instead of focusing on the discharge from the dropper. See Figure 11.4 for an example. In this case, a very heavy object was being carried. The larger drops were from shifting the "body" as the participant walked.

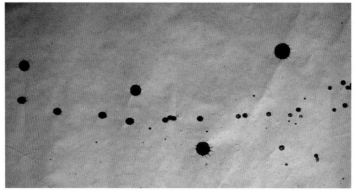

FIGURE 11.4   A butcher paper target used in a drip castoff experiment to show a second article dripping larger drops along the medium-sized drop path.

Walk-and-run exercises show very little difference between the shapes of dripped blood spatters. What is more reliable for speed of travel between walking and running is the spacing of the recorded drips. This type of drip pattern was seen at a double homicide in which a single perpetrator dealt with each victim in separate parts of an office building at different times. One woman, victim A, was the intended victim and was assaulted as she worked at her desk on a holiday weekend. Another woman, victim B, came to work later without realizing victim A had been attacked. Victim B went to the ladies' room near the front entrance of the office building. The assailant accosted her there, stabbing her, and leaving the body. He returned to the office cubicles area to find victim A was not yet dead and had gotten up to run toward the back exit door. He chased her, caught her at the inside of the exit, and slit her throat, cutting her carotid artery. She was carried back to a conference room. Victim B was also not killed by the initial knifing. She exited the ladies' room cautiously, dripping blood. When she saw the assailant, she started to run. Blood drips remained about the same size and shape because they were recorded on thick industrial carpet. The difference was the spacing between drips. Drips close together showed her walking carefully, and then the widely separated drips showed her running for her life.

The paddle fan device was discussed previously in Chapter 7. This exercise has applications for research but is not recommended for 40-hour workshops. The velocity of the fan is a castoff, centripetal (note that it is not *centrifugal*) action. Blood is cast off the fan blades at the speed of rotation. Saying that the size of blood drops and distance traveled in the fan exercise is equivalent to blood drops distributed by gunshot is false. Gunshot involves the impact of a bullet and the gases that propel the bullet out of the muzzle of the firearm. No such gas explosion occurs with the paddle fan. The composition of the fan blades affects the distribution, while the same thing is not considered for gunshot. The distance traveled and size of the drop have application only as an approximation of the blood drop mass, speed of the fan blade rotation, and the fan blade surface characteristics. These are considerations for castoff distribution, not firearms missile impact.

Another common exercise for a bloodstain pattern workshop is the use of a spring trap device to illustrate reproducible impacts (see Figure 11.5). These devices are easy to make for department training programs and provide a setting for variations. The construction requires a base, a mouse or rat trap or spring, and top and bottom lip plates. The trap provides a spring mechanism between the base and the lip plates. A pin through an eye clip on the upper lip can hold the trap open while blood

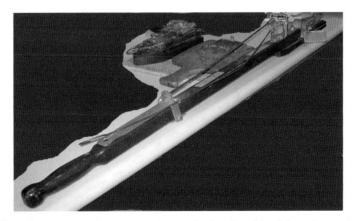

FIGURE 11.5   A variety of spring trap devices that break up blood drops into various sizes.

is placed on the base. When the pin is pulled out, the trap springs closed and impacts the blood source, causing impact distribution of blood drops. The best base to use for the device is a wooden bread board because it provides a handle to hold down the device to prevent the trap from bouncing when the pin is pulled. Being able to hold the handle while removing the pin can also be considered a safety measure, especially if the trap is manufactured with a strong spring closure.

The problem with using this experiment in a workshop is that the resulting bloodstain is called a "medium velocity impact." Depending on the springs and traps used in manufacturing the device, the impact force can be strong enough to distribute blood drops as small as those resulting from gunshot or as soft as that for a hand slap. The strong traps use an auto coil that can crush bones if mishandled. The "velocity" label is very subjective. Tensor force sensors could be used to determine the amount of force and the relative amount of breakup of a given composition of blood.

Part of the confusion in applying the patterns seen with the spring trap is that a line of blood is often applied to the entire front edge of the bottom lip. The impact thus distributes blood drops along a line, rather than as an area more closely resembling that of a blunt force attack during a crime. The square shape of the lip creates a linear arrangement of impact origin. Depending on the width of the lip, the impact could resemble the whole pattern distribution for a wide weapon. The problem is that the width will most likely exceed the width of any comparable injury. The width can be adjusted on the trap by making a small circle of blood in the middle or on an edge of the lip. Refer to Figure 11.6 for an example of placement of blood on the spring trap. The important feature is that the spatters are arranged as distributed away from a central area, which is the area of convergence on each adjacent target surface. This shows the size and shape of the impact that distributed blood drops. The trap dynamics are good, but using it as a pattern match to memorize is not applicable.

FIGURE 11.6   Blood placement on the lip of a spring trap device.

This experiment is beneficial in showing students that the size of the origin of an impact with blood is not a point source. This provides a more realistic concept for later reconstruction of the spatters to the origin.

Allowing the Sacramento workshop participants to select obstructions to place between the traps and a target resulted in an excellent application to casework resulted. The obstruction creates a blockage pattern. This helps participants appreciate the use of blockage in rearranging, removing, and/or replacing items around a crime scene. Too often investigators focus on the size and shape of spatters and miss the fact that something was present (or absent) when the blood drop distribution occurred. Knowing what was moved or removed has more investigative application than recognizing spatters from an assault that is already known.

Most workshops include a castoff-oriented exercise. Although these exercises are excellent, as pointed out in *Bloodstain Pattern Evidence, Objective Approaches and Case Applications* (Wonder, 2007, pp. 294–295), the participants' mindset while doing the exercise is essential. Workshop participants tend to view the exercise as an opportunity to create bloodstains on the ceiling of an enclosure. The action is to roll a chosen weapon (hammer, crow bar, wrench, ball bat, etc.) across a blood-soaked sponge. The weapon is then jerked backward to throw blood drops at the ceiling. The return of the weapon to the sponge is not forceful because the objective is just to pick up more blood to distribute on the back swing. Crime scenes do not involve this approach to action as an assault. There is, however, an exception to crime application. Staging does involve this approach; thus, it can be an essential observation to alert investigators to possible staging after the crime. During the initial approaches to the crime scene work-up, one needs to understand the dynamics of how castoffs are distributed during an assault versus during staging events later.

In workshops, the castoff arrangement may have a "V" arrangement at the reverse of the swing. This is caused by a snap when the weapon is reversed after traveling back away from the blood source and then abruptly changing direction. The distribution is more like cessation castoff than a swing at that point of travel reversal. Confusion has resulted from bloodstain pattern workshops that associate the "V" with the position of the victim, which could be the interpretation from an impact spatter pattern. Arrangements on the ceiling are less likely to be misidentified, but the arrangement on walls can present interpretation problems. More important, the "V" that occurs, like the flicking of a wet towel in shower room play, can indicate that the swing castoff was staged after the assault rather than as part of it.

In a workshop, participants can learn to differentiate these two different dynamics by thinking in terms of beating someone to a bloody pulp versus just making bloodstains on the enclosure ceiling. The issues to notice are the size of the drops, which depend on the ability of the chosen weapon to carry blood from the blood source, and the directions of travel for each leg of the swings. One needs to note which way the force is directed and the degree of force behind the swings. If participants do not make this consideration, interpretation with respect to crime scenes can result in error.

Transfer patterns are easily studied, and little needs to be added. Blockage patterns appear to be underutilized in casework. A very important application of blockage patterns, in addition to that discussed in relationship to impacts, is the folds of clothing on the victim's body. On the initial approach to the scene, it is especially important to observe and photograph apparent blockages due to folds in the victim's clothing after bleeding (see Figure 11.7). These blockages can often help in determining if the victim moved after the assault or if the body was moved.

FIGURE 11.7   Folds in the victim's clothes suggest the body was repositioned after bleeding profusely and perhaps carried to the dirt shoulder of the road later.

Moving transfers are readily recognized and easily studied in workshops but not often used in forming investigative leads later. In the workshop exercise, a target is spattered with blood drops and a material or an object is drawn through the existing wet spatters. This is a wipe moving transfer pattern. If the action is back and forth through the spatters, it becomes a smudge, where direction of travel cannot be concluded as one direction. If the bloody object or cloth is drawn across a clean surface, it represents a swipe. What often happens during exercises in workshops is a target will be spattered with blood drops and then the object or cloth drawn through the wet blood. The action, however, doesn't stop at the end of the blood-spattered area. What started as a wipe becomes a swipe as the object or cloth continues beyond the wet spatters. This is a combination of wipe going into a swipe. This distinction is important at a crime scene when one is interpreting an attempt to clean up the scene versus an accidental brush against and through existing blood. In other words, the interpretation based on which action is identified may become important to an investigation.

Splash-type exercises are fairly well understood. Several variations on design have been used in workshops, and all have some usefulness. There is a need to understand that the streaks and exclamation marks from a splash exercise are not equivalent to gunshot distributions. In some case examples, incompletely trained individuals assumed blood streaks on a floor could be measured for impact origin reconstruction. A rule of thumb with measuring stains for impact spatter reconstruction is that anything under 10 degrees is too elongated to be an accurate estimation of angle of impact.

The importance of the streaks also differs between splash and gunshot distribution. With splash, streaks occur because the distribution is at a very narrow angle to the floor where it is recorded. The streaks for gunshot occur because the explosive gases behind the bullet accelerate the blood drops so fast that forward movement does not cease for a length at contact; instead, the remainder of blood from the drop is pushed along a surface to form a streak/exclamation mark spatter.

Any exercise that indicates to participants that there is such a thing as a standard-sized blood drop is a waste of time and leads to confusion in application. The establishment of a standard value is applicable to a laboratory setting only. There is no crime scene application, and the assumption that it can be used for casework is misleading. The inclusion of such exercises wastes time and money in training that can be better filled with case examples showing how the exercises from a workshop may be applied to actual casework later.

Most workshops do not include an exercise illustrating the results of arterial damage distribution. One hopes that participants learn to recognize such results through lecture cases showing known arterial damage at crime scenes. Unfortunately, this method does not encourage a 3D mindset. It suggests a pattern match type of solution and one based on viewing photographs later. Arterial damage blood drop distribution creates a wide range of patterns depending on the conditions of injury and movement of the victim after assault. The importance must be emphasized because, as investigative leads, arterial patterns have nothing to do with the assailant after the artery is breached. Showing the link between this dynamic and what to look for in a crime scene is not easy.

Three acceptable approaches have been shown in research and workshop programs:

1. *Syringe with forced pressure expulsion.* If this exercise is used to illustrate the stream of arterial-propelled drops, the needle size must be large. A bone biopsy needle with a blunted tip is preferred to provide some safety from needle stick during demonstration. Use a large syringe, 30 to 50 cc from a morgue or coroner's lab.

2. *Peristaltic pump forceful extrusion.* This approach reproduces the pulse but in a reverse manner. Arteries are under continued pressure with spurts of additional pressure from the heartbeat. The peristaltic pump breaks the pressure at given intervals while forcing a column along. The reason for using this technique is that such pumps are common in laboratories and thus are easily set up and controlled. An additional advantage is that smaller amounts of blood may be used. The difference in dynamics is of little concern to the advantages of including the exercise for training.

3. *Recirculating pump with hand pump addition.* This, of course, is the best demonstration, and it's fun for participants. However, it has a number of disadvantages. The reservoir that holds blood is open and requires a large amount of blood compared to the other two techniques (see Figures 11.8 and 11.9). This open reservoir presents a safety hazard and thus requires full gown, mask, shower cap, and shoe protectors for at least two participants. Two additional people need to gown up if they are to record what is happening during the exercise and shut off the pump quickly. The advantage to the exercise is that it gives participants a good idea of the blooding possibilities of an arterial damage assault. Many, if not all, possible arrangements from a pinhole puncture of a major artery may be reconstructed within a minute or two. An alternative way to use this exercise in training is to perform the spraying in a shower stall while videotaping the spray. Then show the video to workshop participants during lectures for arterial damage bloodstain patterns. More details about the design of this and the preceding experiments are included in *Bloodstain Pattern Evidence, Objective Approaches and Case Applications.* (Wonder, 2007, pp. 298–301).

IV. APPLICATION

FIGURE 11.8   Construction of recirculating pump and reservoir containing blood. Tested transfusion-quality blood must be used for safety reasons.

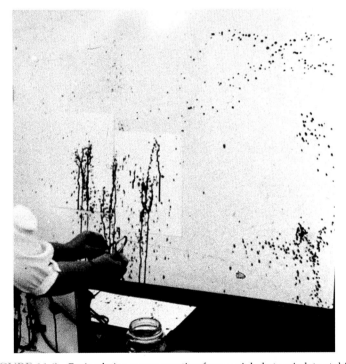

FIGURE 11.9   Recirculating pump spurting from a pinhole tear in latex tubing.

The essential parts to illustrate what participants may see at crime scenes are the pulsing effects of an arterial system, uniformity of alignment, and size ranges for parts of the patterns. As the victim moves or remains stationary, other parts of overlapping patterns will vary. Lectures often focus attention on size of stains from arterial injury, mainly because arterial injury can involve large quantities of projected blood. The quantity of blood is characteristic, but the size of injury may not be if breach is achieved via aneurysm. The parameters influencing size are movement and type of injury. Type of injury will not be known and/or verified until after autopsy. Thus, the involvement of arterial damage must be recognized before autopsy so that the autopsy physician may be requested to look for arterial breach if it is not immediately obvious. Unfortunately, some experts feel they must see indication of arterial damage on an autopsy report before looking for it at the scene or in photographs of the scene. As previously mentioned, pathologists do not always feel a need to mention, nor even look for, arterial injury, especially if it has resulted from an aneurysm after blunt force trauma and is not directly linked to the cause of death.

Workshop examples as exhibits may help show the variety of arrangements for arterial injury, but hands-on pulsing exercises provide a better experience with the total range of possible recorded arrangements (see Figure 11.10). Any photograph- or exhibit-only presentation will encourage a

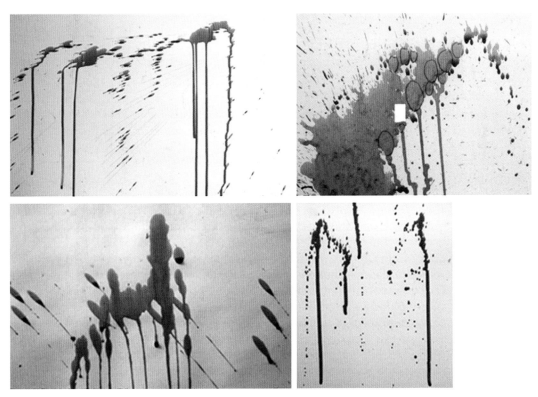

FIGURE 11.10 Variations of arterial damage patterns created from experiments with a recirculating pump.

IV. APPLICATION

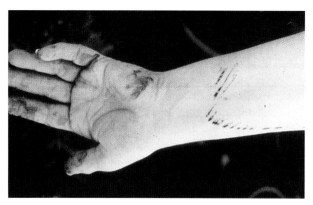

FIGURE 11.11   Arterial damage pattern on the arm of a demonstrator using the pump. This observation could verify suicide by cut wrists.

2D approach. In Figure 11.11, note where the demonstration resulted in an arterial-type projection toward the demonstrator. Note the absence of staining to the hand that could be holding a knife. The arterial pattern could correspond to a cut to the opposite wrist. In this case, right-handedness versus left-handedness and interpretation of what is seen or not seen in the patterns would be strong clues as to suicide versus homicide.

THE IMPORTANCE OF THE 3D APPROACH

The two most important considerations for applying bloodstain pattern analysis learned from workshops to crime scene casework are competent training and a 3D observation approach. The worst way to apply the evidence is to immediately begin measuring spatters at the scene. Perhaps this is why homicide detectives have occasionally shown an advantage over crime scene investigation personnel in solving mock crime scenes in workshops. Detectives usually do not like to measure spatters and thus rely on CSIs to do it for them in casework. Those CSIs who are oriented toward fingerprints tend to examine the evidence for pattern matches, with measurement guidelines predominating initially. A highly regarded forensic scientist once said, "Don't miss the forest for the trees." This is the best mindset to apply to bloodstain pattern analysis. This type of analysis is not a pattern match type of evidence to be lumped with fingerprint identification.

A television program titled *Cold Justice*, which premiered in 2013 on the TNT channel, illustrates an excellent application for bloodstain pattern analysis. The program focuses on old cases, which also illustrates that use of the evidence originally may have benefited the investigation so that it didn't become a cold case. The CSI star of the program always re-enacts the crimes and compares them to the autopsy/medical reports and what physical evidence was available at the time the crimes were discovered. The play acting as it relates to the injuries listed on the autopsy and timeline puts the crime scene in a 3D framework. In this way, those involved can recognize unlikely scenarios by getting a feel for viewing the actual events, and thus those events are less likely to lead to wasted time and effort.

Some excellent training workshops also include a mock crime scene as a final exam in the course. The important criteria for mock crime scenes are that they are as close as possible to the way a real crime scene would result but are duplicated as safely and as contained as possible. The benefit of the Sacramento semi-annual workshops, which commonly included one to two people from a wide range of departments, was that the participants had learned well enough from previous students to be able to point out inconsistencies regarding actual crimes as portrayed in the construction of mock crime scenes. This showed that graduates not only learned information for their own casework but also passed it on to others in their departments. If a program is repeated exactly the same way, as is characteristic of many law- and law enforcement–designed courses, participants from each agency need to be sent to different courses. The sum of the knowledge gained will benefit the entire department.

The 3D approach was used in the final exam of early workshops, which distributed a paper fold-up of an alleged crime scene. Unfortunately, when this fold-up was used as a final exam, any misconceptions among participants were pointed out only after the course was over. No time was devoted to going over the answers. The instructor recorded students' failure to understand the 3D nature of crime scenes perhaps as a weakness for future court testimonies opposite the students trained, more so than to gauge the success of the instruction of the workshop.

So how does one apply bloodstain pattern information in a 3D context? The best approach is to visit the crime scene as soon after discovery as possible. If the first line patrol have had an introduction to bloodstain pattern evidence, that greatly advances the ability to gather information before the scene changes from investigative transfer. All bloodstain pattern analysts use photographs to finalize their interpretations, but a visit to the scene sets in motion the 3D concept for viewing the photographs later. One needs to stand back from bloodstains to gain information regarding the shape of the arrangement of spatters within. This often tells whether it's a single pattern or if overlapping patterns are represented. In fact, viewing a crime scene as three dimensions and considering how the events occurred in that context benefits an investigation by indicating overlapping events not seen in bloodstain pattern workshops and possibly missed on examination of photographs. Being at the scene frequently indicates to investigators that more photographs need to be taken, including whole patterns, parts of patterns, and the reference structures and context of the dynamics and blood distribution during the crime.

Apply sequencing to recognizable patterns. For example, begin by identifying a swing castoff pattern. Follow directions of travel for the spatters, locating the position of the victim and the end of the reverse swing. Look for indications of impact spatters at the victim, cessation castoffs showing self-defense or lack of self-defense, and drip castoffs indicating injuries that may be bleeding. This is the time and place to note inconsistencies. The sooner staging is identified, the better the chance of locating the best indication of a person or persons of interest.

Locate the amounts of blood in patterns. A few spatters and no drips can indicate the beginning of the assault, with progression toward more blood involved in the pattern formations showing the direction the victim moved while being assaulted. Video recordings of a crime scene are not as informative as stills unless there is some play acting showing the probability of events during the assault. In other words, sweep the video across a wide angle of the scene. Then have a person of the right height and weight as a suspect re-enact the assault. Stop at each whole bloodstain pattern and then telescope in to details and references to still photographs. Some day, virtual reality reconstruction photography may be possible. Such technology would have application in both casework and training modules to encourage 3D concepts to investigations.

Three-dimensional photography would be excellent if applied with bloodstain pattern analysis. Unfortunately, this may be too costly for small departments. Presentations at forensic meetings have included 3D autopsy photographs showing cadaveric spasms, which could be co-related to the victim's position at the moment of traumatic death. Chapter 12 discusses this observation further regarding examining and cross-examining pathology witnesses. For the purpose of applications at CSI work-up of the scene, the body should be photographed as soon as possible after a death is discovered. Pathologists can then identify and describe cadaveric spasms from photographs taken within an hour of death, even though autopsy may not be conducted for hours later.

Previous chapters also described stringing at a crime scene. This is a step taken after impacts are identified. Initially, CSI personnel take photographs with and without numbers to identify location when compared to a wide-angle shot before and after placement of numbers. Some time ago, a technique was described using dotted tape. This method is an alternative to strings for finding the area of convergence. A downside to using the dotted tape, however, is the fact that it encourages a 2D approach to spatters. Examples have been shown in which the tape is applied to spatters from castoffs and arterial damage patterns but missing the true identification and suggesting an interpretation inconsistent with the true dynamic event distributing blood drops. Tapes with straight lines or, cheapest yet, household string or thick black thread can be used for areas of convergence.

APPLICATIONS TO REVIEW WITHIN A 3D CONTEXT

In the follow-up to crime scene recording and collection, it is perhaps difficult to keep a 3D mindset regarding the dynamics of the crime. The reason is that analysis shifts from the actual scene to 2D photographs and written documents. Interviews, investigator logic in developing a scenario, and various reports from the crime lab and autopsy are all 2D in nature. This can lead to thinking of the case as 2D logic. The process may go something like this:

> A victim was shot with a hand gun (autopsy), neighbors all say the victim and person of interest had problems (interviews), a bloodstain pattern on the wall is high velocity impact spatter (labeled because death was by gunshot), and in conclusion a person of interest is to be arrested. Inconsistencies may exist and be ignored, such as the bloodstain patterns not from gunshot impact but rather from a nose bleed from an earlier fight. One of the neighbors also fought with the victim, and there was money owed. The autopsy also lists blood in the nose, trachea, and larynx. If the crime had been viewed in a 3D context, it might have been noted that the person of interest was not of the correct height for the angle of the gunshot to result in the assumed high velocity impact spatter pattern on the wall. Re-examining the impact spatter pattern shows dynamics characteristic of respiratory distribution. Confirm with autopsy and re-interview neighbors.

One way to achieve a 3D review of the evidence is to use a 3D HumanCAD (HumanCAD Version 2.5, 2013) type of program. An advantage to this program is that after drawing the victim as found and finding possible prior positions, one may shift the eye view to examine the scene from different angles. This is a strong 3D concept application, but it also can aid in understanding the dynamics of the crime as they relate to injuries and bloodstain patterns. Not all departments would be able to afford this software, but a central agency, such as state or federal government or international private laboratories, could make the application available.

An example of reviewing a case in a 3D context was discussed in *Bloodstain Pattern Evidence, Objective Approaches and Case Applications.* (Wonder, 2007, pp. 175–180). A woman was found in a warm waterbed with gunshot wounds to three different areas: the right-side rib cage, the right temple, and the back midline of the skull. The rib cage shot would not be immediately fatal, but shots to either the temple or back of the skull would be. The rule of thumb is that you can't successfully kill someone twice. The shot to the side was reconstructed by having a volunteer of a similar size wear the nightgown the victim was wearing when shot. Refer to Figures 11.12 and 11.13.

FIGURE 11.12   Volunteer sitting as suggested by the crime lab when the victim was shot in the side.

FIGURE 11.13   Volunteer wearing the victim's nightgown while standing at the moment of the gunshot to the side.

IV. APPLICATION

FIGURE 11.14   Victim carefully arranged in a warm waterbed after the two shots to the right side.

The white dot in the figure is the bullet hole through the nightgown that corresponds to the entrance wound and direction of the bullet path found at autopsy in the victim's side. Because this shot wasn't immediately fatal, it can be considered the first shot, with either of the two fatal shots coming afterward. The victim was still capable of some defensive action. However, the assailant could move in with the shot to the temple. In Figure 11.13, the position of the victim is reaching downward toward a drawer in the waterbed where a Beretta handgun was said to be located. This is more consistent with the location, orientation, and blood flow noted on the nightgown. A shot in the same location killed the woman's son two years prior. This is not immediately ignoring the skull shot but was a consideration to be evaluated further. Note the flow of blood from the side wound. It is suggested that immediately following the shot, the victim fell forward, yet she was found on her left side in the bed.

The body was found carefully arranged in the waterbed (see Figure 11.14). The pillow case, which was found over her head, showed a characteristic "V" arrangement of spatters from a gunshot. This was arranged so that the pillow was on her head and the gun was positioned under the pillow aimed toward the back of her head. This position confirms the gunshot to the skull being fired after the body was arranged on the waterbed. Later, the autopsy physician verified the shot to the back of the skull was post-mortem, confirming the order of injuries interpreted from bloodstain pattern evidence.

Approaching the information in a 3D context helps determine the sequence of gunshots with the autopsy. Both of the other shots were premortem. All of this information was useful in the trial of the victim's husband, who had killed his son and two years later killed his wife by a premeditated plan. The husband had admitted earlier in the death of his son that he was familiar with body temperature in determining time of death. He had an alibi for a time period following the shooting of his wife. The purpose of the waterbed was to facilitate keeping the body temperature up. Initial scenarios included a burglary that went wrong and that the victim was killed because she woke up from sleeping in the waterbed and was shot. The DA brought in an outside expert when too many inconsistencies were recognized in the death of woman/wife/mother. The case on the son, which was originally called suicide, was reopened.

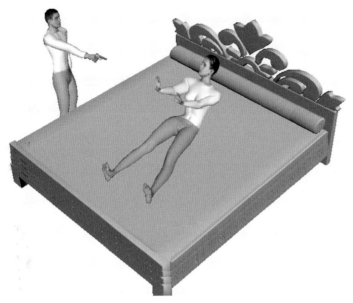

FIGURE 11.15   HumanCAD drawing of the crime lab suggestion.

FIGURE 11.16   HumanCAD drawing of alternate position during the shot to the side.

HumanCAD could have been useful in a case such as this. A 3D drawing of the figures should show that the angles of shots for the side and temple wounds were not logical from the position of the body as found (see Figure 11.15). If the victim was seated upright, as suggested by the crime lab, the assailant would still be too high for the wound straight across to the side. Figure 11.16 illustrates

IV. APPLICATION

an alternate position of the body during the shot to the side. More important is that the entry to the bedroom is to the left of the foot of the bed. The assailant would have to walk in the door, around the bed to the right side of the victim, and shoot her in the side as she faced the foot of the bed. Not only is this an unlikely position for the victim being accosted by a stranger, as alleged at the beginning of the investigation, but it is an impossible position for the body as found. After the shot, the victim would not fall in the position found, and why would a burglar artfully arrange the body with covers after shooting? The shot to the skull was overkill but possibly to justify the position in which the victim was found.

A final note regarding this case is that a hutch cabinet was located on the left side, as viewed from the foot of the bed. Any burglar entering from the opposite side of the bed would be very unlikely to wait until he walked around the bed to shoot the victim as she sat up in the bed. If that had happened, then the question remains: Why did she not get up immediately if she saw a burglar within the bedroom? All in all, the interrupted burglar assumption wasted time and money in the investigation. Also, calling the son's case a suicide on the basis of the father's statements provided no economy later.

REFERENCES

HumanCAD Version 2.5, 2013. NexGen Ergonomics Inc. Available at www.nexgenergo.com.
Wonder, A.Y., 2001. Blood Dynamics. Academic Press, London. pp. 20–21.
Wonder, A.Y., 2007. Bloodstain Pattern Evidence, Objective Approaches and Case Applications. Elsevier, San Diego, CA. pp. 175–180, 294–295, 298–301, 348, 363 (Appendix D).

Bloodstain Pattern Application in Court

Before you can solve a problem, you must first understand it. Although both lawyers and scientists employ logic, lawyers apply logic in different ways than scientists. They have different viewpoints derived from law school. Lawyers are trained to respect precedent and the majority view. That viewpoint comes into play when they work with experts. They tend to accept an expert's theory if they believe courts have previously recognized that theory as a proper basis for testimony. It is true that *Daubert v. Merrell Dow Pharmaceuticals, Inc.* (Daubert v. Merrell Dow Pharmaceuticals, Inc.) formally abandoned the *Frye* (Starrs, 1982, p. 684) general acceptance test. However, a close reading of *Daubert* reveals that trial judges are still supposed to consider general acceptance as a factor, and any realistic survey of the case law indicates that trial judges ascribe a great deal of weight to that factor. Of course, trial judges are most likely to be lawyers. In contrast, scientists revel at the prospect of shattering previously accepted principles. To name just a few, Newton, Einstein, Lister, Pasteur, Edison, and Jobs all pioneered breakthroughs that upset the conventional wisdom. Although the legal system usually progresses by a gradual refinement of long lines of precedent, the evolution of scientific thought is dictated by ongoing empirical research that often overthrows previous beliefs. The difference is a question of degree, and it is nevertheless a significant difference.

HISTORY FROM THE LEGAL VIEWPOINT

The recognition of bloodstain pattern analysis as evidence to apply to adjudication in the United States belongs with Dr. Paul L. Kirk, who implemented the criminology degree at the University of California at Berkeley, established the beginnings of the profession of criminalistics, and applied techniques previously developed in Europe to cases of violent crime in the United States. He applied rudimentary research, or reconstructions, for bloodstain patterns, called blood dynamics, as a technique for court presentation. Dr. Kirk lectured to lawyers, encouraging them to view the importance of the evidence in trials. Appearing in court as an expert witness in blood dynamics also provided a source of income for Dr. Kirk, and this lucrative role as an expert witness has been passed on to others learning the field, in addition to their forensic work or as a retirement occupation. In his correspondence, he appeared to have encouraged others to further the science but not to have contributed additional information from his own studies. He also apparently did not discourage erroneous assumptions in applied principles, at least based on those from his own scientific background.

Other documents reviewed at the Bancroft Library at the UC Berkeley campus and a review of appellate decisions regarding some of his casework and testimony show that Dr. Kirk predominantly followed earlier European studies (Piotrowski, 1895, pp.5–62) in which reasonable facsimiles of weapons were used to beat blood sources, usually a blood-soaked sponge or sacrificed animal, to create recognizable patterns (Balthazard et al., 1939). He emphasized the arrangement of spots, termed "spatters," to identify the way an assailant used a weapon involved in a violent assault. Later instructors shifted training to imply pattern match identification, allowing participants in workshops to attempt to memorize simplified exercises and afterward apply their memory of such exercises to crime scenes. This approach has carried over into the concepts for reconstruction experimentation of casework.

INTERACTIONS BETWEEN LAWYERS AND BLOODSTAIN PATTERN ANALYSIS EXPERTS

The first paper this author delivered at a Pan-American Conference science meeting in 1982 (Wonder, 1982) began with this sentence: "There are two ways to view blood dynamics, forward and reverse." After more than 30 years gaining much more knowledge and experience, the author believes that opening statement has had considerable verification and applicability. If everything worked well to the point of consideration for court, there should be no surprises or problems. That is, if identification has met specific criteria, as Dr. Kirk advocated from his lectures to lawyers, interpretation with scientific logic has been periodically updated, and that logic is applied to the investigation from the onset, trial presentation should be simple and straightforward. This is the point where the reverse comes in: historically, bloodstain pattern evidence in the United States has been used in *reverse order*. That is, the experts, upon instructions from the lawyers who hire them, start the sequence of applying bloodstain pattern interpretation, rather than have it begin before initial case work-up. Rather than the bloodstain pattern interpretation applying to the investigation, each side of the bench in the adversarial process interprets the evidence as benefits its case presentation. Interpretation—and often even identification of which dynamic act occurred—is shoe-horned into testimony to prove whatever is desired by the legal counsel putting the witness on the stand. This occurs during the trial rather than the evidence being used in an unbiased way at the onset of the investigation. An officer or expert may be encouraged to say what is desired for a future "atta boy" (a commendation from the department) or possibly to protect his future of being hired or involved in major crime cases.

Many examples of this scenario exist. One was the case previously presented in Chapter 9, where arterial damage bloodstains were found on a freezer in a garage but ignored during prosecution presentation at trial. If the true identification of bloodstain patterns had been admitted at the beginning of the investigation, it should have been available to the defense during mandated discovery. The argument could then be applied to contradict the prosecution's scenario that the brother, who had a key to the front door, which was found locked, had to be the killer. The defense would then have the option to argue that a killer could have entered the garage while the garage door was open rather than entering the front door. Some well-regarded forensic scientists and law enforcement assigned experts claimed in their testimony not to mention stains in the garage because they didn't recognize the substance as blood. It was the defense expert who brought up the pattern identification of arterial blood distribution in the garage for the attorney defending the case. This example is an application of bloodstain pattern analysis working in reverse, not as it should have been as part of the fact finding in the initial case work-up.

It is difficult, if not impossible, to prove someone is lying when testimony is offered as an opinion, albeit that of an expert. The alleged expert may truly believe what he or she is saying based on training that focused on simplified principles and out-of-context basics. Relying on specific sizes for identification of which dynamic event occurred makes this possible. Because most events involve a range of sizes that overlap per type of event, one can select in a biased way, intentionally or unintentionally, that size of spatter to conform with what is desired, ignoring anything contradictory.

The solution to abuse in expert testimony as it relates to bloodstain pattern evidence requires understanding how each player in the drama of the courtroom views the evidence. This evidence may be a primary consideration to experts in the discipline, but to most other law players in the court process of violent crime, blood splatters [sic] are of little or no importance to the entire proceedings. Some highly qualified and regarded prosecutors claim never to use it. This is a sad comment that an economical procedure for speedy resolution of violent crimes is being ignored, if not outwardly abused, in application. It is regarded as a post-event expert opinion brand of evidence presented at trial rather than as a primary investigation technique, such as fingerprints, tool marks, and DNA collected for profiling. The decision is not that this evidence may be important and economical to include in an investigation, but rather whether the case justifies the time and expense of consulting with an accepted expert in the discipline.

The adjudication process, as trials are classed, in countries that practice the adversarial procedure (i.e., the accused are allowed to defend themselves), includes the following players: the judge, prosecutor, defense counsel, defendant, lay witnesses, law enforcement (beat officers, CSIs, and detectives), crime lab forensic scientist, medical doctor or medical officer who may be a pathologist, a jury (if the trial is by jury versus bench/judge), and assorted expert witnesses as called by either side. The first consideration is whether a bench trial or a jury trial is better in those jurisdictions where there is a choice between the two. Judges will be less influenced by bloodstain pattern evidence than juries, with at least one exception. Extremely bloody assaults may influence juries in an adverse way, which may result in their disengaging when the evidence is shown. (Neilson and Winter, 2000, pp. 223–250). By contrast, later during deliberation, the jurors may feel reluctant to let a possibly violent offender go free. They may decide to find the accused at least partially guilty of the horrendous crime and convict to a lesser degree instead of setting him or her free. Judges have usually heard such details before and are less affected by the gore of a case.

There is indication that a negative shift in attitude toward bloodstain pattern evidence may be occurring, perhaps as a result of publication of abuse and recognition that the subject may be applied as "instant evidence" when other physical evidence is not available. In this latter situation, an attorney selects an expert to testify that bloodstains are *consistent with* the opinion the attorney favors for trial. This may be a law enforcement–assigned expert or person from the government crime lab subservient to the prosecutor. It can also be a defense attorney selecting what the industry calls a "liar for hire." Keeping such individuals off the stand has not proven successful, thus reviewing their analysis and showing their opinion as not based on scientific fact are preferred approaches.

IV. APPLICATION

However, challenges to pure scientific principles should not keep qualified investigative information out of a trial. Years of experience and number of cases processed by the expert should not be the only accepted qualifications for the opinion presented at trial. This means that the expert should not automatically, on the basis of previous casework, be assumed to have the correct opinion in regard to identification of the bloodstains, as well as how the patterns were interpreted in their meaning when found at the crime scene.

IMPORTANCE OF PRETRIAL MOTIONS

Because pretrial strategies such as Frye challenges are not successful in keeping some experts off the stand, it becomes more advantageous for both sides of the bench to specify what areas the experts may include in their testimony by way of pretrial *motions in limine*. Trace evidence, firearms experience, and medical background all may enter into testimony regarding bloodstain patterns recorded at a crime scene. It is a waste of time and an additional frustration to wait until the moment of testimony to see whether these subjects will be admitted from the same expert with bloodstain pattern evidence. Once the boundaries of expertise associated with a bloodstain pattern analysis are established, the testimony may proceed to cover the sequences of the entire crime. When evidence may be presented with using just one witness, it will result in saving the time and expense of establishing testimony from more than one expert. This reason can also be argued to permit testimony from the bloodstain pattern analyst relative to how, when, and why bloodstain patterns were interpreted as they were as provided in testimony.

This author's many encounters with attorneys at forensic meetings and holiday office parties show that there is a level of contempt for "blood splatters" [sic] and individuals professing expertise in such evidence. Some of this contempt is deserved, but a lot of it should not be. Historically, bloodstain pattern evidence has been, and may continue to be, viewed as evidence to apply when other physical evidence is lacking. DNA is often seen as the "miracle evidence" to link assailants with crimes. The problem is that DNA merely shows who was there, not necessarily when or what those persons did while there. The extreme sensitivity of current testing protocols can be misinterpreted when found with bloodstains. There is no way to show how DNA was deposited without the addition of pattern evidence such as skin print, wipe, swipe, and spatter arrangements. Even when fingerprints are associated with DNA, the reason could be that the DNA was left over or under a previous or subsequent print, and not part of the crime itself.

The majority of cases will be tried by jury, whether or not the option existed to request a bench trial (or trial by a judge alone). In countries practicing the adversarial process, the prosecution will first present their side of the issue, and the defense will be able to cross-examine, rebut, and/or refute what the prosecution supply. If the prosecution team are unsure of the strength of their case, they may offer a plea bargain to the defendant to save time and the cost of the trial, or more likely to gain some sort of conviction when there is a fear that a jury might set the accused free in the end. Unfortunate as it may be, the fact remains that the cost of a trial should be very much a consideration for both the prosecution and the defense. It is the economy of using bloodstain pattern evidence that should be a factor for both sides long before trial. For the most economic advantage, it is tantamount that application of this evidence be part of investigations, not held back until trial.

APPLICATION OF EXPERTISE EARLY IN THE CASE

Considerations for the prosecution include the speed of finding the correct person of interest in a crime, plus eliminating surprises such as codefendants and eyewitnesses and bringing charges against the wrong person. Bloodstain pattern evidence may show what happened, and this information can be used with other evidence such as trace, tool marks, and DNA. Too often the defense will consider bloodstain pattern evidence only if the prosecution first indicate that such testimony will be entered. This is a huge loss to the defense team because the evidence can supply at least three advantages, regardless of whether the government recognizes the probative value for their side:

1. Bloodstain pattern evidence can show the attorney if the client is lying and help avoid getting blindsided, which could occur from the prosecution during trial.
2. Bloodstain pattern evidence can show mitigating circumstances that will benefit the client's case even though he or she may be guilty of some part of the accusations. Presenting this information to the client can encourage him or her to accept a negotiated plea, which saves everyone time and money. This may be seen either in refuting deliberate intent as a person accused of premeditated murder rather than as manslaughter resulting from nonintentional events involving the accused prior to the death of the victim. Such mitigating circumstances may be involved with acts by individuals who are streetwise to the criminal justice process. Unfortunately, although innocent, these latter individuals may lie even when lying is not necessary or may even be harmful for their case.
3. Bloodstain pattern evidence can show the accused was not guilty as charged. No matter what kind of person the client is, there may be evidence of innocence for the events of the crime as charged. If the client has been guilty of other events or events leading to, but not concluding with, the one under consideration, he or she may continue to lie, feeling that doing so will help with the greater charge. Although the concept of "innocent until proven guilty" is well known, juries may still feel that if the person is arrested and charged, he or she must share at least some of the guilt. Bloodstain pattern evidence has exonerated some innocent individuals.

An example of exoneration occurred when a couple attempted to frame a neighbor for an accident perpetrated by the husband (see Chapter 6). The couple claimed a young man broke into their house and pistol whipped the husband, yelling for his drugs. The couple claimed the kid was an associate of their daughter's boyfriend, of whom they disapproved. The police arrested the boy, and the assistant district attorney assigned to the case planned to proceed to trial after filing assault charges. Bloodstain patterns showed that the husband was not pistol whipped, but rather fell and hit his head on the door knob of the front door and that he staggered into the house but did not struggle with an assailant. When the district attorney reviewed the case, a new ADA was assigned, agreeing that the charges should be dropped.

All trial strategy advantages are more likely to occur when considered early in a case. Waiting until after the opposing side provides expert testimony puts a time constraint on subsequent analysis. Case review is then focused on confirming specific arguments rather than total fact finding. The effectiveness of testimony decreases when the jury members see the evidence as a simple difference in opinions between experts. The facts become less important for consideration than the resumes of the experts.

As mentioned earlier, previous casework may have nothing to do with the case under consideration. One standard approach by attorneys is to show for the benefit of the jury that the expert is beholden to the prosecution or is a professional defense expert. A better approach, which is not yet practiced, is to have the expert testify for the court as opposed to representing a specific side of the case. In other words, the expert works for the court or for a private lab that is employed to do work for both sides, not one specifically used for the prosecution or defense. If the expert's salary comes from the agency desiring specific testimony, it is impossible to prove total lack of bias in regard to bloodstain pattern evidence.

QUESTIONS FOR KEY WITNESSES IN BLOODSTAIN PATTERN ANALYSIS (BPA) CASES

The primary witnesses for the prosecution will be the detectives, CSIs, and forensic lab staff. One standard approach is that the attorney asks whether the expert had his or her work reviewed. This question relates to claims in government labs that someone signs off on all work. What is not presented is that the signing off usually occurs as part of a simple administrative review that the work is complete. This means a supervisor looks for grammatical and punctuation errors and that certain steps in an applicable protocol are listed. Lab managers seldom are trained in bloodstain pattern evidence and may not have been shown the logic which led to the report that is being signed. Most experts within departments or private labs have received training from a course taught by someone who may be in the profession of testifying for income. Review is not possible unless the former instructor is hired for the case. This is a good argument for training several people from each agency at different courses and requiring them to share their knowledge and review each other's analyses. Listing alternatives to an interpretation may suffice to provide, or refute the possibility of, an error rate for the scientific discipline of bloodstain pattern evidence.

A major component of the application of bloodstain pattern evidence at trial is laying the groundwork for the expert testimony. Although the prosecution may feel there is no need, doing so is advisable for both sides of the bench. Setting the framework for conclusions is essential for defense expert witnesses. The most important opening is from the pathologist, or a medical doctor if death was delayed or not involved. In bloodstain pattern analysis, there must be a source of blood. Obviously, blood comes from inside a victim, bystander, or assailant during or following an attack. Where and how those injuries occurred can be paired with patterns at the crime scene to show exactly how those involved in the violence moved during and after injuries.

Following are some of the questions that should be asked; they require answers from a medical doctor/pathologist either before trial or during cross-examination. These are suggestions for deposing the various individuals who are involved with testifying in cases of violent crime.

Questions for Deposing Pathologists

1. Was an artery breached? If the pathologist fails to mention or denies having seen an injury to an artery during the autopsy, especially when arterial patterns were identified at the scene, it becomes important that blunt force trauma be mentioned and explained in regard

to damage to arterial cell walls prior to testimony by a bloodstain pattern expert. Blows that were delivered to the head may weaken the arterial vessels that are located over bone around the skull. If this weakening happens, a bulb is pushed out along the artery, much like blowing up a balloon. This, in turn, results in what is called an aneurysm. Subsequent blows to the same area along the artery may tear skin and rupture the bulb of the aneurysm. This type of breach may be as small as a pinhole, thus not clearly visible to the autopsy physician. If the pathologist refuses to identify an arterial breach, it becomes essential that he or she be asked to describe how blunt force can create and pop an aneurysm. Efforts are being made to make arterial involvement a part of standard autopsies (Wonder, 2005; Discussions and considerations for the Scientific Working Group...). Even if it becomes listed in a standard forensic autopsy protocol, years will lapse before such changes in procedure are included for all autopsies and training of new pathologists who will be doing autopsies. Autopsies performed by a clinical pathologist may still not follow forensic protocols. If the victim was admitted to an emergency room prior to death, emergency care records are more likely to identify arterial breach because of the seriousness of such injury.

2. When was the autopsy performed relative to time of death? When one is asking questions regarding time of death, it is beneficial also to ask or cross-examine regarding whether and when the autopsy was performed relative to time of death. For example, a condition known as cadaveric spasm occurs with death during extreme stress. When it is important to associate the position of the victim at death with the bloodstain patterns at the crime scene, it is mandatory that a pathologist explain what this condition is and when it is seen. Pathologists who routinely do not perform autopsies until several hours after receiving the body at the morgue may never encounter this condition. One can find an explanation of what the condition entails using an online search engine; here, in brief, it can be described as that condition which consists of immediate rigor setting in the extremities, such as arms, hands, and fingers, at or close to death. If the body is photographed soon after death, the position of the limbs recapitulates (i.e., shows the same) the position of the victim as at the moment of death. Even if it was not part of the original autopsy, this information can be brought out in testimony from the pathologist by using crime scene photographs.

Figure 12.1 shows a victim in the back seat of a car. The man was cornered by four members of a rival gang as he left a business. He ran from his attackers and dove head first into the back seat of an auto while receiving gun shots to the shoulder and legs. Not one of the shots prior to his entering the car was immediately fatal. Notice that glass on top of the victim shows he was in position when the shots were fired to the car windows. One shot, which occurred after he was in the back seat, was to the exterior carotid artery at the left side temple. This shot to the head would be expected to be immediately fatal when the victim was in considerable fear for his life.

Figure 12.2 shows the body as removed from the auto within minutes of responding officers' arrival. The positions of the hands and arms are due to cadaveric spasms and thus provide the position of the victim at the moment of the fatal shot to the head.

Figure 12.3 shows the X-ray of the victim's temple area, which confirms the bullet to the temple. The view is face up, with the scattered skull fragments on the left side of the head respective of the victim.

IV. APPLICATION

FIGURE 12.1   Victim in back seat of car.

FIGURE 12.2   Body removed from car.

According to a definitive work on firearms injuries, the bullet should not fragment upon entry. (DiMaio, 1999). The fragments visible in the X-ray in Figure 12.3 are of bone fragments of the skull shattered by the missile/bullet track. Identification and explanation of these fragments should be made through testimony from the autopsy physician.

Figure 12.4 shows the victim at autopsy.

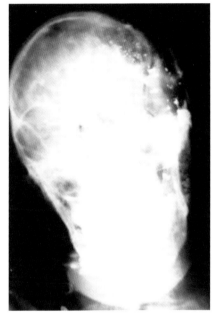

FIGURE 12.3   X-ray of the victim's temple area.

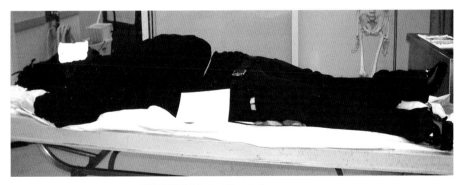

FIGURE 12.4   The victim at autopsy.

IV. APPLICATION

It is understandable that a pathologist prefers to autopsy a victim after rigor mortis recedes. That time can be 6 or even 12 to 24 hours after death. Regular rigor comes on after cadaveric spasms diminish. This information can be obtained from the pathologist during testimony or by cross-examining after initial testimony. The important issue is that pathologists do not mention cadaveric spasms because they may seldom, if ever, see this condition. Primary photographs of the crime scene, especially of the victim, must be shown to the testifying pathologist to identify the phenomenon and provide interpretation regarding primary position of the victim soon after death.

3. How long would the victim have lived after specific injuries? This question is very much related to interpretation of bloodstain pattern evidence. This information can be applied to sequence the injuries in regard to recognized bloodstain patterns around the scene. The sequence of injuries can then be used to confirm or edit possible scenarios regarding criminal intent. Many pathologists appear not to want to be specific as to the order of injuries, especially if more than one injury could have been fatal; i.e., it is unknown which injury actually led to death. If this is the situation, bloodstain pattern evidence should be included with the pathology report to help sequence injuries. If such information is not included in the autopsy report, then cross-examination of the pathologist prior to putting a bloodstain pattern expert on the stand is advisable.

4. What were the angles of blows, gunshots, and knifings? Autopsy reports are good for determining this information. Strength and angle of attack are essential both in identifying a person of interest and in proving claims of self-defense against deliberate attacks. Historically, the reconstruction of bloodstain patterns was to determine angles and strength of assaults with various weapons. Understanding how a specific weapon distributed blood drops is still relevant to investigations as well as the reconstructions of how an assailant used the weapon. However, it is also essential to bring out specific injury to the respiratory system: nose, mouth, throat, larynx, trachea, and lungs. Such injuries can lead to bloodstain patterns from coughing, wheezing, breathing, and sneezing after injury opens a blood source. This is linked to how long the victim could live after injury and if he or she moved around the crime scene. Misidentifications of bloodstain patterns occur with wheezing versus gunshot impact arrangements. Identifying injuries to respiratory organs can show the possibility that labeled "high velocity impact spatter" patterns actually may have come from the victim wheezing, panting, and/or breathing after injury.

5. What medical information was collected at the time of autopsy or during prior medical attempts to save the victim's life? This information comes under the expertise of the pathologists, too. In one case previously described in Chapter 10, a person was charged with assault and homicide, but the victim's death was listed on the autopsy report as toxicity due to *Pseudomonas aeruginosa*, especially virulent bacteria in the victim's blood that are resistant to antimicrobials. The victim was a homeless alcoholic. Deaths from *P. aeruginosa* septicemia, a blood infection, occur in the alcoholic homeless without any assault.

Victims with hepatitis, AIDS, and/or other forms of venereal disease can pass on the disease to their victims or assailants with markers that may identify the source of the infecting agent. The presence or absence of these markers may benefit the case for either side. The autopsy reports need to be reviewed and verification obtained in testimony from the testifying physicians. Cross-examining the autopsy physician can open up testimony as to pre-death health factors that contributed to death.

6. What is the blood composition? If it is known in advance that the prosecution will include bloodstain pattern testimony, the pathologist should be asked questions regarding blood composition. The main issue should be to raise the point that blood is not a uniform substance and does not behave the same as water. Events such as coagulation and the behavior of blood when mixed with water may be seen in bloodstain patterns, but prior description should be established with medical testimony. This does not mean that the expert on bloodstain patterns cannot testify as to blood behavior, but this information rather endorses and strengthens such testimony in front of the jury.

7. Were X-rays taken of the victim? If so, why aren't they included as part of testimony? When gunshot injury is part of the autopsy, X-rays of the victim are always taken. Surprisingly, these X-rays are almost never entered into evidence with the autopsy report and may not be part of the mandatory discovery. Tracking bullets and/or shattered bone fragments is essential in mapping the bullet path, which leads to the angle of the shot. The height and angle of a shot—whether or not the accused was able to deliver it—help determine the position of a firearm when a shot is fired. Preferably, the X-rays should be examined alongside the autopsy description of injuries. Contradictions have been found in which bullets were fragmented and redirected within the body, leading to erroneous conclusions by the autopsy physician regarding the number of bullets, wounds, and angles possible for gunshots. Bone fragments can also cause arterial breaches, which may be identifiable in the X-rays. For skull injuries, X-rays are required to show whether breach occurred in the subarachnoid space, the area where cerebral spinal fluid covers the brain, which would involve pressure and clear spinal fluid diluting blood in projected spatters.

Pathologists tend to be focused people. On one hand, what they say during testimony in regard to the autopsy is based on training grilled into them, so they may provide language without analyzing its effect on the jury. On the other hand, when a prosecutor requests information not phrased as directly related to the autopsy, pathologists may fall back on their civilian mindset and vocabulary. In one example, an autopsy reported no blood was found in the victim's mouth. During testimony, the pathologist said there was blood in the mouth. This statement was not a contradiction to the pathologist because he had viewed the mouth at autopsy differently from the appearance of the mouth in question while testifying. The defense expert in bloodstain pattern analysis explained the contradiction. Blood had seeped between the victim's lips and was deposited on the teeth, i.e., in the mouth. During the autopsy examination, no blood was found in any of the respiratory system, throat, nose, larynx, trachea, tongue, or "mouth" (i.e., behind the teeth). The pathologist was a clinical doctor, not forensically trained in crime autopsy standards, which may make a difference in autopsy reporting. During testimony, the pathologist was shown a picture of the victim with blood on the lips and provided with a reminder that blood was on the teeth behind the lips, and thus blood was in the mouth.

Questions for the CSI, Evidence Technician, and/or Identification Technicians

Crime scene investigators (CSIs, often called identification technicians) are an important part of the prosecution's case when application of bloodstain pattern evidence is used. The problem of viewing the evidence as a pattern match format was discussed previously. From experience, the author has found these individuals are very skilled and reliable if they have received good training. Some have a background in science, although that background may have been general science courses years previous to the law enforcement applications. What may be a vulnerability is the current scientific foundation for the specific evidence. In an ideal world, different parts of the investigation would work together for the whole case resolution. Identification technicians would describe the evidence they collected, photographed, and interpreted. Forensic scientists from the crime lab would explain the scientific principles behind the evidence, if such is required. Only those scientific basics that influence the evidence presented need be explained. Including out-of-context, out-of-date principles weakens the evidence as a whole, and they should not be part of testimony in the interpretation of bloodstain patterns associated with the case under consideration. CSI training may be simplified and include junk science principles rather than hard-to-understand technical data. The better approach would be to have criminalists trained in the true science of the evidence provide the explanations during trial when necessary.

From the prosecution's viewpoint, including antiquated scientific basics, with a focus on terminology without understanding the science of the evidence, may provide fodder for a skilled defense attorney to destroy essential physical evidence in a trial. The government needs to protect its experts as much as the defense team needs to provide background for theirs. Keeping up-to-date and informed on the background of the scientific discipline of bloodstain pattern evidence benefits all.

1. If testimony has been given in pattern classification using terms such as "high velocity impact spatter (HVIS)," questions should include (a) How do you know it is high velocity? (b) Is sneeze also high velocity? (c) Is size the only criterion you used to determine the identity of the bloodstain pattern? (d) If you learned that the victim was beaten at the position of the pattern you identified but shot someplace else, would your classification as high velocity impact spatter be the same?
   The objective is to determine whether the expert is merely spouting memorized terminology. A misapplication occurs when the case involves a victim of gunshot injury, and it is assumed that any groups of spatters found at the scene must be labeled as gunshot. HVIS is commonly equated with the results of gunshot although spatter sizes may occur with other events. Respiratory and high-pressure arterial release may distribute blood drop size ranges classified as mist, which is defined by post-1970 terminology as resulting from high velocity impact but with emphasized application excluding dynamics other than gunshot. Dr. Kirk's definition was that accelerated blood drops at a high velocity impact a target surface. Kirk's term retains the identification of *high velocity impact spatter* whether from gunshot or other events that may project blood drops at high velocity. In cross-examining an expert in bloodstain patterns, one needs to learn whether the expert's use of the term relates to any event that would distribute high velocity blood drops in addition to gunshot.
2. If size of spatters alone is used to justify the identification of a bloodstain pattern as to what dynamic event distributed the drops forming it, the obvious question is this: how many spatters from the arrangement were measured? This question prevents claiming the interpretation from a specific size that is considered consistent with the desired scenario. Thorough experts may use a grid to analyze spatter patterns. This is good technique, but any report based on this application should include the number of spatters per square and location of the grid square with respect to the convergence of impact-distributed spatters.

3. The expert might say that blood is a fluid like any other fluid and obeys the laws of physics and mathematics. In that case, these questions should follow: (a) Which laws of physics do you mean? (b) Are you aware that the mathematics of the string reconstruction of the origin are flawed? (c) If blood is like all other fluids, why can't other fluids be transfused to save lives? (This is a good question but one that the court may not allow.)

Blood is unique; that is why no acceptable substitute has been found to replace blood when blood loss is critical. Physics laws governing concepts such as surface tension are applied to stationary substances, not necessarily projected fluids and especially not blood drops. Water is governed by surface tension yet includes considerable wobble, or oscillation, in flight. Blood drops are much more steady in flight and thus must involve stronger internal forces than mere surface tension. The string reconstruction concept, in which it is assumed that a blood drop will leave an oval-shaped bloodstain with width equal to the diameter of the blood drop in flight before being recorded, is like the transference of a shadow, not a liquid drop traveling at an angle at impact. See Chapter 7 of this book for further explanations. There is no way to slice a sphere to get an oval shape with the same diameter as the drop that was distributed toward the recording surface.

4. The expert says that the pattern is castoffs. This is a primary error found in many CSI identifications. It is essential that background for arterial involvement be laid with the autopsy physician first. Then one might ask these questions to bring out the error in identification with the crime scene work-up: (a) How do you identify a castoff pattern? (b) How do castoff patterns differ in appearance from arterial spurts? (c) What is the difference in interpretation between castoffs and arterial spurts when they are seen at a crime scene?

The last question here is the most important. Castoffs are interpreted as violent swings of a bloody weapon, whereas arterial spurts occur without any involvement of the assailant beyond a possible initial blow. It's also within reason to have the assailant be the cause of an arterial breach, such as with fist blows to the head, and then leave the scene before the victim succumbs. Claims that the accused left the victim alive may be true as far as the accused remembers. If an assailant was responsible for the rupture of an artery, he or she could have caused the injury that led to death without knowing he or she did so; this could relate to criminal intent. Juries can be shown that the difference between castoffs and arterial injury is recognized through bloodstain pattern interpretation and can lead to conclusions regarding whether or not premeditation was part of the crime. Earlier chapters of this book presented ways to identify each pattern.

5. If the expert has done reconstruction experimentation, it is essential to bring out the logic involved. Questions include (a) What were you reconstructing with your experiment? (b) What was the composition of the material you used to simulate blood? (c) What were the differences between your experiment and the crime alleged?

Reconstructing the same size spatters provides no information regarding a crime event. The exact conditions of the crime events cannot be replicated or made to be substantially similar as required by legal standards. Reconstructing alignments and distribution of sizes, however, can provide an understanding of what happened in the crime events. Using an aqueous (water-based) substance for blood does not guarantee the same behavior as blood. Providing the differences between experimental design and the understanding of the crime scene events is a good way to provide an error rate for bloodstain pattern evidence. It is impossible to reconstruct an event without involving injury and loss of safety considerations, yet providing information on how an experiment differed or followed the actual crime allows the jury to make a decision regarding how close the reconstruction was to the alleged crime.

6. If photographs of bloodstain patterns are shown, questions should be asked regarding areas where there were no bloodstains. These questions provide information regarding blockages, absences, and arrangement of doors, windows, furniture, and objects around the scene at the time of blood drop distribution. Photographs showing environmental shadows are good sources for positioning the victim and surroundings at the moment when photographs are taken, after the crime scene is found. Flashes may block shadows from sunlight but not entirely. If environmental shadows are seen in photographs, it may be necessary to ask if pictures were taken without flash and what time of day photographic work-up was completed.

7. If testimony includes frequent use of the word "droplet," the expert should be asked to explain the difference between a "drop" and a "droplet." The original application was to differentiate a droplet as a part of the breakup of a standard drop. The degree of breakup was supposed to relate to the velocity of the force contacting the blood source. The term has been retained even though it is widely recognized that there is no such thing as a standard drop size. If there is no standard drop size, then the breakup of the fictitious drop to form droplets has no relevance or meaning. Fixation on terminology may suggest that the expert isn't keeping up-to-date with scientific principles but may be concentrating on speaking the language without necessarily understanding the evidence.

   Whether or not this line of questioning continues depends on how obstinate the expert may be. If the definition is that the term "droplet" is retained for historical significance—i.e., "that is what we say because that's what we've always said"—questioning would seem redundant and foolish to the judge and jury. The questions should end. If the expert continues to define the term as a breakup of a standard drop, then these questions can be asked: (a) How was the standard size determined? (b) What is the meaning? (c) What is the logic regarding the estimate of the size? The original determination of a standard drop size was illustrated by using chemistry laboratory burettes to disperse measured aliquots of donated blood, counting the drops necessary to reach the measured levels, and then dividing the number of drops distributed into the volume measured.

   For example, say 20 drops fell from the burette to make a measured volume of 1 cubic centimeter. Divide 1 by 20, and you get 0.05 cc, or the size of the drops in the blood sample used was 0.05 cubic centimeters. However, that value depends on the composition of the blood sample and the size of drops delivered by the burette. Different blood compositions will provide different-sized drops, and different burettes/pipettes markedly differ in size of drops. The conclusion is that this information is useless in application to actual crime scene evidence. It is, however, sometimes retained out of habit.

8. If the CSI testifying uses the expression "passive stains" to mean blood dripping without added force, the question is this: do you regard gravity as a force? If not, a number of lines of questioning can be applied. The first one is that gravity and gravitation are not necessarily the same thing (Parker, 1998, p. 905). Gravity is simply weight. Gravitation is also called gravitational force. The universal formula for force is $F = ma$, where F is force, m is the mass of something, and a is acceleration during free fall. Gravitation is written as $F = mg$, where g is the attraction of gravity toward the earth (Parker, 1998, p. 824). In other words, the acceleration is the force of gravitation.

Questions for Responding Officers and Early Investigative Personnel

If responding officers give testimony, some of the preceding questions may be relevant to the first sight of the crime scene. Additional information or questions may be applicable:

1. Was there any water, or moisture, around the scene? This question applies to the accusation that the accused cleaned up the scene and/or premeditated the assault with a planned follow-up. Blood mixing with water called PABS/Mix (physiologically altered bloodstain/mixed with another substance) patterns can be a source of information relative to the time line of the crime.

2. Do you recognize clotting of blood? Did you see any evidence of clotting in the blood around the scene? If the expert does not understand or recognize clotting, then his or her testimony is limited to fresh-shed blood, which limits the knowledge for investigative leads, identification, and interpretation of bloodstain pattern evidence in testimony. If an expert claims to recognize clotting bloodstain patterns, it is a good idea to find out how he or she learned this application. Workshops may fail to point out behavior of blood during coagulation, such as passing through specific stages and being delayed with agitation.

3. Was blood flowing or dripping at the scene? If blood was fresh, it should still be liquid and possible to flow when viewed at the scene. This information acts with the time line but also indicates the possibility of more bloodstain patterns occurring after assault. Not all actions may involve an accused. Some bloodstain patterns may be attributed to those coming to the assistance of the victim. A big error in viewpoint of some law enforcement personnel is to feel that a person of interest who has blood on his or her person is automatically involved in the assault. This view can be refuted by asking paramedics and emergency room personnel if they have ever obtained bloodstains on their clothes without being involved in an assault.

4. Was blood flowing from the victim, a bystander, or a person of interest? Individuals claiming to be assaulted but not involved in the crime do lie on occasion. The flow and spread of blood can show what type of involvement the person had to sustain bloodstains on his or her person. Explanations inconsistent with the bloodstain patterns are excellent sources to determine the truthfulness of persons of interest.

5. Did you seal the scene immediately upon arrival; i.e., did first line response officers seal the scene before paramedics, coroner's staff, and primary detectives arrived?

6. Did the seal of the scene include all bloodstains found, including those patterns identified later in the investigation? It should not be embarrassing that a scene was not completely sealed if the victim was still alive. Any area outside the seal should be identified early as an area where contamination and/or investigative transfer could occur. Sometimes investigative transfer can be used to draw a time line for the investigation. Every piece of information can have its use. Ignoring information is never the best approach to testifying regarding scene work-up.

Following are some common errors that may show up in the viewpoint of law enforcement personnel with regard to bloodstain pattern interpretation and construction of a crime scenario:

1. First line officers may focus on helping the victim to the extent that they contaminate the crime scene. Such contamination is labeled *investigative transfer*, to differentiate it from contamination by other noninvestigative individuals. Paramedics are classed with law enforcement officers in leaving investigative transfer. This is not a criticism but merely an explanation of changes to the evidence that must be considered when interpretation is applied later.

2. Although most detectives are suspicious people, they still tend to believe some of what they encounter at interviews. They tend to believe the victims, yet victims have occasionally been found to lie, be involved in the crime, and/or protect others who were responsible for the crime. An indication of lying may be the attempts to explain bloodstains around the crime scene and on those present. Identifying the dynamics from the bloodstain patterns at the scene before interviews can help sort out truth and fiction later. In one example, a suspect claimed his wife fell and hit her head on a bathtub. The detective saw the scene prior to the interview and thus was able to point out to the man that he was lying. The man was told that based on prior viewing of the crime scene, it was known that his wife's head was hit three times on the tub and then her body was moved to the position where she was later found. The man, shocked at the fact that his actions were known, responded with "the bitch deserved it."

3. Law enforcement personnel who attend lectures given by fellow officers tend to accept the principles presented without question even though the instructors may not have sufficient scientific background to be experts themselves. If lectures are given by non-law-enforcement instructors, opinions from such lectures are not necessarily believed over any previous ones by fellow law enforcement personnel.

4. For some reason not fully understood by the author, law enforcement primary investigators sometimes tend to ignore the victim's body unless photographing it for others to review. A possible explanation is that although law enforcement may harden responders to the scene by frequent exposure to violent death, they retain sensitivity to the loss of human lives. Photographs of the body are essential to a full investigation and should be taken as soon as possible after discovery. Angled shots, close-ups, and the whole expanse of the scene should be included. Flows should be photographed from different angles so that the directions of flows may be followed when showing pictures to the jury later.

5. Most experienced law enforcement officers are proud of their years with the force. They will willingly state the number of years they have been investigating violent crime. Questions of these officers should include (a) Have you had special training in bloodstain pattern evidence? (b) If training was obtained by attending a bloodstain pattern workshop, when did this occur relative to the years of experience? If training was within a year or so and experience is claimed over many years, there is a question regarding what was learned in the workshop. Participants may feel they already knew all they needed to know. These types of people probably attended a workshop to learn the terminology, not the applications, and will be easily confused when asked questions involving how the different events are identified with bloodstain pattern evidence. Sometimes this attitude causes participants to block out what they are being taught during a workshop. No instructor wants to be credited with teaching material inconsistent with the application of a scientific format, yet some participants may take away that misconception. Terminology does not teach how to apply the evidence to investigations.

6. The most common vulnerability to an investigation is to approach the crime scene and thus the crime in a 2D context. This approach may concentrate on words, not visual images of the crime committed. The influence of law helps shape this approach for more experienced investigators because of their many years of dealing with court testimony. Detectives may learn to think in terms of how the case can be presented in court with words, terminology, and interpretation. For example, a suspect has blood on his shirt. Rather than think in

terms of what caused the bloodstains and whether the suspect's explanation is possible, a detective may be thinking blood on the suspect means he committed the beating, and the bloodstain pattern was a medium velocity impact because the victim was assaulted with a blunt weapon. The terms to use are "medium velocity impact spatter [MVIS] from a blunt weapon." Lawyers may accept this description because words are their logic. The bloodstains on the suspect may, however, actually be from the victim still breathing and wheezing blood prior to death. The MVIS terminology is subjective. Questions regarding alternative possibilities should be included, even if only to exclude them as possibilities in a particular case.

7. Belief that any blood on a person is a symbol of guilt is a big error, as discussed previously. Claims that the blood was from another source can be refuted with DNA evidence. On one hand, claims of the accused not having been there at all will not be accepted given contrary DNA evidence. On the other hand, claims to offering assistance, having found the scene earlier, or having been present when the victim was injured at another time could be true and should not be ignored.

Questions for Laboratory Personnel

It is an unfortunate fact that many crime lab administrators feel bloodstain pattern evidence is a subject of police work, but many police identification officers and detectives feel it is too technical for cop work. Bloodstain patterns get lost between these two when, in fact, it is all of the above. On one hand, the law enforcement crime scene work-up is the first approach, and officers must be trained to obtain and apply investigative leads information. On the other hand, the true scientific discipline of bloodstain pattern evidence involves basics that are beyond the requirement of law enforcement background. Early training was simplified to prevent the technical basics from confusing workshop participants, but such limitations also alienated many qualified criminalists trained in science. When attorneys on either side of the bench can find an alleged expert to testify that whatever is desired by the employing party is consistent with the bloodstains, the result is that lawyers have less respect for the importance of the evidence as evidential leads. The solution begins with recognition that bloodstain patterns are scientific-based evidence but must continue to be established as an important application in court.

1. When one is examining clothing, an identification of bloodstains may be given as right or left. It is essential that everyone understands how the concept of right and left is applied. This description can be *as viewed* (i.e., the examiner's right or left) or *as worn*, for articles of clothing. An example of this error was encountered when a criminalist examined a bow tie worn by an accused assailant. A report was given to the prosecution stating the tie had blood spatters on the underneath left side of the tie, which was considered consistent with the tie being worn while the accused beat the victim located to the assailant's left. When the bow tie was presented to the defense expert, it was pointed out that the original criminalist viewed the tie flipped over, horizontally and vertically, so that at examination and interpretation, the underneath *right side as worn* became the *left side up as viewed*. The position of the spatters and interpretation were as if they were on the underside of the left. The spatters were actually on the underside of the *right as worn* by the accused, which would have been opposite the position of the victim during the beating (see Figure 12.5).

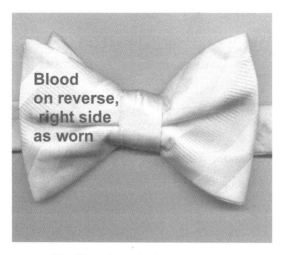

Tie flipped vertical, up to down
to view reverse side.
Description as examiner saw it.

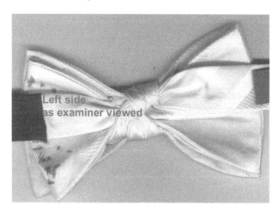

FIGURE 12.5   A bow tie is shown with blood spatters applied to the right side as worn. The interpretation was the left side as viewed.

No typing or DNA profiling was performed to identify the source of the blood. The accused was photographed carrying his injured, but very much alive, son with the boy's head on the father's right shoulder. Wheezing and contact blood from the child could have stained the bow tie on the right side. Bloodstains on the accused's right shoulder as photographed added confirmation.

The same types of questions should be applied to clothing examiners who identify bloodstains as blood spatters. The question is whether the spatters are seen on the inside or the outside of garments. Sometimes it is obvious where the stain occurs (see Figure 12.6). This is a transfer from inside the garment, i.e., as worn. An injury to the shoulder existed,

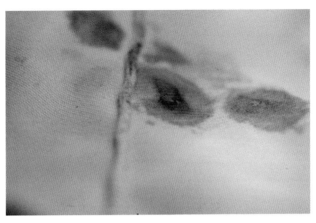

FIGURE 12.6   Bloodstain transfers are seen on the inside surface of a nightgown.

and when the garment was put on, part of the clot and still-wet blood was transferred to the garment. The same thing happened in Figures 12.7 and 12.8. Which side the blood touched first is not always apparent, nor is what dynamic event created the first wet bloodstains. If an expert claims to always know which side of a fabric is involved, it might be beneficial to show him or her unknown exhibits to identify. If doing so is not possible, requesting how the identification was made is necessary—just as an opinion of the examiner can be called into question.

Also notice the bloodstain to the far right, as viewed in Figure 12.8. The white specks show that the bloodstain came from beneath the fabric, not on it. All the stains seen were from scratch wounds under the T-shirt fabric. The little one resulted from a double transfer; i.e., the injury was blotted and then touched the shirt a second time when less blood was present.

This approach could be useful for justice if impact spatters are identified on the shoulder of a garment usually worn by the victim but occasionally worn by the suspect. This may happen with roommates, siblings, and parent/child relationships, among others in a modern family. To prevent misuse, one should note the area of the victim where scrapes or scratches could transfer blood drops. The lack of scars or an indication of any previous injury would nullify the explanation of spatters on the garment.

2. Working in a crime lab is no protection against using a 2D approach to evidence. In fact, many trace techniques include matching shapes, so that approach may be favored without knowing it. Although a criminalist may have the academic background to apply scientific technique, it is surprising to find that many accept the pattern match concept of identification for bloodstain pattern evidence. Visits to the original scene, re-enactments, HumanCADs, and mock crime scenes help and/or remind criminalists viewing the evidence in a 3D context.

3. Clinical and forensic labs have much in common. One common trait is the preference for measurement and/or instrumentation to validate the work. This technique is viewed as a

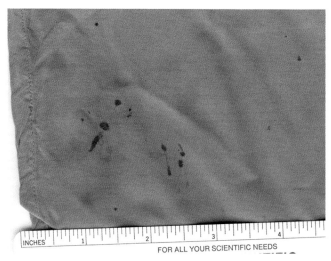

FIGURE 12.7   Transferred bloodstains are seen on a silk blouse.

FIGURE 12.8   A T-shirt is shown with transferred bloodstains from a fingernail scratch injury on the wearer.

safeguard so that one is able to say, "That's the result I found" or "I didn't make a mistake; the machine malfunctioned." Because bloodstain pattern evidence does not involve instrumentation—rather, it requires considerable logic—many experienced forensic scientists shy away from it. This is unfortunate because the lack of required costly instrumentation in the application of bloodstain pattern evidence should be recognized as a strong positive economic factor.

4. An argument offered by those in the crime lab who do not wish to learn the technical basis for bloodstain pattern evidence as a true scientific discipline may be that the subject can't be learned because it is too subjective. This is another way of looking at the inherent preference

for instrumentation to provide answers, rather than an opinion based on a lot of logic from an understanding of the evidence. Training and exposure to academic presentations have a lot to do with how those in a crime lab view bloodstain patterns. If the more experienced personnel and supervisors in a lab form derogatory opinions, they pass these along to others in the lab. Not everyone in a crime lab has the same academic background, unless the administration favors hiring personnel with only one type of background. A lab will greatly benefit from a variety of backgrounds if those with various educational histories interact and communicate well. Younger people and recent college graduates may have more recent updates on scientific foundations of benefit in recognizing that earlier incorrect concepts have changed.

5. Of course, the biggest vulnerability is a lab that, or individual who, frequently looks for evidence, or justification for evidence, against a specific person of interest while ignoring other possibilities. This may be in the mindset of the criminalist to please the prosecutor, or it may be from instructions from police and/or prosecutors. Defense lawyers are well aware of this possibility of abuse, so they cross-examine to bring it out if the focus was solely on the accused. Although of a lesser degree of injustice, some defense attorneys may focus on experts who routinely provide testimony to benefit clients; otherwise, they are not hired. Either way may put the expert under an economic burden to find as told, not to provide a true analysis.

Questions for the Bloodstain Pattern Expert, Excluding or Limiting Testimony

Examining or cross-examining an expert in bloodstain pattern evidence may involve approaches that differ from standard legal guidelines. Because of the lack of concern regarding the probative value of bloodstain pattern evidence, lawyers often fail to prepare in advance for examining the evidence and focus on the person testifying as an expert. The fact that the author has encountered the same approaches by lawyers in trials with widely different courts and cases shows that there may be little preparation to address the evidence itself. The expert with prior experience may be judged as sufficient. The examinations during trials usually involve one or more approaches:

1. Attempts have been made to exclude the evidence based on *Frye, Frye/Kelly in California,* and *Daubert* (Wikipedia.org), or legal standards of admissibility of scientific evidence. None of these cases are presently successful in excluding bloodstain pattern evidence testimony in today's courtrooms if the expert has even the slightest prior training. There has been too much training and testimony and too many articles in journals claiming scientific research for the argument that bloodstain patterns are not part of the forensic tools used in investigations. An interesting approach may be to ask the expert whether he or she believes bloodstain pattern evidence is a scientific discipline. Some alleged experts claim it is not, thereby creating an approach that disqualifies them from giving a scientific opinion based on bloodstain patterns. That belief, that bloodstain pattern evidence is not a science, also indicates that the expert has not had adequate scientific training in the discipline.

2. Claiming an individual does not have expertise to provide testimony regarding where blood sources are available inside the body is also not acceptable in modern times. This

claim is outdated. Nowadays forensics specialties exist for nurses, clinical technologists, and physicians who may be qualified to testify on bloodstain pattern evidence as well as provide explanations regarding how blood leaves the body to form identifiable (as to dynamics of projection) resultant patterns. To deny admission of the source of blood for patterns could be like discussing a traffic accident without being able to point out malfunctions of the automobile. Blood does not exist in arrangements of spatters without some prior event opening a blood source and causing drops to be projected away. How blood is exposed and leaves the body is a major factor in understanding the arrangements recorded at the crime scene. Experts who accept the limitation may not have a good understanding of how bloodstain patterns occur. Ironically, this argument can be reversed for testimony from pathologists. If a bloodstain pattern analyst is barred from discussing blood inside the body, the pathologist should be barred from discussing bloodstain patterns outside the body. The resolution of this issue turns on the scope of the testifying expert's education, experience, and training.

3. Because instrumentation and protocols involving chemicals are not required for bloodstain pattern analysis, anyone, regardless of background, can claim to have expertise in the evidence. The only requirement is showing knowledge beyond the normal individual. Showing the jury how to measure stains may suffice in the minds of judges and prosecutors, but this does not actually demonstrate that the individual is qualified to identify and draw conclusions regarding the significance of specific bloodstain patterns. In fact, measuring bloodstains is not precise even among participants and trainers of workshops. Variance occurs and may or may not be within acceptable ranges, nor be applied to applicable spatters.

4. An essential part of being an expert in bloodstain patterns is to be able to work with other evidence examinations. Crime labs may be required to work with too small of a budget to have individual forensic scientists specialize in one discipline, especially one that is limited to specific types of violence. Before the explosion of DNA forensic technology, bloodstain pattern evidence was included with serology and trace evidence. Serology is no longer a necessity in a well-organized crime lab. Serologists either retired, went into DNA, or branched out into other specialties such as trace evidence, but, if trained, retained focus on bloodstain patterns. The same arguments against the approach as 2D (measure and classify) evidence applies to all expertise.

5. A clue to the cross-examination approach of the expert is how an analysis is completed. Any review solely with observations of photographs and statements from interviews shows a preponderance of attention to 2D exhibits. Visits to the scene and re-enactments show an appreciation of the 3D context of the crime when blood is distributed. Some experts claim to ignore the autopsy reports because of dissatisfaction with information provided by pathologists. It is true that some testimony by physicians may be in error, whether or not it is based on autopsy or medical records prior to death, but it is not wise to ignore the reports. It is better to review autopsies and medical reports prior to trial and clarify any perceived errors or disagreements in testimony. All involved in jurisprudence need to remember that the trial records are kept for years and may be involved in litigation decades later when it may be impossible to resolve questions of error and/or possible contradictions.

6. The best approach to testimony by an expert is to teach the judge and jury how bloodstain pattern arrangements result so that they understand the evidence and the probative value. In the Alexander Lindsay hearing (The Honourable Mr. Justice Lovejoy, 1991), an opposing expert demanded that the expert on the stand state that bloodstains seen at a beating were

medium velocity impact spatters. Before the testifying expert could answer that the size ranges could be from any of several dynamic events other than beating with a blunt weapon, the judge asked the barrister representing the visiting expert whether he meant impact, castoff, or arterial. The judge was seeing how to identify patterns with his own eyes and was less confused by subjective labeling. Using specific criteria is a better way to teach recognition of pattern categories. Measurements do not have direct association to events and may confuse rather than educate. Exact velocity gradients are not known for the time of the crime, and thus can be confusing, especially when the expert himself or herself does not understand the historical applications.

7. The use of court exhibits is an important part of the testimony. The legal guidelines are to not overuse pictures of gore. To include many grossly bloody scenes with obvious grievous injuries may result in exclusion by the court because the prejudicial effect on the jury is deemed to outweigh the pictured probative value. The average person is not accustomed to seeing bloody crime scenes and may turn off attention to avoid thinking about what happened to victims during the crime. Pictures should be limited to specific points. Black-and-white photographs with colored areas showing specific bloodstains may be used. The colors should not include green, brown, or pastels. Green is the color of the international symbol "Mr. Yek," a symbol of poisons for children; brown is symbolic of defecation; and pastels may be regarded by jurors as silly and out of context with blood substances. Red, blue, or purple can be used to illustrate bloodstain pattern arrangements. The reaction of the jury should be viewed when evidence is presented and adjustments made accordingly regarding bloodstain pattern classifications.

8. It should be the crime lab forensic experts who deal with the jurors' concept of the "CSI Effect." In television programs, actors speak the language in a context that may not be found in crime labs. A common illustration is multiple in-line arrangements that are characteristic of arterial spray but called castoff by the actor. These programs are designed to solve a crime case within one or two program lengths. In real life, it may take days, months, or even years for all of the evidence in a case to be recognized for the value it holds in the investigation of violence. Providing all of these details in a television program could adversely affect the audience and the show ratings. It must also be remembered that violent criminals watch CSI programs. It behooves crime lab experts to attempt to dispel any CSI Effects in court. If they do so early in the trial, they can also point out to the jury that staging may occur from the suspect's beliefs in the CSI Effects.

SUMMATION

Court applications are complex, yet the application of bloodstain pattern evidence during trials has been experienced as relatively repetitive. This indicates that the primary users of the evidence, the lawyers, may not fully understand the uses, abuses, and probative values for applications, both prosecution and defense, from the investigative process to the courtroom. To make matters worse, but hopefully improved in the end, may be the present finding by appellate courts to consider false testimony from expert witnesses as grounds for granting retrials. ("Ryan Ferguson: Innocent Man Freed after Years in Prison"). The issue becomes who will point out to the court what is false expert testimony. If that is based on popular vote of any organization, the validity of the science is not necessarily being considered. A rule to remember is that if the testimony is to be offered in trial, it is essential that the attorneys understand it before putting a witness on the stand.

Throughout this chapter, reference has been made to updating the science. Research projects are considered methods of updating, yet there are many criticisms to research as applied to bloodstain pattern analysis. The various considerations regarding this issue are discussed in the following section for the benefit of the future experimental design. It remains essential that when new applications are found, legal counsels are alerted to the expanded applications.

REFERENCES

Balthazard, V., Pierdlievre, R., Desoille, H., Derobert, L., 1939. Etude des gouttes de sang projecte. Presented at the 22nd Congress of Forensic Medicine. France, Paris.

Daubert v. Merrell Dow Pharmaceuticals, Inc. 509 U.S. 579 (1993).

DiMaio, V.J.M., 1999. Gunshot Wounds: Practical Aspects of Firearms Ballistics and Forensic Techniques, 2nd ed. Taylor and Francis, Boca Raton, FL.

Discussions and considerations for the Scientific Working Group on Medical Death Investigations. Requests and comments have been supplied by the author to include comments regarding arterial damage in all autopsies where found. http://swgmdi.org/index.php?option=com_content&view=article&id=90&Itemid=103

The Honourable Mr. Justice Lovejoy, 1991. Report of the Enquiry held under Section 475 of the Crimes Act 1990 into the conviction of Alexander Lindsay (formerly Alexander McLeod Lindsay).

Neilson, W.S., Winter, H., 2000. Bias and the Economics of Jury Selection. International Review of Law and Economics 20 (2), 223–250.

Parker, S.P. (Ed.), 1998. Concise Encyclopedia of Science and Technology. 4th ed. McGraw-Hill, New York, NY, pp. 824–905.

Piotrowski, E., 1895. Ueber Entstchung, Form, Richtung und Ausbreitung der Blutsuren nach Hiebwunden des Kopfes. Vienna University Publications, Vienna. Exhibits taken from the 1992 English translation by Golos Printing, New York, NY, pp. 35–62.

"Ryan Ferguson: Innocent Man Freed after Years in Prison," ABC News Nightline. Last modified November 13, 2013. http://blogs.ajc.com/news-to-me/2013/11/13/innocent-man-free-after-10-years-in-prison-for-murder/.

Starrs, J., 1982. A Still Life Watercolor, in Frye v. United States. Journal of Forensic Science 27, 684.

Wikipedia.org is a good source of online descriptions for these precedent-setting cases.

Wonder, A.Y., 1982. Recent Research Methodologies in Bloodspatter Evidence. Presented at the Pan-American Conference on Forensic Sciences, Sacramento, CA.

Wonder, A.Y., 2005. An Expert Witness Requests Re-evaluation of SOP in Autopsy Reporting, Supported With Case Examples. Paper presented at the American Academy of Forensic Sciences, 57th Annual Meeting, New Orleans, LA, before the Pathology Biology Section.

RESEARCH FOR THE FUTURE

Reinventing the Wheel

It is not the purpose of this book to discourage any research in bloodstain pattern evidence. The objectives for the material presented here are for advancing identification, interpretation, and application of the discipline as an economical forensic science tool in the investigation and resolution of violent crime. Some approaches to research presently available in the literature, however, add little, if anything, to advance the discipline as an investigative methodology. It is believed that such projects were well intended and might have been conducted differently if the redundancy and omissions of experimental design were better understood when developed. The following criticisms, reviews, examples, and suggestions are offered for consideration before future projects are undertaken. Implementing some of these suggestions, one hopes, will improve the scientific recognition and application for bloodstain pattern evidence.

How Dr. Paul L. Kirk evaluated his experiments and how similar projects are perceived and concluded now differ. Many individuals, including some who have taken 40-hour workshops, believe that the sizes of any spatters found at a crime scene are all that is necessary to identify the criminal events. This belief cannot be found in any of the papers in the Paul L. Kirk archives at the University of California Bancroft Library. What is understood from the literature review is that Dr. Kirk examined and described the arrangement of spatters distributed by different events, with size viewed as part of the analysis but neither the whole nor the most important parameter.

It is possible that some of the emphasis on impact velocity as a parameter of event identification came from studies regarding the resulting wounds from gunshot. It should be clarified that the discussion of velocity in those textbooks dealing exclusively with gunshot are correct in limiting their discussions to velocity impact of the projectiles. However, with bloodstain pattern evidence, limiting identification of patterns to impact velocity is acceptable only if it is fact that only gunshot wounds are involved and not the possible additional distribution of blood spatters from dynamics other than the results of a bullet. A misconception has developed into any crime that involves blood drop distribution from gunshot being described in terms of *velocity of impact.* Even with death by gunshot, prior assault and movement following injury may involve blood drop dispersions not related to an impact-type event. Respiratory distributions and high-pressure arterial release are noteworthy differences in dynamic acts not resulting from the velocity of an object at impact.

In identification schemes using the pattern match approach, identification is limited to the size of drops from an event. Size of individual spatters recorded is important as a degree of action but not sufficient to classify blood drop–distributing events into assault by blunt instrument, gunshot versus respiratory, knifing, or secondary distributions such as blood dripping into blood. Dr. Kirk can be regarded as the best scientist to study the relatively new forensic discipline in the United States. After his death, some approaches to researching the evidence have deviated from true scientific concepts.

A number of problems can be found within published research projects brought to this author's attention. Proposed protocols of projects to be worthy of a claim of scientific qualification will, hopefully, lead to applications for crime scene investigation methodologies. A scientific-based research study should include specific steps. The following are examples of steps that can apply to any research project:

1. Identify and limit the specific problem or question to be understood and/or resolved with the project.
2. Conduct a literature search for applicable scientific foundations.
3. Construct an experimental design for the project.
4. Acquire and/or manufacture instrumentation and devices, and compile a formula for reagents as necessary.
5. Identify what and how records of the project results will be kept and distributed.
6. Conduct the project.
7. Review results, interpret information gleaned, and draw conclusions.
8. Suggest modifications for future projects to deal with unsuspected results and extend understanding.

Perhaps in another subject, another country, or at a different time, this list for scientific study would be followed. In the present discussion with regard to bloodstain pattern evidence, some of these steps are sadly lacking in the assumed scientific research published in the literature.

The following sections discuss how each of the preceding steps can be applied and where they might have gone wrong.

1. IDENTIFY AND LIMIT THE SPECIFIC PROBLEM OR QUESTION TO BE UNDERSTOOD AND/OR RESOLVED WITH THE PROJECT

Most college advisors are good at emphasizing this first stage. The concept may be phrased as "choose your battles wisely." On one hand, too broad of a subject can be overwhelming to researchers. On the other hand, too narrow a subject may be subjective and viewed as the result of bias. The results become a desire to "reinvent the wheel." Unfortunately, there is another academic phrase, thought but rarely stated: "It didn't work out, but we can get a paper out of it." This latter phrase indicates bias in thoughts regarding a project that will be designed to find expected results. When the expected results do not occur, the experiment is considered a failure and abandoned, or it is shelved until the design can be altered to achieve the expected results.

Beware of answering other people's questions rather than one's own. For example, the often-encountered question of what influences the diameter of a drip of blood spatter has been the subject of many so-called research projects. Because of the common errors in logic surrounding this concept, the projects to determine an answer may end up derailing the train of thought. This author has been caught in this same wrong approach to identifying a subject of study and thus speaks from experience. The initial concept was that previous studies were applicable, and the principles could be assumed to be fact. The first projects centered around the belief in the existence of a standard-sized, later called typical, blood drop. The concept was to study blood drops in free fall and find those parameters that would affect the estimate of how far the drop traveled to the recording surface.

Two errors in logic exist in the original publications and have been retained in many subsequent ones: first is the misconception that blood is a uniform substance. Blood composition has been adequately proven not only to vary between different individuals but also to vary within the same body, especially over time during blood loss (Albert et al., 1965, pp. 20–21; Wonder, 2007, p. 3f67). The second error in logic is that the only characteristic influencing blood drop behavior upon contact with a recording surface was the individual blood drop's surface tension. These assumptions have been the subject of many studies, including a Ph.D. dissertation (Ramon and Smith, 1996, pp. 161–171). The beginning premise was that a blood drip resulted in a diameter of blood spatter that could be equated to the distance the drop fell if the target surface texture was considered. Later studies acknowledged the size of the original drop falling, but they did not adequately identify what parameters led to different sizes in drops. Dropper size was recognized, effects of the surface from which blood dripped were tested, and oscillation in flight was an assumed parameter based on studies of water drops. Later studies considered the presence of spines around the circumference of the stain (Attinger et al., 2013, pp. 375–396), which should also require attention to the target surface where the bloodstain was recorded.

Because the author was a medical technologist working with blood 40 hours plus per week, the variations seen after laboratory distributions with blood from many donors made the logic behind such studies doubtful. Perhaps the best way to understand mistakes is to make them oneself and admit to doing so. The realization that blood is not and cannot be considered a uniform substance led to an awareness that the red cell concentration influences the drop behavior and thus the diameter of dripped bloodstains. Projects were thus designed to investigate the effect of different blood compositions upon the diameter of the bloodstains formed from dripping blood.

It should go without saying that a research project should contribute something of benefit for the future applications of the evidence. Because law enforcement crime scene technicians will be the primary users of any information regarding identification of bloodstain patterns, it follows that the information should be applicable to their protocols in crime scene work-up. Experience with training workshops has shown that meticulous techniques in measurements are less likely to be applied by detectives, who might miss the importance of measurements in instruction for collection by technicians. Criminalists from crime laboratories, by contrast, may focus on measuring a few individual blood spatters while ignoring the overall arrangements. The point is bloodstain pattern evidence is a teamwork type of evidence wherein different viewpoints and techniques can be beneficial to the whole investigation. From this, one must keep in mind that any research project that will benefit and later be applied should be understood by people with a wide range of academic backgrounds.

Keep it real. It appears sometimes that what is thought to be a scientific project is actually only science in theory. One must keep in mind that the purpose of bloodstain pattern research is to find ways to understand the dynamics of actual crimes, which will assist in solving the acts of violence. Nothing shows this gap in logic like the studies of swing castoff bloodstain patterns, especially when one relies on computer illustrations. It should be understood that computers can create images that are impossible in reality. The way that blood drops leave a moving blood carrier can be imagined as in tandem lines of blood drops of identical size, when such would not occur if the carrier was a blunt weapon being used to inflict bodily injury to a victim. The shifts in direction of the swing are the means to dislodging blood drops, not the angular momentum imagined as a smooth arc. High-speed photography for collecting the images is better at illustration, but the conclusions should be from actual observations, not shoehorning what was expected from ideal, imagined events.

Repeating someone else's project or planning one that is an extension thereof is not a bad idea as long as one keeps an open mind while conducting such. Assuming a previous paper was complete and accurate can lead to bias in forming an experimental project. It is wise to question previous studies and list areas that may show variance if parameters are to be questioned. One parameter for most of the previously completed studies would be how the ratio of red blood cells affects blood drop behavior within the experiment (see Figure 13.1). This author conducted preliminary studies prior to a master's degree thesis project (Wonder, 1982, p. 41). Later exercises by the author have also found the age of blood can influence some spatter characteristics.

If the project is to be conducted in an academic environment, such as a college, it is an essential consideration that the faculty advisor respects the evidence discipline. On one hand, if the course project is within Criminal Justice or pre-law Forensic Science departments, instructors may not have the necessary scientific background. On the other hand, some academic-based individuals feel bloodstain pattern evidence is police work and not a science. The viewpoint and direction of this advice may fail to focus on scientific principles for the research study. Students may be directed to

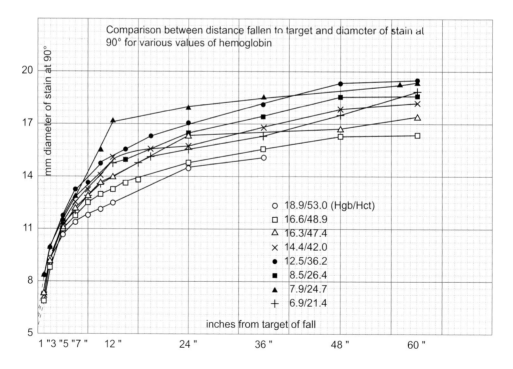

FIGURE 13.1 Preliminary study of the effects of hemoglobin (RBC concentration) versus diameters of blood drips on plain white cardboard.

law enforcement literature rather than science. The suggestion is to find a different project or a different advisor, as that advisor is unlikely to be interested in research in bloodstain pattern evidence.

The best way to identify a project may be to find a subject that is not present in the literature. This indicates that information may not be available, and a project will definitely fill the gap of necessity. There are many projects designed to study the estimation of drop size distributed by different dynamics. Most, if not all, reviewed by the author to date ignore the composition of blood substance, which definitely affects interpretation at crime scenes. There are studies questioning the estimation of the distance fallen by a dripping blood source. None of these studies reviewed would provide investigative leads information because one cannot know the composition of the blood dripping. There are other attributes of bloodstain patterns that are not found within literature written specifically about the evidence.

2. CONDUCT A LITERATURE SEARCH FOR APPLICABLE SCIENTIFIC FOUNDATIONS

A literature search is a must for any project to be considered for scientific application. By literature search, we mean searching several recognized publishers of scientific articles. Law enforcement journals and newsletters are not necessarily classed as scientific publications. This is not to slight the benefits of such material, but to point out that the focus of law enforcement journals and newsletters is on problem solving and applications in police work, and not those articles designed to enhance the acceptance of the discipline as scientific-based forensic evidence. Books and periodicals in medicine, engineering, fluid mechanics, biochemistry, and medical technology offer much material with scientific background. Too often references used for math and physics tend to be favored, but these textbooks are often editions from the individual's years in school. Facts in math and physics are viewed as steady, but changes in concepts do occur. One such concept is non-Newtonian behavior and flow. The main progress in understanding occurred after World War II, 1943 and after. Instructors who gained their scientific background prior to 1945 were not exposed to new engineering problems caused by the historical assumption that all fluid flowed according to the same principles governing water behavior.

Research literature can be loosely grouped into four areas: pre-1942 (pre-WWII), 1943–1979 (postwar developments), 1980s (rapid technical and medical discoveries), and the computer age. Each group has benefits and detriments in logic to apply to research. Pre-WWII literature provides history and an understanding of how professors and scientists thought when their background was anchored in the understanding of that time. This was the initial period when Dr. Kirk received his college education. Between 1943 and 1979, many advances occurred in engineering and medicine. Physics concepts may have changed, as in the shift from classical physics to modern physics. During the 1980s, engineering, mass production, and medicine came to many new understandings, including the recognition of non-Newtonian fluid behavior and how blood does not flow homogeneously (evenly) mixed in the body. In the present day, the focus is shifting away from library references and toward online, cyberencyclopedia sites. One usually learns, however, that not all data online is complete and/or accurate. Double-checking between online statements and published works before accepting information as fact is advised.

What is used from publications will develop from a list of keywords. Presently, the keyword *bloodstains* will include references that predominately use the same historical works and concepts. Although it is essential to be aware of these publications on the subject, it is not wise to use the same ones for new research. Because there is a lack of material included in research projects dealing with the *non-Newtonian nature of blood*, this is an excellent keyword to include in a literature reference. *Rheology* is applicable to blood behavior, whereas *hydrology* is not. The latter term deals with water and aqueous substances, not viscoelastic materials such as blood. *Surface tension* and *cohesion* are good keywords to further understand the difference in blood behavior not being a function solely of surface tension. Medical references on injuries, trauma, cadaveric spasms, arterial bleeding, and head wounds are good sources for understanding crime scene evidence.

An approach that has been frequently encountered includes using one or two references written specifically about bloodstains, selecting one statement within as fact and focusing on expanding what may have been an erroneous concept in the beginning. A method of evaluating a reference is to look at the bibliography first. Check for the references used in that publication. References should include scientific material from other fields as well as those from forensic science textbooks. Some forensic science textbooks are written for those with less academic backgrounds. There are many textbooks available dealing with bloodstain pattern evidence, and a few were written by highly respected forensic scientists. Some were written by law enforcement people who have had many years of experience with crime investigation but not so much academic background in biological subjects or those fields dealing with blood substance. The science of the evidence may be of less importance to them than the use of knowledge obtained from workshops to put violent criminals away. Unfortunately, lack of scientific basics may make the approach to the evidence vulnerable to misunderstanding, misperceptions, and misapplication. It is unwise and can be embarrassing to simply use the bibliographies of other authors, assuming their quotation was accurate. If a reference is to be used, it is essential that the reference be read to verify the accuracy of prior quotations.

An argument can be presented that there was little literature on the science of blood behavior applicable to bloodstain pattern evidence in the early years of research. In that situation, some preliminary experiments would provide information to help understand which parameters influence blood drop behavior. This author used blood samples collected in a hospital clinical lab to determine whether red blood cell concentration affected the diameter of blood drips on different material. Although the results were not published beyond a master's degree thesis, the same type of preliminary study could be available to anyone checking the same parameters before designing a research project. An alternative to collecting a variety of hemoglobin/hematocrit values is to spin tubes with normal values and either remove plasma or add analogous (from the same patient) plasma.

Another observation with regard to reviewing literature prior to designing experiments is to note the scale used in any graphs. For example, this author's thesis plot of distance fallen and hemoglobin values shows a spread of 4 mm between low concentration of hemoglobin and high. The spread does not look impressive because the scale was not large. A spread of 4 mm in stain diameter for estimating distance fallen depends on where in the total range the difference of 4 mm occurred. The larger drops show a greater error in estimating distance fallen from the diameter of the resultant stain than the small drops. However, the smaller the drop diameter, the greater the possibility that it is a secondary or satellite spatter, not from the original blood drop contact with a target. In other words, the smaller drop could result from a parent drop, not be an indication of the incident angle to the original distribution. Experience with both research and actual crime investigations brings to mind many considerations necessary before a project can be designed.

3. CONSTRUCT AN EXPERIMENTAL DESIGN FOR THE PROJECT

Here is a major problem with many past research studies. It is a well-known fact—but seldom, if ever, admitted in print—that one can prove anything one wishes to prove if one designs the experiment in the way to prove it. This is a serious consideration for bias, intentional or not, in reconstructions of crime scene evidence. For example, say an expert wishes to "prove" a suspect killed the victim. The victim died from blunt force trauma. The experimental design could be to beat a bloody sponge with something, anything that may bear no resemblance to the weapon or method used, and then point to spatters on the clothes of the demonstrator saying, "See, I proved that the suspect beat the victim." Spatters can be acquired from the victim's wheezing or pin-point breach arterial spurting on investigators, paramedics, and/or innocent bystanders after assault. An example of blood distribution having nothing to do with criminal events at the moment blood drops were being recorded was presented in *Blood Dynamics* (Wonder, 2001, p. 72). Other views of the same event are presented in Figures 13.2 and 13.3. The figures show a victim of a beating sitting in a police agency explaining the nature of a fist assault. Blows were apparently struck to the eyebrow area, where an artery lies over skull bone. The small artery was apparently ruptured via aneurysm, described previously. The officers weren't aware of spurting until they saw bloodstains appearing on their persons.

Reconstruction guidelines of crime scenes have made progress in attempts to become sufficiently similar to the crime alleged, but it is a fact that one cannot legally duplicate fatal assault injuries to a human. Use of animals is commonly regarded as a cruel and unusual act and is greatly discouraged. Animals are now put down in humane ways that will not duplicate a criminal assault. It follows that a reconstruction of criminal events to prove a specific side to the case cannot duplicate the event and thus should not be considered open-minded research. Information gleaned from reconstructions, however, is useful in developing ideas for future projects.

An essential part of designing a project, which may apply to reconstruction experiments as well, is to include controls. With bloodstain patterns, including controls is not as easy as it

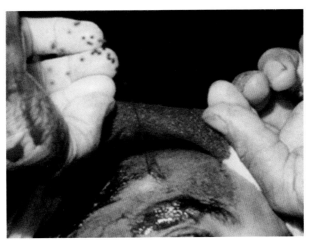

FIGURE 13.2   Victim with small artery spurting blood while being interviewed by a detective. *(Photograph supplied by Anaheim Police Department)*

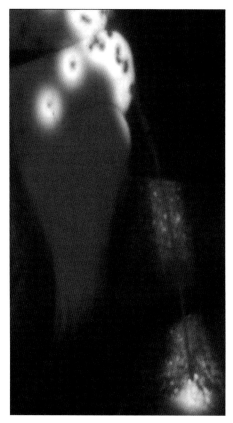

FIGURE 13.3   Highlighted column from arterial injury showing separation after blood exited under pressure from an artery. No impact to break up the blood occurred. *(Photograph supplied by Anaheim Police Department).*

would be with chemical or microscopic tests. One method would be to consider the variance range of the project. This could be in the angles involved in a beating, the weight of weapons, the velocity of bullets, or the pressure behind an arterial spurt. Tests for variance can act as controls in showing effects of the parameters on the project. It should be noted that the variance considered as a control must be other than the parameter being studied for the project. Reconstruction type exercises use controls that are (1) as the law enforcement investigators claim; (2) as the suspect claims; and (3) as the bloodstain patterns indicate, which may differ from both 1 and 2 (Epstein et al.).

A study presented at a symposium in 1989 claimed to estimate the volume of blood in small bloodstains (MacDonell and De Lige, 1989). A number of problems in the logic should have been noticed but were not provided with the handout for the presentation. No information was described regarding the blood sample used beyond calling it "typical." Objectives centered around propagation of small drops, removal from a surface by capillary action, determination of volume from capillary measurements, and correlation with standards. The drop propagation was from brush bristles of undetermined nature. The nature of the bristles—plastic, nylon, animal hair, or other—could affect the size of the drops. This overall action, would produce small drops, but the mass of the drops would not be known without the information regarding the blood sample and surfaces of the brush bristles used. Removal of the drops by capillary action would be influenced by red cell concentration and age of the blood. Variation in capillary aspiration occurs with different samples of blood, as pointed out in *Blood Dynamics* (Wonder, 2001, p. 7).

The most significant error in logic was that the study might apply to the specific conditions of the experiment but would not be applicable to blood lost at a crime scene. Unfortunately, the criterion that was being studied—volume of blood forming a drop—was influenced by the same parameters (diameter of the spatter) that were used to determine drop distance traveled and the identity of the event that distributed blood. In the handout material, the conclusion was that "if the diameter of a bloodstain is known, it is possible to estimate the volume of blood required to produce that stain...." Rather than provide information, this was a loop that contributes confusion that cannot be applied to crime scene investigations involving bloodstain analysis (see Figure 13.4). Looking at the design of this project, we can organize it as follows:

a. The distance the drop traveled and the dynamics of distribution are estimated from the diameter (size) of the spatter formed.
b. The diameter (size) of the spatter will depend on the volume of the drop.
c. The volume of the drop will depend on the mass (weight/volume) of the red blood cell concentration of the blood in the drop.
d. The red blood cell concentration will influence the diameter (size) of the drop.

Part of the author's master's degree thesis published in 1982 included using standard blue capillaries to aspire blood samples. Two attempts to construct a standard curve using hemoglobin adjusted with outdated transfusion service blood were compared to one series of freshly collected random patient samples from a clinical laboratory. The interesting results were in regard to older blood bank blood values that, when plotted against capillary heights, tended to provide linear correlations. Fresh blood, anticoagulated with EDTA used within 16 hours of collection, provided a log curve when plotted versus capillary heights (see Figure 13.5). Later, the same log curve relation was seen with fresh EDTA samples adjusted for hemoglobin values with homologous plasma. Thus, it is considered that age of the blood may affect behavior. Obviously, fresh, dried, or coagulated blood will likely be found at crime scenes.

The concern about the assumption for the presentation previously described regarding estimating small drop volumes (a subject applicable to the 1989 symposium) is that the size of the drop does not in and of itself identify the dynamic event that distributed drops. Until that identification of an event is determined, the size of drops involved does not provide any investigative information. After the identification of the event is made, such as gunshot, wheeze, arterial breach, rapid blood into blood dripping, etc., the size of drops involved may provide information regarding the amount of force involved in the blood source breakup. Again, for clarity, size of spatters should be used for the amount of force, not the type of force.

Regarding controls and variance for the project, it should be noted that this can act as the variance of error rate required for scientific evidence by the National Academy of Sciences. For such to be available with investigative applications, records must be provided with the study. Records can't be available unless prior design includes collection and presentation of results.

V. RESEARCH FOR THE FUTURE

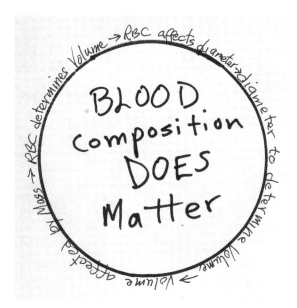

FIGURE 13.4   A loop in logic regarding RBC ratio and distance blood drops traveled.

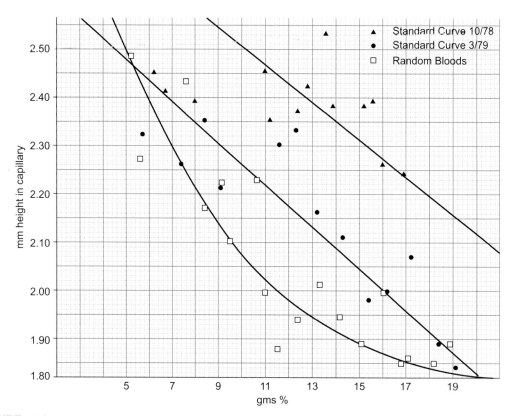

FIGURE 13.5   Correlations of capillary aspiration versus hemoglobin values for fresh versus stored blood. All tubes were anticoagulated with ethylenediaminetetraacetic acid (EDTA).

V. RESEARCH FOR THE FUTURE

4. ACQUIRE AND/OR MANUFACTURE INSTRUMENTATION AND DEVICES, AND COMPILE A FORMULA FOR REAGENTS AS NECESSARY

Sometimes the experimental design is arrived at in reverse after finding devices and so on to provide reproducible actions. It is well understood that to identify and study applicable parameters, and variance of these, one must be able to reproduce the distributing event in a repetitious but substantially similar manner as may occur at crime scenes.

Of course, the most important reagent for projects in bloodstain pattern evidence is the blood sample. Because of concern for blood-borne diseases, substitutes for blood have been widely suggested. The fact that blood is unique may be ignored or denied. Anything can be used to illustrate fluid dynamics as long as the claim is for illustration only and thus limited to characteristics that will remain similar between substances. This goes back to selecting the subject to study and relates to what records of the experiment would be collected. Pig blood has been mentioned as exhibiting close to the same behavior as human blood, yet swine diseases may carry over to humans. Blood tested for but rejected from transfusions for reasons other than medical history provides the best source. Packed red blood cells provide patterns consistent with crime scene exhibits. It is not correct to insist on whole blood for reconstruction. As explained earlier, blood does not flow homogeneously (evenly) mixed in the body. Blood flows with the core of red cells in the middle of the vessels, and plasma with circulating platelets flows around the core. This was explained in detail in *Blood Dynamics* (Wonder, 2001, p. 30) from medical references. (Albert, 1971, pp. 49–50; Nubar, 1966, p. 3). When injury occurs, healthy blood vessels constrict to stop blood loss (Sohmer, 1979, p. 2). For this reason, blood lost at a crime scene may not be whole blood but may be representative of a higher concentration from the red cell core.

Packed red blood cell pouches for transfusion purposes have two other advantages. Removing the plasma from donated units decreases the carrier medium of infectious diseases and thus may decrease biological hazards of whole blood. It must be understood that only those units tested for blood-borne diseases should be used in research projects in schools and workshops where safety is tantamount. A second advantage to requesting packed red blood cells from blood banks and transfusion services is that packed cells are more commonly available as outdated units to be discarded. Whole blood units are not routinely stored for random transfusions. They may be kept as autologous transfusions (drawn from a patient for use by that patient alone) that are not available to donate or sell to researchers. Another suggestion is that requests for blood be for discarded neonatal and/or pediatric units so as not to waste full units for adults. Drawing blood from workshop participants is not advised for the simple reason that it is unknown whether or not the donor has been exposed to such hazards as hepatitis. Workshops conducted by the author in the 1980s through 1990s found a majority of participants claimed exposure to hepatitis. Law enforcement and crime scene investigation involve biological hazards out of proportion to routine population exposure. Safety procedures did not become common until after the identification of AIDS at crime scenes. Individuals may pick up and transfer some viruses without showing outward signs of illness.

After the source of blood for the project is resolved, a consideration must be made, the same as for any research: the criteria of reproducibility. The fact that a single experiment may be designed to obtain a specific confirmation is not a scientific study but a possible biased reconstruction. Because this is possible, it has led to claims of subjectivity in bloodstain pattern evidence as a whole. Random deviations of results that do not reoccur in repeated experiments have less influence on the conclusions. It is suggested, however, that they still be acknowledged. Studies in all scientific projects depend on the results repeating and becoming predictable for applications as protocols for methodologies. To make a project repeat for bloodstain pattern study, one may need to use a device or instrument that will perform an action repeatedly in the same manner. An example is the common spring trap device used to deliver an impact to an aliquot of blood. This device, used both in studies and in training, can have variance of amount of blood, the way the sample is positioned on the trap lip, and in composition of the blood aliquot. Angle of impact and position with respect to the recording surface can be varied as parameters.

Some previous studies have attempted to design reproducible swing castoff patterns. The need for a reproducible device is obvious because workshop examples are performed by participants, which results in a variety of heights, strengths, and methods of application. Even when the same volunteer and same weapon are used to cast off, drops may not be reproduced. Focus should be on simulating grievous bodily injury to the blood source without necessarily attention to reproducing the swings. A problem will occur between the difference in the way a device will cast off blood drops and the amount of blood between swings versus the way distribution would result during a crime of violence. The blood drops that are flicked off at the end of the release of an object, brush, rod, etc., may be closer to cessation castoffs than swing. The dynamics in these studies are to investigate how drops are distributed from criminal application of swings. This would still be acceptable if the differences were recognized as part of the conclusions. Unfortunately, conclusions have been interpreted as refuting scientific principles of swing castoff dynamics, and the analysis of the concept is regarded as providing contradictory conclusions in scientific explanations. Imagined illustrations of some expected results show parallel alignment of same-sized spatters, which was not representative of true crime scene swing castoffs.

The author has received many devices for reproducibility designed and engineered by a very talented father. Several of the items in training and casework were shown in *Bloodstain Pattern Evidence, Objective Approaches and Case Applications* (Wonder, 2007, pp. 334-342). The newest item in the Wonder Institute collection was designed by a plastic manufacturer for photographing the behavior of blood drops at free fall (see Figure 13.6). The top sheets can be hooked together to form slanted surfaces from horizontal, or flat, to 60-degree angles at half-degree increments. Plates of glass, plastic, or cardboard can be slid into grooves on the angled plastic sheet.

An earlier model made out of a cardboard box failed to admit enough light for clear photography of blood drop behavior upon impact with the slanted plate of the device. An advantage to many of the devices featured in *Bloodstain Pattern Evidence* was that the design was varied to see whether changes would influence the results. Single exercises may not represent the whole possible range of results in research, especially those designed to provide a specific example of a case. Repeats are essential. The lack of variance may end up being a liability because the act doesn't show the range of behavior. There will always be exceptions to the rule, and it is essential to find out where they are likely to occur, including why and how they happen.

FIGURE 13.6   Plastic angle box for photographing drips at an angle.

5. IDENTIFY WHAT AND HOW RECORDS OF THE PROJECT RESULTS WILL BE KEPT AND DISTRIBUTED

Another very important component of any research project is to identify and design how and what records to be compiled. Early research, in 1895, attempted to record the overall arrangement of spatters that resulted from various blunt force–type assaults to animals. The events were less controlled so that variations occurred but were not necessarily recorded for future projects (Piotrowski, 1895, pp. 36–48). The sketches of alignment for spatters were not accurate, thus denying some of the information that would be useful later in applications to crime scenes. Modern research projects also sometimes seem to be devoid of details regarding arrangements and alignments of spatters after different dynamic events. With these results, there appears to be a preoccupation with the size of spatters resulting from blood drop distribution and the distance they traveled. Overlap of size ranges for different types and degrees of force distributing blood drops of unknown mass makes such information inapplicable to crime scene investigation. The whole pattern includes how the individual spatters are recorded as well as the distribution of the size ranges.

Much more is being understood with the application of high-speed photography. Most of these observations, however, focus on lateral, or side, views of the behavior of blood drop distribution and impacts with a surface. This has led to implications that blood drops form ovals upon contact. Blood drops form tight spheres in flight, as shown in Figure 2.5 and the cover of this book. The distortions leading to ovals at contact are claimed based on water and water-based fluids oscillating. The loose attractions within water drops permit distortions in flight that may be recorded as ovals and other shapes. Such observations are not necessarily applicable to blood drops. When a blood drop makes contact with a surface, it is in the shape of a circle with the distortion of oval, teardrop, or exclamation mark formed as a result of continued forward momentum. Dropping blood of different hemoglobin/hematocrit values, however, showed that contact shape can be affected by the ratio of red blood cells. Plasma is Newtonian (water-like), whereas red blood cells are non-Newtonian (viscoelastic).

The blood used in the drip exercise was six tubes of freshly drawn blood tested by a clinical lab to be 13.6 mg% hemoglobin. Aliquots of plasma were removed from two tubes and added to two tubes, making two tubes of 5.5 mg% hemoglobin and two tubes of 19.8 mg%. Drops of all three samples were made with Beral® one-piece plastic droppers that deliver uniform drop sizes per sample of blood. The shapes of the drops at impact with the surfaces varied slightly based on the red cell concentration. Fewer red cells means less internal cohesion, which allows for some distortion of shape in flight and at impact with the target. High red cell concentration formed tight spheres, which always left a rounder shape. These were all dropped at an angle of 30 degrees. The rounder shape did not flow after contact and thus stayed in the round shape of first contact (the footprint of the blood drop) with the target surface. The absorption in fabric greatly depends on the ratio of red blood cells. Liquid plasma may migrate through fabric with ease, carrying some of the red cells. Strong cohesion holds the red cells in a single sphere and does not permit migration of liquid with free red cells (see Figure 13.7).

When and where a project will be presented are essential to preliminary planning of the work. Several science publications are available, and the submission requirements should be checked before starting a research project. Presenting a paper at meetings or symposiums is good, but the information from them may not be available to all applicable fields of interest over a long period of time. Publication is the best way to distribute the results of research for future benefit. Because some groups limit oral presentations if results were published previous to presentation, it is necessary to check these guidelines or be sure to present the paper before submitting for publication. Papers, whether spoken or published, are accepted or rejected after the project is completed. Having a focus and objective in mind is good for organization and record keeping during the project. Government grants allow for pre-project funding and require periodic updates. Obtaining grants, however, may require more politics than scientific value for future applications.

In the author's experience, every experiment leads to a need for more experiments. What records are kept can provide the beginning for the next project. In bloodstain pattern evidence, all projects

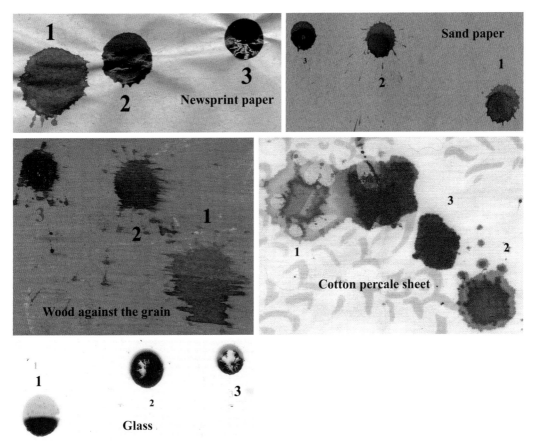

FIGURE 13.7 Random drops of blood with variable hemoglobin values on different material from 24 inches height and on 30-degree angle slants.

seem to revert back to some of the conclusions from the 1970s and may not acknowledge the many scientific discoveries in other fields since then. Organizations formed for the benefit of bloodstain pattern evidence may favor legal agendas to keep the discipline consistent with previous trial and case applications rather than further the subject as scientific evidence. This approach is understandable but perhaps not the most economical application of the evidence in the detection and resolution of violent crime.

6. CONDUCT THE PROJECT

Step 6, conducting the project, is the point at which most performed research focuses and is the easiest of the steps. Experimental design should be evaluated with each repeat to see whether variations in results occur and if design influences those results. Funds may not be available for adequate repeats to determine whether the aberrations are the rule or if exceptions occur infrequently. This is why it is advantageous for different research groups to repeat the same projects and supply all the results, even those that are unexpected and may be viewed as one-time aberrations. Workshops make this possible if the content is changed over time, and exceptions to expected results are also studied. Although the project may have been done by another group, it is still recognized as research to verify that a different group in a different location can obtain the same or different results. The mock crime scene scenarios utilized in workshops have repeated tests to show the applications of string reconstruction to actual crime scenes.

The two most important parts of conducting research are space and time. Completing projects hastily may prevent the degree of attention to details in the results that will benefit future projects. Space—the location where blood will be used—requires not only cleanup but also disinfection for biological hazards. Bleach, antimicrobial soaps, and washes apply to disinfection, whereas water and water-based soaps may be used in cleanup. It is important to allow disinfectants to dry on a surface for the time period noted in the instructions for use of the agent. Clumps of dried blood need to be cleaned and then disinfected and cleaned again. Disinfectant is insufficient if blood clumps are dried and protect microbes within the lumps.

Blood-stained material may not be discarded in routine trash bins. Alternatives are to burn cardboard and other burnable items. Blood containers may be discarded at transfusion services such as blood banks, clinical laboratories, and hospitals. If none of these options are available for discarding specific items, hazardous waste agencies may be located online. There is usually one charge for picking up a given weight of material and discarding it in hazardous waste dump sites.

7. REVIEW RESULTS, INTERPRET INFORMATION GLEANED, AND DRAW CONCLUSIONS

There is a consistency of conclusions for many projects offered in recent years saying, in essence, "we found what we expected to find." This is good for repeated projects but not so good for provision of material for future applications of the evidence. Conclusions should be directed to what was learned and not known before the research project was conducted. Were past conclusions in error? Was new information from the literature search incorporated into the project so that the knowledge of blood behavior is expanded? Were the results truly analyzed, or was the conclusion that "more work needs to be done before we can conclude anything"?

The term *interpretation* has been criticized because it is perceived as subjective. This may be an unfair assumption. A parallel in application can be understood between the clinical laboratory and a forensic lab. Technicians may run instruments in a clinical lab and supply the numerical values provided. They do not interpret the results. Technologists also may run instruments, but they are trained to interpret results as requiring that they alert the physician, retest the instrument, or ignore the readout. They also run controls on the instruments to verify satisfactory operation. Crime labs may have the same division of labor in that criminalists interpret results and draw conclusions regarding the importance of the information obtained from instrumentation, chemical tests, microscopic exams, or CSI-collected material. The problem with interpretation is that it requires thought and logic. That can be by way of subjectivity—as the thought and perceived logic of the individual—but it does not need to be that way. A way to check for logic in evaluating a research project is to examine it for cause and effect. What is the effect found after the project?

We've now come back to the first step: limit the project to a manageable exercise. So, including too much in the conclusions to be specific and applicable for the actual results nullifies the benefit from the research. For the subject of bloodstain pattern evidence, the results will be some kind of bloodstain pattern. Drawing conclusions based on the size of spatters can be applicable only if the project included various events so that size ranges of spatters can be compared. Under various conditions, almost any event can have overlapping size spatters so that one size alone cannot identify the event. Conclusions cannot show a size as specific for an event if only one event was studied. Distribution of sizes over a range of the pattern, alignment of directions of travel, and configuration of the entire group of spatters representing the array from blood drops distributed can be recorded as results. If these are then compared between repeats of the experiment and/or similar but different dynamic acts, information applicable to crime scenes will be made available.

8. SUGGEST MODIFICATIONS FOR FUTURE PROJECTS TO DEAL WITH UNSUSPECTED RESULTS AND EXTEND UNDERSTANDING

The obvious caution with this part of a research study is that answers for unexpected results require repeated experiments to verify the accuracy of any proposed solution. An example of a process that does not follow this caution occurred during a trial. In testimony, an expert said that an article of clothing was worn by the accused when she shot the victim. The visible spatters on the article were not in the mist and small size ranges. The expert identified the clothing as being worn during the homicide based on mist spatters being present. In testimony, the expert claimed that the mist could not be seen, but it was there because it was a gunshot fired by the suspect. There was no report or indication that the expert examined the clothing with a microscope. If the mist couldn't be seen, how did he know it had to be there? The same problem exists with research conclusions. If the expected isn't there, the absence must be verified and any explanation for the absence tested for applicability. Hunches may be right, but they must be proven so. The same applies to explanations of variance by red cell concentration and non-Newtonian behavior. If it doesn't matter, one must have proof that it doesn't matter.

An additional project objective should be added for research in forensic science. Any completed study should have discussion regarding how it can be applied to crime scene investigation. With that requirement, it becomes clear that some perceived projects are not favored for research study including research papers dealing with the following issues with respect to bloodstain pattern evidence:

a. Studies of any parameters to add to the concept that a drip bloodstain can be measured to determine how far the blood drop fell before being recorded during an actual crime event.
b. Studies of blood spatter sizes as identification without consideration for the arrangement and distribution of groups of spatters for the type of dynamic event that distributed them.
c. Studies using water or water-based (aqueous) fluids to determine size and shape of blood spatters from blood drop distribution.
d. Studies using a bloody sponge and random weapons to duplicate the distributions from traumatic injury involving arterial damage.
e. Studies involving one dynamic, such as gunshot, blunt force, or arterial injury, to understand a different dynamic, arterial injury, gunshot, or blunt force. The most common is an effort to duplicate assumed castoff patterns that were, in fact, arterial spurting.

REFERENCES

Albert, S.N., Jain, S.C., Shibula, J.A., Albert, C.A., 1965. The Hematocrit in Clinical Practice. Charles C. Thomas, Springfield, IL. pp. 20–21.

Albert, S.N., 1971. Blood Volume and Extracellular Fluid Volume, 2nd ed. Charles C. Thomas, Springfield, IL. pp. 49–50.

Attinger, D., Moore, C., Donaldson, A., Jafari, A., Stone, H.A., 2013. Fluid Dynamics Topics in Bloodstain Pattern Analysis: Comparative Review and Research Opportunities. Forensic Science International 231 (1), 375–396.

Epstein, B., Laber, T., 1983. Minnesota Bureau of Criminal Apprehension staff. A procedure advocated in "Experiments and Practical Exercises in Bloodstain Pattern Analysis" Callen Publishing Co. Minneapolis, MN.

MacDonell, H.L., De Lige, K., 1989. Presentation and IABPS Meeting, Dallas, TX.

Nubar, Y., 1966. The Laminar Flow of a Composite Fluid: An Approach to the Rheology of Blood. New York Academy of Sciences, New York, NY. p. 3.

Piotrowski, E., 1895. Ueber Entstehung, Form, Richtung und Ausbreitung der Blutsuren nach Hiebwunden des Kopfes. Vienna University Publications, Vienna. pp. 36–48.

Ramon, A., Smith, E.R., 1996. Oscillating Blood Droplets—Implications for Crime Scene Reconstruction. Science and Justice 36 (3), 161–171.

Sohmer, P.R., 1979. The Pathophysiology of Hemorrhagic Shock. In: Hemotherapy in Trauma and Surgery. American Association of Blood Banks, Washington, D.C, p. 2.

Wonder, A.Y., 1982. The Effects on Geometric Human Bloodstain Design by Hemoglobin Concentration and Time Sequence of Moisture Exposure. California State University, Sacramento, CA. p. 41.

Wonder, A.Y., 2001. Blood Dynamics. Academic Press, London. pp. 7, 30, 72.

Wonder, A.Y., 2007. Bloodstain Pattern Evidence, Objective Approaches and Case Applications. Elsevier, San Diego, CA. pp. 334–342.

14

Research Project Examples

COLOR USED TO DETERMINE AGE OF BLOODSTAINS

During preparation for a murder trial, the author was informed of a claim by a criminalist employed by a government crime lab that the age of a single blood spatter found in a kitchen sink, seen in Figure 14.1, would be used to place the accused at the scene at a specific time, days earlier. The associated injury to the accused was a finger cut, which was allegedly received during a struggle with a knife between the accused and the victim while in the kitchen. Because the claim was for a very specific time period, and other claims by the same criminalist had been disproved when the background regarding the protocol for a conclusion was applied, the author decided to try a reconstruction experiment to test the validity of the use of bloodstain color to determine age of the stain.

Case Reconstruction Protocol Study Number 1

For the purposes of this experiment, white ceramic tile was believed to be substantially similar to the surface characteristics of a porcelain kitchen sink for a quick illustration. A finger puncture system for diabetic testing was available to deliver a uniform injury to a finger. A digital readout satellite clock was used for timing. At zero hour, a puncture was applied to the fingertip and allowed to dislodge a single free-flow drop on to the tile from a height of about 4 inches. Distance of fall was not exact. Photographs at time periods thereafter were collected. In each exhibit, a color circle was included to verify which time period applied to the example shown. A collection of the series was available for cross-examining the witness who claimed to be able to assign a specific time based on blood spatter color appearance. The results of the experiment were not required after the prosecution decided not to apply the conclusions from the witness at the trial. See Figure 14.2 for the series of photographs resulting from this reconstruction.

Although the purpose of this rough experiment was mainly to determine validity of the claim of time estimation from the appearance of the spatter, a few other items of information became available. The photograph of the blood spatter in the kitchen sink was probably taken at least 4 days after the alleged crime. This information was based on the last time the victim was seen, when the body was found, and when the scene was photographed. The estimate was to place the suspect at the scene at the time of an alleged rape and subsequent death. DNA confirmed the source of the

FIGURE 14.1   Crime scene photograph of a kitchen sink at the home of a murder victim. A single spatter is located by a placed number placard.

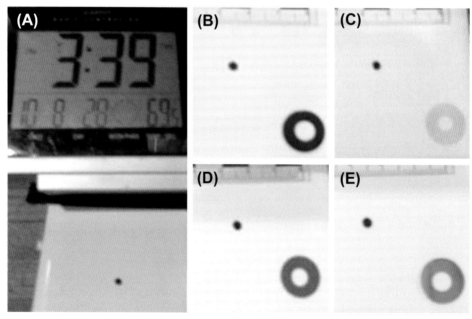

FIGURE 14.2   Photographs A through E show drying time periods for a single blood drop deposited on a ceramic wall tile. Time periods were confirmed by inclusion of a radio-controlled clock with a color circle to verify the drying time each represented.

spatter, but the suspect was known to the victim and, in fact, had fathered two children by her. The injury claimed was a very small nick to the side of a finger. Unfortunately, the focus was not good on the author's camera, with lack of sharpness not noticed until after the series was completed. The interpretation, however, was based on the appearance, primarily the color, of the spatter. Because the proposed testimony was dropped, no further testing was conducted nor conclusions made at the time the series was collected.

The meaning of the color circles was related to the time after the drop was deposited. No anticoagulant was used; no color circle was present at zero hour of deposit. A blue circle was used 18 hours later; yellow, 24 hours later; red, 30 hours later; and green, 48 hours later. Initially, the color of the blood was visible as bright red, but it began to darken slightly as the single bloodstain dried. By 24 hours, very little change occurred, and the color remained pretty much constant for the rest of the time, up to a week later.

Bloodstain Color Study Number 2

When one is reading crime scene work-ups, it is not uncommon to see estimates of the age of bloodstains identified. There are several random thoughts regarding the usefulness and construction of a project to study further the reliability of this observation. The amount of blood in the drop would influence the shading of the color. Also seldom mentioned in forensic reference material about blood substances is the fact that red blood cells are respiring organs (Dailey, 1998, p. 25). Blood may take up or give off oxygen even after it leaves the body. Obviously, we need to understand more about the parameters that go into estimating time periods of bloodshed after spatters are distributed. The following are some factors to consider:

1. What is the source of blood color changes? Red blood cells take up and release oxygen, which changes the color of hemoglobin.
2. Differences exist between arterial and venous blood sources because arteries carry oxygen to body organs, whereas veins carry oxygen-depleted red cells back to the heart and then lungs to pick up oxygen.
3. What is the amount of blood? The depth of stain is also involved in the release or absorption of atmospheric oxygen in a pool or spatter.
4. What is the surface where blood was deposited? Plasma may be absorbed through fabric, which may increase the concentration of red blood cells in the original pool or spot. If red cells are able to migrate through fabric weave, drying may occur faster and possibly lock in color sooner.
5. What is the time period? Longer time to dry may result in more loss (or possibly gain) of oxygen.
6. The possibility that blood may be mixed with other substances such as saliva, semen, vaginal fluid, water, or respiratory mucus will affect color of stain.
7. Blood color may be influenced by the background target surface of nonporous materials.
8. Are there other parameters involved not considered here?

The first consideration is what causes color changes. The red blood cells in blood are classed as respiring organs just like the liver, kidneys, heart, lung, etc. Hemoglobin is a red pigment trapped within the protein makeup, called the protein coat, of the red blood cells. The function of the red blood cell organ is to pick up oxygen in the lungs and transport it by way of arteries from the heart to all other organs of the body. Venous blood then carries the red cells back to the heart and to the lungs to pick up more oxygen. Because red blood cells are the most numerous and visible components of blood, what happens to them determines the changes in pigmentation observed. When red cells pick up oxygen in the lungs, they turn a bright fire-engine red. This red cell/oxygen combination flows along arteries throughout the body. As oxygen is lost to body organs, or the atmosphere outside the body, the color shifts to a darker bluish red, becoming the bluish color seen within veins under the skin along the arms, hands, and legs. It is therefore essential to a study of blood spatter color that we choose the source that we start with carefully, whether arterial or venous blood.

As blood dries at crime scenes, it may change to a number of colors and shades, including rust, burgundy, and tar black. An area of the body where arterial and venous blood may be lost in small non-life-threatening amounts is the fingertips. The fingertips contain the arterioles that are the smallest of arteries and provide the location that facilitates the shift from the arterial system to venous for return to the heart. This is the reason heart patients have a clip on their fingers to measure oxygenation from the fingertips during testing for heart function.

It is essential that finger blood be used for any study of the behavior of color changes for three reasons. First, the blood must be freshly shed and not held so that it coagulates or respires to lose or take up oxygen before the timing begins. Second, samples containing ethylene diamine tetra-acetic acid (EDTA), the lavender top blood draw tubes, can never be used because the anticoagulant is also a color preservative sometimes found in food products when color is essential for customer appeal (Wikipedia.org and several other online references). Other blood draw tubes could be used, but they would not prevent coagulation and/or color changes due to exposure to the additives or lack of. Such a tube could be the gray top, or blood alcohol/glucose tube, which contains sodium fluoride preservative. The third reason for using finger blood is the seriousness of using blood from direct arterial puncture. Arterial blood draws are more difficult and require that care be taken to prevent inclusion of any coagulation. Doing so could create an emboli or intravascular clots, which could cause a heart attack or stroke. Because arterial blood is the best for this study due to the fact that the release of oxygen over time will result in a wider variation of color, the fingertip puncture is ideal (see Figure 14.3).

The amount of blood is very important in the color changes that will occur with blood over time. The case example previously cited involved a single drop probably flicked during a struggle. Although we cannot know the volume of blood that resulted in that spatter, it provides an easier concept of volume to study, i.e., a random drop distributed from a small injury. Crime scenes where copious blood volumes have pooled and dried may be as dark as black tar. The depth of the pool could prevent uptake or release of oxygen from the bottom of the pool after being shed, but oxygen could still be given up from the surface. To keep the study simple, we'll retain the single drop from a fingertip for volume to be studied. It must be emphasized that there is no such thing as a standard, or typical, blood drop at crime scenes. Movement involved with bloodshed, as well as the source of injury providing blood, will result in drop size variations.

Time after bloodshed is a definite consideration, especially because that may be the parameter applied to determine or suggest a time line after distribution. The rough comparison previously shown provided information that the criminalist saying he could tell exactly when the suspect shed blood was not supportable, but a question exists whether or not spot appearance could be used as a time line under other circumstances. This does provide parameters for study. Whether or not color changes in a predictable and reproducible manner has not been concluded.

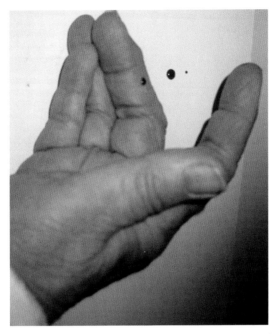

FIGURE 14.3   The location of punctures to the side of a finger (venous blood) and to the tip (arteriole blood) are shown using the right hand of a volunteer.

Controls for the study are always necessary for research. Those that could influence this study but would be kept the same throughout are the red cell concentration measure as hematocrit, distance of drop free fall, and environmental conditions. Cardboard and ceramic tile were considered, but other surface materials were omitted in this study. Because the blood is from a finger stick, the hemoglobin/hematocrit value was known for the donor to be within the 8–9 mg% value when tested by clinical lab protocol later. Distance of free fall for drips was not measured or recorded. Size of the drips and measurements of the resultant stain were not considered.

The validity of using color alone is doubtful, but other information can enhance the prediction of time after bloodshed. That is added to the information not resolved with an exact figure of time. Coagulation may be more reliable, but testing for coagulation is questionable, especially in a crime scene approach for investigative personnel. The standard workshop method of drawing sticks or a glass rod through a pool is not a reliable index of crime event coagulation time. Disturbing the pool will prolong clot initiation, as will diluting blood with other fluids, including cerebral spinal fluid. Safety considerations and delays due to putting on safety equipment must be factored in the time considerations. If the scene is fresh, most likely the first concern will be the victim's survival. Pools of blood under the victim that are large enough for coagulation to proceed at a crime scene do not bode well for the victim and will likely be ignored even if a scene protocol could require testing upon the arrival of first line officers.

V. FOR THE FUTURE

Next, we considered whether there was any literature on the use of color for determining age of bloodstains. Bevel and Gardner provided good information for developing a time line based on studies by Chisum and Rynerson (Bevel and Gardner, 2002, pp. 50–51), with the emphasis on use of major events predominantly gleaned from interviews. Bevel and Gardner did not mention use of the characteristics of bloodstain patterns to determine events for the time line sequence. Drying times were noted, and emphasis was placed on it being wise to use caution (Bevel and Gardner, 2002, pp. 245–246) in drawing conclusions regarding time lines. There appears to be an open subject for future projects regarding estimation of time for dry stains to age; that is, after the stain dries, how does it age, and do color changes occur? Any time that is spent studying bloodstain pattern evidence has shown that the color of bloodstains changes as drying bloodstains remain undisturbed for periods of time.

James and Eckert (1999, pp. 90–93) discussed experimentation with blood drying after capillary action on variations of fabric types and weaves. Some confusion may exist in their conclusions regarding whether it was serum or plasma, and what the ratio of red blood cells was in the fresh blood samples they used. If the hemoglobin/hematocrit was low/low normal, aspiration up fabric strips would definitely be affected. The fewer the red cells, the faster the column of liquid can migrate through fabric, and the faster liquid migration will allow faster drying. If drying time was to be interpreted from the aspiration along fabric and/or amount of drying estimated, the red cell count would need to be known. Unfortunately, the ratio of red cells at a scene where blood was shed cannot be known. The difference between plasma and serum is the removal of salts by the clotting mechanism. Salts will prolong drying with plasma aspiration in fabrics. It should be noted too that dry weight will be greatly affected by retained salts from dried plasma versus dried serum. Salt takes up moisture to the extent that weighing blood spatters in humid climates may fluctuate day to day.

A reference for drying times on different media has been made a part of bloodstain pattern workshops provided by Barton Epstein and Terry Laber (1983, pp. 54–58), which included a format to record and retain information from the workshop exercise. Again, no details beyond the fact that blood was freshly drawn were provided regarding blood composition. In at least one workshop session, blood was drawn from volunteers into sodium fluoride (blood alcohol vacutainers) with no clinical testing possible to determine the red cell concentration.

Drying Time Color Changes

We need to construct an experimental design, which should be easy after the preliminary one was performed as a case reconstruction. Time and color change are the two variables to be studied. Volume is varied for two smaller stains but kept constant for two other exhibits. Epstein and Laber presented a format that will be modified for specific information here. White cardboard versus ceramic tile only will be compared. Free-fall drips from a fingertip, representing arterial blood, will be compared to a drop/smear from the side of the finger, a venous example. The results will be solely based on perceived color differences.

Figures 14.4A–G (H not shown) represent different drying times on ceramic tile after deposit of fresh blood drips. The top-left and -right large drops are full-sized free-fall drops from the tip of a finger punctured with a blood sugar testing lancet. The lower-right example is a touch to release tiny drops, and the lower-left example is contact to smear a small amount of blood, both from the side (venous blood) of the middle finger after puncture with the same lancet.

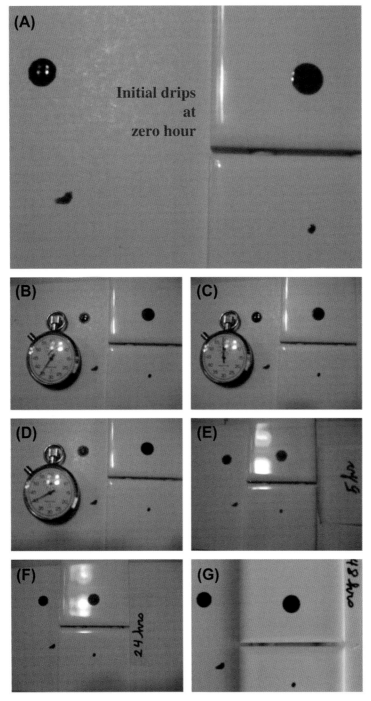

FIGURE 14.4   A collage of seven photos (A–G): ceramic tile on the right, and white, smooth cardboard on the left.

Labels A through H represent the following times and conditions (comments, unless noted otherwise, apply to both ceramic tile and white cardboard):

A. Zero hour drips on cardboard and ceramic tile are shown with one micro-drop and one smear for size drop comparison. Although the light reflection is more prominent on the cardboard drip, the spatter is still darker in perceived color. This is the same blood applied in consecutive drips. The first one was on the ceramic tile and the second on the cardboard.

B. After 7 minutes, drying shows the cardboard target drop is slightly darker to some observers. The tile drop dried faster than the cardboard target drop probably because the cardboard absorbed some moisture.

C. After 10 minutes of drying time, the light reflection on the spatter makes it appear lighter, but that is out of context with the other drying times. This points out the importance of camera angle, light source, and angles when evidence is photographed. This can apply to photographs of bloodstains admitted at trial.

D. After 15 minutes of drying time, the spatters show little difference with regard to color. The smaller drops are even harder to tell age of drying. It is unlikely that an investigative protocol would suggest determining time lapse within 15 minutes of a crime.

E. After 5 hours and longer, the stain on the cardboard is noticeably darker than the stain on the tile. This points out the importance of the surface on which blood dries.

F. After 24 hours, drying shows lack of further changes per surface from that at 5 hours, which draws the question to whether a criminalist could tell which day a blood spatter was left in regard to a time line. Although slight differences may be claimed when tile and cardboard are compared over time, if one doesn't know the initial colors, it is unlikely any change could be identified for crime scene investigation.

G. For 48 hours with different lighting, changes in color still are not apparent. There is some difference with regard to surface on which stain dried. Ceramic tile shows slightly darker stains than cardboard. This may be a factor at crime scenes, i.e., comparison of color for stains on different materials. Interpretation may be that red blood cells on a nonporous surface give up oxygen better than red cells that have dried on a porous surface that absorbed plasma.

H. Exhibit H is not shown because of the apparent lack of change. After more than 2 weeks, the colors were compared with the original drops dried for 2 minutes. Again, the colors were consistent for the surfaces, either tile or cardboard, but drying time per individual spatter was not noticeable. The photograph was observed at the same time of day as the 2-minute photograph.

If the color shading is not obvious to the viewer, it confirms the conclusion that using color appearance to determine when a blood drop was shed is not reliable. This was a blood sample from a single donor viewed at time periods after it was shed. The amount of oxygen saturation and color effect vary per individual, per conditions of drying, and per perception of viewer beyond what was found in this simple exercise.

One parameter kept constant for both of the previous exercises was the hemoglobin/hematocrit value of the blood sample. The donor had a history of anemia, with hemoglobin ranging between 8 and 9 mg%. The concentration of red blood cells will definitely affect the observed color of a spatter and the changes over time during drying. As previously pointed out, the red cell ratio stated as hemoglobin content may also influence the shape of spatters deposited on slanted targets.

V. FOR THE FUTURE

Color Study Number 3 Background

It should be apparent from the color study described in the preceding paragraphs that great expense and time are not necessary for projects that can provide additional information for crime scene applications of bloodstain pattern evidence. Because of the results observed with the first two experiments, a third study was initiated. In this, three types of cloth were viewed with blood drops to see if the fabric nature influenced the color changes over a period of time. Again, the results provided interesting and applicable data for incorporation into CSI parameters.

Three random swatches of household used/worn fabric were cut into rectangles: a terry cloth towel, a cotton T-shirt, and a percale bed sheet. A fingertip was punctured once with a diabetic lancet. Drops were allowed to free fall from about 5 inches onto each swatch. One flick occurred on the T-shirt material. See Figure 14.5 for time at zero.

The set was photographed at 15 and 30 minutes and again at 1 and 24 hours (refer to Figure 14.6A–C). More of our questions are answered. One is that the amount of blood makes a difference, but the difference is not necessarily related to volume of blood in the drop. Note the small spatter at the 7 o'clock position with respect to the T-shirt drop. The color is darker than any of the other spots, yet this drop occurred at the same time as all the others. An interesting fact is that the T-shirt drop retained the red color longer than the percale sheet fabric.

A trace evidence specialist will ask for the reverse view of the fabrics, which is shown in Figure 14.7. Microscopic examination may be required to determine which side a blood spot is on. Rare occasions may exist in which the side of the blood spot cannot be determined. The context of the whole pattern will be useful in interpretation of dynamics responsible for the blood spatters on fabrics.

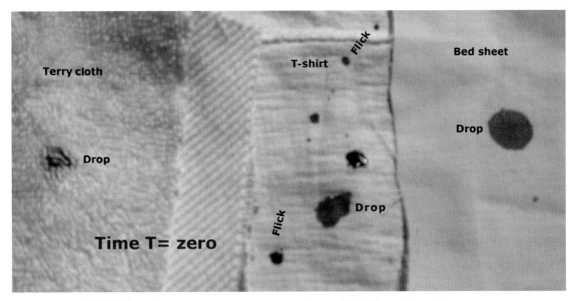

FIGURE 14.5   Three fabric swatches receive drops of blood from a fingertip puncture.

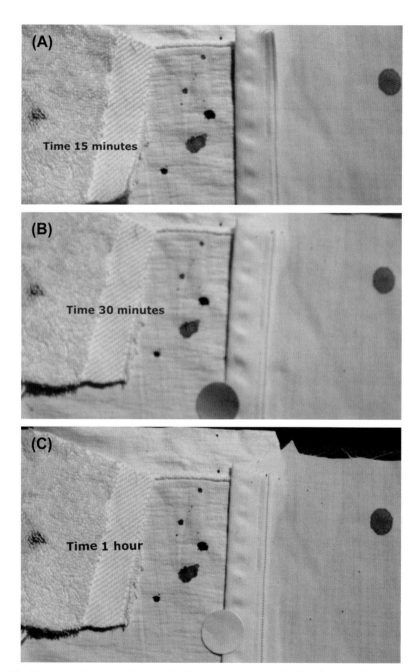

FIGURE 14.6   The fabric swatches were photographed at given time periods after deposit of blood drops.

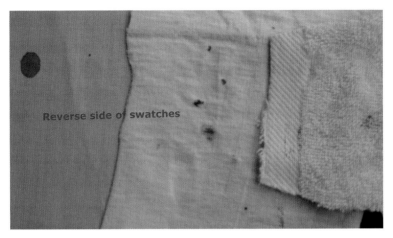

FIGURE 14.7   Reverse side view of fabric swatches and blood drops.

THE INVESTIGATION INTO THE FOOTPRINT OF A BLOOD DROP

The logic behind the string reconstruction has led to the assumption that a drop of blood making contact with a surface forms an oval shape. This is an error in reasoning because the blood drop is predominantly spherical in shape during free fall, and the resultant spatter is spread in a two-dimensional shape, conserving the volume of the blood drop forming it. High-speed photographs of a lateral view have not resolved the question of what shape a drop of blood makes during immediate initial contact with a target. The view that would suggest an answer to that question is one aimed upward beneath the falling drop. A device was designed for this project consisting of a clear plastic box with a slanted top latch (see Figure 14.8). A high-speed video camera was arranged with the lens pointing up (see Figure 14.9).

Random drips from blood with different hemoglobin values falling on the clear plastic slanted target provided unexpected results. The drips were applied to practice using the clear plastic box and slant. Recall that blood is classed as a non-Newtonian fluid, which includes the internal cohesion of red blood cells influencing the tightness of behavior in rounding up to form spherical shapes in flight. Surface tension does not do this, as seen with water drops in flight. Plasma, before any coagulation occurs, is classed as Newtonian, with surface tension influencing drop behavior much like water. The results of free-falling blood drops with less red blood cell concentration resulted in internal cohesion, thus a dense, packed central circle, but behaved according to surface tension from the fluid surrounding the central core upon impact with the target. In other words, plasma with a few red cells, enough to slightly color the fluid, had surface tension broken at impact, forming a beginning to the spatter stain which was still circular but shifting slightly toward oval with the target slant. This result is consistent with the fact that blood flows as a central core in blood vessels, not homogeneously mixed. Venipuncture mixes the blood as it is drawn. See Figure 14.10 for the composite contact of a blood drop of normal red cell count. Figure 14.11 shows a schematic sketch of the two steps in depositing a stain for internal cohesion and surface tension.

The important observation is that the greater the concentration of red blood cells, the larger the central core and the smaller the surrounding area of surface tension rupture. So the next question is:

FIGURE 14.8   Clear plastic box with adjustable slanted top for degrees 20 through 60 (plus 90 with latch horizontal).

FIGURE 14.9   Video camera arranged to view free-falling drops of blood at impact with a slanted surface.

V. FOR THE FUTURE

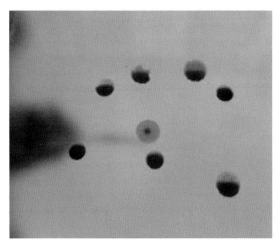

FIGURE 14.10 The forming of a single blood stain from 13.4 mg% hemoglobin value. The dark circle is the footprint of the drop showing the tight internal cohesion of the red blood cells. The lighter ring around the darker circle is the initial layer from surface tension rupture. Note that both are circular at immediate impact of the drop.

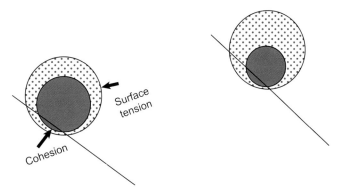

FIGURE 14.11 A schematic sketch of the two steps in depositing a stain for internal cohesion and surface tension.

How does this affect angular bloodstains? Five samples of blood of known hemoglobin/hematocrit were dropped at the angles adjusted with the plastic box. Each stain was measured, the angle of incident calculated, and all angles compared to the set angle for the slanted target. One of the pictures in the video sequence is of interest (see Figure 14.12). In this image, one can see a dot, which is the spherical drop falling before making contact with a darker circular dot beneath it. These two images mark the drop and its shadow. Both, although small, are circular in shape. No ovals are seen before contact, which then results in flow according to the target surface slant.

A condition of drips on slanted targets has been described as *dense zones* (James and Eckert, 1999, p. 87) where excess blood from a drop will flow to the lower edge of the recorded bloodstain. This appearance may be different when viewed with fresh anticoagulated blood versus out-of-date transfusion pouch blood. With the fresher blood, the dense blood area is closer to the original footprint of the drop, i.e., affected by cohesion more than out-of-date red cells. Also, the difference between heavy blood (Hgb/Hct of 18.5/55.1) versus light blood (7.8/22.7) shows the larger

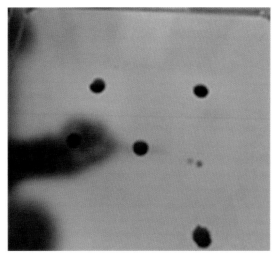

FIGURE 14.12   Image of a single drop falling before contact is made with a target surface. The shapes are seen as circles (spherical), not ovals, with diameters considerably less than the diameter of a resultant bloodstain. Resultant stains are slight ovals due to flow on the target after contact.

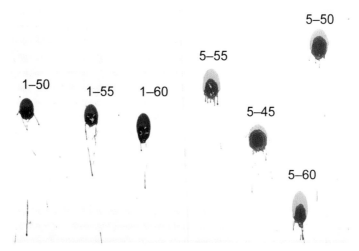

FIGURE 14.13   Comparison of angular drops for heavy blood (labeled 1) versus light blood (labeled 5). Number after the dash on each of these is the drop angle. The dense zones are more rounded for fresher blood than for older samples. Out-of-date transfusion pouches change cohesion with storage, which contributes to the classification as out-of-date for use in human transfusions.

footprint with a smaller light area of surface tension rupture (see Figure 14.13). It is possible that the dense zones at actual crime scenes may indicate the blood drop footprint more so than has been considered with workshop and laboratory experiments. The difference to be studied is the freshness of blood.

Over many years, many research, workshop, and academic individuals and groups all over the world have conducted angular drop experiments. The inclusions here are to add information, not to repeat what is already known. The first consideration must be in regard to the variations in how to measure the drips on angular slants. Angles close to 90 degrees are easier to measure because the footprint tends to be more centered, with the stain filled with blood from the whole drop. As the angle decreases from 90 to 40 degrees and less, the overflow from the drop distorts the leading edge so that interpretation becomes where to cut off elongation of the oval. Rounding off the stain to be a perfect oval shape is not an answer because the impact of the drop was not as an oval. The impact was a circle with the oval shape following from flow of blood based on the speed of the drop at impact. This is why the shape changes to oval as the angle increases. Each drop may have the same amount of blood, but it doesn't exist at the same area on a slanted target. The speed of the drop in free fall will depend on how far it fell and if it reached terminal velocity. Experts in bloodstain pattern analysis learn how to cut off the bottom or leading edge of a spatter so that angular determinations can be reliably used for reconstructing the location of the origin of an impact. It is thus essential to learn this during workshops rather than from reading books on the technique. Practice is definitely advisable, as is the need to apply the technique with constructed mock crime scenes. Still, if the arrangement of spatters is indeed from distribution following an impact of a weapon with a blood source, measuring and calculating angles have been repeatedly shown to benefit investigations.

In a trial conducted using a person with no training in bloodstain pattern analysis, the person measured a series of five blood concentrations dropped at 10 angles. It was found that the first series showed no correlation between the angle of the target and the calculated angle from measurements of the blood spatter. Series 2 through 5 showed an increase in correlation to suggest that it is not only possible but may be easy to train people to measure blood spatters correctly. This is good news because priority may be placed on measurements rather than the importance of interpretation from those measurements.

To avoid the considerable arguments based on how to measure blood drips on slants, Table 14.1 and Figure 14.14 show the results of the study of blood concentration as measured by the author only. The purpose is not to say that blood of any concentration dropped on slants will have the same results, but that blood cell concentration does influence the angular shape under some conditions. Identifying and defining those conditions may provide an estimation that will satisfy data for calculating an error rate of the string reconstruction methodology.

As with any experiment, surprises can result. Although there was a difference of 10.7 mg% hemoglobin, the plot from the three series representing the maximum spread shows little variation. This disagrees with the results of collected patient specimen used in the author's master's thesis project (Wonder, 1982). See Figure 14.15 for graph results from that study. Measurements in the present study did show that the lighter blood had larger measurements, but apparently in this series, the ratio remained comparable. This study used the blood of a single donor freshly diluted or concentrated with analogous (from the same donor) plasma. Both this study and the master's thesis study used blood collected in EDTA. This is good information because previous challenges to different blood compositions have resulted in the answer that it doesn't matter, but there has been little or no presentation of proof to substantiate this claim. Still, another consideration from this small project was that the closer the angle came to 90 degrees, the greater the chance of error. Although this is expected, the results can provide a numerical figure for estimating an error rate.

The range of variation for the angles calculated was within 1 to 10 degrees of the angles arranged on the drop box. For the results of this trial, it can be said that the error in degrees could be plus or minus 5 degrees. This is to say, a blood drip calculated as falling at a 40-degree angle could have actually fallen 35 to 45 degrees with respect to the target surface and without consideration for blood composition. Some may argue that the high and low values for blood hemoglobin/hematocrit are

V. FOR THE FUTURE

TABLE 14.1   Angle Calculations from Measured Blood Drips onto Slanted Targets Versus the Arranged Angle of the Target Support

	1–18.5/55.1	2–8.3/24.4	3–13.4/39.5	4–17.1/50.5	5–7.8/22.7
90	90	90	90	90	90
30	30	30	29	30	30
35	39	38	34	44	38
40	44	41	41	42	38
45	48	48	46	39	47
50	51	56	54	52	54
55	58	62	59	58	54
60	63	65	65	65	61
65	67	76	70	72	76
70	72	74	74	79	68

Columns 1 through 5 are fresh-drawn adjusted bloods in EDTA with the listed hemoglobin/hematocrit values; rows are angles of 30 to 90 degrees set on a drop box. Results in columns are calculated angles from measured spatters. Height of free fall drops was 30 plus or minus 2 inches.

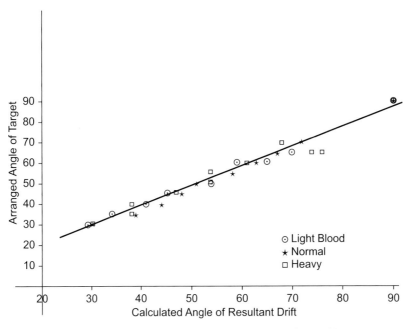

FIGURE 14.14   Graph plots of angular calculations from Table 14.1.

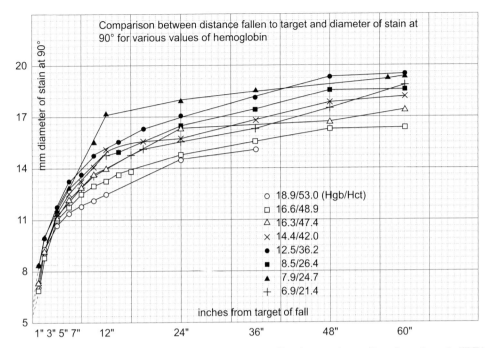

FIGURE 14.15   A master's thesis study of hemoglobin effect from patient-collected specimen in EDTA.

not represented in normal life. The author, ambulatory and conversant, was recently transfused with blood after finding a reading of 6.8 mg% hemoglobin/21.4% hematocrit. Victims of crime, especially drug addicts and the homeless, may show the lower ranges, whereas those in shock or cardiac arrest may show the upper ranges in 18–20 mg% Hgb.

The fact remains that red blood cell concentration is not uniform for individual victims and also not uniform for different injuries on a single victim. Ranges of hemoglobin/hematocrits for that which may result in life or death are hard to state due to the need for more information regarding the ability of individuals to survive. One criterion is how fast or slow the drop is in total blood volume. As pointed out in *Bloodstain Pattern Evidence, Objective Approaches and Case Applications* (Wonder, 2007, p. 367), different organs within a body maintain different ratios of red blood cells, thus hematocrits/hemoglobin values. Loss of blood depends on where the injury occurred and the nature of the injury. There is also a requirement that blood is lost and whether it is internal or external. The organs normally range according to a theoretical 100% column of red blood cells:

Heart: 20%–25%
Brain: 15%–20%
Liver: 40%
Lungs: 35%
Spleen: 80%
Kidneys: 15%–20%
Arteries: 43% (Albert et al., 1965, pp. 20–21)

V. FOR THE FUTURE

When blood is drawn by venipuncture, the separate layers that compose flow are mixed, which results in the normal range of hemoglobin/hematocrit of 14–18 mg%/40%–54% for males and 12–16 mg%/37%–47% for females (Tietz, 1983, p. 258). Normal values vary for different healthcare providers and textbooks (Pagana and Pagana, 1998, p. 254). The preceding experiment suggests that variations per organ may not affect the measurement of stains sufficiently to prevent use in investigative techniques. One situation does provide concern: when injury involves the head, brain, and cerebral spinal fluid (CSF) diluting blood. Head injuries are frequently encountered in casework and usually involve more serious injury quickly during an assault, thus leading to fatal consequences. Being able to identify where CSF and blood were mixed before forming spatters could be advantageous in crime scene investigation.

CSF AND BLOOD PROJECT

If blood is diluted with CSF, it separates the identification of a specific impact to the head from other possible body blows and impact areas. The question arises as to how to determine if head blows resulted, when they occurred, and what part they played in the crime, i.e., assault or homicide. The author has been frequently asked about chemical tests for CSF. The problem is that CSF is essentially a filtrate of blood, thus all, or most, components of blood in the same or lesser concentrations may be found in CSF with or without health.

In one case, a victim sustained multiple blows to the head with a metal baseball bat. A fragment of tissue was found at the crime scene and identified as brain tissue by a qualified forensic pathologist. This fragment was collected by identification technicians and wrapped in a plain paper bindle. Later, when the tissue was examined with an alternate light system along with other items from the scene, it was found that the paper showed bright yellow fluorescence when viewed under Foster & Freeman GG495, with orange filter (see Figure 14.16 and Figure 14.17).

After the tissue was examined, other items were viewed with alternate light sources. Semen stains were expected and found on the victim's underwear. Alternate light source systems are commonly employed to screen for possible semen stains as the stains generally fluoresce. For this reason, an alternate light system was specifically requested prior to a visit to the evidence storage area to identify semen on bed clothing and the victim's underwear (see Figure 14.18). This was compared later with the same light source and a known semen stain as shown in Figure 14.19. The ball bat, however, showed the same fluorescence under blood. The shape and distribution were not consistent with a blow to the genitals but were consistent with one or more blows to the head. The layering of possible CSF with blood under blood would be very consistent with early blows to the head where the skull was breached (see Figure 14.20).

A literature search did not turn up references for determining CSF mixed with blood, with the exception of confirmation that CSF will dilute coagulation factors and thus delay clotting. Discussion with a representative of the alternate light source manufacturer (Foster & Freeman Ltd.) did not provide additional information but did secure loan of the equipment to conduct some preliminary experiments.

The construction of the project involved obtaining CSF samples from three different hospitals. No patient history was possible due to concerns for privacy. It was known that the victim of the homicide who possibly showed CSF mixed with blood distribution at the scene and on evidence collected

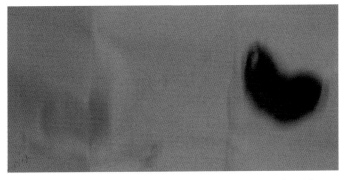

FIGURE 14.16   Identified brain tissue in paper bindle; photographs with normal light.

FIGURE 14.17   Identified brain tissue in paper bindle with fluorescence from 430–440 nm.

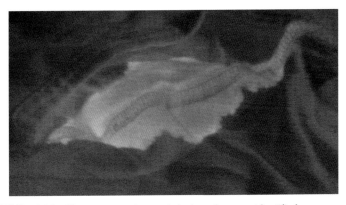

FIGURE 14.18   Fluorescent stain on victim's underwear, identified as semen stain.

V. FOR THE FUTURE

FIGURE 14.19　Fluorescent stain of known semen stain.

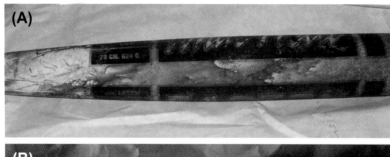

FIGURE 14.20　(A and B) Fluorescent stain under blood on baseball bat.

FIGURE 14.21   Plastic camera box to fit a Canon Power Shot 990 IS camera.

was not treated with any dyes or agents that would influence the CSF's ability to fluoresce. The same could not be said for the samples collected from the hospital. Still, the information is of interest to bloodstain pattern analysis and could provide a scientific basis for future projects in conjunction with hospital clinical laboratories.

The company provided Foster & Freeman GG495 with orange filter over a 2-year time period to examine both the evidence in the one case and samples sent from volunteer labs. The light source was blue: 430–470 nm wavelengths. Orange lens examination goggles were used to observe fluorescence. Because the desire was to record results, a plastic camera box was designed with an orange filter cap to photograph and record data for distribution. Figure 14.21 shows the camera box designed for the project. Only an orange filter was used in this project.

Seven CSF tubes were submitted for examination. The fluid within each tube was viewed with the alternate light source and fluorescence noted. Six tubes showed fluorescence of different levels. One tube did not show fluorescence. Interesting results were recorded in the exhibits constructed, as shown in Figures 14.22 and 14.23.

For comparison purposes, other items found to fluoresce with the Foster & Freeman system included saliva and urine (see Figures 14.24 through 14.26).

Studies with alternate light systems are definitely called for in regard to CSF and blood mixtures. Crime scene investigation using alternative light systems presently exists, and there is a need to recognize when CSF may be the source rather than semen, saliva, urine, or other presently identified material or body fluid. There was one additional observation found 2 years after the experiment described here. A blotting of blood and CSF was constructed but not studied earlier. When the results were reviewed for this book, it was found that the fluorescence remained on the exhibit (see Figure 14.27).

V. FOR THE FUTURE

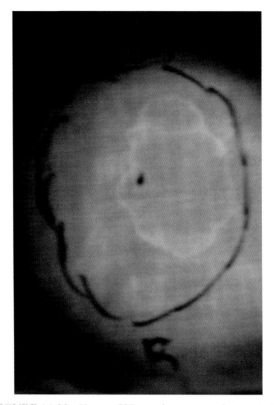

FIGURE 14.22   Known CSF sample on cotton sheet material.

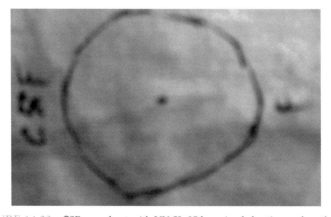

FIGURE 14.23   CSF on a sheet with UV SL-25 long (and short) wavelength light.

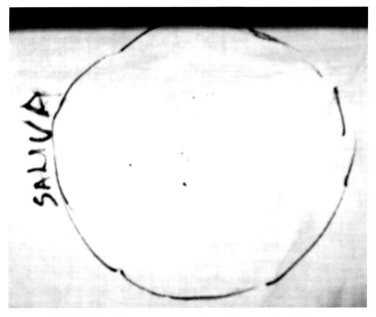

FIGURE 14.24 Saliva viewed in white overhead light.

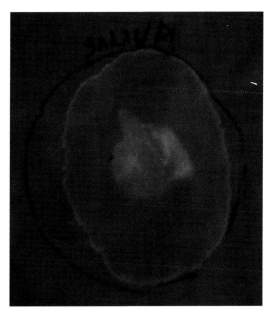

FIGURE 14.25 Saliva viewed with Foster & Freeman system.

V. FOR THE FUTURE

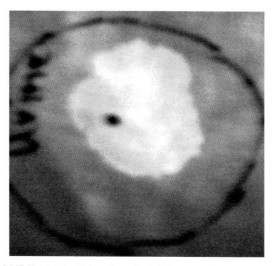

FIGURE 14.26   Urine viewed with Foster & Freeman system.

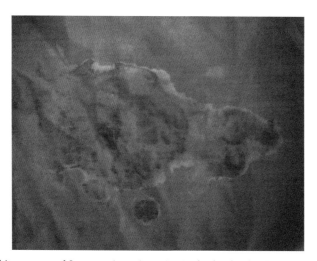

FIGURE 14.27   An exhibit constructed 2 years prior to inserting in this book. Blood and CSF were blotted on cotton sheet material.

The results of this latter project have not been studied in detail nor repeated to determine reproducibility. Parameters, interpretation, and modifications need to be investigated before the results and conclusions can be applied to crime scene casework. It is hoped that the results will interest new students in forensic science and that they will work with medical centers to determine what can be applied to CSI. The objective is to establish scientific bases and expand techniques and applicability of bloodstain pattern evidence.

REFERENCES

Albert, S.N., Jain, S.C., Shibula, J.A., Albert, C.A., 1965. The Hematocrit in Clinical Practice. Charles C. Thomas, Springfield, IL. pp. 20–21.

Bevel, T., Gardner, R.M., 2002. Bloodstain Pattern Analysis with an Introduction to Crime Scene Reconstruction, 2nd ed. CRC Press, Boca Raton, FL. pp. 50–51, 245–246.

Dailey, J.F., 1998. Blood. Medical Consulting Group, Arlington, MA. p. 25.

Epstein, B.P., Laber, T.L., 1983. Experiments and Practical Exercises in Bloodstain Pattern Analysis. Callan Publishing, Minneapolis, MN. pp. 54–58.

Foster & Freeman Ltd. http://www.fosterfreeman.com.

James, S.H., Eckert, W.G., 1999. Interpretation of Bloodstain Evidence at Crime Scenes, 2nd ed. CRC Press, Boca Raton, FL. pp. 87, 90–93.

Pagana, K.D., Pagana, T.J., 1998. Mosby's Manual of Diagnostic and Laboratory Tests. Mosby, Inc, St. Louis, MO. p. 254.

Tietz, N.W. (Ed.), 1983. Clinical Guide to Laboratory Testing. W.B. Saunders Company, Philadelphia, PA, p. 258.

Wikipedia.org and several other online references.

Wonder, A.Y., 1982. The Effects on Geometric Human Bloodstain Design by Hemoglobin Concentration and Time Sequence of Moisture Exposure. Master's Thesis, California State University, Sacramento, CA.

Wonder, A.Y., 2007. Bloodstain Pattern Evidence, Objective Approaches and Case Applications. Elsevier, San Diego, CA. p. 367.

V. FOR THE FUTURE

Summation and Review

What more can be said in summation for bloodstain pattern evidence? Perhaps a great deal. There is much that is still to be learned from casework, research, and application to the investigation as well as resolution of crime. More research should be planned for the future expansion of methods of identification, interpretation, and applications. The great strides in DNA evidence show that forensic science is not a static science to remain consistent with principles from past decades. Such limitations may exist for some investigative techniques, but for other disciplines there is a required continual input in which pure scientific fields are making great strides. The study of blood and how it flows within the human body is essential to understanding how it may exit during dynamic assault to form identifiable arrangements on recording surfaces.

IT ALWAYS COMES BACK TO HISTORY

What may be considered controversy in the discipline of bloodstain pattern evidence perhaps has a parallel in the field of DNA profiling evidence. Russian genetics in the 1930–1940s was set back many years because the government backed a favored expert, Lysenko. Lysenkoian genetics was a refusal to accept progress and changes to principles laid down in Mendelian genetics (Maloy and Hughes, 2013, pp. 286–288). Professor Lysenko adhered to concepts from his own academic origins and refused to accept the beliefs of other scientists. Sadly, or perhaps beneficially, not all communist countries followed suit (Hagemann, 2002, pp. 320–324). The Western world moved on with great strides, which ultimately found their way into forensic applications, and the rest is history.

WHO IS AFFECTED BY DISCOVERIES IN BLOODSTAIN PATTERN EVIDENCE?

It is essential that fields of interest appreciate the probative importance of the evidence as pointed out in Chapter 10, "Expanding Applications in Bloodstain Pattern Evidence." Who needs to know about bloodstain pattern evidence? And why? Perhaps this should be a first consideration, but those who appreciate bloodstain pattern evidence tend to be specialists rather than generalists. Specialists in associated but different disciplines need to have their interests supported by bloodstain pattern applications in order to appreciate what the evidence training can do for their fields. Chapter 10 pointed out the application possibilities of bloodstain pattern training although the most cost-efficacious methodologies are to identify, classify, and determine leads for homicides. Any review of the evidence suggests attention to what will apply to every duty station, department, or bureau.

First Line Officers Benefit from Using BPE Training

There are basically three ways that first line officers can apply their training even if that training was a mere hour or two during basic academy courses:

1. Glean information by viewing cases of vandalism involving spreading of paint, tar, eggs, sewage, or other fluid materials. From this information, one may determine where the perpetrator stood, how he or she distributed material, and which hand he or she used from what relative height.
2. Help to initially and immediately suggest whether the scene represents accidental, suicidal, or homicidal events. It has long been appreciated that initial interviews with witnesses and others may contain lies, misunderstandings, and misinformation. If the first line officer sees discrepancies in the scene, correcting statements stops the tendency to lie, refreshes memories, and relieves those who may feel a need to change statements to protect others.
3. Of course, the most important function of some preliminary training is to introduce new patrol officers to the importance of preserving a scene when they encounter a bloody aftermath.

Detectives Benefit from BPE Training

Even if the detectives responding to a scene are not necessarily oriented toward homicides, they benefit from some exposure to BPE training:

1. Property crimes do occasionally lead to vandalism involving distribution of fluids.
2. Aggravated assaults occasionally involve arguments as to who started the fight, with initial bloodshed as a factor.
3. Being aware of BPE can show where rescue attempts have contaminated the scene.

Identification Technicians Benefit from BPE Training

Identification technicians are usually the most likely to be trained, and little needs to be answered regarding the benefits.

1. As previously mentioned, the knowledge of fluid distribution can be applied to vandalism crime scenes.
2. Breaking and entering scenes can involve vandalism.
3. Traffic accident investigations can often benefit from BPE training.
4. Differentiating between accident, suicide, and homicide can provide information to be relayed to the appropriate detectives and prosecutors.
5. These technicians are the first line people in warning detectives of contamination and staging.

6. Interpreting BPE can lead to other evidence, such as fingerprints and palm prints, that should be recorded and collected.
7. If the ID people don't record and collect, the crime lab won't have evidence to process.

Crime Lab Scientists Benefit from BPE Training

It's unfortunate that some individuals with science qualifications involved in investigations may feel BPE training is not within their necessary expertise. There are benefits to many of the specialist departments:

1. DNA shows who was there but not what they did. Bloodstain patterns show how blood was distributed and may show where it came from.
2. Position and pattern are essential to trace evidence, so training involving those parameters will benefit the mindset of criminalists specializing in trace.
3. It is essential that those with a scientific background act as support for other individuals involved in the investigation who may lack an academic background in pure sciences.

Profilers and Reconstructionists Benefit from BPE Training

In recent years, new specialties have arisen in law enforcement, criminalistics, and private investigations, which can benefit from expanded training courses:

1. Serial murderers may repeat the same approach to assaults, which result in remarkably similar bloodstain patterns. This becomes a signature that is best understood through an ability to classify patterns.
2. Illustrating scenarios of crimes requires experimental design beyond merely using the same items and surfaces. Identifying the dynamics from bloodstain patterns improves the accuracy of reconstruction.

Internal Affairs Investigators Benefit from BPE Training

Sociological and psychological approaches to investigations of law enforcement events may fail to be fair either to the officer or to the public:

1. Training in physical evidence levels the playing field to provide fairness to the officer and the public opinion.
2. Any officer-involved shooting should require an investigation by someone not directly associated with the agency from which the shooter originated. This could be Internal Affairs or a different agency such as the FBI, U.S. Marshals, State or sheriff versus police.

Pathologists Benefit from BPE Training

It is unfortunate that many pathologists feel they would have no use for BPE training. Those who spared the time have found information very applicable to their functions as medical officers:

1. Although autopsies deal with inside the body, blood that has been drawn by violent events provides clues as to how the violence was perpetrated.

2. Through BPE training, pathologists can see the importance of mentioning blood vessels not directly involved with the cause and manner of death.
3. Training in bloodstain pattern evidence can help bridge the gaps in education and experience between forensic and clinical viewpoints.

Prosecutors Benefit from BPE Training

Although the first thought from lawyers would be that examining BPE experts would be the most important, other considerations should take precedent long before trial:

1. The most important player in the drama that will become a trial is the prosecutor in bringing the correct charges against the correct assailant. Recognizing staging to frame another individual is crucial.
2. Recognizing overzealous performance by any of the investigative team is also important. This can be seen in jumping to interpretation that is not verified in the bloodstain pattern evidence.
3. Of course, BPA training benefits prosecutors in their cross-examination of defense experts and may prevent later embarrassment at trial if they are able to see accuracy in defense expert reports.

Defense Attorneys Benefit from BPE Training

Speaking of defense expert reports, there are several things to be said regarding their need to know:

1. It is essential that attorneys understand what their experts are saying.
2. It is equally important to understand the point of view of prosecution experts, their weaknesses as well as strengths.
3. Perhaps an unstated benefit for defense attorneys is that clients who may be guilty of many things may not be guilty as charged. Putting on a good defense can include a finding of lesser than the charge at bar.

Defense Experts Benefit from BPE Training

Any increase in application of bloodstain pattern analysis in initial investigations will require an equal availability for the defense:

1. Provide a safeguard against overzealous interpretation of crime scene evidence.
2. Provide an alternative interpretation in casework where complex patterns are found.
3. Know when a client is lying and use that knowledge to persuade him or her to accept a negotiated plea.

Television Writers Benefit from BPE Training

Most readers would question why television writers would be included in a list of those who need to know or at least understand the nature of BPE. There are, however, some good reasons:

1. Be aware of the "CSI Effect." This is caused by viewers watching television programs and equating actual trials with the principles displayed. So much weight is placed on DNA that

jurors may miss the fact that DNA only tells who was there. When they were there and what they did may have nothing to do with the crime.

2. Accuracy in portraying BPE in mystery and crime programs can shorten the time necessary to instruct the jury when experts need to testify. Shortened time saves money.

College Instructors Benefit from BPE Training

Teachers from secondary levels on up can provide benefits to tender young minds:

1. The first benefit, of course, is in inspiring curiosity so that some of those students will go into the professions that will deal with investigating, solving, and resolving crime.
2. For psychology instructors and college majors, study may involve profiles to test for those people with a propensity for violence out of context with societal norms—a predisposition to violence pretest, so to speak.
3. BPE training will provide an introduction that can lead to students evaluating subsequent training and lectures, which will benefit them in their choice of profession in investigation.

It should be clear that many different disciplines of investigation can benefit from bloodstain pattern training, discussions, and continued updates of information. It has been the objective of this book to provide additional information and alternatives to the existing literature on the subject. The objectives initially stated were as follows:

1. Clarify misperceptions and misunderstandings from previous publications, presented papers, and lectures.
2. Re-emphasize recent scientific discoveries. Update, and further explain, a need for correction in logic for bloodstain pattern interpretation and research.
3. Repeat and confirm the importance of blood substance composition, mainly as non-Newtonian fluid influenced by red blood cell content, in applications for bloodstain pattern analysis in casework and research experimental design.
4. Provide an interpretation scheme for the purpose of obtaining initial, beneficial economic investigative leads before persons of interest are identified.
5. Encourage and extend legal applications of bloodstain pattern analysis as an economical methodology before, during, and after trial.

REVIEW

The following is a review of what was supplied to accomplish objectives in each section of this book.

Section I: Introduction

Chapter 1, "Introduction," provided some historical shifts in the viewpoint of crime labs and attitudes toward bloodstain pattern evidence. One can consider that the political shift suggests a revisiting of Dr. Paul L. Kirk's original approach to the evidence. National Institute of Standards and Technology (NIST) selections of Organization of Scientific Area Committees (OSAC) could be instrumental in setting up forms to update principles and scientific basis as research from fields such as medicine, biorheology, and vascular science. These fields could support a shift back to Kirk's objectives. This chapter presented the viewpoint that bloodstain patterns are not pattern match. The shift in VIS terms pre- and post-1970s is important to identification, classification, interpretation, and application of the forensic discipline. The chapter also addressed the economics of providing some exposure to various investigative branches.

Chapter 2, "The Science of Bloodstain Pattern Evidence," pointed out that blood is non-Newtonian and why this is important to bloodstain pattern evidence. What contributes to non-Newtonian behavior? Namely, red blood cell ratio. The chapter presented some clarification and modification that viscosity is not all that matters in the nature and behavior of blood. The importance of blood's composition is defined both inside and outside the body. The importance of non-Newtonian flow and arterial bloodstain patterns was discussed, with the lesser importance for castoffs and lack of importance for impact spatters. Discrediting surface tension as the sole explanation for blood drop behavior was justified with science and literature searches.

Chapter 3, "Discussion on Terminology," provided an in-depth discussion of past, present, and perhaps future terminology. The focus on bloodstain pattern evidence has been on forming a terminology that is written in stone for mandatory applications. For a field that is viewed from as many perspectives as the preceding lists, determining only one terminology list fails to acknowledge the scope of applications and duty stations involved.

Section II: Identification

Chapter 4, "Review of Historical Approaches to Bloodstain Pattern Identification," revisited the historical approach to identifying patterns, discussed how the process has shifted, and made suggestions to bring back some of the old process in a modern criteria-based framework.

Chapter 5, "Differentiations Between Similar Patterns," provided suggestions for dealing with patterns that resemble each other in some aspects but should lead to very different interpretations.

Chapter 6, "How Many Pieces of Evidence?" presented an approach to identification that focuses on obtaining investigative leads. The benefit is in applying the technique to approaches to the original crime scene.

Section III: Interpretation

Chapter 7, "Information for Interpretation," offered many suggestions for developing time lines, story lines, and interview questions from the identification of bloodstain patterns.

Chapter 8, "Investigative Leads: Suggested Questions and Answers," furthered the idea of using the information for initial crime scene work-up in preparation for application.

Chapter 9, "Staging," examined a frequent involvement in the crime itself, which may have developed from criminals watching CSI-style programs as much as jurors requiring "CSI Effect" evidence at trial.

Section IV: Application

Chapter 10, "Expanding Applications in Bloodstain Pattern Evidence," took the information possible to a new level by applying it to many different situations besides use as expert witness testimony at trial.

Chapter 11, "Applications of Bloodstain Pattern Evidence to Crime Scene Investigation," revisited the main applications for the evidence and training of various duty stations in the techniques.

Chapter 12, "Bloodstain Pattern Application in Court," provided approaches and techniques to extend the applications in court beyond expert opinions stated as "consistent with." This chapter considered methods of examining and cross-examining the various players in court drama.

Section V: Research for the Future

Chapter 13, "Reinventing the Wheel," suggested cautions in developing scientific projects that provide nothing useful for practical applications.

Chapter 14, "Research Project Examples," described research projects and ideas for more studies and examples of projects that need to be further tested to provide information for the future of the science of bloodstain pattern evidence.

Chapter 15, "Summation and Review," has provided an in-depth review of the book.

CONCLUSION

At the beginning of each workshop at the Public Safety Center in Sacramento, California, participants were presented with a list of objectives in their handout material. At the end of the 40-hour program, the list was repeated to the class for agreement, discussion, and disagreement regarding whether the course content had achieved the objectives. No class, out of 32, felt the objectives were not met. It is this conclusion which is the author's desired result from readers of this book. The reward for the time in compiling the information presented here is that many different viewpoints find applications to economically serve the course of justice.

REFERENCES

Hagemann, R., 2002. How Did East German Genetics Avoid Lysenkoism? Trends in Genetics 18 (6), 320–324.
Maloy, S., Hughes, K. (Eds.), 2013. Brenner's Encyclopedia of Genetics. Elsevier, Amsterdam, pp. 286–288.

Index

Note: Page numbers with *"f"* and *"t"* denote figures and tables, respectively.

R

Realignment process, 5
Recirculating pump, 231, 232f
Reconstructionists benefit, 313
Red blood cells, 49
Reinventing wheel
  acquire and/or manufacture instrumentation, 277–278
  bloodstain pattern evidence, 267, 269
  formula for reagents necessary, 277–278
    plastic angle box, 279f
  impact velocity, 267
  interpret information gleaned, 282–283
  literature search, 271–272
  modifications suggesting, 283
  pattern match approach, 267–268
  project conducting, 281–282
  project result records management, 279–281
  resolving with project, 268
    academic environment, 270–271
    drop size estimation, 271
    errors in logic, 269
    hemoglobin effects preliminary study, 270f
  review results, 282–283
  scientific-based research study, 268
Research literature, 271
Research projects, 268–269
  blood drop investigation, 295–302
  blood project, 302–308
  bloodstains age determination using color, 285
    case reconstruction protocol study, 285–287
    color studies, 287–290, 293
    drying time color changes, 290–292, 291f
    fabric swatches, 293f–295f
    finger punctures, 289f
    kitchen sink photograph, 286f
  CSF, 302–308
Retraction, 49
Reverse order, 242
Rheology, 20, 271–272

S

SAD. See Shape, Alignment, Distribution and/or Density
Satellite spatter, 49–50
Scientific foundation, 172–173
  in civilian science disciplines, 5
  conducting literature search for, 271–272
  for forensic discipline of BPA, 3–4

Scientific Working Group on Bloodstain Pattern Analysis (SWGSTAIN), 31
Scientific Working Group on Medicolegal Death Investigation (SWGMDI), 92
Scientific-based research study, 268
Secondary spatter, 50
Serum, 50
Serum stain, 50
Shadowing, 51
Shape, Alignment, Distribution and/or Density (SAD), 87
Simple direct transfers, 51, 162, 177–178
Smear, 51
Smudge. See Smear
South African cave painting, 6f
Spatters, 51–52, 161–162, 175, 242
Splash, 52
Splash-type exercises, 230
Splatter, 52
Spring trap devices, 227–229
  blood placement on lip, 228f
  break up blood drops, 227f
Spurt, 171–173
Staged crime scenes, 210
Staging, 185
  arterial damage bloodstain patterns, 187
  bloodstain pattern evidence, 185
  bloody sponge, 186–187
  castoffs, 187
  elimination, 191
    drapes at living room front window, 194f
    freezer door corner, 191f
    smears and wipes, 195f
    wall between door, 192f
  PABS, 188–189
  transfer patterns, 187
  volume stains, 190
String reconstruction, 53, 150
  assumed velocity, 151
  blood drop diameter, 152f
  chords of sphere, 153f
  confirmations, 156
  cutting off stains, 154f–155f
  errors, 152
  with forethought and confirmation, 155–156
  increases in error from wrongly placing victim, 156f
  limitations to interpretation, 150
  size of blood spatters, 151

Thixotrophic blood, 21
3D approach, 234–236. *See also* Bloodstain pattern
    evidence (BSP evidence)
  applications, 236–240
    HumanCAD drawing, 239f
  arterial damage patterns
    on arm, 234f
    variations, 233f
Three-dimensional photography, 235–236
Trace evidence, 175
Transfer patterns, 44, 54, 229
  in BSP evidence, 161–162, 175–179
  moving, 107–109
  regarding staging, 187
  simple direct, 51
  swipe moving, 53
  wipe moving, 55, 230
Transfers, 146

V
Vandalism investigations, 209
Vector, 32
Velocity impact spatters, 8, 146–147
Viscoelasticity, 20–21
Void, 33, 54
Volume bloodstain, 54
Volume stains, 190

W
Whole pattern, 38, 55, 102
  alignments of spatters, 69
  identification, 61
Whole stain, 153
Wipe moving transfer pattern, 55, 230